Hiking and Backpacking *Trails of* TEXAS

WALKING, HIKING, AND BIKING TRAILS FOR ALL AGES AND ABILITIES!

SIXTH EDITION

Hiking and Backpacking
Trails of
TEXAS

WALKING, HIKING, AND BIKING TRAILS FOR ALL AGES AND ABILITIES!

SIXTH EDITION

Mickey Little

Taylor Trade Publishing
Lanham • New York • Boulder • Toronto • Oxford

HIKING AND BACKPACKING
Trails of
TEXAS

SIXTH EDITION

First Taylor Trade Publishing edition 2006

This Taylor Trade Publishing paperback edition of ***Hiking and Backpacking Trails of Texas, 6th ed.,*** is an original publication. It is published by arrangement with the author.

All photographs are by the author unless otherwise indicated.

Published by Taylor Trade Publishing
An imprint of The Rowman & Littlefield Publishing Group, Inc.
4501 Forbes Boulevard, Suite 200, Lanham, Maryland 20706

Distributed by NATIONAL BOOK NETWORK

Library of Congress Cataloging-in-Publication Data
Little, Mildred J.
Hiking and backpacking trails of Texas : walking, hiking, and biking trails for all ages and abilities! / Mickey Little.—6th ed.
p. cm.
Includes bibiliographical references and index.
ISBN 1-58979-205-X (pbk. : alk. paper)
1. Hiking—Texas—Guidebooks. 2. Backpacking—Texas—Guidebooks.
3. Trails—Texas—Guidebooks. 4. Texas—Guidebooks. I. Title.
GV199.42.T49L57 2006
917.64'0464—dc22

2005019732

The paper used in this publication meets the minimum requirements of American National Standard for Information Sciences—Permanence of Paper for Printed Library Materials, ANSI/NISO Z39.48-1992.

Manufactured in the United States of America.

CONTENTS

Region 3 89

Region 4 117

Backpacking Trails 143

PREFACE

As indicated by its title, the emphasis of this new edition of *Hiking and Backpacking Trails of Texas* remains the same. However, since the newest trend in trails is to construct or adapt existing trails so they are multi-use and can accommodate bicycles and/or horses, numerous trails for those two user groups are now included in this guide. This sixth edition has added 21 additional parks/areas for mountain bikers and 13 additional parks/areas for equestrian users.

The introduction section of this guide continues to include information on "Hiking and Backcountry Ethics" and the "Hiking/Backpacking Checklist." After all, this information is quite appropriate for any trail user no matter what the mode of transportation—i.e., feet, bicycle, or horse. What this guide does not include are topics related specifically to bicycles or horses, other than where the trails are located. In actuality, the explosion in popularity of mountain biking and horseback riding that created the need for multi-use trails has greatly benefited the hiker and backpacker.

While every effort has been made to ensure the accuracy of the information in this guide, neither I nor the publisher assumes liability arising from the use of this material. Because park and trail policies are subject to change, trail users may want to verify the accuracy of important details before beginning a trip. May this sixth edition of *Hiking and Backpacking Trails of Texas* serve you well in the years ahead in your quest for fun and fitness through these outdoor adventures.

Mickey Little
Johnson City, TX

ACKNOWLEDGMENTS

I am indebted to and wish to thank the following individuals and agencies for information in the form of maps, brochures, books, articles, telephone conversations, and personal interviews, without which this revision would not have been possible.

Armand Bayou Nature Center
Big Bend Natural History Association
Carlsbad Caverns–Guadalupe Mountains Association
Fort Worth Nature Center and Refuge
Gay Ippolito, National Forests & Grasslands in Texas
Houston Arboretum & Nature Center
Lavaca-Navidad River Authority
Lower Colorado River Authority
Lubbock Lake Landmark
Michael Owen, Fort Worth District, U.S. Army Corps of Engineers
National Wildlife Refuges, Southwest Region
National Forests & Grasslands in Texas
National Park Service
Parks and Recreation Departments of numerous Texas cities
Sabine River Authority
Texas Department of Transportation, Travel Division
Texas Parks and Wildlife Department
Texas Forestry Association
Trinity River Authority
U.S. Army Corps of Engineers, Fort Worth District
Wild Basin Wilderness Preserve

Mickey Little
Johnson City, TX

INTRODUCTION

The one thing that hiking, backpacking, mountain biking, and horseback riding have in common is that they are most often performed on TRAILS. And, of course, the purpose of this guide is to tell you where these trails are located and provide directions for getting there. You will discover information about the popular trails as well as the lesser-used trails, ranging from nature trails several tenths of a mile in length to expedition trails of many miles suitable for extended backpacking or horseback riding trips.

Throughout the United States, people are realizing the physical and recreational benefits of hiking, backpacking, bicycling, and horseback riding, and they are seeking areas where they can participate in these activities as they enjoy the outdoors. In Texas, the opportunities for participating in these activities are numerous.

The newest trend in trails is to construct or adapt existing trails so they are multi-use trails and can accommodate mountain bikes and/or horses. Texas has 4 state trailways that are multi-use trails. Three of them, called rails-to-trails, are located on abandoned railroad corridors: Caprock Canyons State Trailway (64+ miles), Lake Mineral Wells State Trailway (20 miles), and Lost Creek Reservoir State Trailway (20 miles) with a trailhead at Fort Richardson State Park. Lake Somerville State Trailway (13 miles) connects the 2 state parks at the west end of Lake Somerville. All four of these trailways are designated for hiking, mountain biking, and equestrian.

The newest trailway is the 20-mile Ray Roberts Lake State Park Greenbelt that begins at Elm Fork Satellite Park Unit below the Ray Roberts Dam and ends at the headwaters of Lake Lewisville. The trail includes 12 miles for equestrian, and 10 miles for hike and bike use. Another trailway is the 8-mile Denton Branch Rail Trail, a hike and bike trail from Denton through Corinth, that can be accessed from at least 18 street intersections.

This sixth edition of *Hiking and Backpacking Trails of Texas* covers the full gamut of trails, and is substantially updated with new maps, address changes, and new parks/areas with trails, as well as the addition of trails for different user groups at parks already having a trail system. Twenty-one additional parks/areas that have mountain bike trails and 13 additional parks/areas that have equestrian trails now appear in this new edition.

Three parks that have added significantly to their trail system include Guadalupe River State Park (7 miles of multi-use trails), Big Bend Ranch State Park (Contrabando Trail—an 11-mile multi-use trail with a primitive campsite), and Canyon of the Eagles, on Lake Buchanan, with 14 miles of hiking trails.

Two of the national forests have created new trail systems: a 54-mile Piney Creek Horse Trail with 5 loops is located in the Davy Crockett National Forest, and 3 loops of marked multi-use trails totaling 80 miles are on the Sam Houston National Forest.

Extensive trail systems have also been established on the Caddo and LBJ National Grasslands. Twenty miles of trails in 3 multi-use loops are on Caddo National Grasslands with access from the Bois d' Arc Trailhead. The LBJ Multi-Use Trail is 75 miles in length and consists of 5 loops with access from TADRA Point Campsite, Valley View Group Campsite, or numerous dispersed campsites.

It almost appears as though the Corps of Engineers has received a mandate to establish more multi-use trails. Numerous parks that border their lakes have added trails of varying lengths, but the 5 lakes with the longest trails are Bardwell, Belton, Lavon, Lewisville, and Stillhouse Hollow. Bardwell has an 8-mile multi-use trail at Waxahachie Creek Park; Belton has 10 miles of nature trails at Miller Springs Nature Area; Lavon has a 9-mile trail for equestrian and hiking only called the Trinity Trail, and a 6-mile hike and bike trail at Sister Grove Park. Lewisville Lake has an 8-mile (Pilot Knoll) and a 6-mile (Elm Ford) trail; both are designated for equestrian and hiking. Stillhouse Hollow Lake has a 15-mile multi-use trail at Dana Park.

Take time to peruse this guide thoroughly so you can make wise choices in your decision regarding the location of your next recreational outing or camping trip. One of the greatest things about hiking and backpacking in Texas is that you can choose exactly what appeals to you: rugged mountains or thorny deserts, the shorelines of placid lakes or flowing rivers, sandy beaches, or the pine-hardwood forests of East Texas. Needless to say, the avid mountain bikers and the equestrian riders have their own

set of criteria to help determine the location of their next adventure.

Let's look more closely at the state of Texas and what it has to offer to the outdoor enthusiast. In elevation, the surface of the state varies from sea level along the coast of the Gulf of Mexico to 8,749 feet at the summit of Guadalupe Peak. Terrain varies from the subtropic Rio Grande Valley to the Great Plains in the far north, from the lush pine forests of East Texas to the mountainous Trans-Pecos region of West Texas. In straight-line distance, Texas extends 801 miles from north to south and 773 miles from east to west. The tidewater coastline extends 624 miles.

The weather is generally characterized by mild temperatures. Average annual rainfall varies sharply, from more than 56 inches along the Sabine River to less than 8 inches in the extreme west. Included in Texas' 26 million acres of woodland are 4 national forests with 675,855 acres. The most important forest area of the state is the East Texas pine-hardwood region, known as the "Piney Woods." It extends over 43 counties.

Texas has 91 mountains a mile or more high, all of them in the Trans-Pecos region. Guadalupe Peak, at 8,749 feet, is the state's highest mountain. The longest river in the state is the Rio Grande, which forms the international boundary between Texas and Mexico and extends 1,270 miles along Texas. The next longest river is the Red River, which extends 726 miles.

Of the 50 states, Texas ranks second only to Alaska in the volume of its inland water—more than 6,000 square miles of lakes and streams. Toledo Bend Reservoir, on the Sabine River between Texas and Louisiana, is the largest reservoir in Texas or on its borders, with 185,000 surface acres at normal operating level. The largest body of water wholly within the state is Sam Rayburn Reservoir, with a normal surface area of 114,500 acres.

Texas is fortunate, indeed, to have so many agencies vitally interested in providing and maintaining such excellent trails for the public. Nine parks administered by the National Park Service, and 94 of the parks operated by the Texas Parks and Wildlife Department, have designated trails located within their boundaries. Trails are located on the shorelines of 24 lakes under the jurisdiction of the U.S. Army Corps of Engineers or some other river authority, and numerous nature trails are located on the 9 wildlife refuges that are administered by the U.S. Fish and Wildlife Service. Each of the 4 national forests in Texas have trails suitable for backpacking trips: the 129-mile Lone Star Trail in the Sam Houston National Forest, the 28-mile Trail Between the Lakes in the Sabine National Forest, the 20-mile 4-C Trail in the Davy Crockett National Forest, and the 5½-mile Sawmill Trail in the Angelina National Forest. These trails are administered by the U.S. Forest Service.

More than 90 of the parks operated by the Texas Parks and Wildlife Department have designated trails.

The Texas Forestry Association, a private agency, has designated woodland trails of various lengths at many sites throughout East Texas. Other trails in Texas are administered by Municipal Parks and Recreation Departments. I apologize for any major trails that have been omitted and welcome information on them for future inclusion.

For the individual who wants to learn more about all aspects of backpacking, I would recommend that you learn it by some means other than by trial and error. Consult some of the best books on the subject, secure a few equipment catalogs that describe the most recent innovations in equipment, consult a reputable backpacking store, talk with folks who have done a great deal of backpacking such as those in a local outing or hiking club, or maybe even take a course in backpacking from a nearby college. A backpacker's checklist to aid you in this endeavor appears at the end of this section. Careful and adequate planning can mean the difference between a terrible trip and the trip of a lifetime!

The joys of hiking and backpacking are many, as are the joys of biking and horseback riding. Remember to travel and camp by the rules of "low impact." Be prepared to take care of yourself and the environment. I know you have heard it said before, but I will repeat it here: "Take nothing but pictures; leave nothing but footprints!" With this philosophy, nothing but good times are in store for you. Happy Trails!

How to Use This Guide

The state has been divided into 4 geographic regions as shown in the illustration. Within each region the parks, lakes, forests, and cities that have designated trails are arranged alphabetically. Each of the four regions begins with a map that locates the parks/trails within that region and gives the page numbers for them. A list of "other trails" appears at the end of each region. Many of these trails are nature trails that are shorter in distance than one mile; they are ideal for easy strolls. Be sure to look at these lists because they include trails at 27 state parks, 8 lakes, 4 national parks, 5 national wildlife refuges, and numerous cities.

In addition, the 29 areas that have trails designed for backpacking are grouped in a special section that begins on page 143. Keep in mind that portions of trails designated as suitable for backpacking are also good for day trips. So don't forget to check this section of trails when you are planning your next outing. All parks, lakes, forests, and major trails (if named) are cross-listed by name and city in the index.

As the name implies, the major focus of this guide is on hiking and backpacking trails in Texas. At least, that's been the emphasis since its first edition in 1981. However, due to the popularity in recent years of mountain biking and horseback riding, and because there are still lots of folks who enjoy tent camping in a more wilderness setting than a developed campground, a listing of parks that include these activities/facilities are listed according to geographic regions. So, if biking, horseback riding, and walk-in tent sites are "your thing," you can now tell at a glance where you need to head for your next outing.

All trail users need to spare the land and travel by the rules of "low impact." You are encouraged to read the section entitled "Hiking and Backcountry Ethics" because the information is applicable to all trail users—whether your trip lasts an hour, a day, or a week. A "Hiking/Backpacking Checklist" is also included to serve as a guide in choosing the proper gear whether you hike, bike, horseback ride, or camp.

The last item in this introduction is a display of the universal symbols that are used on the maps. You are probably familiar with most of the symbols but a glance at them will prove beneficial. Most of the maps also display a campground from which a trail starts and ends. Because this guide is not intended to be used as a camping guide, many symbols have been removed from the campground map. In the case of the camping area itself, only a campground symbol is shown. Likewise, all picnic areas (shelters, group, group shelters, etc.) are shown merely as a picnic area. To determine all of the facilities at a park, please consult the companion to this book—*Camper's Guide to Texas Parks, Lakes, and Forests*.

All information reported in this guide has been supplied by the respective operating agency, either through literature distributed by them, through verbal communication, or through secondary sources deemed reliable. Mailing addresses and phone numbers have been given in the event that you need additional information. Also refer to "Resources for Further Information" at the end of the guide.

The trail signs at Aransas National Wildlife Refuge are quite informative.

Bicycle and Equestrian Trails

Due to continued increases in popularity of mountain biking and horseback riding, numerous trails have been constructed or adapted in Texas to accommodate these recreational users. Because both are compatible with hiking and backpacking trails, it seems appropriate to include this information. After all, trails exist or are created to be used for a variety of recreational activities. It matters not whether the trail user is walking, hiking, jogging, biking, or riding on a horse.

Mountain bikes are "fat-tire" bicycles designed to use on dirt surfaces, whereas paved or surfaced bike trails are needed for bicycles with the narrow tires. Mountain bikes are usually allowed on hiking trails but in some locations are not allowed on equestrian trails. Bikers should always yield to hikers, and pass slowly and considerately; they should also yield to horses and make their presence known well in advance.

Trails designated as equestrian trails are multi-use in that hikers may use them; on some trails, bikers may also use them. Hikers should always yield to horses. An equestrian trail has regulations regarding grazing, watering, tying horses to trees, and camping; contact the park for specific information.

Bicycle and equestrian trails are located at the following sites:

MOUNTAIN BIKE TRAILS

MOUNTAIN BIKE TRAILS *(continued)*

Pedernales Falls State Park, 109, 191
South Llano River State Park, 111

Region 4

Big Bend Ranch State Park, 118, 153
Caprock Canyons State Park, 125, 156
Caprock Canyons State Trailway, 125, 156
Copper Breaks State Park, 126
Davis Mountains State Park, 127, 161
Franklin Mountains State Park, 130
Palo Duro Canyon State Park, 137
San Angelo State Park, 139
Seminole Canyon State Park & Historic Site, 140

Texas Parks and Wildlife Dept. © 2004

Numerous equestrian trails have been constructed or adapted in recent years to accommodate the increased popularity of horseback riding.

SURFACED BIKE TRAILS

Region 1

Lake Mineral Wells State Trailway, 33, 185
Meridian State Park, 40
Ray Roberts Lake State Park, 41
  Isle du Bois Unit, 41
  Johnson Branch Unit, 42

Region 2

Bastrop State Park, 52, 144
Brazos Bend State Park, 58
Buescher State Park, 59
Huntsville State Park, 66
Lake Livingston State Park, 69

Region 3

Garner State Park, 97
Goose Island State Park, 115
McKinney Falls State Park, 106
San Antonio Missions NHP, 116

EQUESTRIAN TRAILS

Region 1

Bardwell Lake, 45
Benbrook Lake/Horseback & Nature Trail, 12
Caddo National Grassland, 14
Cooper Lake State Park (South Sulphur Unit), 18
Dinosaur Valley State Park, 21, 168
Fairfield Lake State Park, 23, 170
Grapevine Lake, 28
Lake Arrowhead State Park, 31
Lake Mineral Wells State Park & Trailway, 33, 185
Lake Texoma Big Mineral Equestrian & Hiking Trail, 187
Lavon Lake/Trinity Trail, 36
LBJ National Grassland, 45
Lewisville Lake, 37
Lost Creek Reservoir State Trailway, 25
Loyd Park at Joe Pool Lake, 38
Ray Roberts Lake State Park, 41
  Greenbelt, 43
  Isle du Bois Unit, 41

Region 2

Big Thicket National Preserve, 53, 155
  Big Sandy Creek Unit, 57
Davy Crockett National Forest, 60, 162
  Piney Creek Horse Trail, 61
Huntsville State Park, 66
Lake Houston State Park, 68
Lake Livingston State Park, 69
Lake Somerville State Park Trailway, 70, 71, 186
McKinney Roughs Nature Park, 73
Sam Houston National Forest, 78, 193
  80 miles of multi-use trails around north end of Lake Conroe, 78
Stillhouse Hollow Lake, 87

Region 3

Canyon Lake, 114
Guadalupe River State Park, 98
Choke Canyon State Park (North Shore Area), 158
Hill Country State Natural Area, 182
Pedernales Falls State Park, 109, 191

Region 4

Big Bend Ranch State Park, 123, 153
Caprock Canyons State Park, 125, 156
Caprock Canyons State Trailway, 125, 156
Copper Breaks State Park, 126
Davis Mountains State Park, 127, 161
Fort Griffin State Park and Historic Site, 129
Franklin Mountains State Park, 130
Guadalupe Mountains National Park, 131, 171
Monahans Sandhills State Park, 141
Palo Duro Canyon State Park, 137
San Angelo State Park, 139

Walk-in Primitive Tent Camping

Tent camping remains fairly popular in Texas. The "bottom line" is that everyone doesn't own a motor home, a fifth-wheeler, a camp trailer, or a pop-up tent trailer. Many tent campers prefer to camp away from campgrounds that supply electrical and water hook-ups but offer little privacy. Some parks offer the opportunity to tent camp in a "developed" area; that is, each site has a picnic table, grill, lantern post, and access to a nearby restroom with flush toilets and showers. Some developed tent campsites may even require a walk-in of several hundred yards. Fees charged are usually less than those charged at campsites offering more services.

However, for those who want to tent camp in a more secluded area but don't want to hike a great distance, the primitive walk-in campsite is the answer. There are presently 34 state parks that offer walk-in tent camping along a trail covering a distance of up to 1½ miles. A trail of this length is usually not considered a backpacking trail, but obviously a pack of some sort will be of great assistance in carrying the equipment needed for an overnight stay. The state parks that offer walk-in primitive camping, other than those that are considered backpacking campsites, are:

Campsites that require a short walk-in are usually classified as either "primitive" or "developed."

Region 1

Cedar Hill State Park, 15
Cooper Lake State Park (South Sulphur Unit), 18
Fort Richardson State Park & Historic Site, 24
Lake Bob Sandlin State Park, 32
Martin Creek Lake State Park, 39
Possum Kingdom State Park, 45
Purtis Creek State Park, 45
Ray Roberts Lake State Park, 41
  Isle du Bois Unit, 41
  Johnson Branch Unit, 42

Region 2

Bastrop State Park, 52, 144
Brazos Bend State Park (Youth Group), 58
Buescher State Park, 59
Lake Houston State Park, 68
Mother Neff State Park, 75
Sea Rim State Park, 81
Village Creek State Park, 85

Region 3

Bentsen-Rio Grande Valley State Park, 91
Choke Canyon State Park, 158
  Calliham Unit, 113
  North Shore Unit, 158
Colorado Bend State Park, 159
Devils River State Natural Area, 167
Enchanted Rock State Natural Area, 169
Guadalupe River State Park, 98
Hill Country State Natural Area, 182
Inks Lake State Park, 100
Matagorda Island State Park, 115
McKinney Falls State Park, 106
Mustang Island State Park, 115

Region 4

Big Bend Ranch State Park, 123, 153
Caprock Canyons State Park, 125, 156
Fort Griffin State Park & Historic Site, 129
Franklin Mountains State Park, 130
Palo Duro Canyon State Park, 137
San Angelo State Park , 139

Backpack Camping

The backpacking trails section beginning on page 143 is for those who prefer backpacking and primitive camping rather than day hiking and camping in a developed campground. The 29 areas in Texas that have trails designed for backpackers are grouped in a section following the 4 regions that feature nature and hiking trails. As a cross-reference, these 29 areas with backpacking trails are also cited on the 4 region pages. The areas detailed in the backpacking section of this sixth edition are located in 18 state parks, 4 national parks, 3 U.S. Army Corps of Engineers lakes, and 4 national forests. Even if you don't plan to camp along the trail, keep in mind that portions of trails designated as suitable for backpacking are also good for day trips. So don't forget to check this section of trails when you are planning your next outing.

Hiking and Backcountry Ethics

Rules imposed by those who administer the various trails are common sense rules meant to control actions that may damage natural resources. In recent years, the term "going light" has taken on new meaning. To a backpacker, "going light" is the skill of paring down the load and of leaving at home every ounce that could be spared. But "going light" also means to spare the land and travel and camp by the rules of "low impact." The following information has been suggested by the U.S. Forest Service and is given here for your consideration as you hike and backpack so that your trips on the trail will, indeed, be ones of "low impact."

Backpackers headed into the backcountry should always check the information board at the trailhead; the information posted there can be invaluable.

General Information

1. Don't shortcut trails. Trails are designed and maintained to prevent erosion.
2. Cutting across switchbacks and trampling meadows can create a confusing maze of unsightly trails.
3. Don't pick flowers, dig up plants, or cut branches from live trees. Leave them for others to see and enjoy.

Plan Your Trip

1. Keep your party small.
2. Take a gas stove to help conserve firewood.
3. Bring sacks to carry out your trash.
4. Take a light shovel or trowel to help with personal sanitation.
5. Carry a light basin or collapsible bucket for washing.
6. Check on weather conditions and water availability.
7. Before your hike, study maps of the area, get permits if necessary, and learn the terrain.

Setting Up Camp

1. Avoid camping in meadows; you'll trample the grass.
2. Pick a campsite where you won't need to clear away vegetation or level a tent site.
3. Use an existing campsite, if available.
4. Camp 300 feet from streams or springs. Law prohibits camping within ¼ mile of an only available water source (for wildlife or livestock).
5. Do not cut trees, limbs, or brush to make camp improvements. Carry your own tent poles.

BREAKING CAMP

1. Before leaving camp, naturalize the area. Replace rocks and wood used; scatter needles, leaves, and twigs on the campsite.
2. Scout the area to be sure you've left nothing behind. Everything you packed into your camp should be packed out. Try to make it appear as if no one had been there.

CAMPFIRES

1. Use gas stoves when possible to conserve dwindling supplies of firewood.
2. If you need to build a fire, use an existing campfire site. Keep it small. Before you leave, make sure it is out.
3. If you need to clear a new fire site, select a safe spot away from rock ledges that would be blackened by smoke; away from meadows where it would destroy grass and leave a scar; and away from dense brush, trees, and duff, where it would be a fire hazard.
4. Clear a circle of all burnable materials. Dig a shallow pit for the fires. Keep the sod intact.
5. Use only fallen timber for firewood. Even standing dead trees are part of the beauty of wilderness, and are important to wildlife.
6. Put your fire cold out before leaving: let the fire burn down to ashes, and mix the ashes with dirt and water. Feel it with your hand. If it's cold out, cover the ashes in the pit with dirt, replace the sod, and naturalize the disturbed area. Rockfire rings, if needed or used, should be scattered before leaving.

PACK IT IN—PACK IT OUT

1. Bring trash bags to carry out all trash that cannot be completely burned.
2. Aluminum foil and aluminum lined packages won't burn up in your fire. Compact it and put it in your trash bag.
3. Cigarette butts, pull tabs, and gum wrappers are litter, too. They can spoil a campsite and trail.
4. Don't bury trash! Animals dig it up.
5. Try to pack out trash left by others. Your good example may catch on!

KEEP THE WATER SUPPLY CLEAN

1. Wash yourself, your dishes, and your clothes in a container.
2. Pour wash water on the ground away from streams and springs.
3. Food scraps, toothpaste, even biodegradable soap will pollute streams and springs. Remember, it's your drinking water, too!
4. Boil water or treat water before drinking it.

DISPOSING OF HUMAN WASTE

1. When nature calls, select a suitable spot at least 100 feet from open water, campsites, and trails. Dig a hole 4 to 6 inches deep. Try to keep the sod intact.
2. After use, fill in the hole completely burying waste. Then tramp in the sod.

EMERGENCY ITEMS

1. According to conditions, carry extra warm clothing such as windbreakers, wool jackets, hats, and gloves. Keep extra high-energy foods like hard candies, chocolate, dried fruits, or liquids accessible. Don't overload yourself, but be prepared for emergencies.
2. Travel with a first-aid kit, map compass, and whistle. Know how to use them.
3. Always leave your trip plan with a member of your family or a close friend.
4. Mishaps are rare, but they do happen. Should one occur, remain calm. In case of an accident, someone should stay with the injured person. Notify the nearest state, local, or federal law enforcement office for aid.

Water obtained from springs should be treated or boiled before drinking.

HIKING/BACKPACKING CHECKLIST

This list is not meant to be all inclusive or necessary for each trip. It is a guide in choosing the proper gear. Although this list was prepared for the hiker/backpacker, it is quite appropriate for anyone using the backcountry, whether they are traveling by foot, canoe, bicycle, or horse. Parentheses indicate those optional items that you may not want to carry depending upon the length of the trip, weather conditions, personal preferences, or necessity.

TEN ESSENTIALS FOR ANY TRIP:

___ Map
___ Compass
___ First-aid kit
___ Pocketknife
___ Signaling device
___ Extra clothing
___ Extra food
___ Small flashlight/extra bulb & batteries
___ Fire starter/candle/waterproof matches
___ Sunglasses

DAY TRIP

(add to the above):

___ Comfortable boots or walking shoes
___ Rain parka or 60/40 parka
___ Day pack
___ Water bottle/canteen
___ Cup
___ Water purification tablets
___ Insect repellant
___ Sun lotion
___ Chapstick
___ Food
___ Brimmed hat
___ (Guidebook)
___ Toilet paper & trowel
___ (Camera & film)
___ (Binoculars)
___ (Book)
___ Wallet & I.D.
___ Car key & coins for phone
___ Moleskin for blisters
___ Whistle

OVERNIGHT OR LONGER TRIPS

(add the following):

___ Backpack
___ Sleeping bag
___ Foam pad
___ (Tent)
___ (Bivouac cover)
___ (Ground cloth/poncho)
___ Stove
___ Extra fuel
___ Cooking pot(s)
___ Pot scrubber
___ Spoon (knife & fork)
___ (Extra cup/bowl)
___ Extra socks
___ Extra shirt(s)
___ Extra pants/shorts
___ Extra underwear
___ Wool shirt/sweater
___ (Camp shoes)
___ Bandana
___ (Gloves)
___ (Extra water container)
___ Nylon cord
___ Extra matches
___ Soap
___ Toothbrush/powder/floss
___ Mirror
___ Medicines
___ (Snakebite kit)
___ (Notebook & pencil)
___ Licenses & permits
___ (Playing cards)
___ (Ziplock bags)
___ (Rip stop repair tape)
___ Repair kit—wire, rivets, pins, buttons, thread, needle, boot strings

MAP SYMBOLS

BIKE TRAIL
CABINS
CAMPGROUND
EQUESTRIAN SITES
HIKING TRAIL
HORSE TRAIL
NATURE/INTERPRETIVE TRAIL
PARKING
PARK OFFICE
PICNIC AREA
PRIMITIVE GROUP SITES
PRIMITIVE SITES
RANGER STATION
RESTROOMS
SCREENED SHELTERS
TOILETS FOR PRIMITIVE SITES

REGION 1

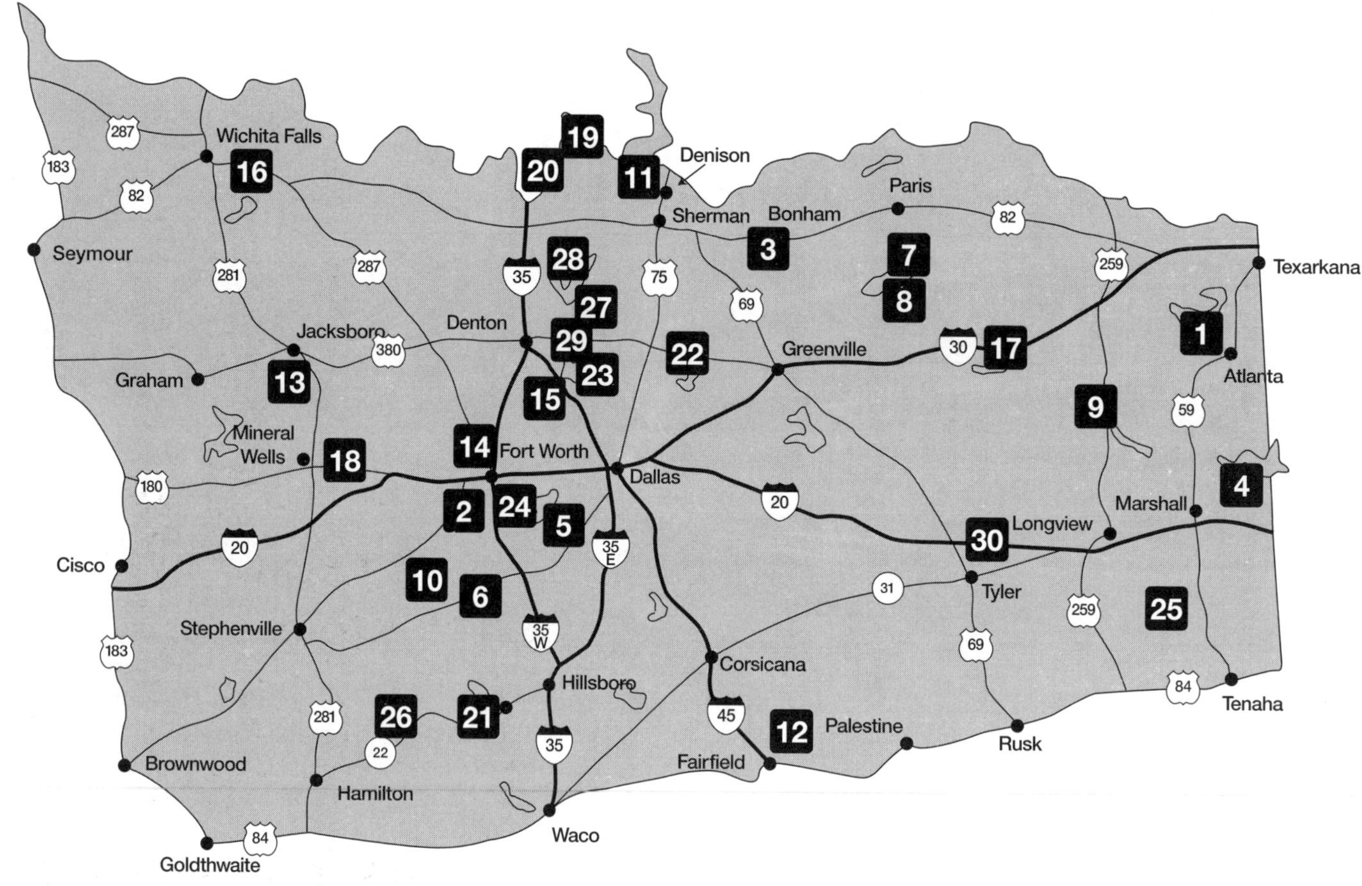
Wichita Falls
Denison
Sherman
Bonham
Paris
Seymour
Texarkana
Jacksboro
Denton
Greenville
Atlanta
Graham
Mineral Wells
Fort Worth
Dallas
Marshall
Longview
Cisco
Tyler
Stephenville
Corsicana
Hillsboro
Palestine
Rusk
Tenaha
Fairfield
Brownwood
Hamilton
Waco
Goldthwaite

Atlanta State Park

FOR INFORMATION

ATLANTA STATE PARK
927 PARK RD. 42
ATLANTA, TX 75551
903/796-6476

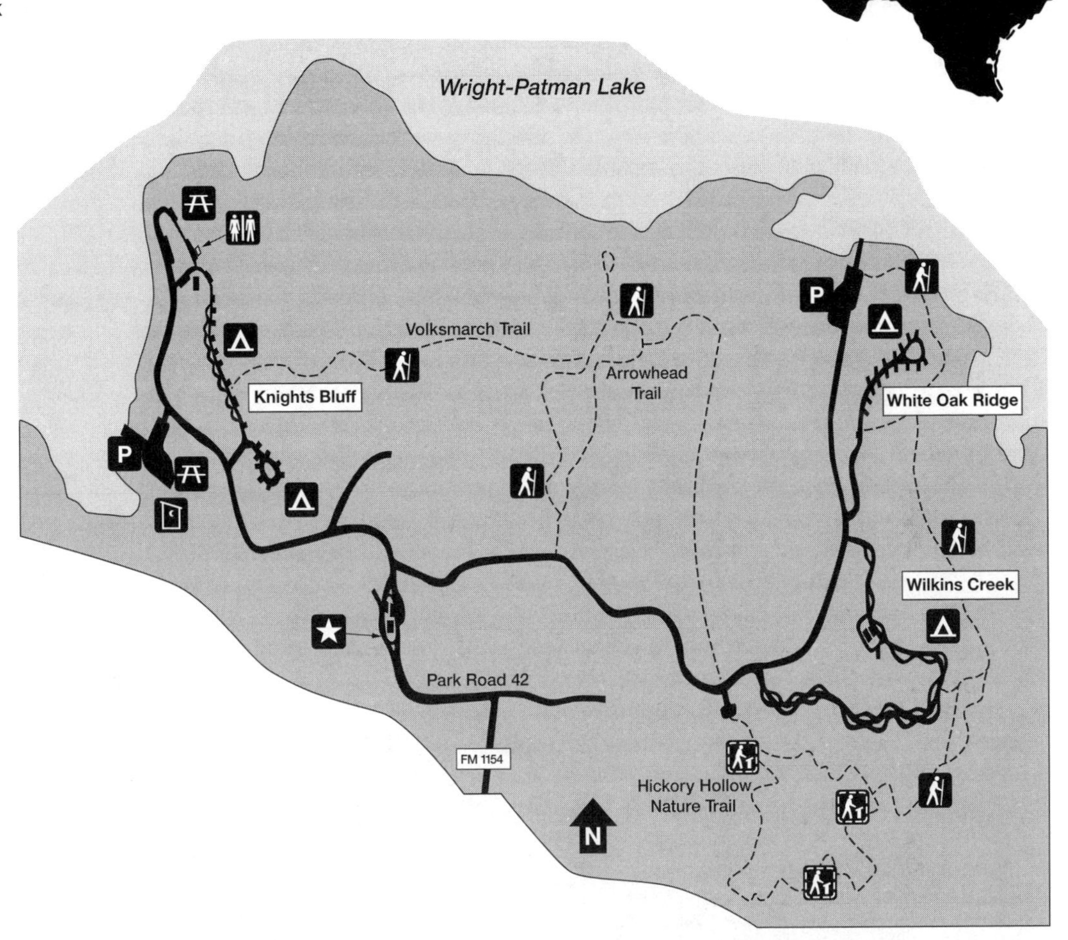

LOCATION

Atlanta State Park is located approximately 11 miles northwest of Atlanta. Drive 6 miles west of Atlanta on TX 77 to FM 96 and then north on FM 96 for 6 miles and north on FM 1154 for 2 miles to Park Road 42. The 1,475-acre park is located on the shores of 119,700-acre Wright-Patman Lake.

TRAIL NOTES

The 1.2-mile nature trail and 2.6-mile hiking trail in the eastern portion of Atlanta State Park wind through an undeveloped area. Several extensions of the trail form loops, which allow for outings of short duration. The trail meanders through a scenic portion of the pine forest and hardwood bottomlands and passes by a small creek, Wilkins Creek. Eventually, the trail terminates with a short extension along the shoreline. A 1.2-mile-loop hiking trail is in an undeveloped area near the center of the park; a Volksmarch Trail intersects this trail.

These young hikers are awed by the structure of this magnificent tree.

Benbrook Lake/Horseback and Nature Trail

FOR INFORMATION

Benbrook Lake
P.O. Box 26619
Ft. Worth, TX 76126-0619
817/292-2400

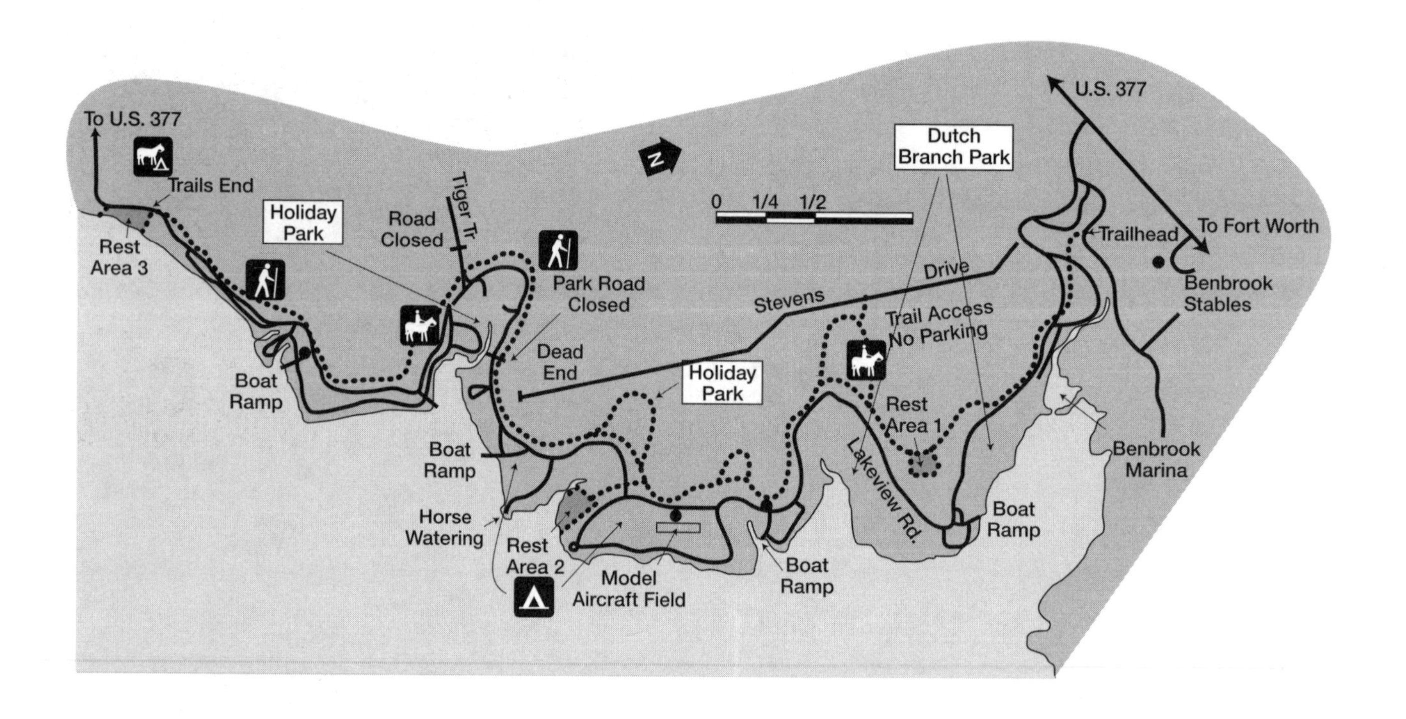

TRAIL NOTES

Benbrook Lake is located southwest of Fort Worth on the Clear Fork of the Trinity River and is administered by the U.S. Army Corps of Engineers and the city of Benbrook.

A 7.3-mile horseback and nature trail is located on the west side of Benbrook Lake. It takes between 4 and 5 hours to ride the trail round-trip. The terrain includes flat open spaces, rolling hills, beautiful wooded areas, and challenging slopes. The trail offers many panoramic views of the lake and surrounding countryside.

The horseback trail has 3 enclosed rest areas, designated Rest Area #1, Rest Area #2, and Trails End, as well as a beginning trailhead. Parking for vehicles and trailers is available at the trailhead, Rest Area #2, and Trails End. No parking is provided at the Stevens Drive access point. Overnight camping for horsemen is permitted only in the Trails End and Rest Area #2. Water for horses may be obtained in Rest Area #2 and at Trails End. Restrooms and drinking water are available at various locations along the trail. The city of Benbrook operates a horse stable near the trailhead. Those interested in renting or stabling a horse should contact the stable manager for this information at 817/249-1176.

There are two other trails at Benbrook Lake: the city of Benbrook maintains a ⅓-mile, paved exercise trail at Dutch Branch Park, and the Corps has a pedestrian-only 1.7-mile trail at the south end of the Holiday Park Campground. It is a flat, river-bottom trail along the north side of the Clear Fork of the Trinity River.

Bonham State Park

FOR INFORMATION

Bonham State park
1363 State Park 24
Bonham, TX 75418
903/583-5022

LOCATION

Bonham State Park is located southeast of Bonham. From Bonham, travel south on TX 78 for 2 miles, then southeast on FM 271 for 2 miles to Park Road 24. The 261-acre park includes a 65-acre lake.

TRAIL NOTES

The park is situated in the Blackland Prairie Region of Texas. Eleven miles of mountain biking and hiking trails traverse the rolling prairies and woodland that encircle the lake. The terrain is dominated by grassland; more luxuriant woodlands occur along water courses and the lake's shoreline. Numerous wildflowers and flowering shrubs cover the gently rolling prairie in the spring, and stands of cedar and mixed hardwoods provide a panorama of multi-colored leaves in the fall.

Caroline West

Luxuriant woodlands encircle the lake; they provide a panorama of multi-colored leaves each fall.

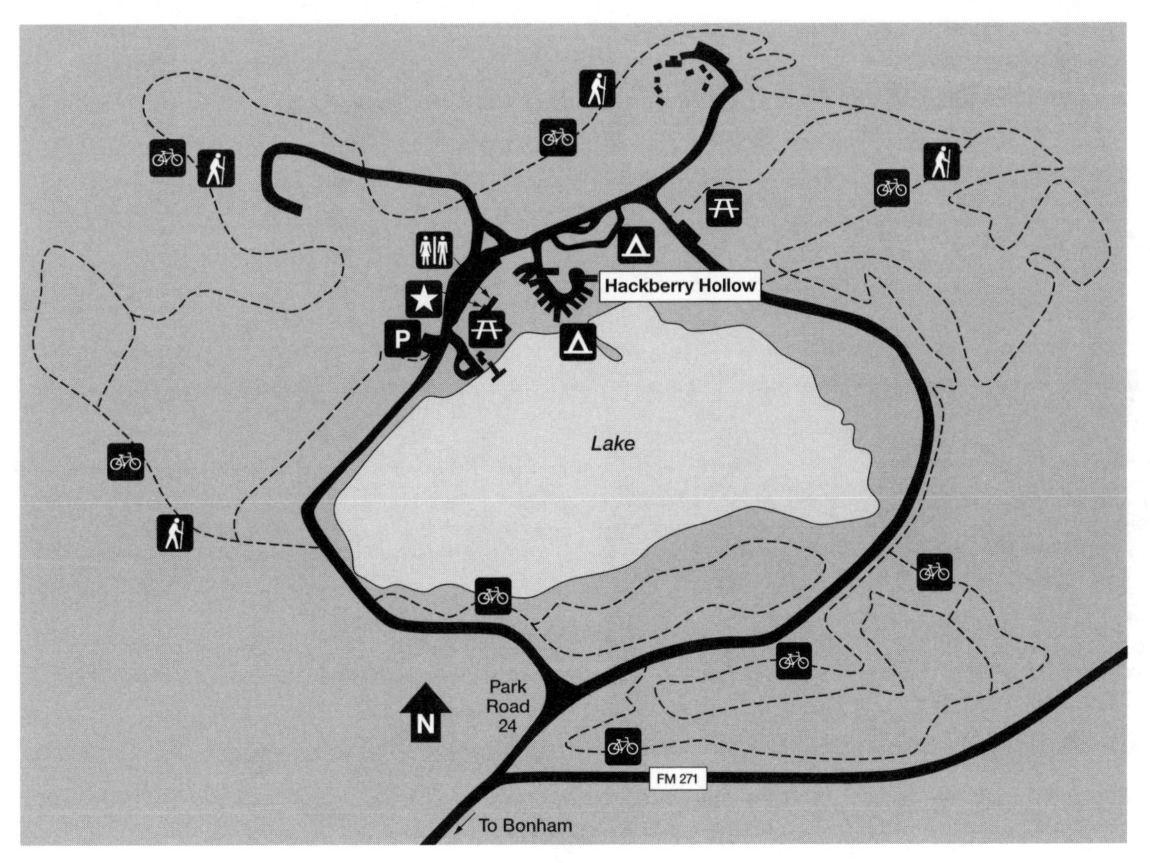

Caddo Lake State Park

FOR INFORMATION

Caddo Lake State Park
245 Park Rd. 2
Karnack, TX 75661
903/679-3351

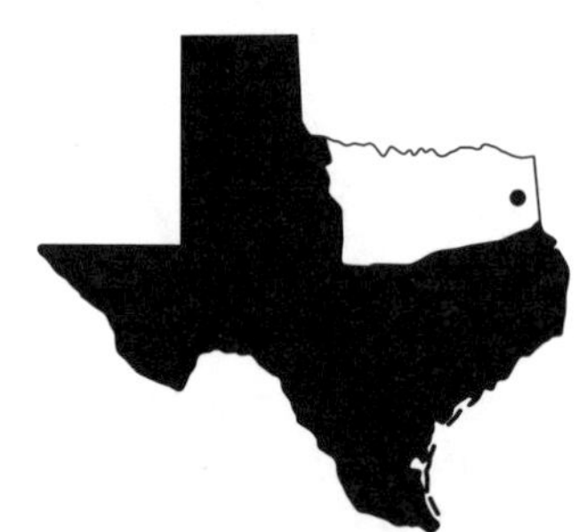

LOCATION

Caddo Lake State Park is located 15 miles northeast of Marshall, .4 mile off of TX 43 to FM 2198 to Park Road 2. The 484-acre park fronts Big Cypress Bayou with access to Caddo Lake.

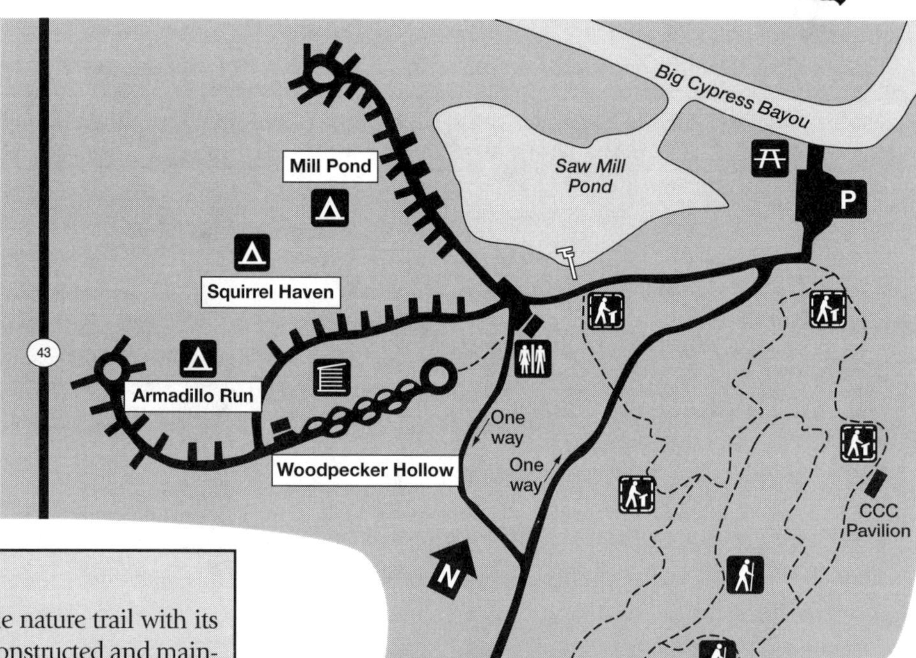

TRAIL NOTES

Caddo Forest Trail, the ¾-mile nature trail with its dense canopy of shade, is well constructed and maintained. Plants commonly seen along the trail are loblolly pine, dogwood, white oak, water oak, red oak, bald cypress, and redbud. An additional hiking trail, 1½ miles in length, adjoins the nature trail.

Park visitors at Caddo Lake enjoy canoeing among the bald cypress trees almost as much as hiking among the diverse vegetation of the nature and hiking trails.

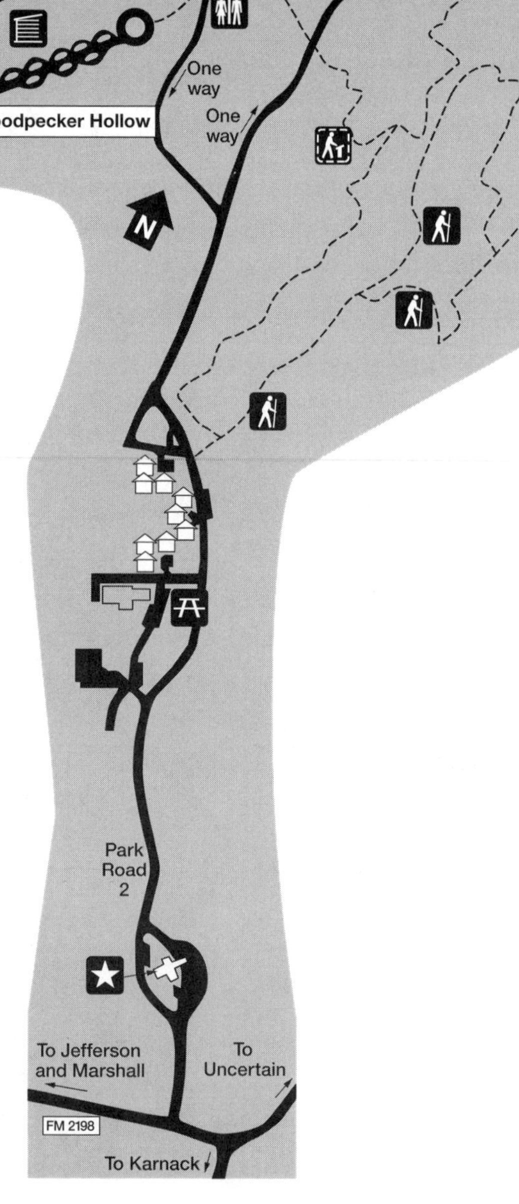

Cedar Hill State Park

FOR INFORMATION

CEDAR HILL STATE PARK
1570 WEST FM 1382
CEDAR HILL, TX 75104
972/291-6641

LOCATION

Cedar Hill State Park, located on the 7,500-acre Joe Pool Lake, is recognized as an urban area park due to its proximity to the Dallas-Fort Worth metroplex. It is located 10 miles southwest of Dallas, 4 miles southeast of Grand Prairie, and 3 miles west of Cedar Hill. The entrance to this 1,826-acre park is from FM 1382. From US 67, exit FM 1382 and travel northwest for 2½ miles. From I-20, exit FM 1382, and travel south for 4 miles south. The park is skirted by FM 1382 and Mansfield Road.

TRAIL NOTES

Two of the hiking trails at Cedar Hill State Park (Pond Trail and Talala Trail) offer primitive campsites. These two trails total 4½ miles; Talala Trail has a self-guided tour booklet. Overlook Trail is a ½-mile hiking trail from Shady Ridge Campground at the north end of the park. The DORBA Trail is a 10.3-mile premier mountain bike trail named for the volunteers of Dallas Off-Road Bicycle Association that built the trail. Over 1,400 acres of prime mountain bike landscape are crisscrossed, providing more than 15 miles of intense riding at the present time. Plans are to gradually double the trail miles. According to the bikers, the trail is located in one of the prettiest parts of the county—the white-rock escarpment. Bikers must pay the park entrance fee to access the trail. The trail is closed after rainfall, so phone 972/291-3900 and press star 2 for trail conditions.

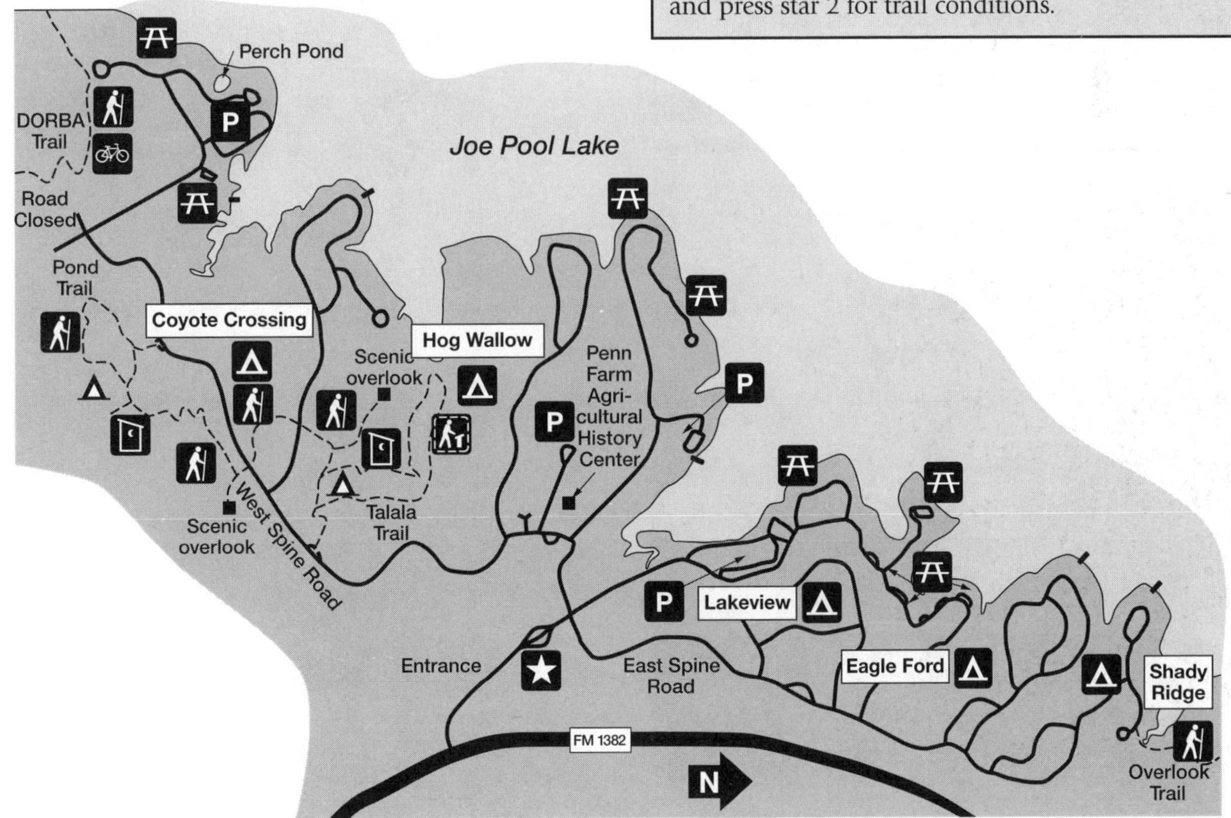

Cleburne State Park

FOR INFORMATION

Cleburne State Park
5800 Park Road 21
Cleburne, TX 76033
817/645-4215

LOCATION

Cleburne State Park is located 10 miles southwest of Cleburne; from Cleburne, take US 67 southwest for about 4 miles, then left on Park Road 21 for 6 miles. This 528-acre park, named for Confederate hero General Pat Cleburne, includes a 116-acre lake of clear, clean water flowing from 3 natural springs beneath the surface of the lake.

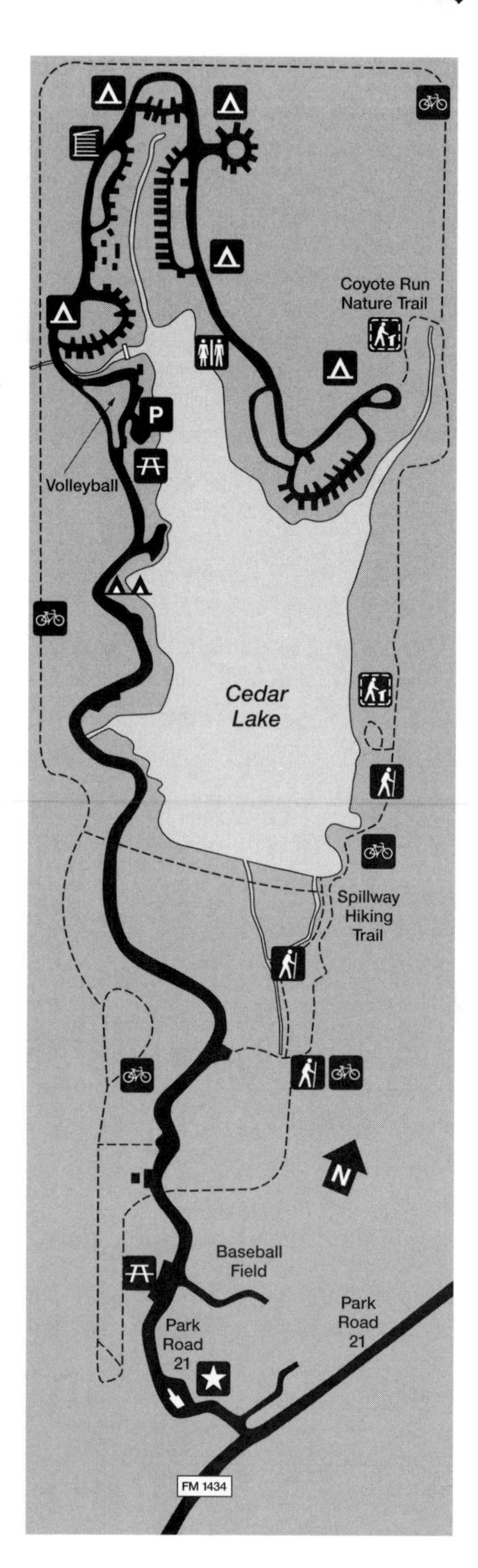

TRAIL NOTES

The Coyote Run Nature Trail is a 2.4-mile round-trip interpretive nature trail that has 18 numbered markers along the trail. A self-guided tour booklet is available at the park headquarters. The trailhead to the Spillway Hiking Trail is from Park Road 21; it is a one-mile round-trip and is also designated as a mountain bike trail. A 7-mile mountain bike trail is located west of Park Road 21 and encircles the park to the north, connecting to the Nature Trail. In early spring there is a carpet of bluebonnets in the open field and over 75 species of wildflowers in the park. In the fall the trees and bushes display colorful foliage.

The Coyote Run Hiking Trail that is adjacent to Cedar Lake along its east side has a scenic footbridge.

COOPER LAKE STATE PARK
DOCTORS CREEK UNIT

FOR INFORMATION

COOPER LAKE STATE PARK
DOCTORS CREEK UNIT
1664 FM 1529 SOUTH
COOPER, TX 75432
903/395-3100

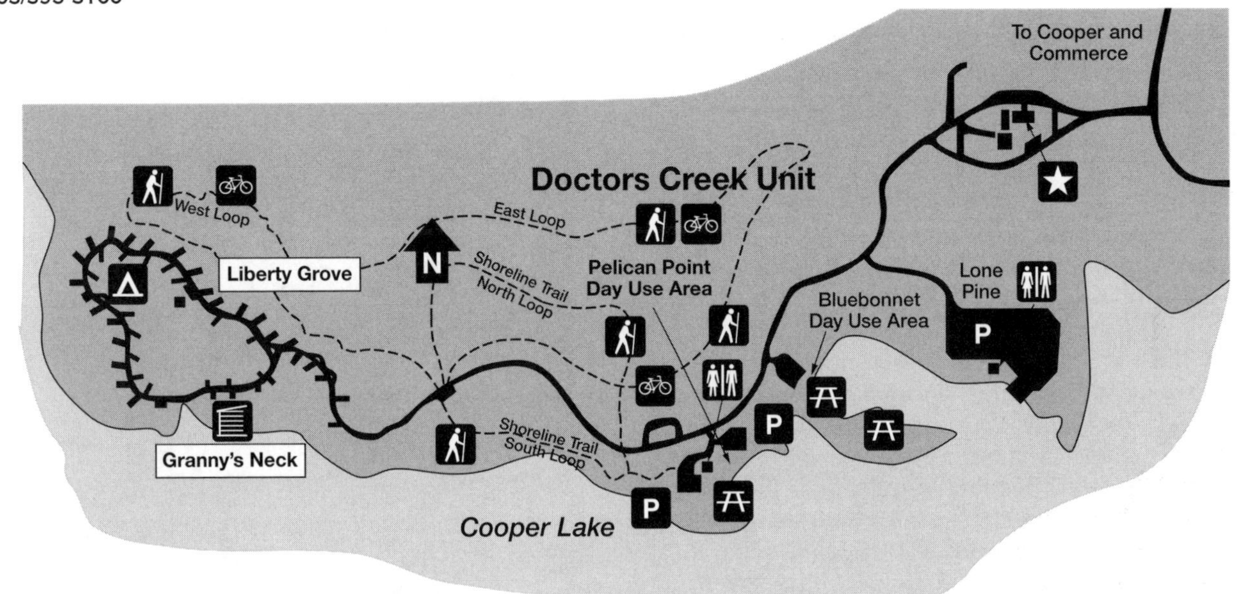

LOCATION

To reach the Doctors Creek Unit of Cooper Lake State Park, travel east on TX 154 from the town of Cooper for 1 mile, then turn right onto FM 1529, and travel 2 miles. Or, from I-30, take exit 122 on the west side of Sulphur Springs and travel north on TX 19 for 14 miles, then west on County Road 4795 for 2 miles to the Corps of Engineers Office; cross the lake dam and drive ½ mile to the park entrance. The 466-acre Doctors Creek Unit is on 19,305-acre Cooper Lake on the Sulphur River.

TRAIL NOTES

The Doctors Creek Unit has a 6.2-mile shoreline; a 1.3-mile hiking trail near the lake offers the opportunity to explore the shoreline habitat. Three miles of trails are located north of the park road and are designated as hike and bike trails.

Many of the parks operated by the Texas Parks and Wildlife Department are located at lake settings.

SOUTH SULPHUR UNIT

FOR INFORMATION

COOPER LAKE STATE PARK
SOUTH SULPHUR UNIT
1690 FM 3505
SULPHUR SPRINGS, TX 75482
903/945-5256

TRAIL NOTES

The South Sulphur Unit has 5 miles of trails designated for hiking and mountain biking, and 10 miles of trails designated for equestrian use. The trailhead for the 5-mile Coyote Run Nature Trail is at the Heron Harbor parking area. The difficulty of the trail is rated easy to moderate. The trail is marked with orange blazes, and the hiking time is estimated at 3 to 4 hours.

The equestrian trails are located in the western portion of the park and begin at Buggy Whip Equestrian Camping Area. There are 15 equestrian campsites with water and electricity. Three trails are available: Buggy Whip, Finley Creek, and Mill Creek. Buggy Whip Trail offers an easy 3-mile loop through the woods with panoramic views of the lake. Finley Creek Trail is a challenging trail that travels 2½ miles through mostly wooded terrain. The trail crosses one major creek and several smaller drainages. The Mill Creek Trail is a 5-mile trail that offers hilltop views of Cooper Lake. Access to this trail is through Finley Creek Trail and is rated more difficult due to terrain and length.

LOCATION

To reach the South Sulphur Unit of Cooper Lake State Park, travel north from I-30 at exit 122 on the west side of Sulphur Springs for 10 miles on TX 19, then west on FM 71 for 4 miles, and then north for 1 mile on FM 3505 to the park entrance. The 2,310-acre South Sulphur Unit is on 19,305-acre Cooper Lake on the Sulphur River.

The 5 miles of hiking trails at the South Sulphur Unit are also designated for mountain biking.

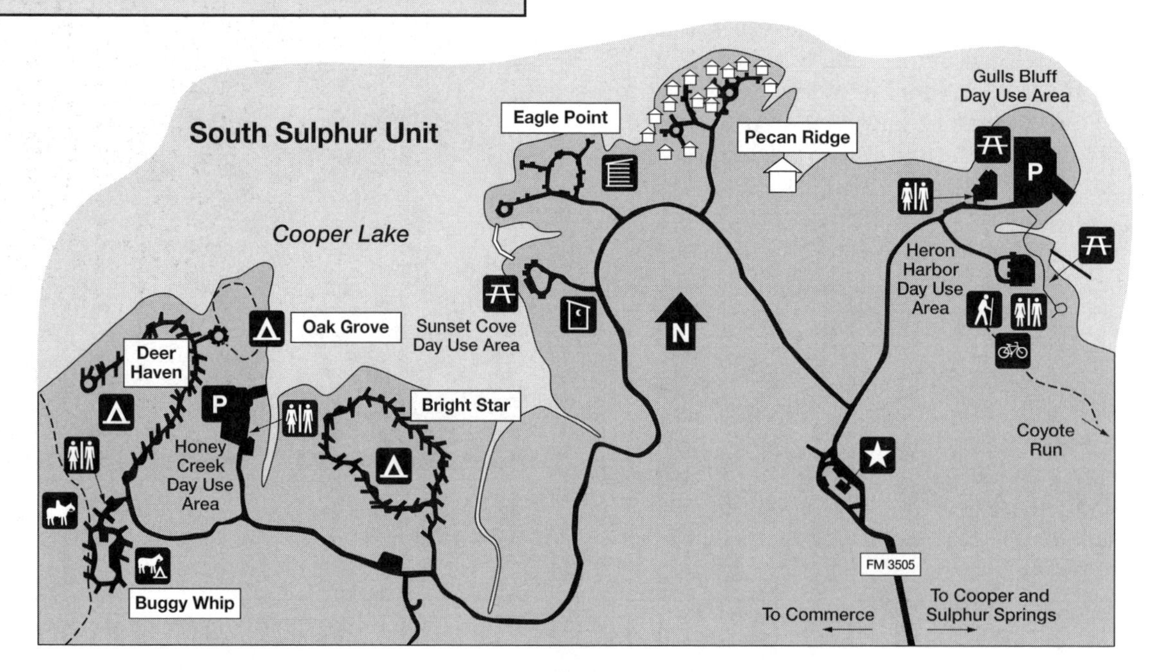

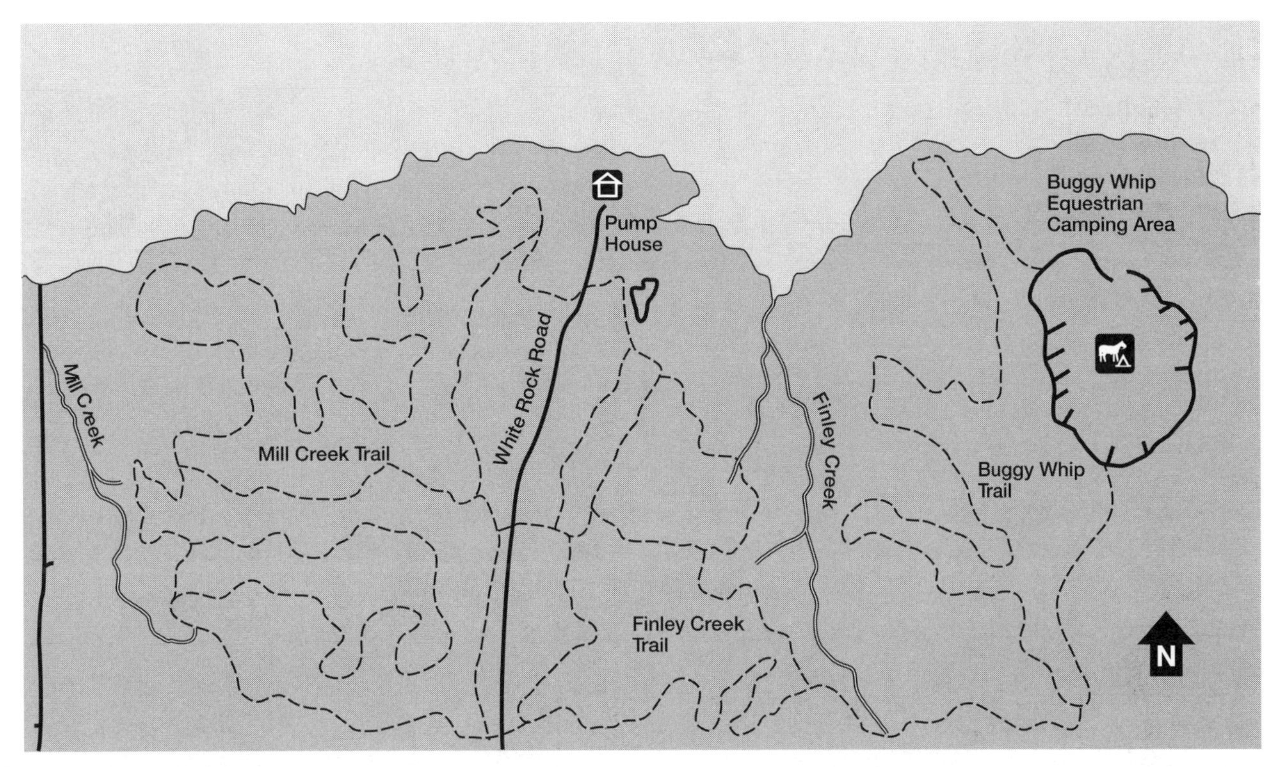

Equestrian Trails

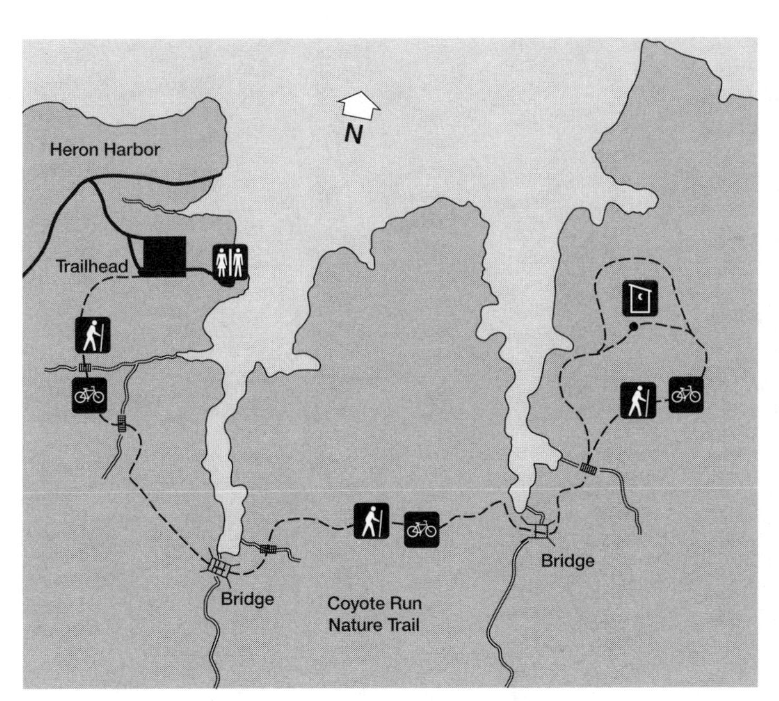

Coyote Run Nature Trail

Marsha Elmore

The 10 miles of equestrian trails at the South Sulphur Unit actually consist of 3 trails: Buggy Whip, Finley Creek, and Mill Creek. Buggy Whip is the easiest and Mill Creek is the most difficult.

DAINGERFIELD STATE PARK

FOR INFORMATION

DAINGERFIELD STATE PARK
455 PARK RD. 17
DAINGERFIELD, TX 75638
903/645-2921

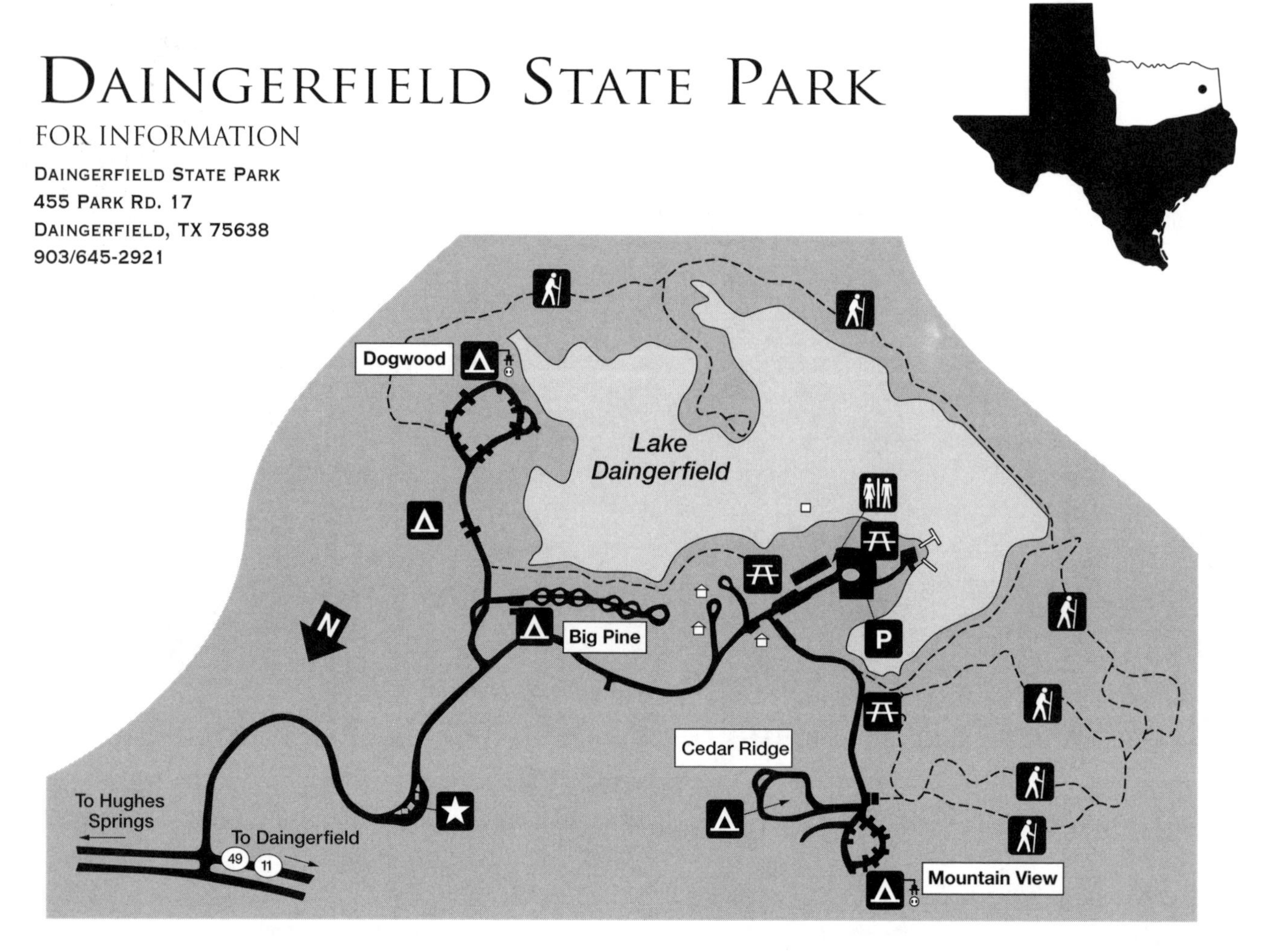

LOCATION

Daingerfield State Park is located approximately 3 miles east of Daingerfield on TX 11 and TX 49, to Park Road 17. The 551-acre park includes an 80-acre lake.

TEXAS HIGHWAYS Magazine

The 80-acre Lake Daingerfield that the 2½-mile hiking trail encircles is quite picturesque in the autumn.

TRAIL NOTES

The 2.5-mile hiking trail encircles a picturesque 80-acre lake. Over 42 different species of trees and other vegetation have been identified along the trail. The scenic beauty of the trail is best evidenced in the spring when the dogwood and redbud trees are in bloom, or in the fall when the leaves of the hardwood trees begin changing colors, contrasting with the deep greens of the pines. Beds of cinnamon ferns grow along hillside seepage areas. Some of the ferns may reach a height of five feet and are common to East Texas. A large old chinquapin tree, once recorded as a state champion, grows alongside the trail.

Dinosaur Valley State Park

FOR INFORMATION

DINOSAUR VALLEY STATE PARK
P.O. BOX 396
GLEN ROSE, TX 76043
254/897-4588

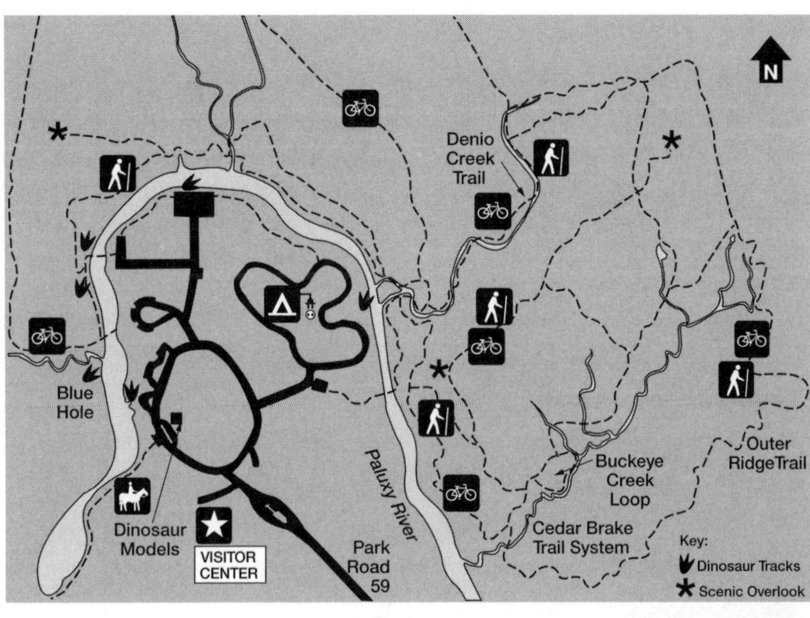

LOCATION

Dinosaur Valley State Park is located approximately 5 miles west of Glen Rose via US 67 and FM 205. The 1,523-acre park is along the Paluxy River.

TRAIL NOTES

A 1-mile hiking trail crosses the Paluxy River and goes to a promontory that commands a view of the park and surrounding countryside. The 5½-mile Cedar Brake Trail System provides access to several scenic overlooks and to 7 primitive camp areas for backpackers; this trail is designated for hikers and bikers. Trail users are aided by a color-coded trail system: some trails are marked in white, some in blue, and some in yellow. Horseback riding is allowed only in the 100-acre South Primitive Area; users must provide their own horses. Hikers and mountain bikers are also allowed to use the South Primitive Area, which is designated for day use only. There are approximately 12 miles of bicycle trails.

The dinosaur tracks found in the park represent some of the best preserved fossil footprints in Texas. There are 3 types of tracks, representing 3 types of dinosaurs.

Texas Parks & Wildlife Dept. © 2004

There are approximately 12 miles of bicycle trails at Dinosaur Valley; some are quite challenging.

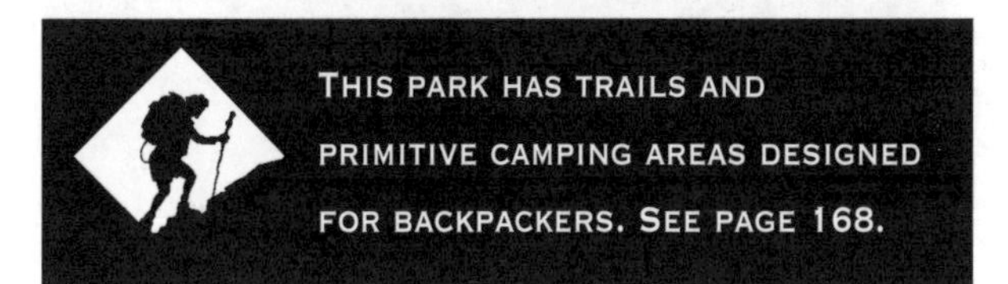

THIS PARK HAS TRAILS AND PRIMITIVE CAMPING AREAS DESIGNED FOR BACKPACKERS. SEE PAGE 168.

Eisenhower State Park

FOR INFORMATION

EISENHOWER STATE PARK
50 PARK ROAD 20
DENISON, TX 75020-4878
903/465-1956

LOCATION

Eisenhower State Park is 5 miles northwest of Denison. Travel on SH 91 to FM 1310, then 1.8 miles to Park Road 20. The 423-acre park is located on the shores of Lake Texoma, Texas' third largest reservoir, formed by the damming of the Red River.

TRAIL NOTES

Eisenhower State Park has 6 miles of trails. The section of trail from the boat ramp east to the Armadillo Hill camping area is for hiking only. The trail running northwest from the boat ramp to Elm Point is designated for hiking and biking. Hiking the trail reveals a wide variety of flora and fauna as well as an abundance of marine fossils. One of the most common fossils found is the ammonite, a rounded spiral relative of the octopus.

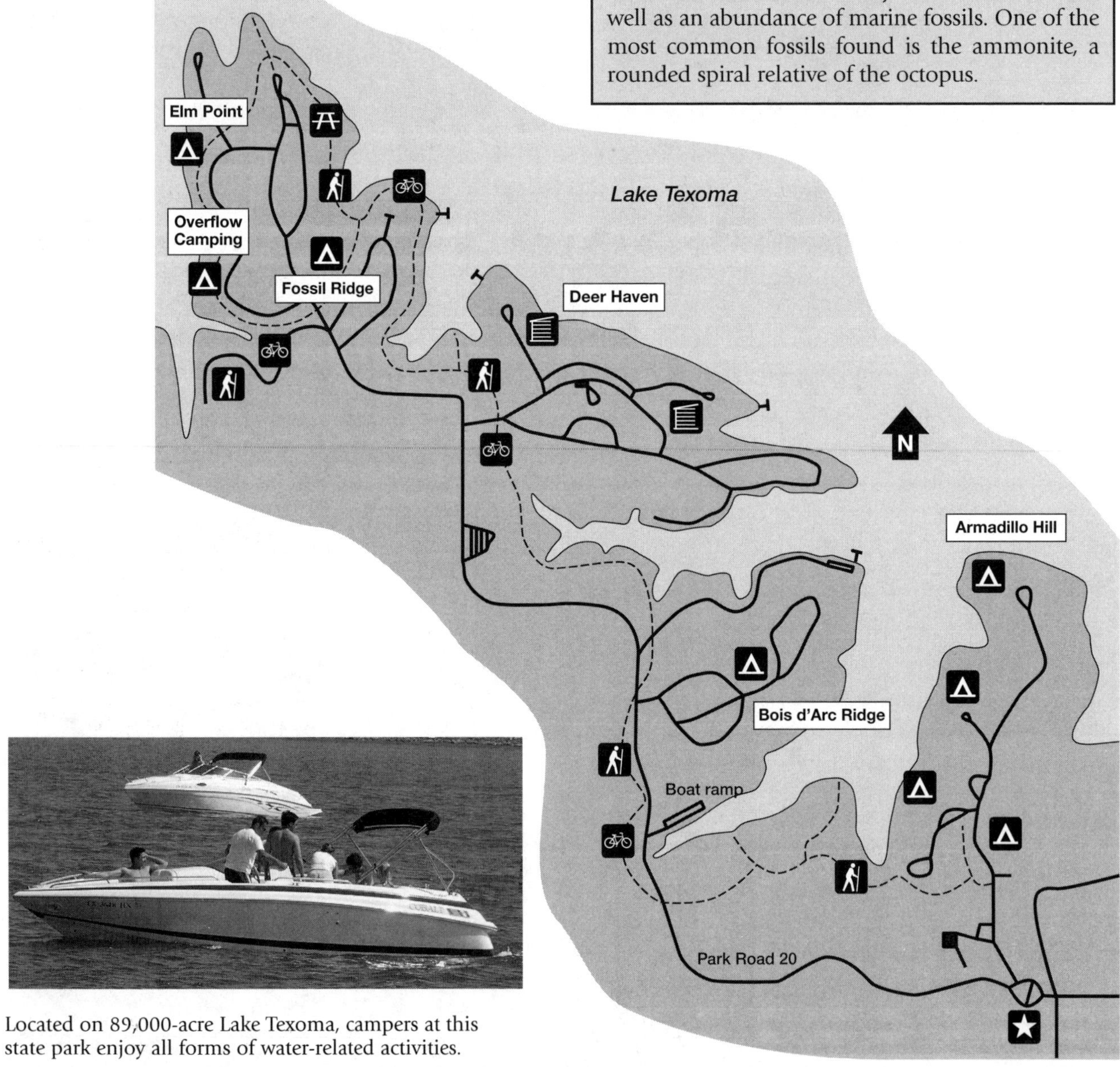

Located on 89,000-acre Lake Texoma, campers at this state park enjoy all forms of water-related activities.

Fairfield Lake State Park

FOR INFORMATION

FAIRFIELD LAKE STATE PARK
123 STATE PARK RD. 64
FAIRFIELD, TX 75840
903/389-4514

LOCATION

Fairfield Lake State Park is located 6 miles northeast of Fairfield. From I-45, exit 197, take US 84 east to FM 488, north to FM 2570, then northeast to FM 3285 and east to Park Road 64. This 1,460-acre park, with its beautiful hardwood forest and rolling hills, is situated on the southern end of the 2,400-acre Fairfield Lake. Bald eagles are winter visitors.

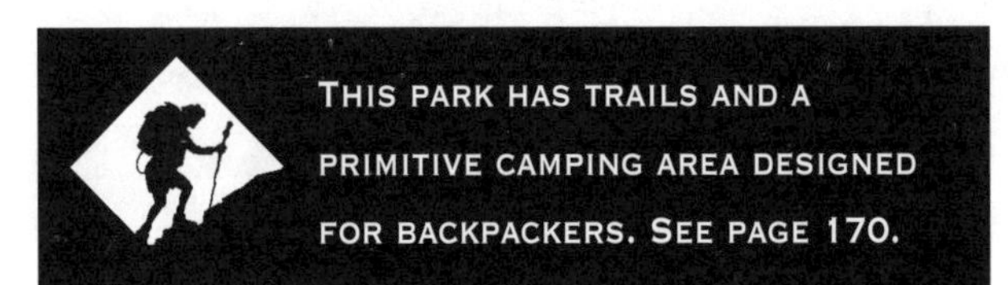

TRAIL NOTES

A 2-mile hike/bike trail is adjacent to the Post Oak camping area; the trailhead to a 1-mile bird-watching trail is west of the main road between the park entrance and the camping areas. Big Brown Creek Trail is a 6-mile round-trip hike/bike trail that leads to a backcountry camping area for backpackers. The first 1½ miles of this trail has interpretive signs to identify many of the trees and other plants; several trailside benches are provided for rest stops.

The Perimeter Trail has recently been completed. One trailhead is from a hike/bike trail that is east of the Post Oak camping area; the other trailhead is near the entrance to the park. This trail, designated as a multi-use trail for hiking, biking, and equestrian, follows a portion of the park's east and south boundary. There are approximately 20 miles of bicycle trails.

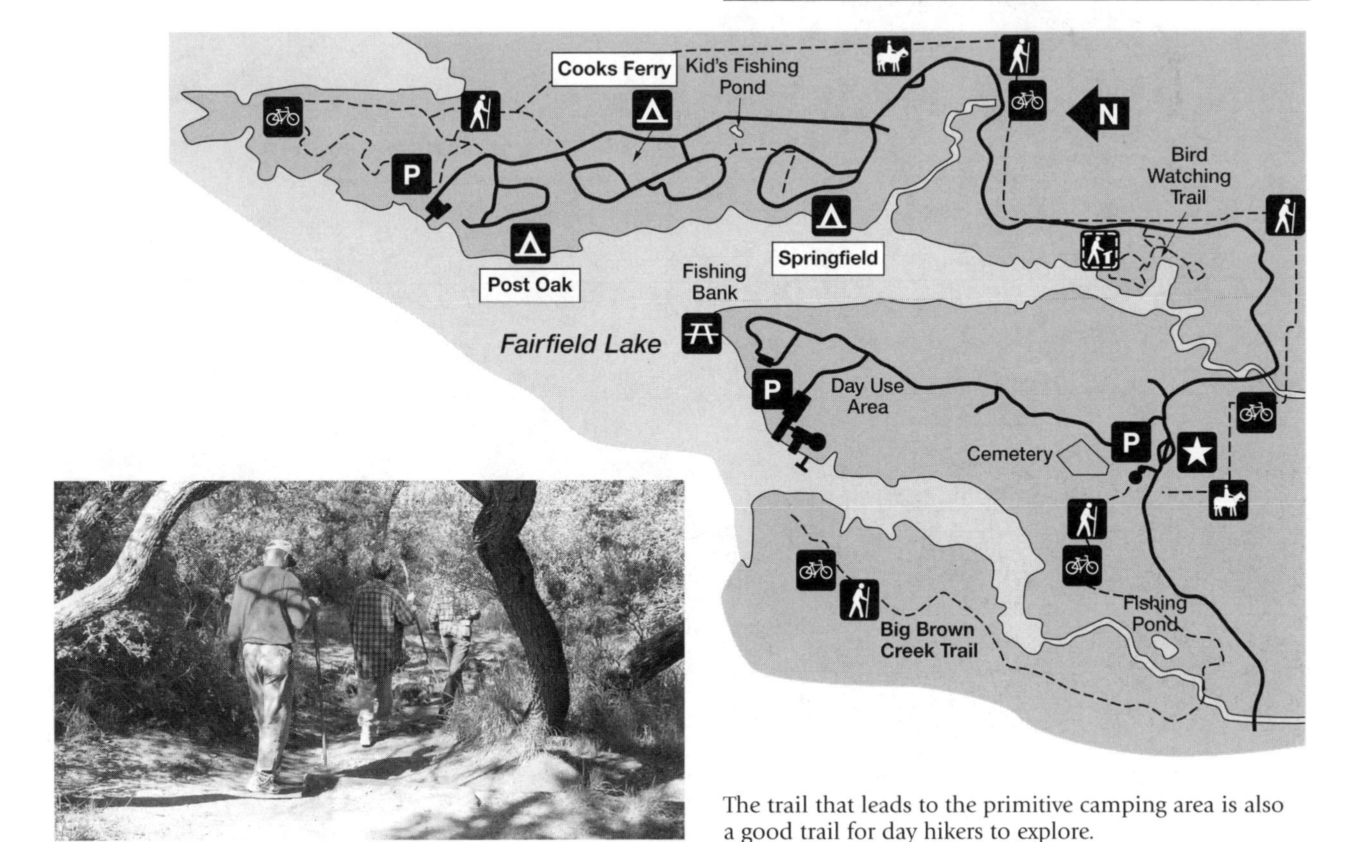

The trail that leads to the primitive camping area is also a good trail for day hikers to explore.

Fort Richardson State Park & Historic Site and Lost Creek Reservoir State Trailway

FOR INFORMATION

FORT RICHARDSON STATE PARK & HISTORIC SITE
AND LOST CREEK RESERVOIR STATE TRAILWAY
228 STATE PARK RD. 61
JACKSBORO, TX 76458
940/567-3506

LOCATION

Fort Richardson State Park and Historic Site is in the Jacksboro city limits, 1 mile southeast of the square with access from US 281. The remains of a federal fort, built in 1867, after the Civil War, include 2 replica barracks and 7 of the post's original structures; an interpretive center has exhibits about the history of the fort. The 402-acre park has an 8-acre lake.

TRAIL NOTES

The Lost Creek Nature Trail is a ½-mile trail that follows the creek along its west bank while the Running Spring Path is a shorter trail that follows the creek along its east bank. The 1.7-mile Prickly Pear Hiking Trail is a loop trail in the open prairie. Twenty walk-in campsites are located in a primitive camping area off of this trail. The newest and longest trail is a 10-mile multi-use trail called the Lost Creek Reservoir State Trailway.

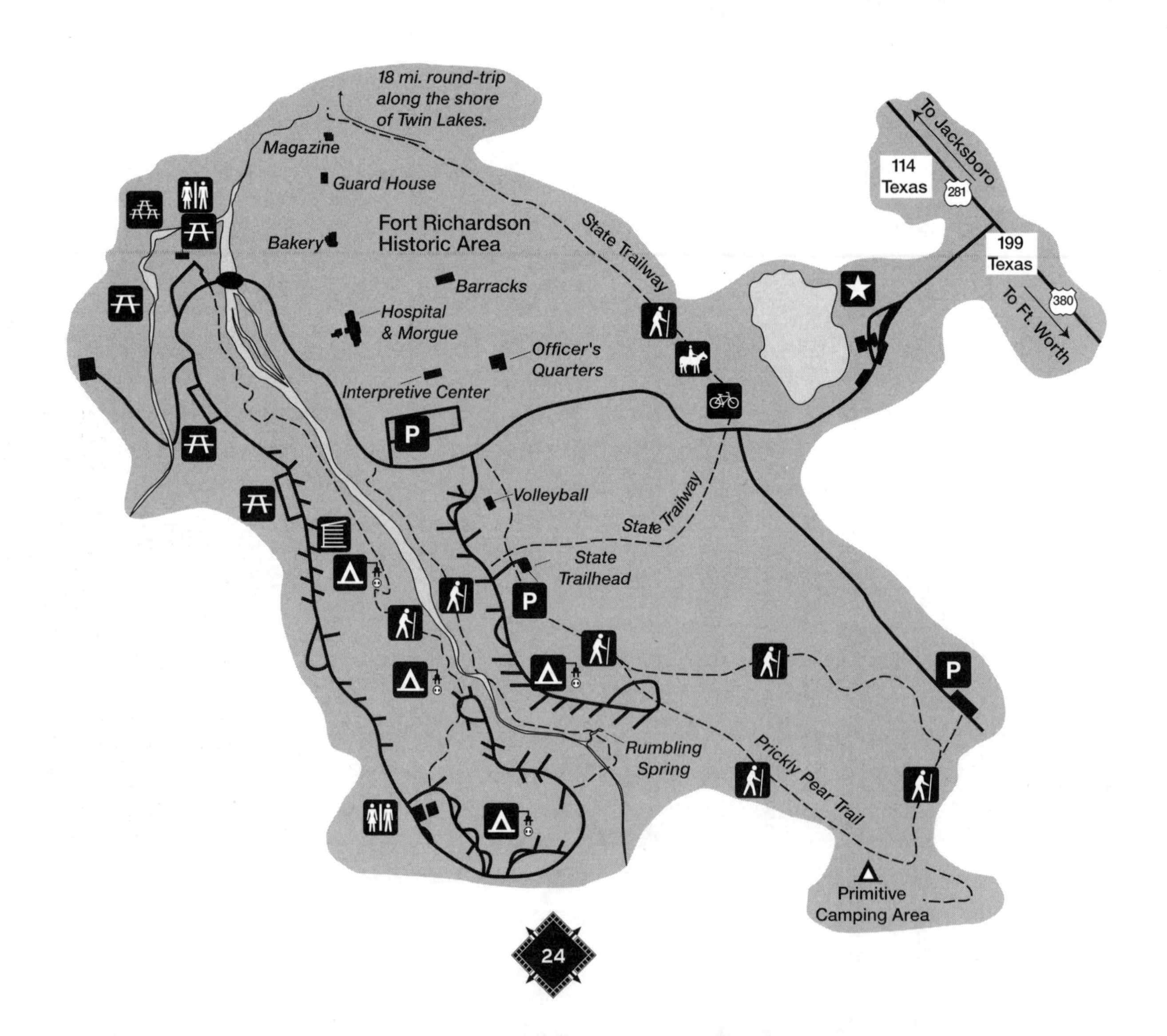

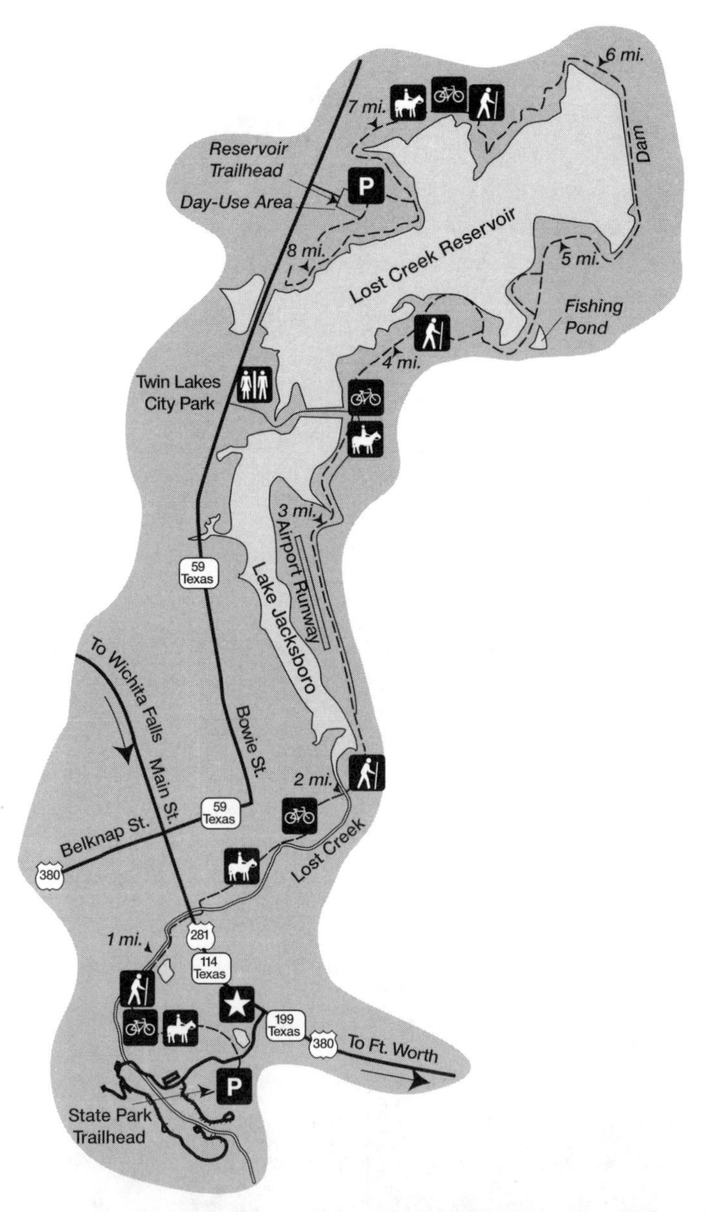

LOST CREEK RESERVOIR STATE TRAILWAY

The Lost Creek Reservoir State Trailway is a hike, bike, and equestrian trail that runs adjacent to Fort Richardson, follows Lost Creek along the east side of Lake Jacksboro and Lost Creek Reservoir, crosses the dam at the reservoir, and winds along the west side until it reaches a trailhead at a day-use area. There are 2 trailheads: one at Fort Richardson and one at Lost Creek Reservoir. The trail is 10 feet wide and has an improved surfacing of base material and a topping of about four inches of screening materials. This type of surface creates a smooth trail for all types of use.

Cyclists should pass other trail users slowly and considerately. Cyclists should wear a helmet and should yield to hikers when meeting from opposite directions. Hikers and cyclists should always yield to horses and make their presence known well in advance, then move aside to allow horses to pass, if meeting from the opposite direction; if passing horses from behind, hikers and bikers should pass on the left after making the rider aware of their presence. Pets are permitted on the trails, but must be under control and on a leash at all times.

Marsha Elmore

There are 2 trailheads to the Lost Creek Reservoir State Trailway: one at Fort Richardson State Park and Historic Site and one at Lost Creek Reservoir.

Fort Worth Nature Center and Refuge

For Information

Fort Worth Nature Center and Refuge
9601 Fossil Ridge Road
Fort Worth, TX 76135-9148
817/237-1111
www.fwnaturecenter.org

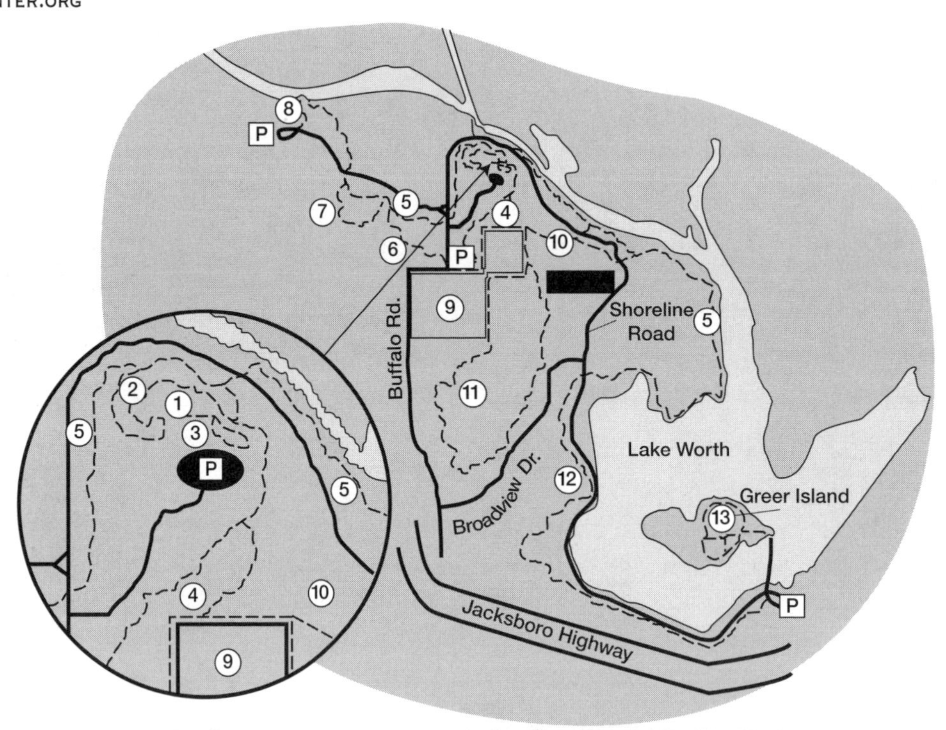

About the Center

A 25-mile trail system provides excellent opportunities to see native wildlife and plants at the Fort Worth Nature Center and Refuge. It is one of the largest nature centers in the United States and its 3,600+ acres of urban wilderness make it one of the most unique natural areas in north-central Texas. Forest, prairie, marsh, river, and limestone outcrops are accessible within the center's boundaries and represent the major ecological habitats of the region. The sanctuary is located 10 miles from downtown Fort Worth; the entrance is at the intersection of FM 1886 and TX 199, 2 miles west of the Lake Worth Bridge. Refuge hours are 9 a.m. to 5 p.m. daily. Visitor center hours are 9 a.m. to 4:30 p.m. Tuesdays through Saturdays; noon to 4:30 p.m. Sundays; and closed on Mondays. Gates close at 5 p.m.

Lillian Morava

In addition to armadillos (the unofficial state critter of Texas), small herds of buffalo and whitetail deer reside at the nature center.

THE TRAIL SYSTEM

1. **Hardwicke Interpretive Center**—All trails can be reached from the Hardwicke Interpretive Center, at the center of various trailheads. The center has exhibits and visitor information; trail maps are available. Trails #2, 3, 4, 5, 6, 7, 10, and 11 start at the center. Restrooms available; wheelchair accessible. Trails are identified by symbols.
2. **Caprock Trail**—Views along a fossil shell outcrop; ½-mile/45 minutes; symbol: fossil shell.
3. **Limestone Ledge Trail**—A short paved trail suitable for short walks; wheelchair accessible; 800 feet/20 minutes; symbol: bluebonnet.
4. **Prairie Trail**—This trail passes through a prairie and passes by the buffalo range; 1 mile/1 hour; symbol: buffalo.
5. **Riverbottom Trail**—This trail leads to either the Marsh Boardwalk Trail (round-trip 3.4 miles), or follows the river, marshes, and forests to connect with the end of Canyon Ridge (round-trip 4.6 miles). Different routes are possible. Accessible from the Caprock Trail or from the Deer Mouse Trail; symbol: turtle.
6. **Wild Plum Trail**—This trail ties together several trails that take you through forest, wild plum thickets, and back to the Hardwicke Center via the Prairie Trail; 3.2 miles/2 hours; symbol: flower.
7. **Forked Tail Creek Trail**—This trail is accessible from the Riverbottom Trail that leads to the Marsh Boardwalk just past the Wild Plum Trail. This trail follows a shaded creek bed lined with Burr oaks, post oaks, pecans, American elms, and various understory trees; 2.7 miles/1½ hours; symbol: fork.
8. **Marsh Boardwalk**—Boardwalk over the marsh and through riverbottom forest; 900 feet/30 minutes; symbol: heron.
9. **Buffalo Range**—Close-up views of a small herd of buffalo, whitetail deer, and prairie dogs.
10. **Deer Mouse Trail**—This trail ties together the Oak Motte and the Riverbottom Trail. A loop can be created by walking the Prairie, Oak Motte, and Deer Mouse trails, and returning upriver on the Riverbottom Trail to the Caprock Trail; 2½ miles/1½ hours; symbol: mouse.
11. **Oak Motte Trail**—This trail meanders through grasslands and clusters of red and live oak trees; 3.2 miles/2 hours; symbol: acorn.
12. **Canyon Ridge Trail**—Ridgetop vistas, shady canyons, and views of the marsh make this a scenic trail; 3 miles one way/2½ hours; symbol: yucca.
13. **Greer Island Trails**—Cross a levee to a forested island with several interlocking trails; 1½ miles/1 hour; symbol: cattail.

This sign says it all: travel by the rules of "low impact" and you'll be taking good care of yourself and your environment.

People aren't the only visitors that enjoy the Refuge.

Grapevine Lake Trails

FOR INFORMATION

GRAPEVINE LAKE PROJECT OFFICE
110 FAIRWAY DRIVE
GRAPEVINE, TX 76051-3495
817/481-4541
817/481-3576 (INFORMATION LINE)

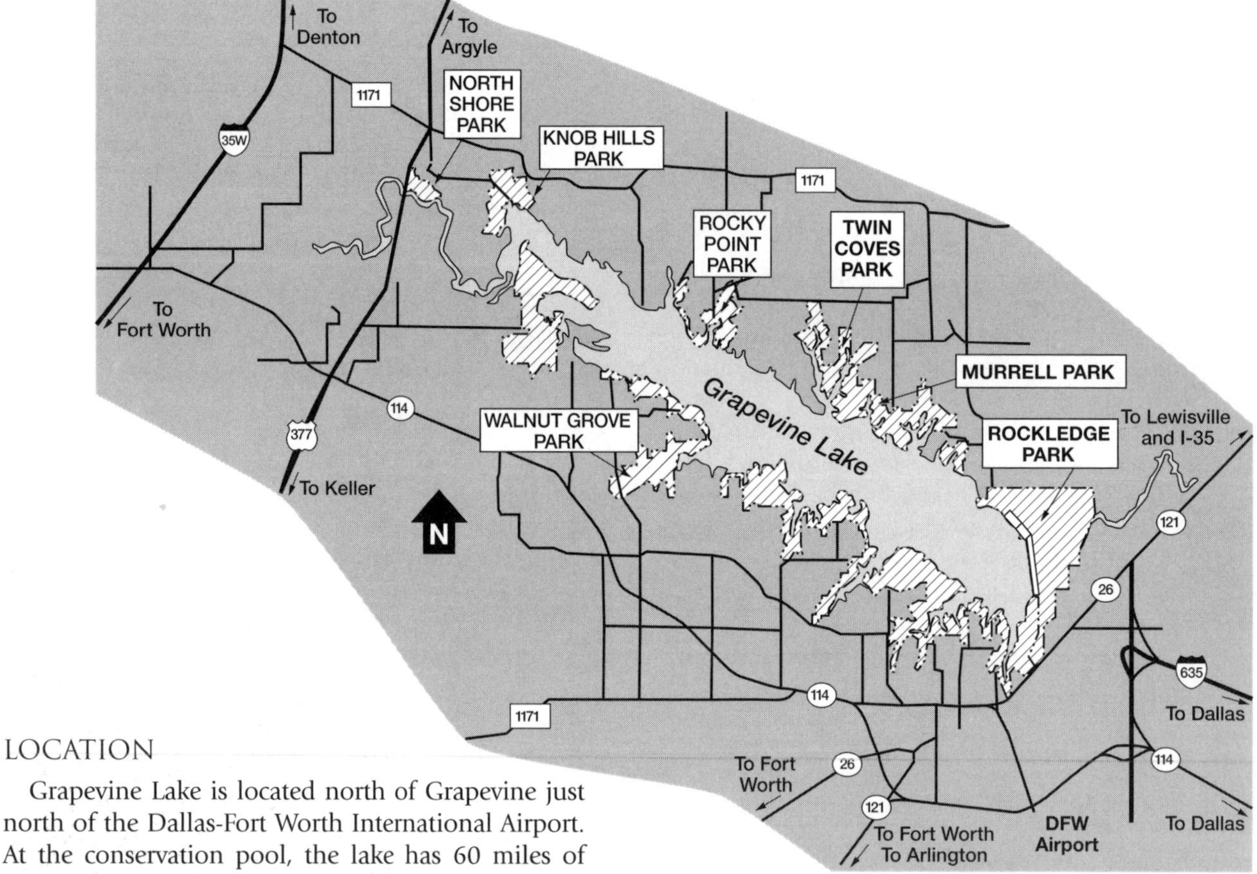

LOCATION

Grapevine Lake is located north of Grapevine just north of the Dallas-Fort Worth International Airport. At the conservation pool, the lake has 60 miles of shoreline with a surface area of 7,380 acres. Twelve parks surround the lake; 7 are developed areas with facilities furnished by either the Corps of Engineers or a concessionaire, and 5 are undeveloped park areas.

Four of the parks at Grapevine Lake have developed campgrounds.

TRAIL NOTES

Trails are located at 7 of the parks—nature, hiking and mountain biking, or equestrian and hiking. Trails designated for horses and hikers are Walnut Grove, Cross Timbers, and Rocky Point. The Northshore Trail and the Knob Hills Trail are hiking and bicycle trails. The trails are located on flood control land and the possibility of flooding exists. Under any wet conditions the trails may be closed to horses and bicycles. To check trail status and conditions, call the Grapevine Lake information line at 817/481-3576.

The **Walnut Grove Trail** is a 10-mile horseback riding and hiking trail at Walnut Grove Park. The park is located on the southwest side of the lake off of TX 114 (Northwest Parkway). A map is available.

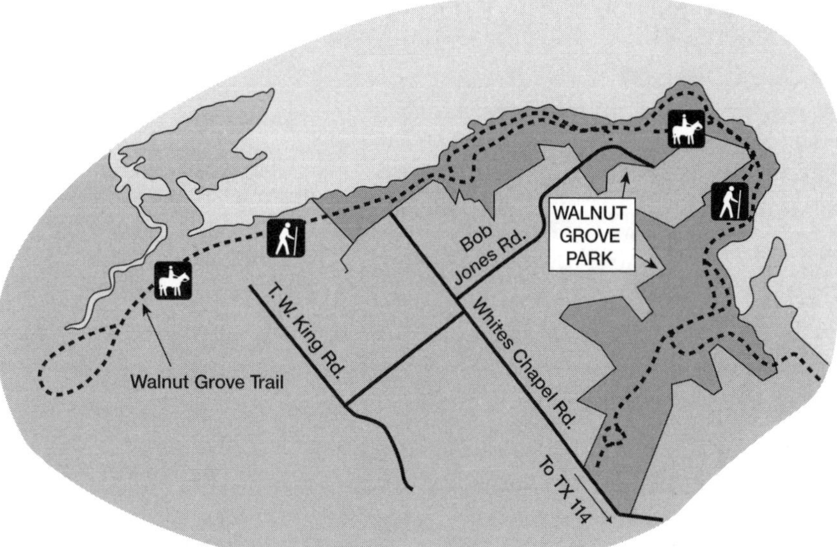

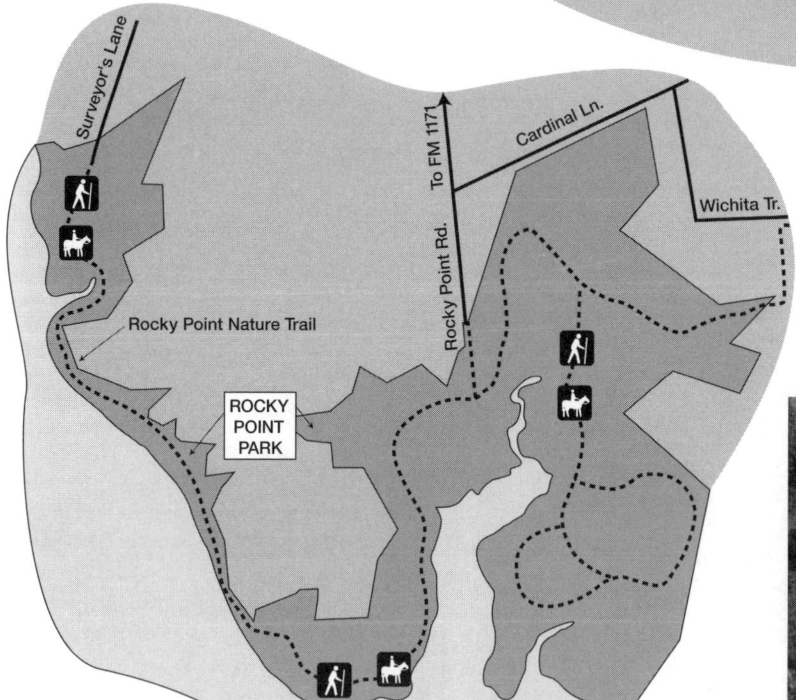

The **Rocky Point Nature Trail** is a 3-mile-long horse and hiking trail that winds around Rocky Point Park and Redbud Point, providing beautiful views of the lake from the bluffs.

These hikers appear to be on a mission!

The **Northshore Trail** was developed for hikers and bicyclists; therefore, horse and motorized traffic are prohibited. The trail is a single track, natural surface trail that begins at Rockledge Park and winds westward along the lakeshore through Murrell Park to end 9 miles later at Twin Coves Park. Several access points to the trail are available via public roads, but due to heavy use, visitors are advised to access the trail in Murrell Park.

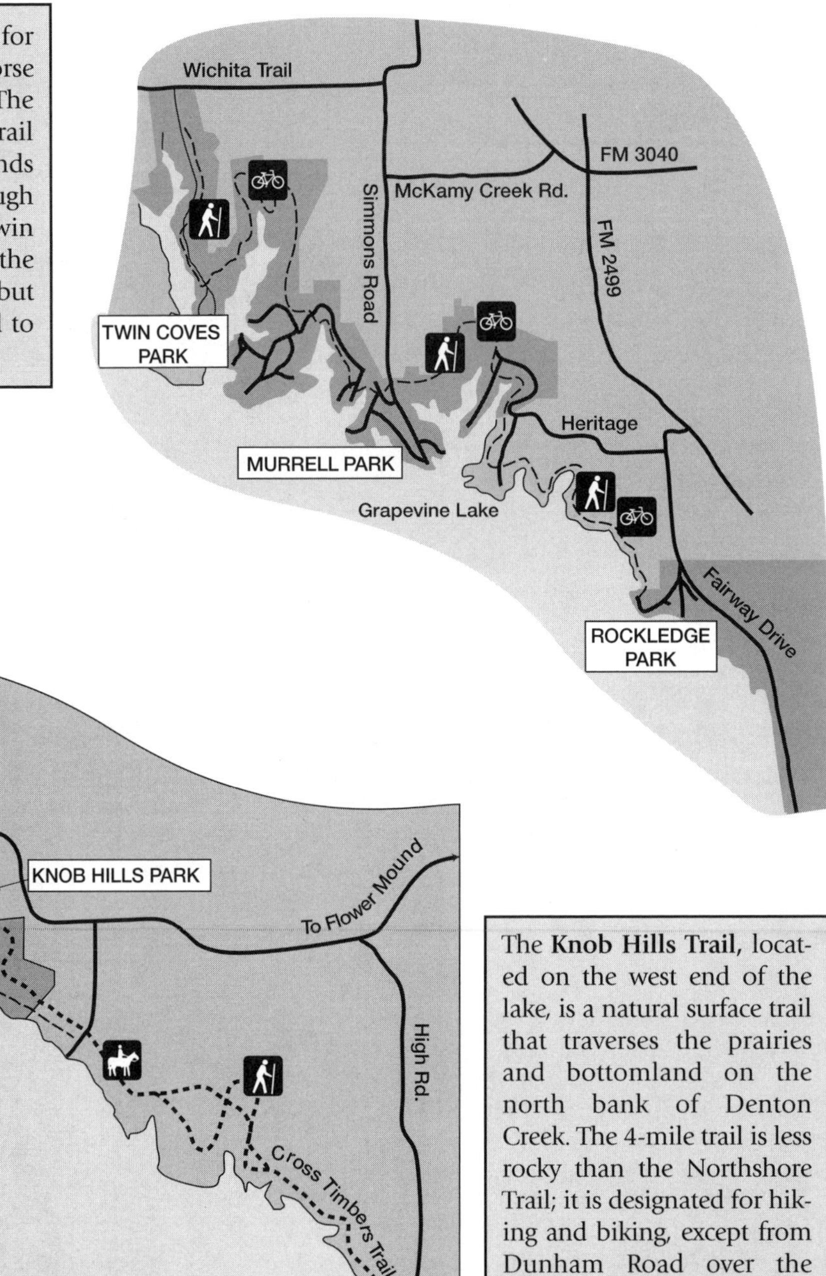

The **Knob Hills Trail,** located on the west end of the lake, is a natural surface trail that traverses the prairies and bottomland on the north bank of Denton Creek. The 4-mile trail is less rocky than the Northshore Trail; it is designated for hiking and biking, except from Dunham Road over the White's Bridge, where it is shared with equestrians.

The **Cross Timbers Trail** is also located along the shoreline at the northwest end of the lake in the undeveloped Knob Hills Park area. This trail is a 5-mile trail for horseback riding and hiking; a map is available.

LAKE ARROWHEAD STATE PARK

FOR INFORMATION

LAKE ARROWHEAD STATE PARK
229 PARK RD. 63
WICHITA FALLS, TX 76301
940/528-2211

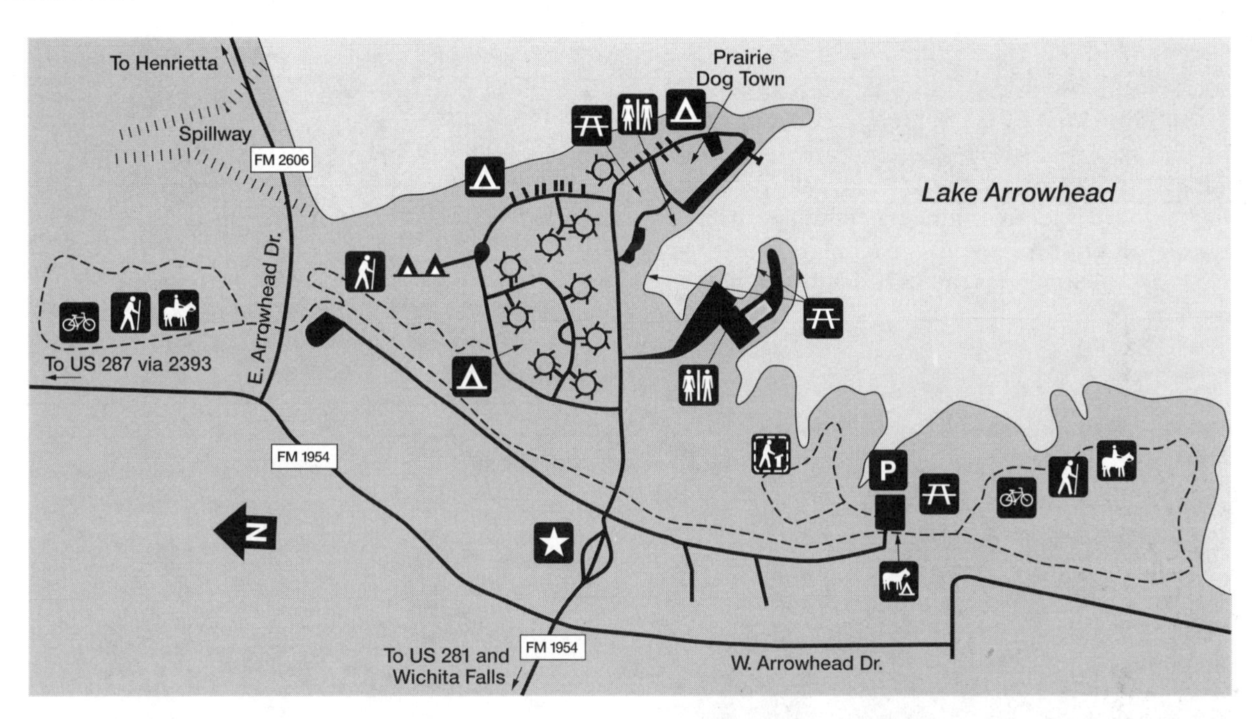

LOCATION

Lake Arrowhead State Park is located southeast of Wichita Falls on the shore of Lake Arrowhead. To reach this 524-acre park from US 281, take FM 1954 east for 8 miles; from US 82/287, take FM 2393 south for 8 miles. The lake is on the Little Wichita River and covers about 16,200 surface acres with 106 miles of shoreline. Large steel oil derricks dot the lake; waters around these structures frequently yield large stringers of fish.

Marsha Elmore

More than 5 miles of trails at Lake Arrowhead are designated as multi-use trails. In addition, there is a 300-acre day-use horseback riding area.

TRAIL NOTES

The park has a variety of trails. One trail is designated as a nature trail, another as a hiking trail, and more than 5 miles are designated as multi-use trails for hiking, mountain biking, and equestrian. There is also a 300-acre day-use horseback riding area with potable water, restrooms, barns, and pens. The land surrounding the lake is gently rolling mixed-prairie, much of which has been invaded by mesquite in recent decades.

LAKE BOB SANDLIN STATE PARK

FOR INFORMATION

LAKE BOB SANDLIN STATE PARK
341 STATE PARK RD. 2117
PITTSBURG, TX 75686
903/572-5531

LOCATION

Lake Bob Sandlin, a 9,460-acre reservoir on Cypress Creek, is southwest of Mount Pleasant and southeast of Mt. Vernon. The 640-acre Lake Bob Sandlin State Park is located along the central portion of the reservoir's north shore. The park may be reached by FM 21, which bounds the west side of the park.

TRAIL NOTES

The park has 4½ miles of trails, with 8 footbridges. Two walk-in primitive camping areas are located on a 1½-mile loop trail. The trailhead to another loop trail is north of the day-use area. The section of trail leading from Fort Sherman Campground to the park road is designated as an interpretive trail. Mountain bikes are permitted on all of the trails.

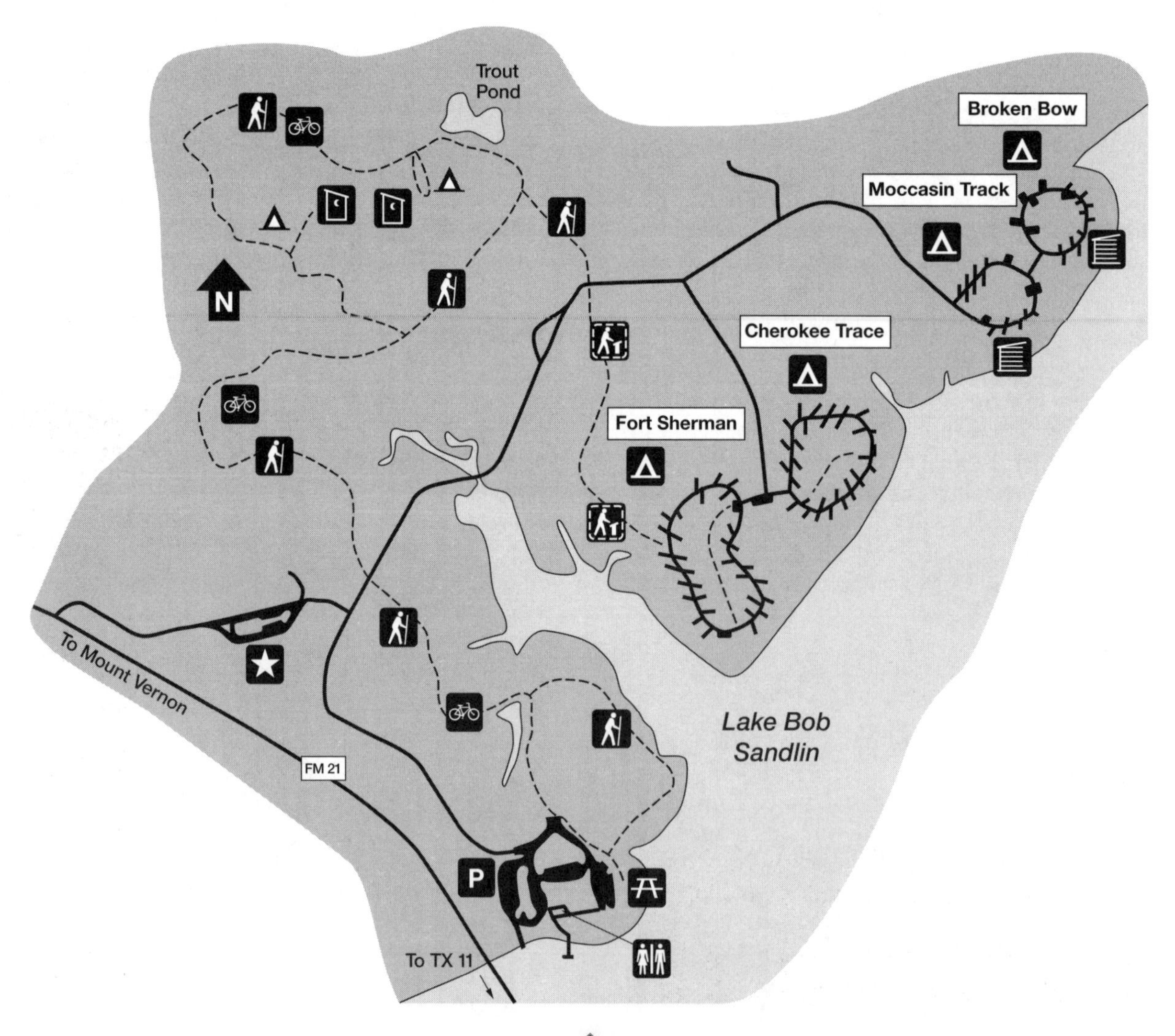

Lake Mineral Wells State Park and Trailway

For Information

Lake Mineral Wells State
Park and Trailway
100 Park Rd. 71
Mineral Wells, TX 76067
940/328-1171

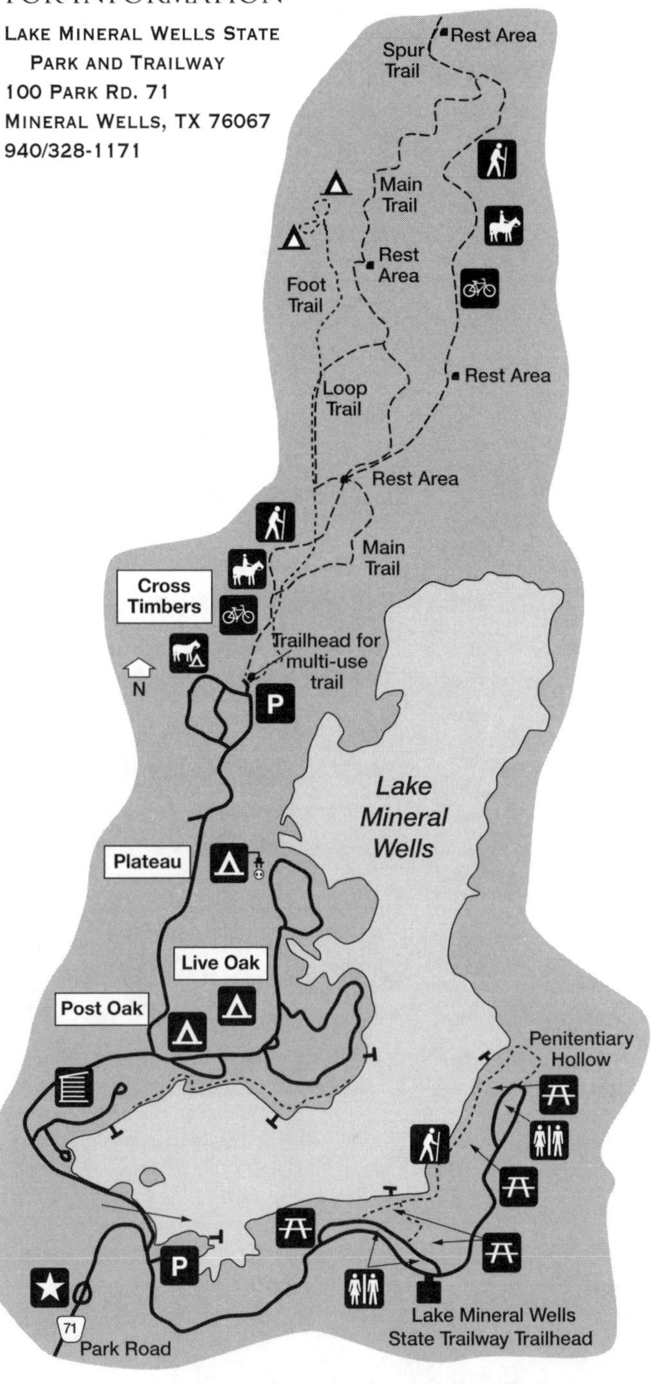

Location

Lake Mineral Wells State Park and Trailway is situated only 4 miles from the center of town. The park contains 3,282 acres, which include the 646-acre lake, and may be reached by traveling 4 miles east from the city of Mineral Wells on US 180 or 15 miles west of Weatherford on the same highway.

Trail Notes

Five miles of hiking trails exist along the water's edge near the camping area as well as in the day-use area. A 2½-mile hiking trail leads to 2 primitive camping areas for backpackers. These two trails do not allow bikes and horses. Horseback riding, bicycling, and hiking are permitted on the main trail north of the Cross Timbers equestrian camping area. This trail is 12 miles round-trip. The terrain consists of hilly, varied soils broken by Brazos and Trinity tributaries.

The hiking trail located along the water's edge is called the Water Trail. Signs like this one are posted at different locations to aid the hiker.

THIS PARK HAS TRAILS AND PRIMITIVE CAMPING AREAS DESIGNED FOR BACKPACKERS. SEE PAGE 185.

LAKE MINERAL WELLS STATE TRAILWAY

The Lake Mineral Wells State Trailway had its grand opening on June 6, 1998, National Trails Day, celebrating the 75th anniversary of state parks. The trail begins northwest of Weatherford and travels 20 miles westward to the downtown district of Mineral Wells. The trailway is connected to Lake Mineral Wells State Park and has 4 trailheads: near Weatherford, in Garner, in the state park, and in downtown Mineral Wells. Fees will be collected at the Weatherford trailhead (staffed station Saturday and Sunday and honor system Monday through Friday). Fees will also be collected at the park headquarters.

The trailway provides a diverse experience for hikers, bicyclists, and equestrians as it winds gently through remote farm and ranch lands and ends in a typical downtown district of an active West Texas community. Because the trailway is located on a railroad bed, the grades are very flat and curves are very gentle. The trailway is 20 miles long and 10 feet wide. The 2 miles of surface from the downtown Mineral Wells trailhead toward the east is asphalt; the remaining 18 miles is finely crushed and screened limestone. Each of the trailway's 4 trailheads has paved parking, drinking water, restrooms, trail information, and accessible parking. All 15 bridges have been decked and railed for safety. *Note: the trailway may be closed during wet weather.*

Marsha Elmore

The Lake Mineral Wells State Trailway opened officially in June 1998. This multi-use trailway stretches for 20 miles between Mineral Wells and Weatherford.

This hiker is exploring Penitentiary Hollow—an area used for rock climbing and rappelling located in the park's picnic area.

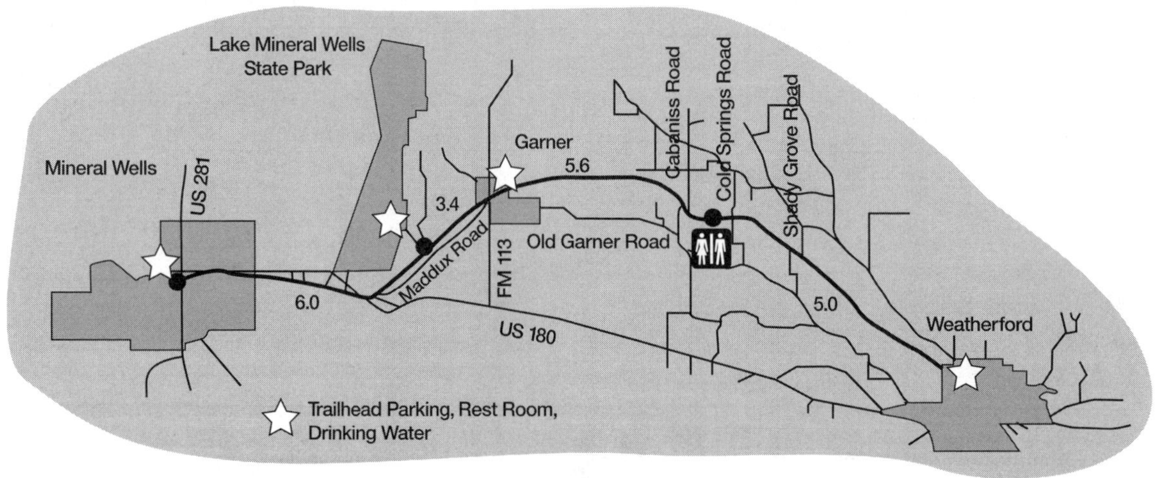

Lake Whitney State Park

FOR INFORMATION

LAKE WHITNEY STATE PARK
P.O. BOX 1175
WHITNEY, TX 76692
254/694-3793

LOCATION

Lake Whitney State Park is located 3 miles west of Whitney on FM 1244. From I-35, take the Hillsboro exit; in Hillsboro take TX 22 west to Whitney. The 955-acre park is located on the shore of Lake Whitney, the fourth largest lake in Texas. The park has scattered groves of post oak and live oak; in the spring bluebonnets and Indian paintbrushes cover the landscape. The crystal water of this 23,500-acre lake provides excellent boating, skiing, and fishing activities.

TRAIL NOTES

A 0.9-mile nature trail winds through open grassland and heavily wooded areas, and along the shoreline of Lake Whitney in the western portion of the park. A 1-mile multi-use trail for hikers and bikers is in the eastern portion of the park.

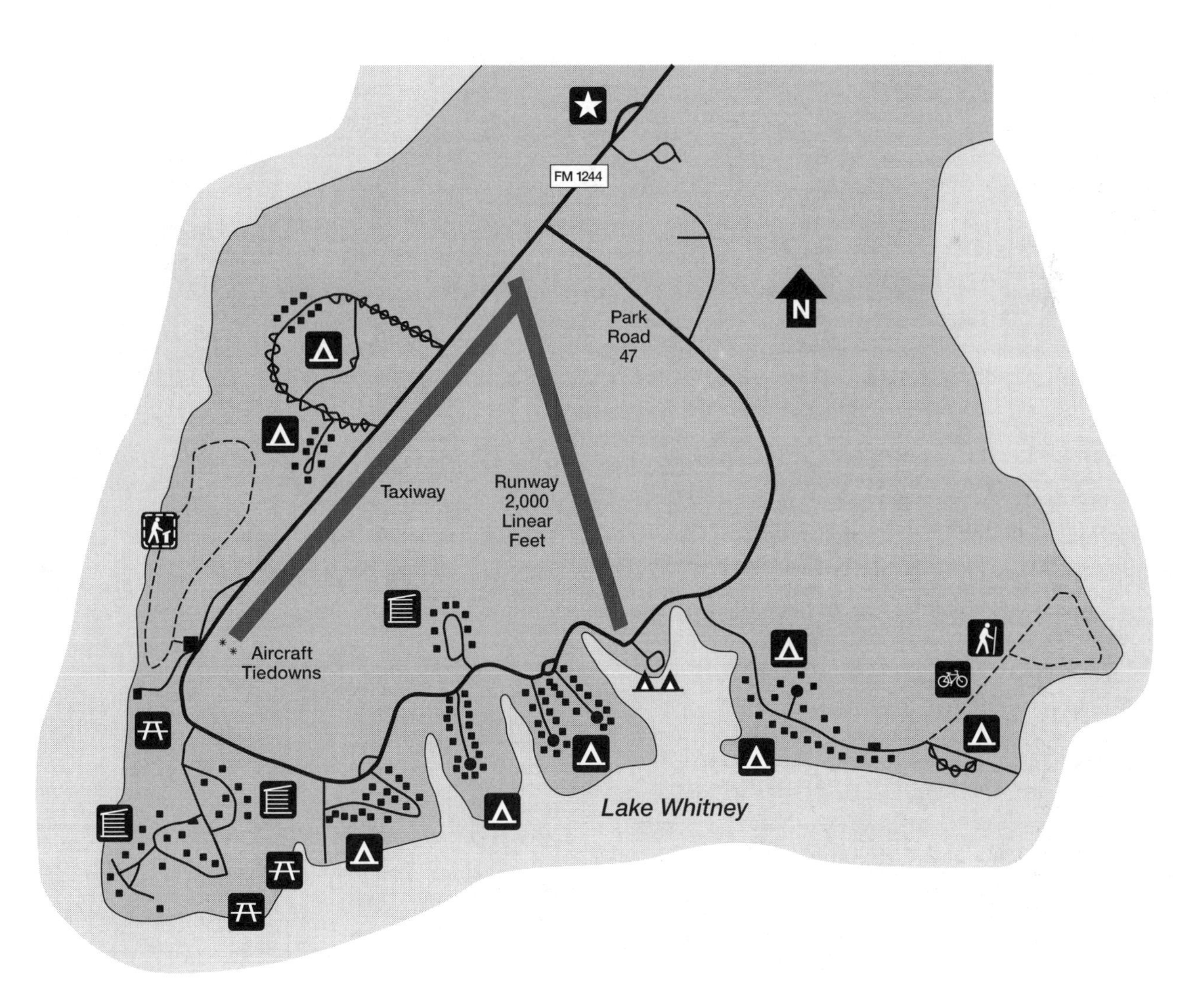

Lavon Lake/Trinity Trail/ Sister Grove Park

For Information

Collin County
825 N. McDonald St., Suite 145
McKinney, TX 75069
972/548-3744
www.collincountytexas.gov

Location

Lavon Lake is located northeast of Dallas via US 75 and TX 78 from Wylie. **Sister Grove Park** is located east of McKinney off of US 380; turn north on CR 559 from the US 380 bridge that crosses the north end of the lake. Then turn left onto CR 561 and left onto CR 562. The park is on the left.

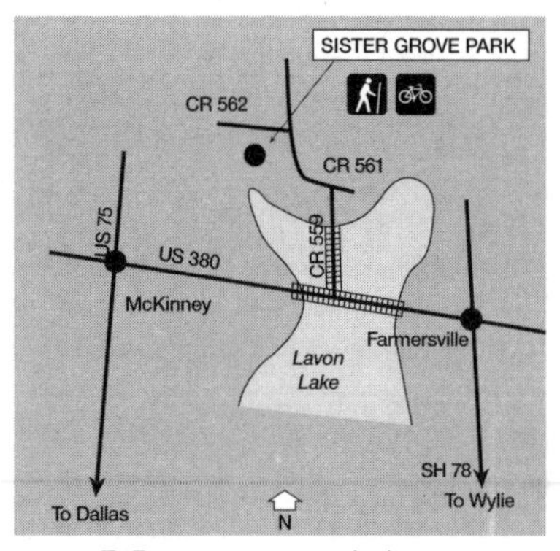

Vicinity Map

Trail Notes

The **Trinity Trail** is for equestrian and hiking use only. This 9-mile trail is on the west arm of Lavon Lake between Brockdale Park and East Fork Park. Groups of more than 25 riders are required to obtain a permit from the Lavon Lake Corps of Engineers office. Trail is closed when wet. Call for status: 972/442-5711. Restroom facilities and picnic areas are available.

Sister Grove Park, located on the northeastern arm of Lavon Lake, is the site of a natural surface 6-mile hike and mountain bike trail. When the trail is wet, it is closed to bikes. Restroom facilities, a covered pavillion, and picnic tables are available.

Both trails are administered by Collin County. The Trinity Trail is maintained by the Trinity Trail Preservation Association.

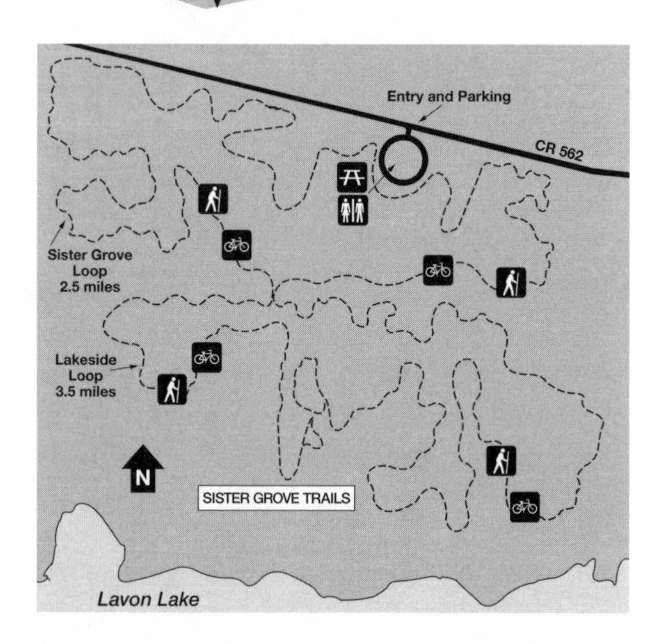

Lewisville Lake Trails

FOR INFORMATION

Lewisville Lake
1801 N. Mill Street
Lewisville, TX 75057-1821
972/434-1666

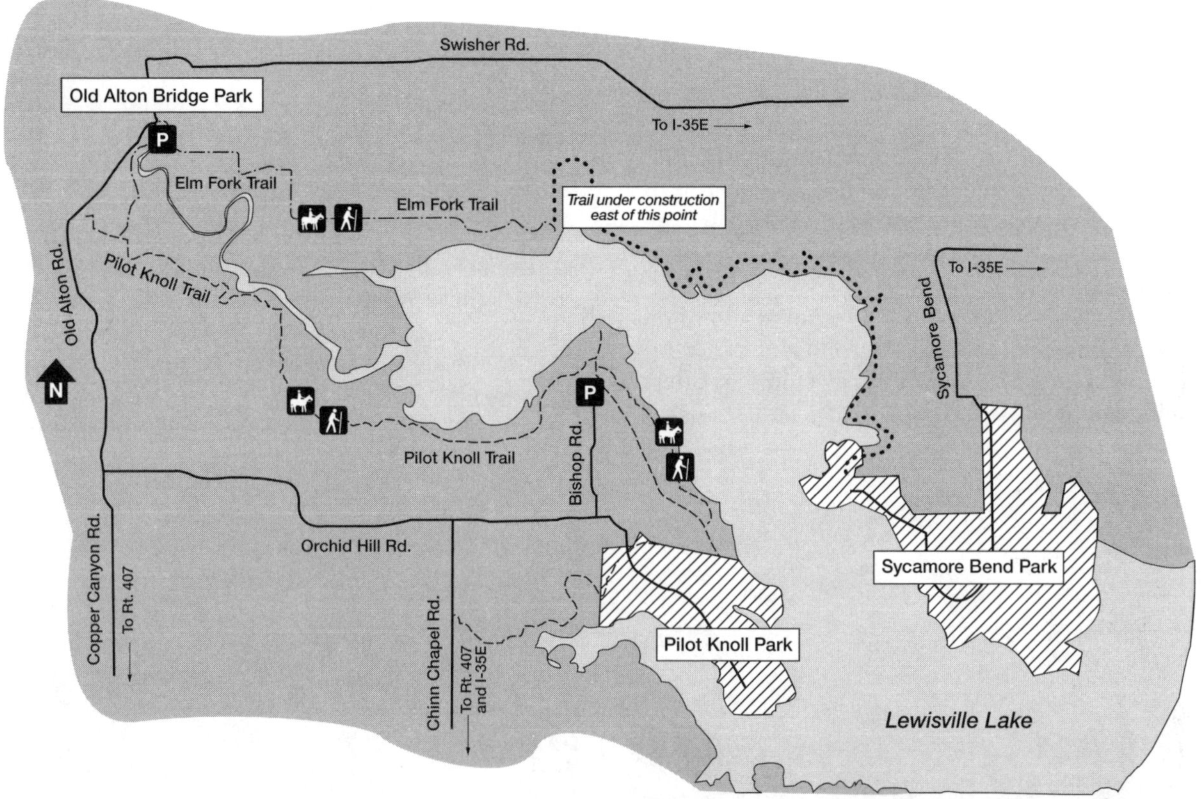

LOCATION

Lewisville Lake is a 28,980-acre Corps of Engineers impoundment on the Elm Fork of the Trinity River with a 187-mile shoreline. The lake is about 27 miles north of downtown Dallas and southeast of Denton. The Elm Fork and Pilot Knoll Horse and Hiking Trails are located on the southwest arm (Hickory Creek) of the lake, just west of I-35E.

TRAIL NOTES

The **Pilot Knoll Equestrian Trail** is located adjacent to Pilot Knoll Campground and is available to equestrians and hikers. The trail is approximately 8 miles in length and is divided into several smaller sub-trails. Bishop Road Trailhead provides horse trailer parking, and Pilot Knoll Park has limited parking outside the main gate. There is also walk-in access off of Chinn Chapel Road.

The **Elm Fork Hiking and Equestrian Trail** is a new trail that connects to the Pilot Knoll Trail and will eventually end at Sycamore Bend. Currently, the parking lot at the historic Old Alton Bridge Park is one access for hikers while horses can gain access from the Pilot Knoll Trail. Work on this new 6-mile tail was still in progress in 2004; at that point in time, horses were required to stop after 2 miles but the entire trail was open to hikers.

The horse and hiking trails at Lewisville Lake are located at the southwest arm of the lake.

Loyd Park
at Joe Pool Lake

FOR INFORMATION

City of Grand Prairie-Lake Parks
3401 Ragland Road
Grand Prairie, TX 75052
817/467-2104

LOCATION

Loyd Park is located about 5 miles south of I-20 off of TX 360 on the west side of the western arm of 7,500-acre Joe Pool Lake. The lake, created by the impoundment of Mountain Creek and Walnut Creek, is south of I-20 between Fort Worth and Dallas, east of US 287 and west of US 67 to Midlothian. The 800+-acre park, operated by the city of Grand Prairie, and named for an early pioneer family, offers camping and day-use facilities.

TRAIL NOTES

There are numerous hiking/biking/equestrian trails totaling about 10 miles. The main trail follows a winding course along Walnut Creek at the upper end of Joe Pool Lake. This trail provides access for fishermen and nature lovers. This trail is relatively flat and winds among native pecans, ash, and elm trees and occasionally into previously cleared bottomland. Other trails in the park pass through overgrown fields, upland post oak forests, and fields of flowers.

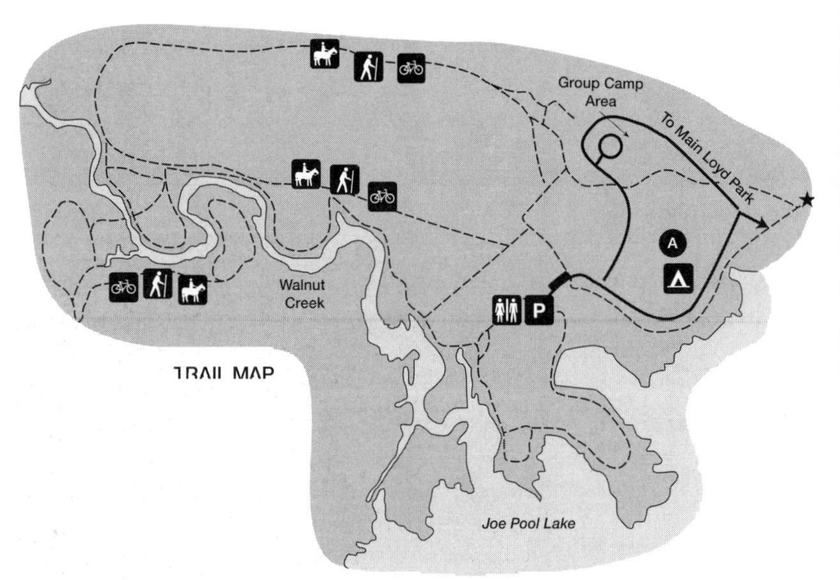

Some trails at Loyd Park pass through overgrown fields.

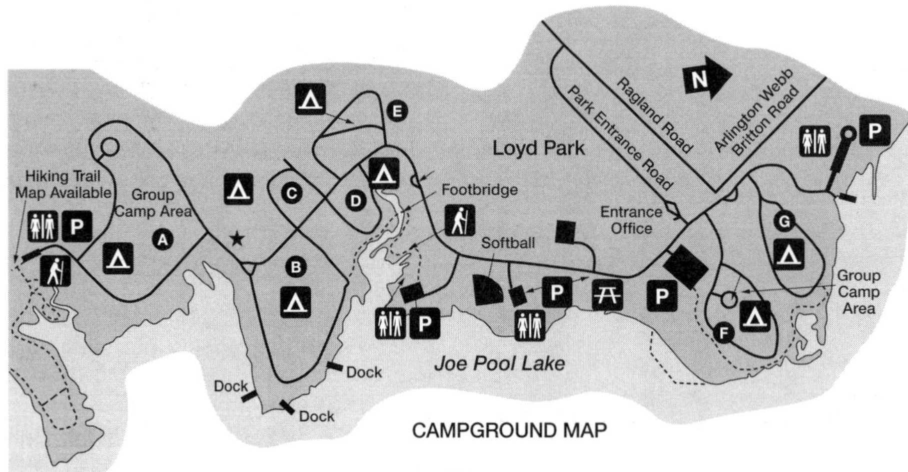

Martin Creek Lake State Park

FOR INFORMATION

MARTIN CREEK LAKE STATE PARK
9515 CR 2181D
TATUM, TX 75691-3425
903/836-4336

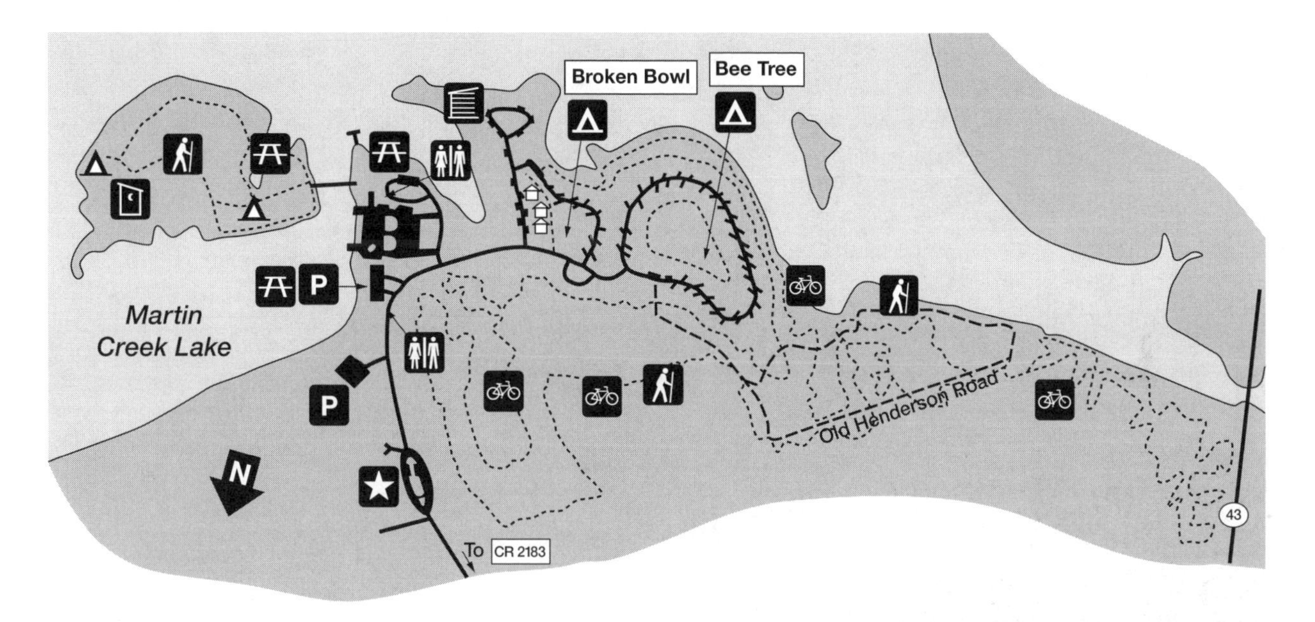

LOCATION

Martin Creek Lake State Park is located 20 miles southeast of Longview. The park may be reached by driving 3 miles southwest of Tatum on TX 43, then turning south on CR 2183. The 286-acre park is on the north shoreline of the 5,000-acre Martin Creek Reservoir, constructed to provide cooling water for a generation plant.

TRAIL NOTES

A 1½-mile hiking trail leads to primitive camping areas on the scenic wooded island that can be reached only by footbridge or boat. The gently rolling terrain and old pastureland provides a good setting for the 6½-mile mountain bike/hiking trail. The trailhead is on the south end of the Broken Bowl camping area. Fall, usually late October through the first two weeks of November, is a particularly scenic time at Martin Creek, with colorful foliage displays from the many varieties of hardwoods.

The 5,000-acre Martin Creek Reservoir provides cooling water for a generation plant as well as the opportunity to fish.

MERIDIAN STATE PARK

FOR INFORMATION

MERIDIAN STATE PARK
173 PARK RD. 7
MERIDIAN, TX 76665
254/435-2536

N
Bosque Trail
Little Forest Junior Trail
To Meridian
22
7
Little Springs Trail
Shinnery Ridge Trail
Entrance
Lake Meridian
To Hamilton

LOCATION

Meridian State Park is located about 3 miles southwest of Meridian off of TX 22. Park Road 7 provides access to the 505-acre park. The campground and hiking trails encircle a 73-acre lake, formed by a rock and earthen dam on Bee Creek, a small but scenic tributary of the Bosque River.

Six of the park's screened shelters are located on the shoreline and adjacent to the 2.3-mile Bosque Hiking Trail that encircles the lake.

TRAIL NOTES

Meridian State Park has 5 miles of trails that include 2 nature trails, 2 hiking trails, and a paved park road for bicycle riding. The 0.4-mile Little Springs Trail and the 0.7-mile Little Forest Junior Trail are loop trails on the east side of the lake. The 2.3-mile Bosque Hiking Trail encircles the lake and the 1.6-mile Shinnery Ridge Trail is located on the west side of the lake. A 250-yard section of this trail is paved and accessible to the handicapped with benches along the trail.

The hiking trails meander through undeveloped areas of the park where the terrain becomes rather rugged. Several interesting features of the trails include a scenic overlook of the lake called Bee Ledge. The park road serves as a scenic and hilly 5-mile round-trip paved "bicycle trail," which is suitable for all types of bicycles.

Ray Roberts Lake State Park

Isle du Bois Unit

FOR INFORMATION

RAY ROBERTS LAKE STATE PARK
ISLE DU BOIS UNIT
100 PW 4137
PILOT POINT, TX 76258-8944
940/686-2148

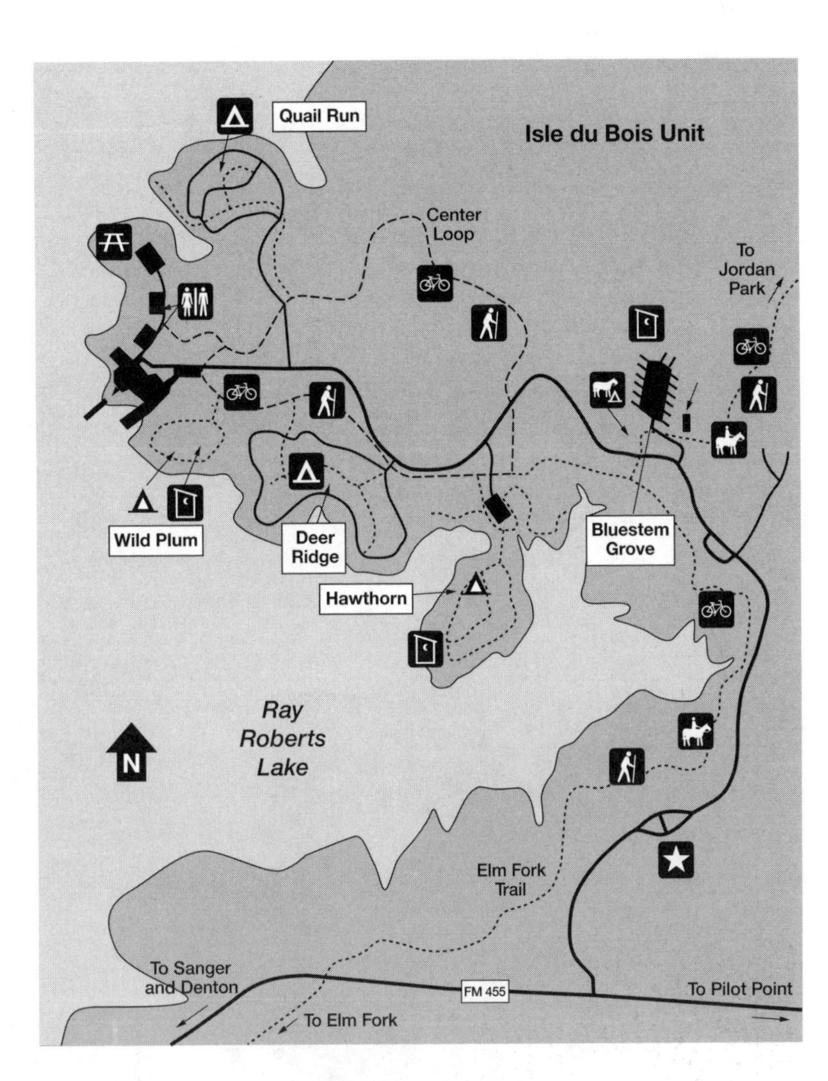

LOCATION

The Isle du Bois Unit of Ray Roberts Lake State Park is located on the east side of Ray Roberts Lake. The lake is a 29,350-acre Corps of Engineers impoundment on the Elm Fork of the Trinity River; it is north of Denton, east of I-35 and west of US 377. From I-35, take FM 455 east from Sanger, travel about 10 miles, and cross the dam to the park entrance. From US 377, the park is 4 miles west on FM 455. The Isle du Bois Unit contains 2,263 acres and has 11 miles of shoreline.

TRAIL NOTES

A 4½-mile improved surfaced hike/bike trail loops through the Isle du Bois Unit and a 12-mile multi-use dirt trail (hike/bike/equestrian) extends from Elm Fork East Satellite Park Unit through Isle du Bois Unit to Jordan Satellite Park Unit. Part of the 4½-mile paved trail is handicapped accessible. *All trail users must remain on established trail.*

Hikers and cyclists should always yield to horses and make their presence known well in advance. Hikers and cyclists should stop well in advance and move aside to allow horses to pass from the opposite direction. When passing horses from behind, hikers and bikers should make the rider aware of their presence and then pass on the left. Never pass a horse too close; try to keep a buffer zone.

JOHNSON BRANCH UNIT

FOR INFORMATION

RAY ROBERTS LAKE STATE PARK
JOHNSON BRANCH UNIT
100 PW 4153
VALLEY VIEW, TX 76272-7411
940/637-2294

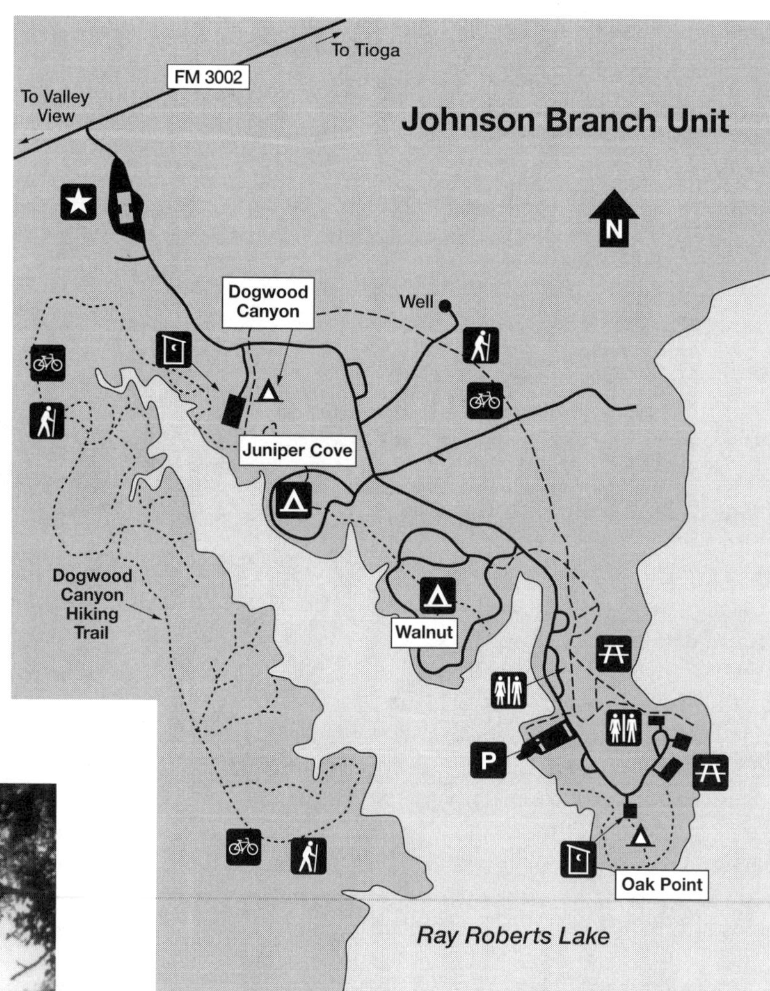

LOCATION

The Johnson Branch Unit of Ray Roberts Lake State Park is located off of FM 3002 east of I-35. From Sanger, travel north on I-35 to Lone Oak Road (exit 483), turn east on FM 3002, and travel 7 miles to the park entrance. This park unit contains 1,514 acres on the north side of Ray Roberts Lake, a 29,350-acre impoundment of the Elm Fork of the Trinity River.

TRAIL NOTES

The Johnson Branch Unit has 14 total miles of trails: 4 miles of paved trails accessible to the handicapped, and 10 miles of trails for backpacking, hiking, and mountain biking.

The Johnson Branch Unit of Ray Roberts Lake State Park has 4 miles of paved trails accessible to the handicapped.

Ray Roberts Lake State Park Greenbelt

FOR INFORMATION

Ray Roberts Lake State Park Greenbelt
100 PW 4137
Pilot Point, TX 76258
940/686-2148

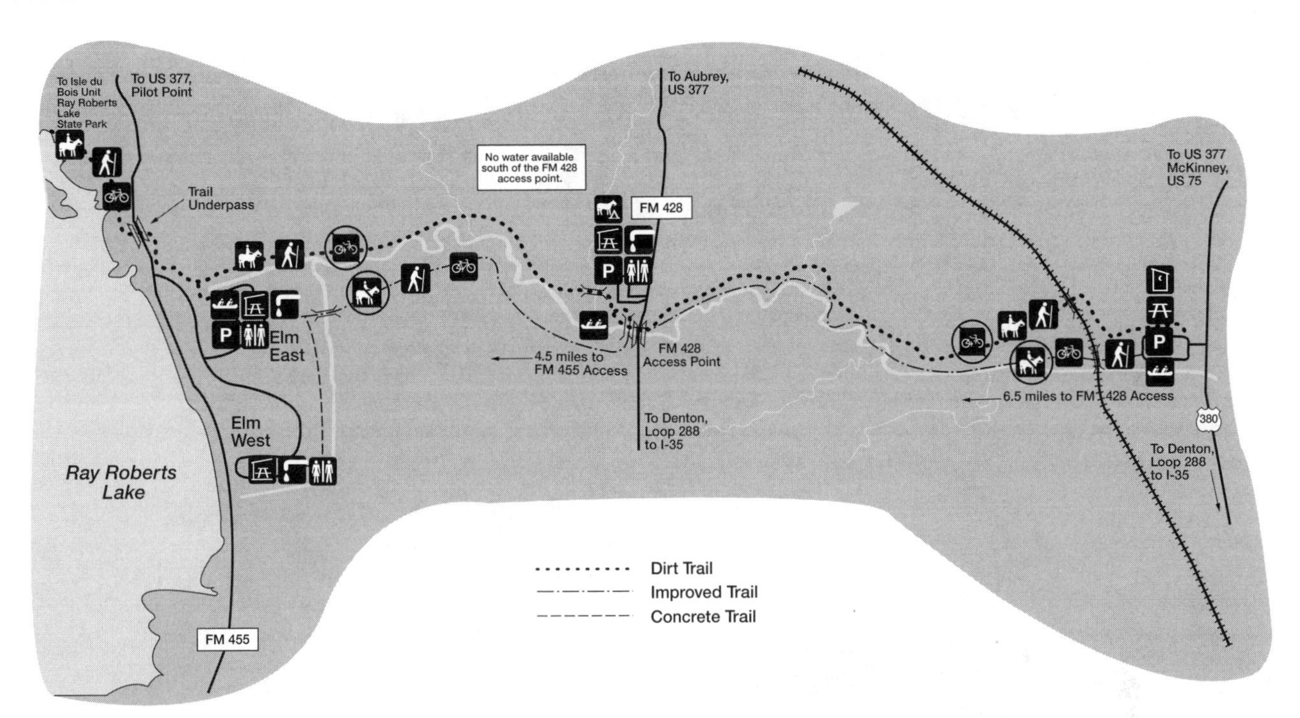

LOCATION

The Ray Roberts Lake/Lake Lewisville Greenbelt Corridor begins at Elm Fork Satellite Park Unit below the Ray Roberts Dam and ends at the headwaters of Lake Lewisville. This corridor meanders along the heavily wooded banks of the Elm Fork Branch of the Trinity River. Access points are FM 455 below the Ray Roberts Dam, FM 428, and US 377/380.

Hikers, bikers, and horseback riders aren't the only folks who enjoy this Greenbelt corridor.

TRAIL NOTES

The **Greenbelt** is a 20-mile multi-use trail system: 12 miles for equestrian and 10 miles for hike and bike use. Canoeists, birdwatchers, anglers, and other outdoor enthusiasts are also welcomed on the Greenbelt. Canoe and kayak rentals are available by calling Greenbelt Canoe Rentals 817/228-9496.

Cyclists should pass other trail users slowly and considerately. Hikers and cyclists should always yield to horses and make their presence known well in advance, then move aside to allow horses to pass, if passing from the opposite direction. If passing horses from behind, hikers and bikers should pass on the left after making the rider aware of their presence. All users must yield to handicapped users. Pets are permitted on the trails, but must be under control and on a leash at all times.

Tyler State Park

FOR INFORMATION

Tyler State Park
789 Park Rd. 16
Tyler, TX 75706-9141
903/597-5338

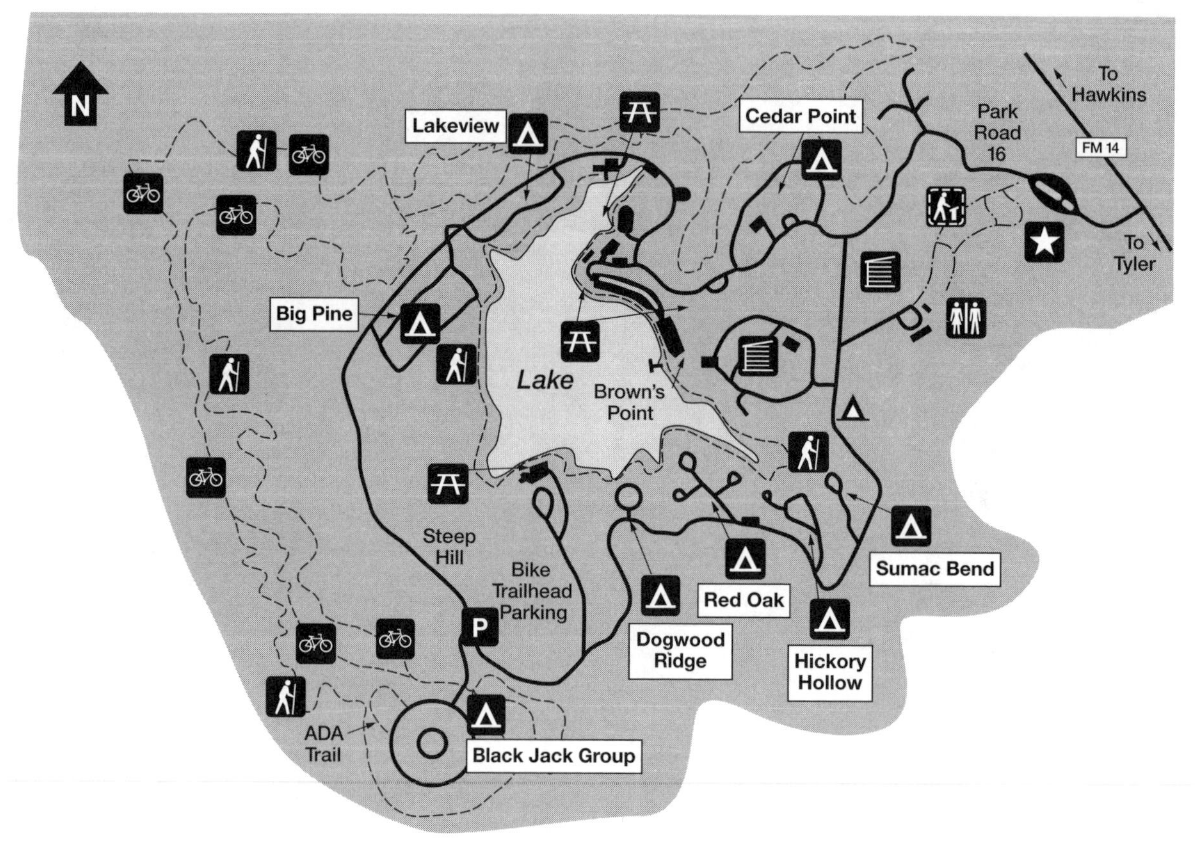

LOCATION

Tyler State Park is 8 miles north of Tyler on FM 14 and 2 miles north of I-20. This 985-acre park has a 64-acre lake.

TRAIL NOTES

A 2½-mile hiking trail that encircles the lake, and a ¾-mile nature trail have been developed for those interested in getting a close-up view of nature. The Whispering Pines Nature Trail has numbered posts along the trail and a guide booklet. The spring-fed lake is lined with maple, ash, and birch that turn to crimson in the fall. Spring fills the park with blossoms from dogwoods and redbuds. Rugged terrain provides the setting for 13 miles of mountain bike trails.

The bicycle trails in the western portion of the park are the most rugged.

OTHER TRAILS IN REGION 1

CADDO **Possum Kingdom State Park**

▲ 1-mile loop trail for hikers at the northwest end of the park past the designated swimming area.

Possum Kindgom State Park
P.O. Box 70
Caddo, TX 76429
940/549-1803

DALLAS **Hike & Bike Trails**

▲ The Dallas Park and Recreation Department has 82 miles of unpaved and hard surface trails in parks and greenbelts; 27 trails are described in a 26-page booklet named *Hike & Bike Trails Directory*. Five of the longest trails are:

11.5-mile White Rock Lake Hike & Bike Trail
10-mile Dallas Nature Center Trail
7.5-mile White Rock Creek Trail
4-mile Lower White Rock Creek Trail
4-mile Katy Trail

City of Dallas
Dallas Parks and Recreation Department
1500 Marilla, 6FN
Dallas, TX 75201
214/670-4100

DECATUR **National Grasslands Trails**

▲ On LBJ National Grasslands—a 4-mile hiking trail between 2 recreation areas (Black Creek Lake and Cottonwood Lake) and a 75-mile long multi-use trail for horses, mountain bikes, and hiking.

▲ On the Caddo National Grasslands—3 multi-use loop trails (for horses, mountain bikes, and hiking) totaling 20 miles from the Bois d'Arc Trailhead.

Caddo/LBJ National Grasslands
1400 N. US Hwy. 81/287
P.O. Box 507
Decatur, TX 76234
940/627-5475

DENISON **Eisenhower Birthplace SHS**

▲ Hiking paths wind through about 10 acres of the Eisenhower neighborhood. Visitors receive a guided tour through the birthplace home and can also arrange for a customized, guided "Ike Hike" through the railroad trails, creek areas, and wooded sections of the park.

Eisenhower Birthplace State Historic Site
607 S. Lamar
Denison, TX 75021
903/465-8908

DENTON **Denton Branch Rail Trail**

▲ The 8-mile Denton Branch Rail Trail is part of the Trinity Trails System that will run from southern Dallas County to the Lake Texoma area. This rail trail passes the southeastern section of Denton and through a portion of Corinth; it is open free to the public and can be accessed from at least 18 street intersections along its route that mosly parallels I-35E. The north trailhead is at the City Hall East parking lot. The trail surface is of a fine crushed limestone, ideal for hiking and biking.

City of Denton
Parks and Recreation Department
321 East McKinney Street
Denton, TX 76201
940/349-7275

ENNIS **Bardwell Lake Trails**

3 trails at Bardwell Lake

▲ 11-mile equestrian and multi-use trail at Waxahachie Creek Park.

▲ a short nature trail in Waxahachie Creek Park.

▲ Tonkawa Trail—trail entrance on north side of Bardwell Dam Road near the east bank of Waxahachie Creek; almost a mile in length.

Bardwell Lake
4000 Observation Dr.
Ennis, TX 75119-1339
972/875-5711

EUSTACE **Purtis Creek State Park**

▲ 1¼-mile hiking trail begins near the camping area and leads to 13 primitive walk-in campsites via a loop.

Purtis Creek State Park
14225 FM 316
Eustace, TX 75124
903/425-2332

FORT WORTH **Hike & Bike Trails**

Hike and bike trails in the Trinity Trail System in Fort Worth include:

▲ 2.5-mile Marine Creek Trail along Marine Creek from Rodeo Park to Buck Sansom Park.

▲ 2.6-mile Overton-Foster Trail from Kellis Park to the Trinity River.

▲ 5.6-mile trail from Cobb South Park through to Quanah Parker Park.

▲ 10.4-mile Trinity River Trail following the Clear Fork of the Trinity River from Pecan Valley Park to Heritage Park.

▲ 13-mile Heritage Trail, connecting the Trinity Trail and the existing trail at the Stockyards.

Park and Recreation Department
4200 South Freeway, Suite 2200
Fort Worth, TX 76115-1499
817/871-5700

FORT WORTH **Japanese Garden**

▲ The Fort Worth Japanese Garden, located at 3220 Botanic Garden Drive, has numerous trails that wind through the garden, which once was the site of an old gravel pit. The garden is open daily; an admission fee is charged. Phone 817/871-7685.

LEWISVILLE **Lewisville Lake**

▲ 0.66-mile Cicada Trail below the dam at Lewisville Lake.

Lewisville Lake
1801 N. Mill St.
Lewisville, TX 75057-1821
972/434-1666

LONGVIEW **Cargill Long Park**

▲ Cargill Long Park, a National Recreation Trail, is located between Hollybrook Drive and Marshall Avenue (US 80) in Longview on an abandoned railroad right-of-way with dense vegetation. The 2.2-mile hiking and bicycle trail, 9 feet wide and surfaced with asphalt, is marked at ¼-mile intervals and varies from flat to gently sloping hills; horses and motorized vehicles are prohibited. A restroom and playground are located midway.

Parks and Recreation Department
P.O. Box 1952
Longview, TX 75606-1952
903/237-1270

PALESTINE **Palestine State Park**

▲ ½-mile self-interpretive nature trail at Palestine State Park begins near playground area, circles around pond, crosses a footbridge, and finds its way back to the picnic and restroom areas.

Palestine State Park
RR 4, Box 431
Rusk, TX 75785
903/683-5126

PURDON **Navarro Mills Lake**

▲ ½-mile Alliance Creek Nature Trail at Oak Park at Navarro Mills Lake.

Navarro Mills Lake
1175 FM 667
Purdon, TX 76679-3187
254/578-1431

QUITMAN **Governor Hogg Shrine Park**

▲ The Old Settlers Nature Trail at Governor Hogg Shrine Park is a 0.4-mile loop trail with 23 numbered stops; a trail guide is available. The vegetation along the trail has been undisturbed since 1900. Park visitors are advised to use insect repellent before starting out. This 26.7-acre park is the only park in the state with 3 museum buildings.

City of Quitman
100 Governor Hogg Parkway
Quitman, TX 75783
903/763-2701

RUSK **Rusk State Park**

▲ ¼-mile self-interpretive nature trail at Rusk State Park begins across from a 15-acre lake and winds its way through to the camping area. A bird blind and viewing area are situated alongside the trail. Rusk State Park also offers walking and bicycling throughout the campground recreation area and around the lake.

Rusk State Park
RR 4, Box 431
Rusk, TX 75785
903/683-5126

SHERMAN **Hagerman NWR**

▲ Five hiking trails, or defined foot access areas, on Hagerman National Wildlife Refuge, including roads open to hiking that are closed to private vehicles. Crow Hill ¾-mile trail has a viewing platform. Also, there's a 2-mile self-guided auto tour. The refuge lies at the south end of the Big Mineral Arm of Lake Texoma, northwest of Sherman. From FM 1417 turn west on Refuge Road (1 mile north of FM 691 or 2 miles south of FM 120) and follow this road for 6 miles to headquarters. Lobby is always open for brochures. Refuge is day use only.

Hagerman National Wildlife Refuge
6465 Refuge Rd.
Sherman, TX 75092-5817
903/786-2826

▲ 2.2-mile nature trail at Herman Baker Park.

City Manager
P.O. Box 1106
Sherman, TX 75091-1106

TEXARKANA **Wright-Patman Lake**

▲ 1.5-mile trail from Rocky Point Park to Piney Point Park.

▲ 1.3-mile Possom Trot Trail at Northshore/Intake Hill Park.

▲ 0.5-mile Charles Gardner Trail and a 0.6-mile trail (from playground to Gate House) in Clear Springs Park; gravel trail surface.

Wright-Patman Lake
P.O. Box 1817
Texarkana, TX 75504-1817
903/838-8781

TYLER

▲ 2-mile nature trail at Southside Park.

▲ A paved nature trail at Windsor Grove Park, just west of the Tyler Rose Gardens on SH 31.

Parks and Recreation Department
Box 2039
Tyler, TX 75701

WYLIE **Lavon Lake**

▲ Hiking trail at Bratonia Park at Lavon Lake.

Lavon Lake
3375 Skyview Drive
Wylie, TX 75098-5775
972/442-3141

REGION 2

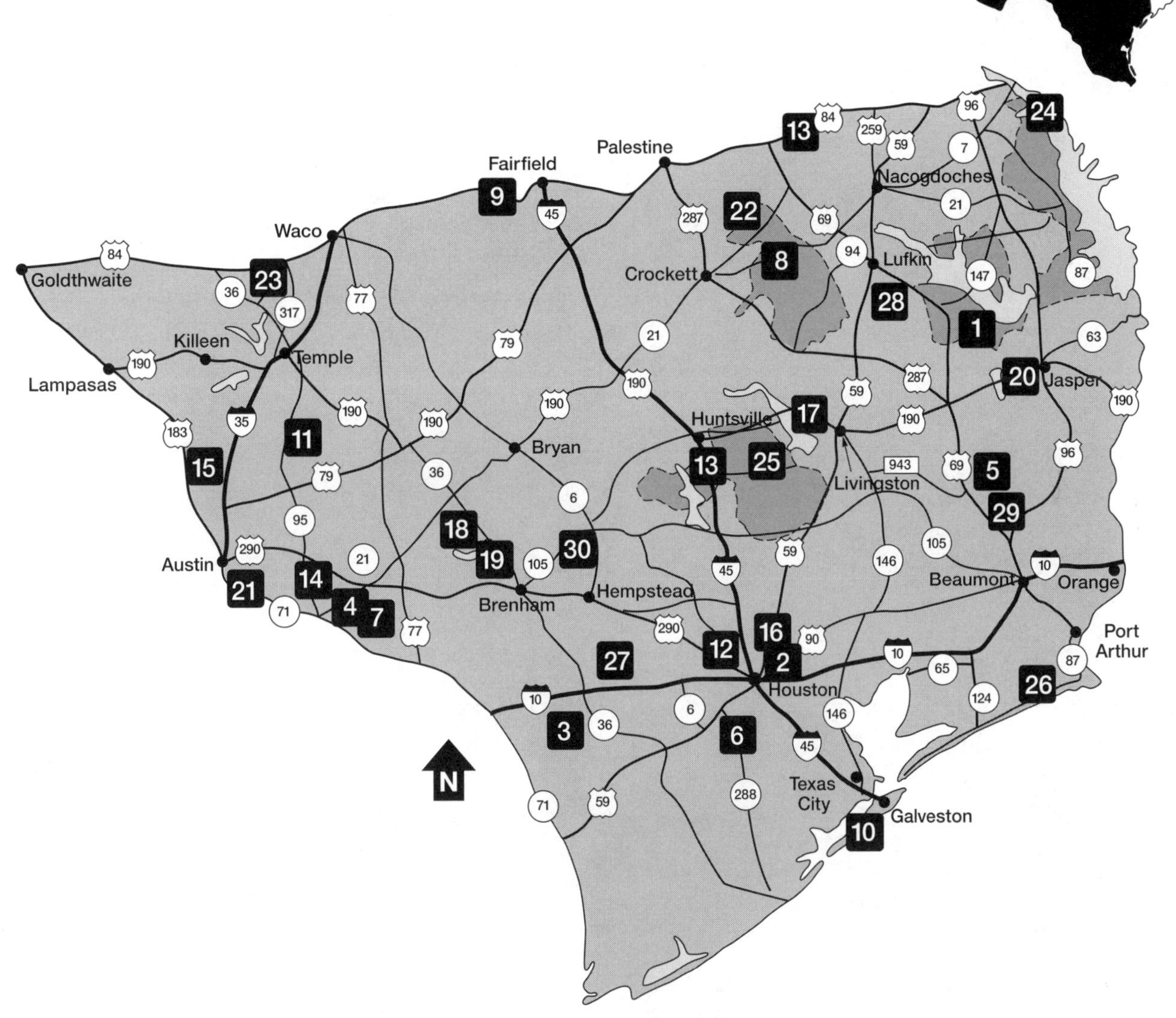
Goldthwaite
Lampasas
Killeen
Temple
Waco
Fairfield
Palestine
Crockett
Nacogdoches
Lufkin
Jasper
Huntsville
Livingston
Bryan
Austin
Brenham
Hempstead
Houston
Beaumont
Orange
Port Arthur
Texas City
Galveston
N

Angelina National Forest

For Information

Angelina National Forest
111 Walnut Ridge Road
Zavalla, TX 75980
936/897-1068

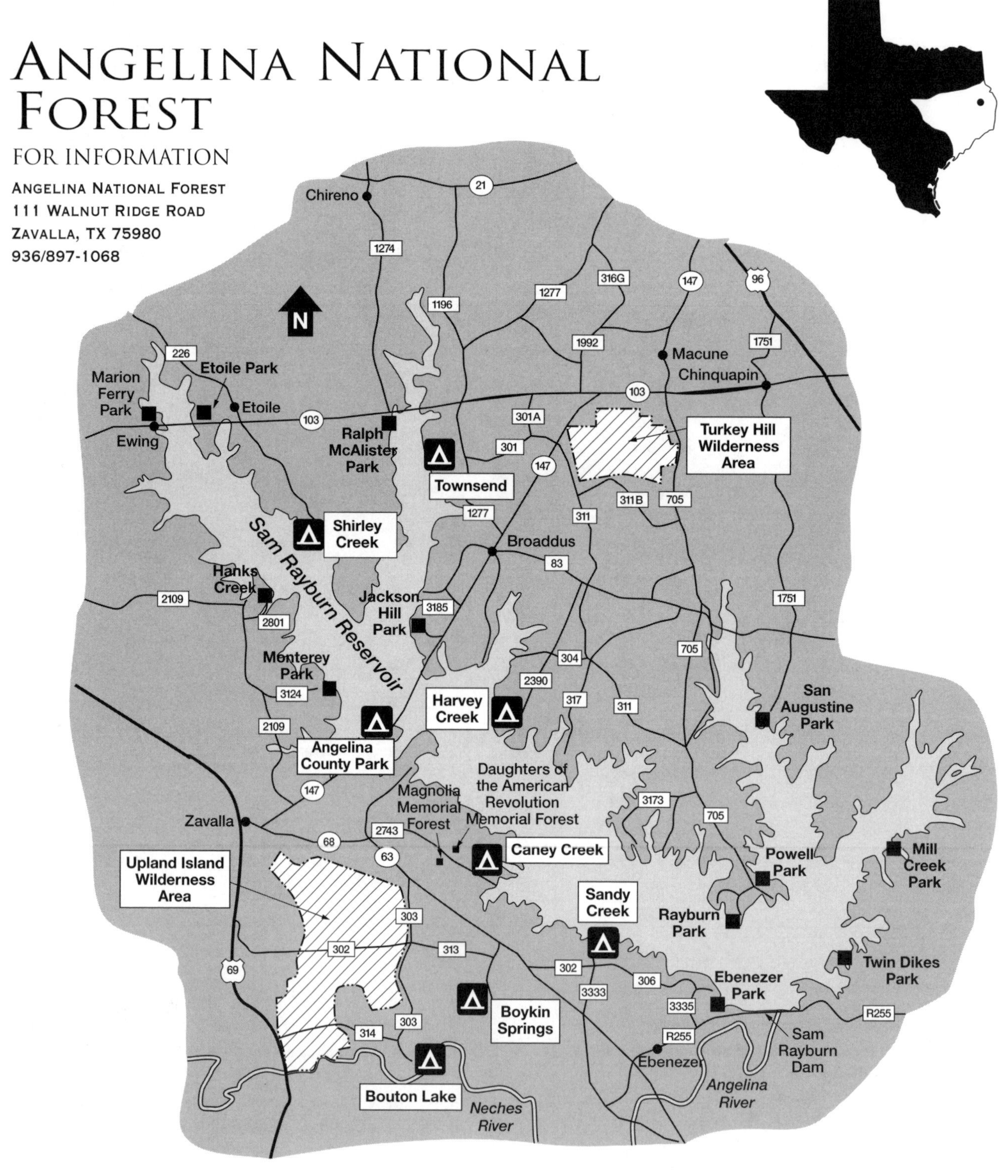

Location

Angelina National Forest, located in Angelina, Jasper, Nacogdoches, and San Augustine counties, is the smallest of the 4 national forests in Texas and contains 153,179 acres. The forest surrounds much of Sam Rayburn Reservoir. The 13,331-acre Upland Island Wilderness Area and the 5,473-acre Turkey Hill Wilderness Area are located on the Angelina National Forest. Hiking and horseback riding are allowed in wilderness areas; bicycles and other wheeled vehicles are prohibited.

Hiking is permitted anywhere in the National Forests in Texas unless otherwise posted. In the Angelina National Forest there are developed trails at Bouton Lake Recreation Area and Boykin Springs Recreation Area; the Sawmill Hiking Trail connects these areas. This hiking trail is used by backpackers.

HIKING/NATURE TRAILS AND LOCATIONS

- ▲ **Bouton Lake Recreation Area:** Take TX 63 east from Zavalla for 7 miles; turn right (south) on FSR 303 for 7 miles. This is the site of one of the 2 trailheads of the Sawmill Trail.
- ▲ **Boykin Springs Recreation Area:** Take TX 63 east from Zavalla for 10½ miles; turn right (south) on FSR 313 for 2½ miles. This area has a 0.7-mile scenic foot trail along Boykin Creek and around the lake. The campground is also the site of one of the 2 trailheads of the Sawmill Trail.

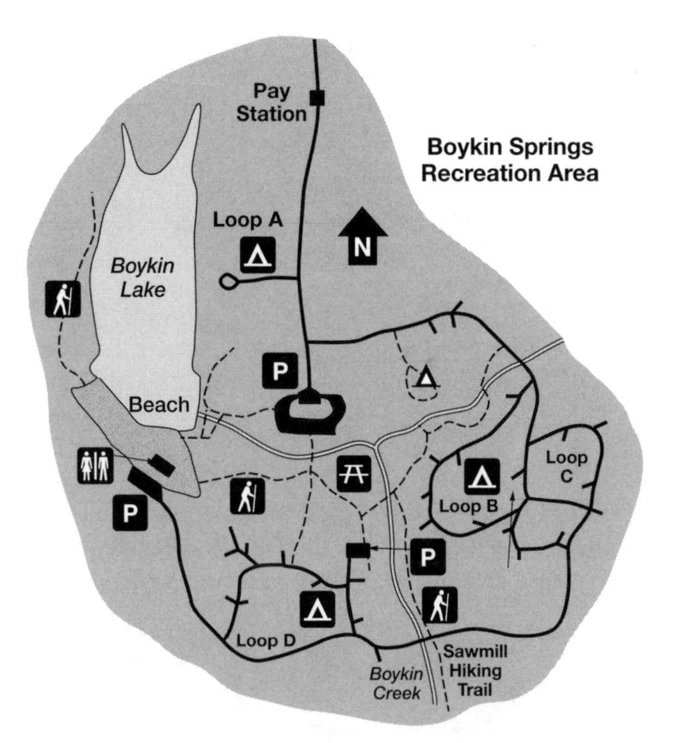

Angelina National Forest/ Sawmill Hiking Trail

FOR INFORMATION

ANGELINA NATIONAL FOREST
111 WALNUT RIDGE ROAD
ZAVALLA, TX 75980
936/897-1068

TRAIL NOTES FOR SAWMILL HIKING TRAIL

The Sawmill Hiking Trail is a 5½-mile trail that begins at Bouton Lake Recreation Area and ends at Boykin Springs Recreation Area. Blue plastic rectangular markings, about head high, indicate the trail's direction. Most of the trail runs along the Neches River bottom and passes two abandoned Aldridge Sawmill sites. A ¾-mile spur leads to the old abandoned Aldridge Sawmill site on the east end. For more than 2 miles the trail follows an old tramway once used as a rail line to haul logs to the sawmills. Hikers can see the Neches River from several points along the trail. Since this trail is also used by backpackers, this map is not duplicated in the Backpacking Trails section.

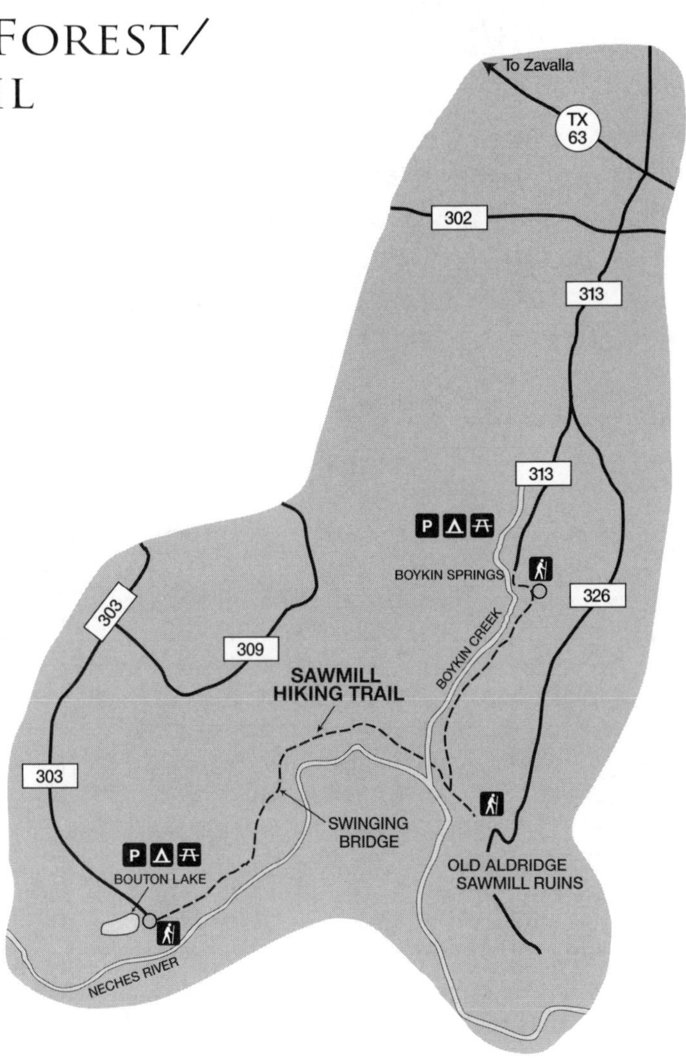

Armand Bayou Nature Center

For Information

Armand Bayou Nature Center, Inc.
(8500 Bay Area Boulevard, Pasadena)
P.O. Box 58828
Houston, TX 77258
281/474-2551
www.abnc.org

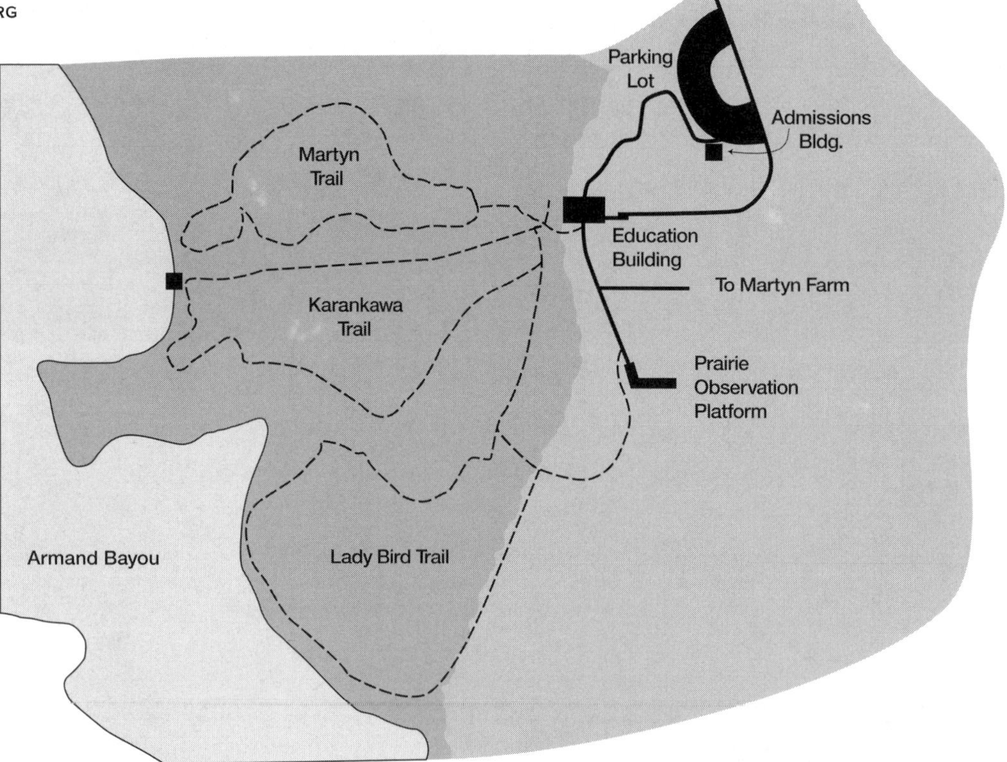

Nature trails lead to the bayou where water birds such as these may be viewed.

Trail Notes

The Armand Bayou Nature Center is located at 8500 Bay Area Blvd., southeast of Houston. The center covers 2,500 acres and is made up of a central building and 5.0 miles of nature trails, which lead down to the bayou and through expanses of both coastal prairie and marshland. The bayou and the center are named in honor of the late Armand Yrmategui, who was one of the best-known naturalists in the state. The center is open Wed. through Sat., 9 a.m. to 5 p.m., and Sun., noon until dark; it is closed on Mon. and Tues.

ATTWATER PRAIRIE CHICKEN NATIONAL WILDLIFE REFUGE

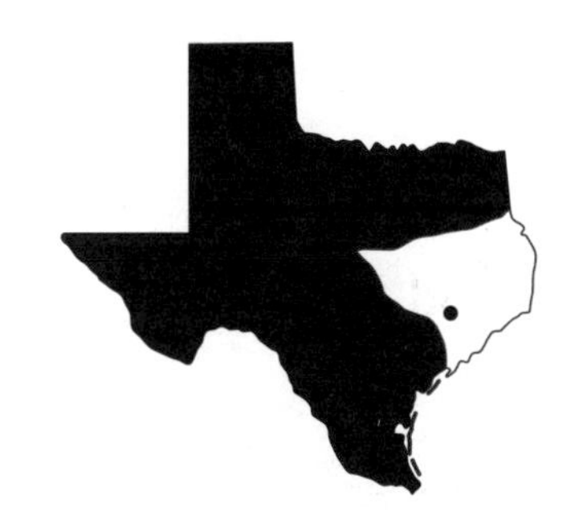

FOR INFORMATION

REFUGE MANAGER
ATTWATER PRAIRIE CHICKEN NATIONAL WILDLIFE REFUGE
P.O. BOX 519
EAGLE LAKE, TX 77434-0519
979/234-3021

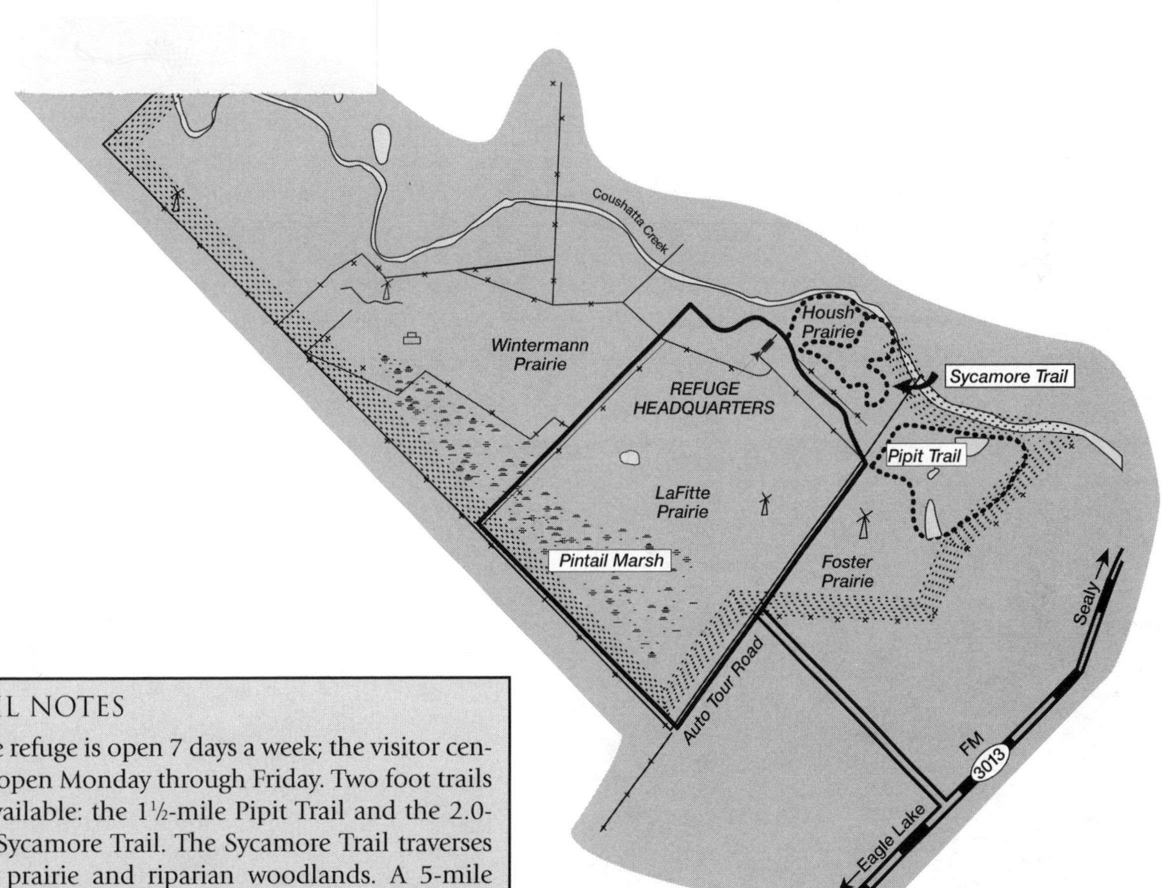

TRAIL NOTES

The refuge is open 7 days a week; the visitor center is open Monday through Friday. Two foot trails are available: the 1½-mile Pipit Trail and the 2.0-mile Sycamore Trail. The Sycamore Trail traverses open prairie and riparian woodlands. A 5-mile auto tour route, accessible in good weather, crosses prairie and wetlands; it is open from sunrise to sunset. Vehicles must remain on the road. Foot travel is permitted along the tour route and all designated paths. Picnicking is allowed at the refuge headquarters only. Fires, overnight camping, hunting, fishing, and canoeing are prohibited.

Though primarily dedicated to the welfare of the Attwater's prairie chicken, the refuge is used by many migratory and resident wildlife species. During the winter, large numbers of waterfowl congregate on the marsh and cultivated fields.

LOCATION

The refuge is located 7 miles northeast of Eagle Lake, off FM 3013, or south of Sealy on TX 36 to FM 3013 and traveling west for 10 miles. Headquarters is reached by driving 2 miles west of the main entrance on FM 3013. The 10,528-acre refuge is currently managed by the U.S. Fish and Wildlife Service.

Bastrop State Park

FOR INFORMATION

Bastrop State Park
P.O. Box 518
Bastrop, TX 78602-0518
512/321-2101

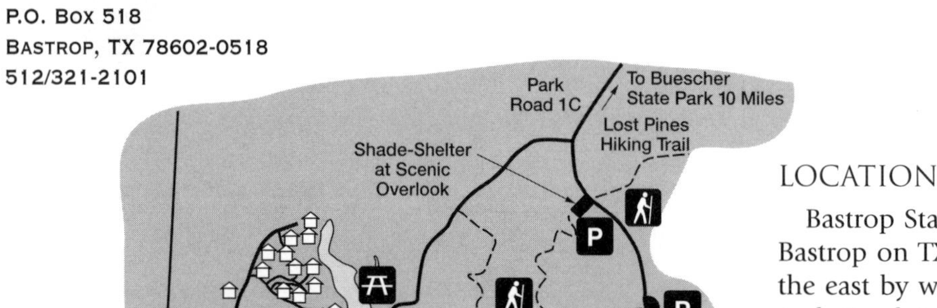

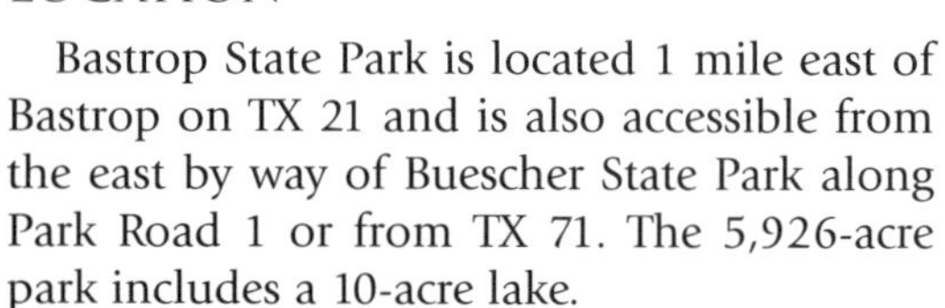

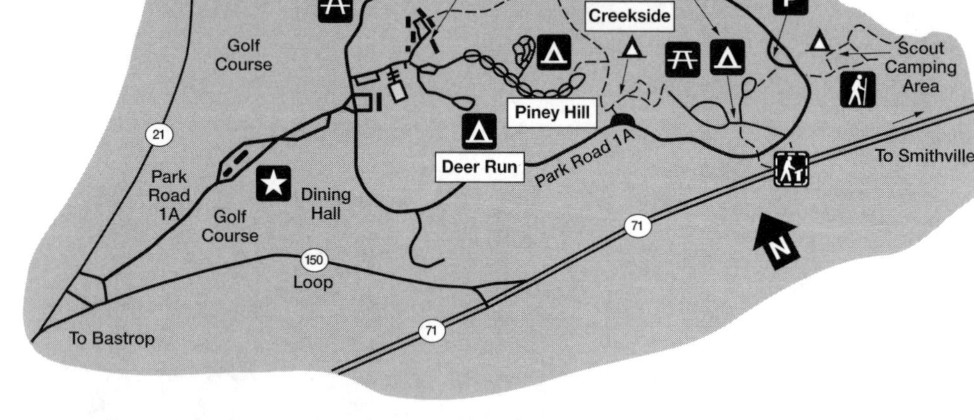

LOCATION

Bastrop State Park is located 1 mile east of Bastrop on TX 21 and is also accessible from the east by way of Buescher State Park along Park Road 1 or from TX 71. The 5,926-acre park includes a 10-acre lake.

The wooded campgrounds and trails provide excellent birding opportunities.

TRAIL NOTES

Hikers enjoy the quiet woodland and rugged hills that make this park one of the most beautiful in Texas. Several hiking trails exist within the area bounded by the loop Park Road 1; they lead to the scenic overlook and the small lake, and connect the various camping areas. The 8½-mile Lost Pines Hiking Trail is east of Park Road 1A; it has several options for shorter hikes. Backpack camping is allowed along this trail. See page 144 for details. Park Road 1C from Bastrop State Park to Buescher State Park has 13 miles of surfaced roads for bicycles. This road is quite hilly and is not recommended for beginners. Because of erosive soils, bicycles are not allowed on any of the park's hiking trails.

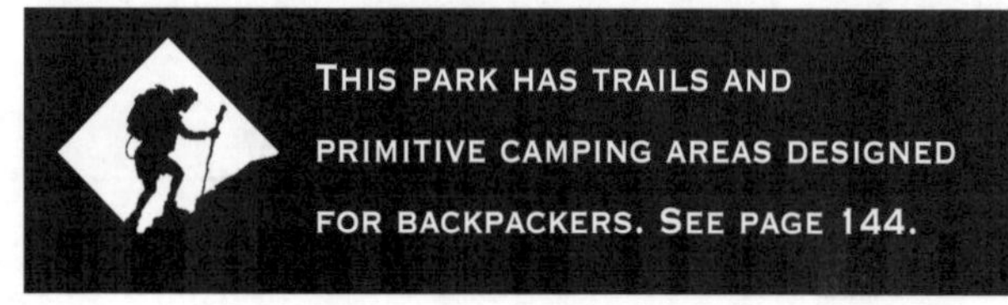

THIS PARK HAS TRAILS AND PRIMITIVE CAMPING AREAS DESIGNED FOR BACKPACKERS. SEE PAGE 144.

BIG THICKET NATIONAL PRESERVE

FOR INFORMATION

BIG THICKET NATIONAL PRESERVE
3785 MILAM
BEAUMONT, TX 77701
HEADQUARTERS 409/839-2689
VISITOR CENTER 409/839-2337

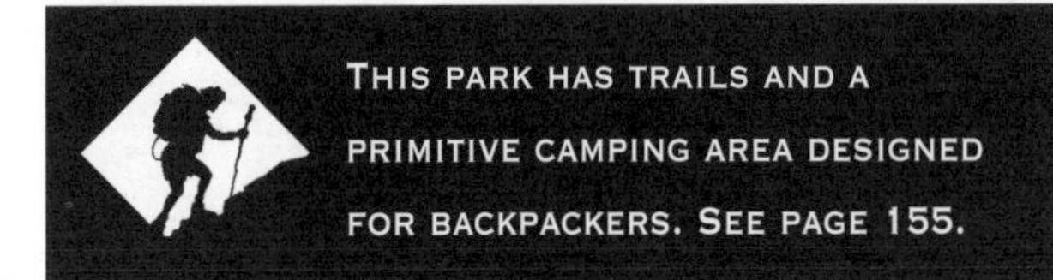

BIG THICKET VISITOR INFORMATION STATION

The Big Thicket Visitor Center is reached by traveling 7 miles north of Kountze on US 69 to FM 420; turn east on FM 420. The station is on the left; it is open daily, from 9 a.m. to 5 p.m. Information on the preserve's resources, recreational opportunities, and facilities is available. A 20-minute video can be viewed. Phone: 409/839-2337.

LOCATION

The Big Thicket National Preserve, composed of 12 units of various sizes and spread over 50 square miles, contains more than 85,000 acres. The units range in size from 550 to over 25,000 acres. Scientists have termed the Big Thicket a "biological crossroads"; it is recognized internationally for its diversity. Factors contributing to this diversity are geology, geography, climate, and water. It is the first area to receive the preserve designation by the national park system, which means it will remain in its natural state. Located in southeast Texas, the 12 separate units are bounded by US 96 on the east, US 90 on the south, US 59 on the west, and US 190 on the north.

Hiking is one of the best ways to experience the Big Thicket. There are presently hiking or nature trails on 5 preserve units. Visitors may select from 9 trails ranging from ¼ mile to 18 miles in length. Back-country camping for individuals or small groups is allowed in designated portions on 9 of the units. See p. 155 for details.

A variety of naturalist activities is offered by the preserve during the warmer months. Reservations are required for all programs, and can be made through the visitor center, 409/839-2337.

These trails include a variety of forest communities, providing glimpses of the diversity that make up the Big Thicket. The trails are open at all times; however, keep in mind that flooding occurs after heavy rains. Permits are not required to hike, but you should register at the trailhead, and you will be provided a detailed trail map there. Parking is available at the trailheads.

For your comfort bring drinking water and wear comfortable shoes that you don't mind getting muddy. Don't forget to bring mosquito repellent during warm weather months. All the trails are on relatively flat terrain and are easy to walk. Pets, camping, and firearms are not permitted on these trails. Horseback riding and mountain bikes are permitted on Big Sandy Creek Horse Trail only.

Refer to the map for the trailhead locations of the following 8 trails—

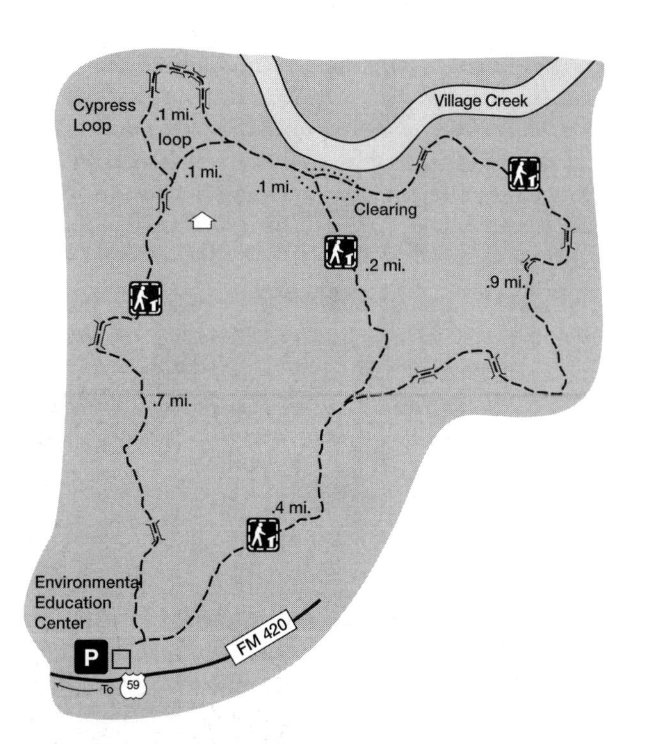

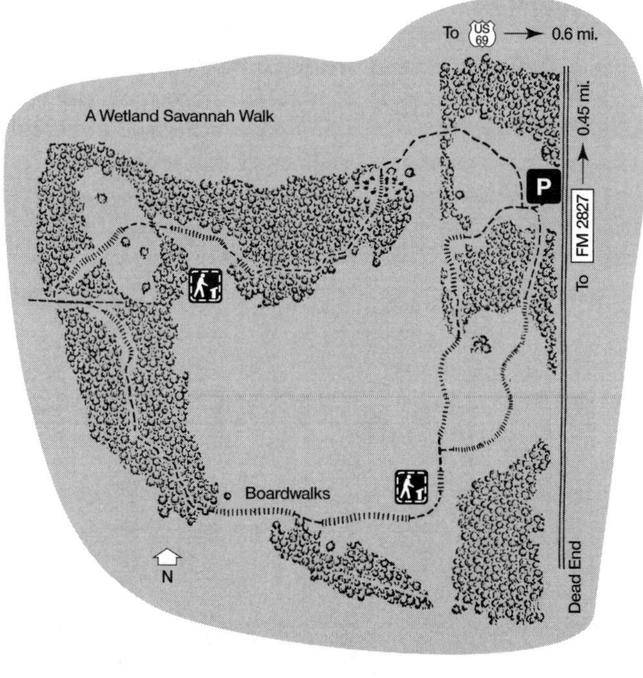

The **Kirby Nature Trail** is located at the southern tip of the Turkey Creek Unit on FM 420, 2½ miles east of the junction of US 69 and FM 420. It begins behind the Staley Cabin. This is a double loop trail with an inner loop that is 1.7 miles long and an outer loop 2.4 miles long. The trail leads through a diverse mixture of hardwoods and pines. Where it passes along sections of Village Creek, there are cypress sloughs and floodplains. A trail guide booklet is provided at the trailhead.

The **Sundew Trail** is located at the eastern edge of the Hickory Creek Savannah Unit, ½ mile south of FM 2827. The dirt road leading to the trail-head intersects FM 2827 ½ mile west of US 69. A trail booklet guides you around a 1-mile loop that leads through an open longleaf pine wetland savanna containing a large variety of wildflowers that bloom long and beautifully. A short, ½-mile-long loop section is fully accessible.

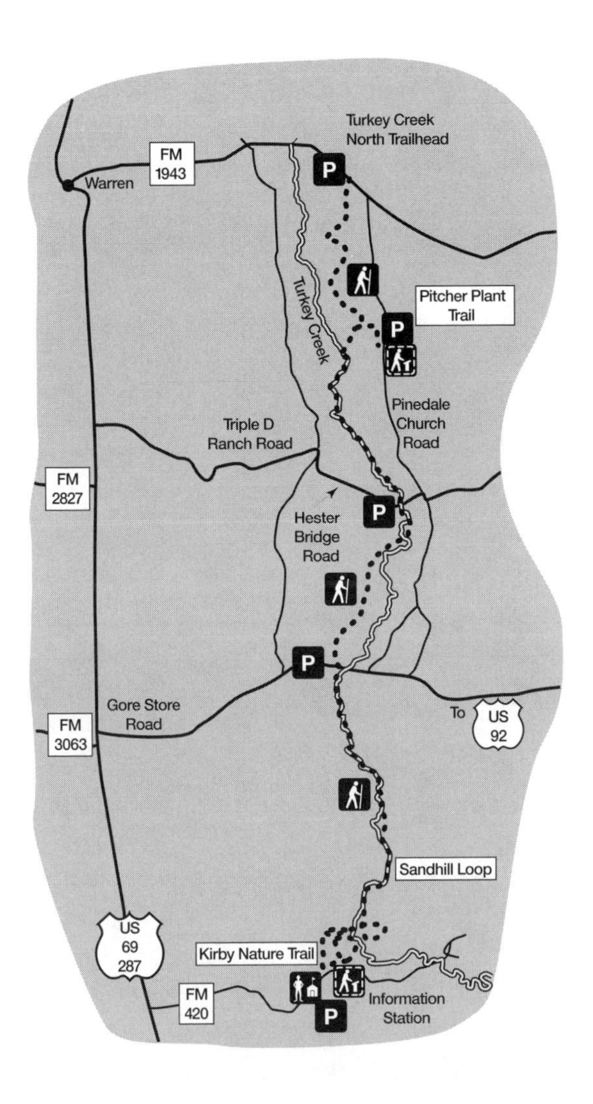

The **Turkey Creek Trail** is a 17½-mile linear trail which roughly parallels Turkey Creek. There are four main trailheads. The north trailhead is 3½ miles east of Warren on FM 1943. The south trailhead is located 4 miles in on Gore Store Road. This road is the first right turn (east) after the US 69/FM 3063 junction. The third trailhead is on the Triple D Ranch Road that crosses Turkey Creek, about 6 miles south of the north trailhead. The Kirby Nature Trail and the Pitcher Plant Trail also provide access. The trail provides diverse views as it winds through the sandy pine uplands, mixed forests, floodplains, and baygalls that surround Turkey Creek.

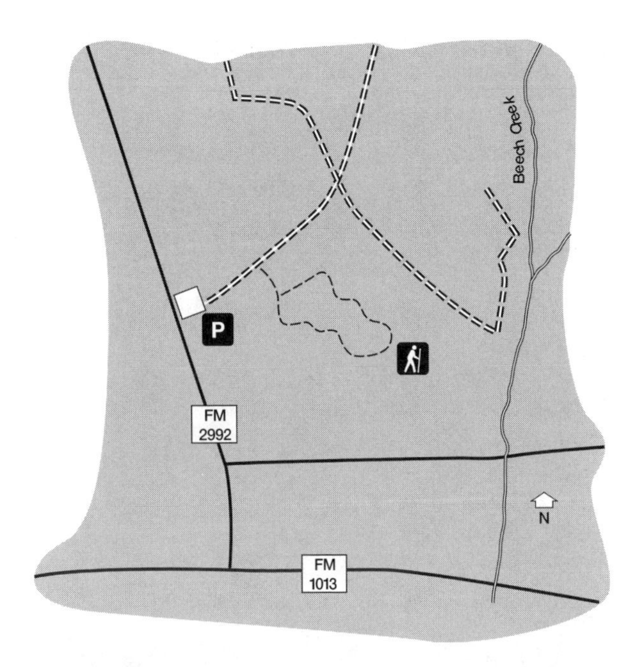

The **Beech Woods Trail** is near the SW corner of the Beech Creek Unit. Access is from FM 2992, 1½ miles north of its junction with FM 1013. A short walk on an old dirt road brings you to the 1-mile loop trail. This trail meanders through a magnificent mature section of a beech-magnolia-loblolly forest.

The Beech Woods Trail provides a 1-mile loop trail through a magnificent mature section of a beech-magnolia-loblolly forest.

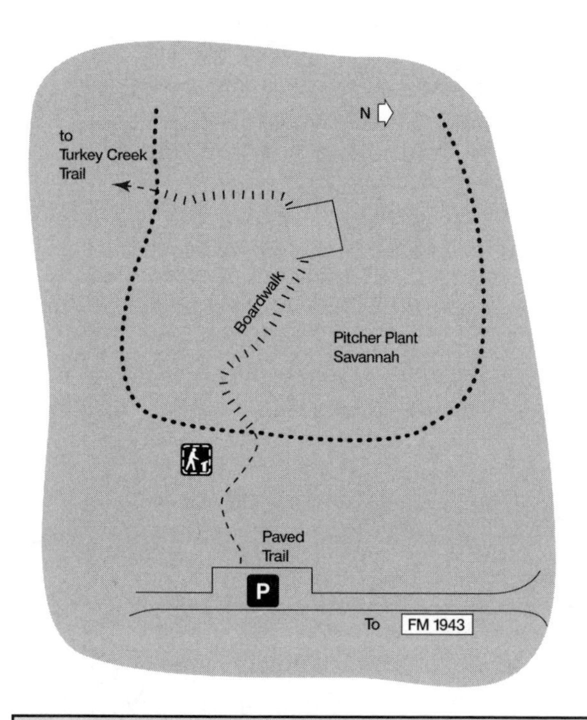

The **Pitcher Plant Trail** is located on the NE side of the Turkey Creek Unit. To reach the trailhead, follow FM 1943 east from Warren 4.3 miles, turn south and continue 1.9 miles along the east boundary of the Turkey Creek Unit. The ¼-mile-long hard-surfaced, fully accessible trail allows you to view close-up several kinds of carnivorous plants, including many pitcher plants.

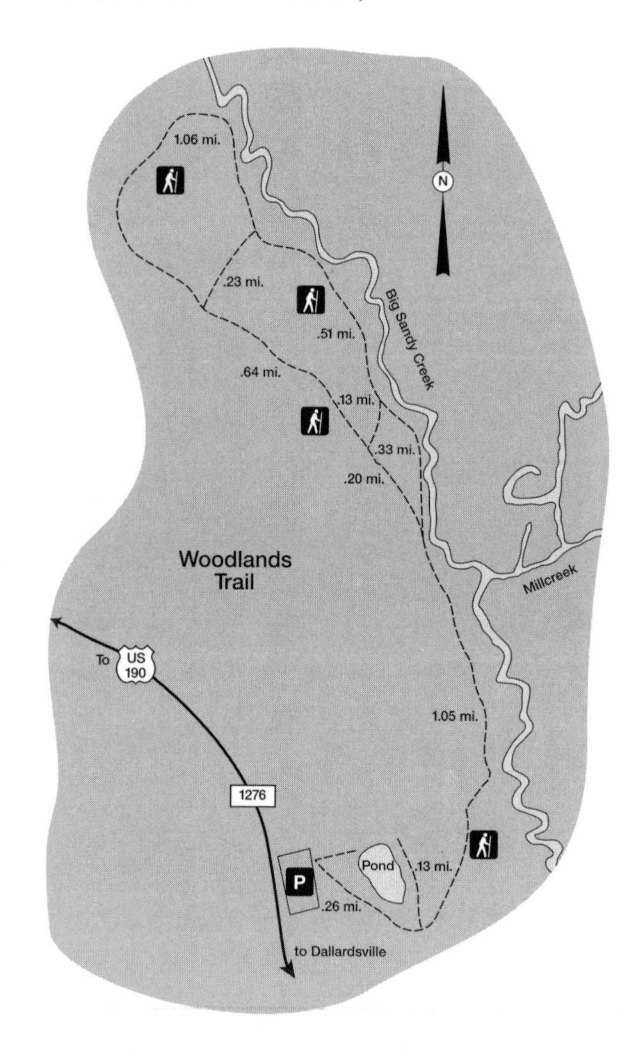

The **Woodlands Trail** is located at the NW edge of the Big Sandy Creek Unit. The trailhead is found on FM 1276, 3.3 miles south of US 190, or 5.9 miles north of Dallardsville. The trail is a 5.4-mile-long loop. Two shorter loops (3.3 or 4.5 miles) can be taken if you desire. There is a noticeable change in elevation as you drop into the Big Sandy Creek floodplain. Huge hardwood trees provide dense shade with sparse ground cover. Portions of the trail cut through upland pine stands and old pastures being reclaimed by nature.

Pitcher plants, like these, can be viewed close-up from a ¼-mile hard-surfaced, fully accessible trail.

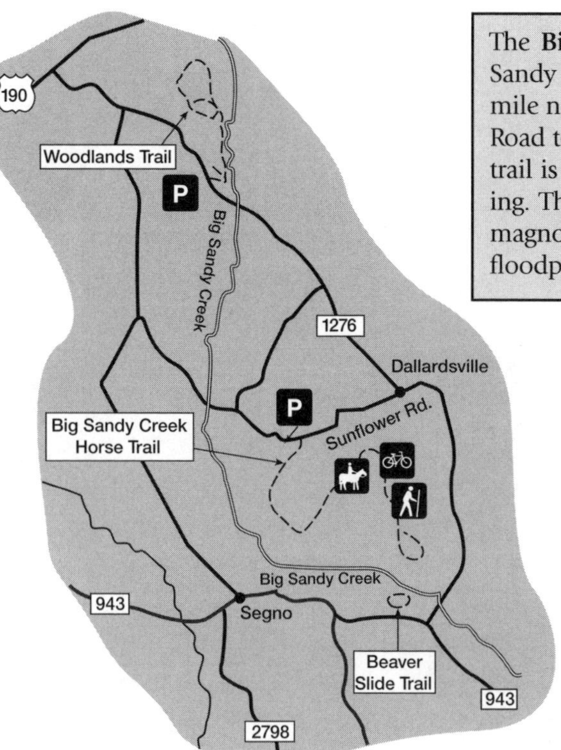

The **Big Sandy Creek Horse Trail,** in the SE corner of the Big Sandy Unit, can be reached by turning left from FM 1276, a half mile north of Dallardsville and proceeding 3 miles on Sunflower Road to the trailhead located on the left. This 18-mile round-trip trail is designed for horseback riding, hiking, and mountain biking. The trail meanders through upland pine forests and beech-magnolia-loblolly pine slopes before crossing Simons Branch to a floodplain forest.

The **Beaver Slide Trail,** in the SE corner at the Big Sandy Creek Unit, is located on FM 943 about a quarter mile west of the FM 1276/FM 943 intersection. This 1½-mile loop trail winds around a series of ponds formed by old beaver dams. The trail provides access to Big Sandy Creek and several excellent fishing spots.

The **Birdwatcher's Trail,** located at the confluence of the Menard Creek unit and the Trinity River, is 3.1 miles (5.0 km) north of Romayor off of FM 2610 on Oak Hill Drive. FM 2610 is west of TX 146 and east of the Trinity River; it can be reached via FM 787 just west of TX 146 or directly from TX 146 just south of the intersection on FM 943 with TX 146. The 0.5-mile long trail offers a panoramic view of expansive sandbars on the Trinity River from high bluffs on the east bank. The trail offers good birding opportunities for shorebirds, raptors, and migrant songbirds.

REGION 2

Marsha Elmore

The Big Sandy Creek Horse Trail is an 18-mile round-trip trail designed for horseback riding, hiking, and mountain biking.

Brazos Bend State Park

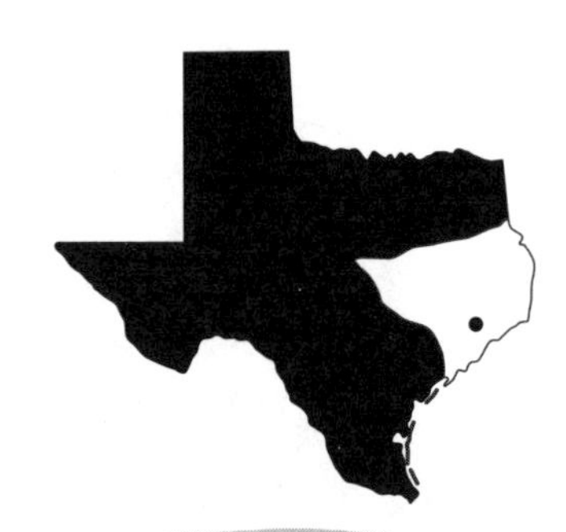

For Information

Brazos Bend State Park
21901 FM 762
Needville, TX 77461-9511
979/553-5101

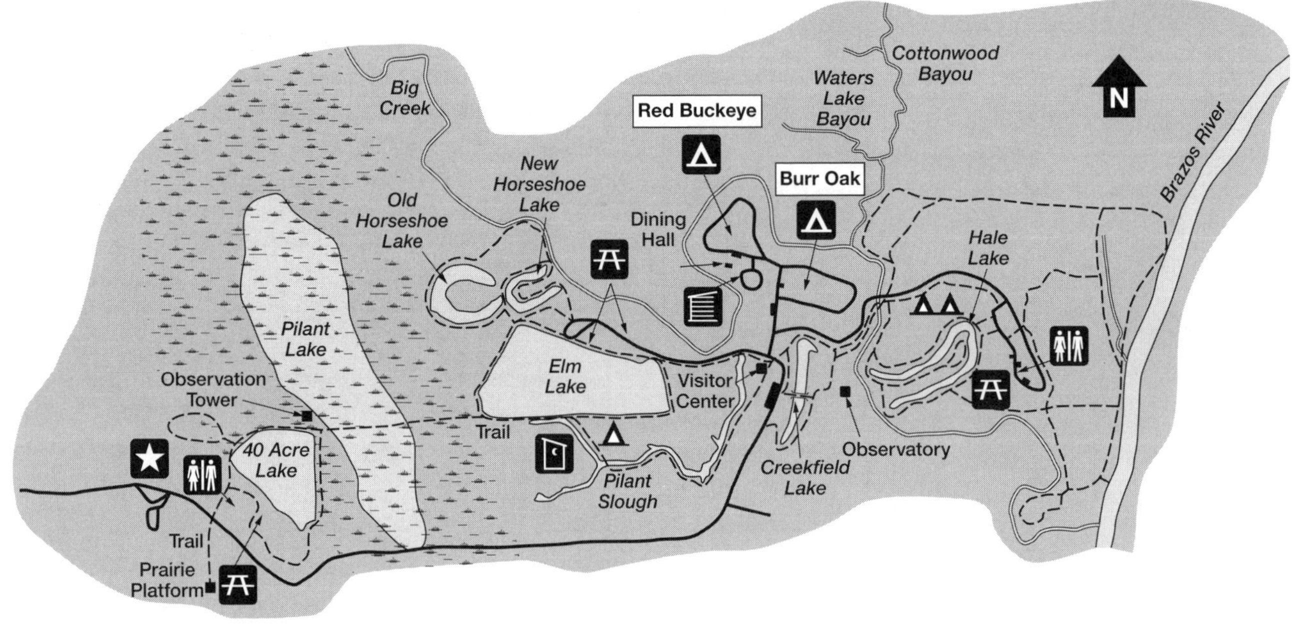

Location

Brazos Bend State Park may be reached by traveling approximately 20 miles southeast of Richmond on FM 762, or by traveling south from Houston on TX 288 to Rosharon, then 11 miles west on FM 1462. The 4,977-acre park has an eastern boundary of 3.2 miles fronting on the Brazos River.

Visitors at Brazos Bend State Park are cautioned to pay due respect to alligators; this pier is an excellent area from which to view them.

Trail Notes

Outdoor enthusiasts delight in the observation tower, platforms for wildlife observation/photography, and the extensive trail system at Brazos Bend State Park. There are 21 miles of hiking/ mountain biking trails; some are surfaced and some are unsurfaced. Some trails are designated as hiking only, while others are designated for either hiking or biking. The map displayed here does not distinguish between the two types of trails. Keep in mind that all trails can be used for hiking, but some trails are not suitable for biking. Obtain a map from the park office and observe the posted signs when biking on the trails. A ½-mile nature trail encircles a portion of Creekfield Lake and is accessible to those with vision, hearing, and mobility problems. Some park lakes are home for the American alligator; visitors are encouraged to view the alligators from a distance, and not to approach or feed them.

Buescher State Park

For Information

Buescher State Park
P.O. Box 75
Smithville, TX 78957-0075
512/237-2241

Location

Buescher State Park is located 2 miles north of Smithville. From TX 71, travel ½ mile north on FM 153 to Park Road 1; Loop 230 provides access to FM 153. The 1,017-acre park, located on the eastern edge of the famous Lost Pines of Texas, includes a 25-acre lake.

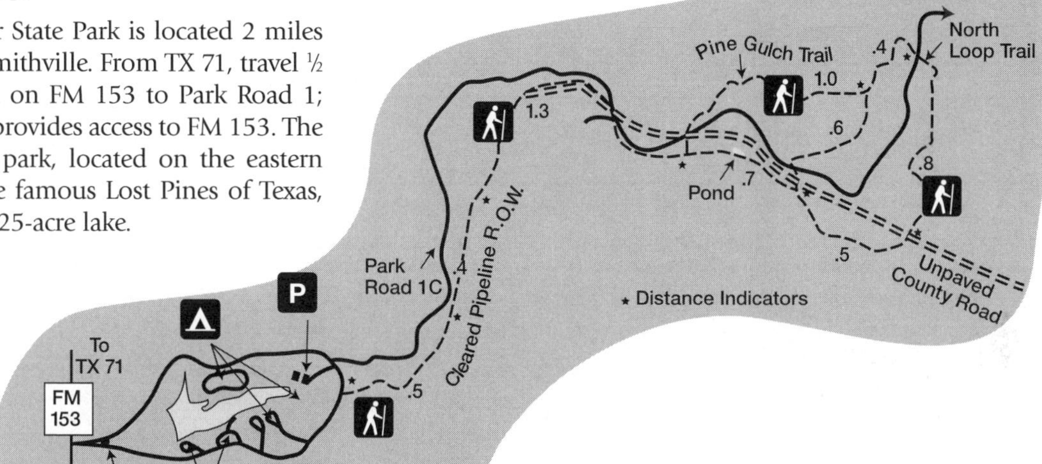

Trail Notes

This 7.7-mile round trip hiking trail, dedicated in February 1988, was constructed in 2 years as a result of nearly 900 hours of volunteer labor by members of the Texas Trails Association and the Sierra Club. The project was coordinated by Dr. Keith McCree of Texas A&M University. This trail allows hikers to enjoy a portion of the famous "Lost Pines" and other natural features of the rugged, hilly terrain.

The trail is for day use only; there is no overnight camping on the trail. Hikers should stay on the trail at all times as the trail was built with drainage and erosion control features to ensure preservation of the park resources. Dogs should be kept on a leash, fires are prohibited, and hikers should carry out everything that is brought with them. No bicycles are allowed on the trail.

Many bikers enjoy the challenge of the ride on Park Road 1C from Buescher State Park to Bastrop State Park; some prefer to combine this venture with a camping trip.

Davy Crockett National Forest

FOR INFORMATION

Davy Crockett National Forest
(in Ratcliff, east side of FM 227, just north of SH 7)
RR 1, Box 55-FS
Kennard, TX 75847
936/655-2299

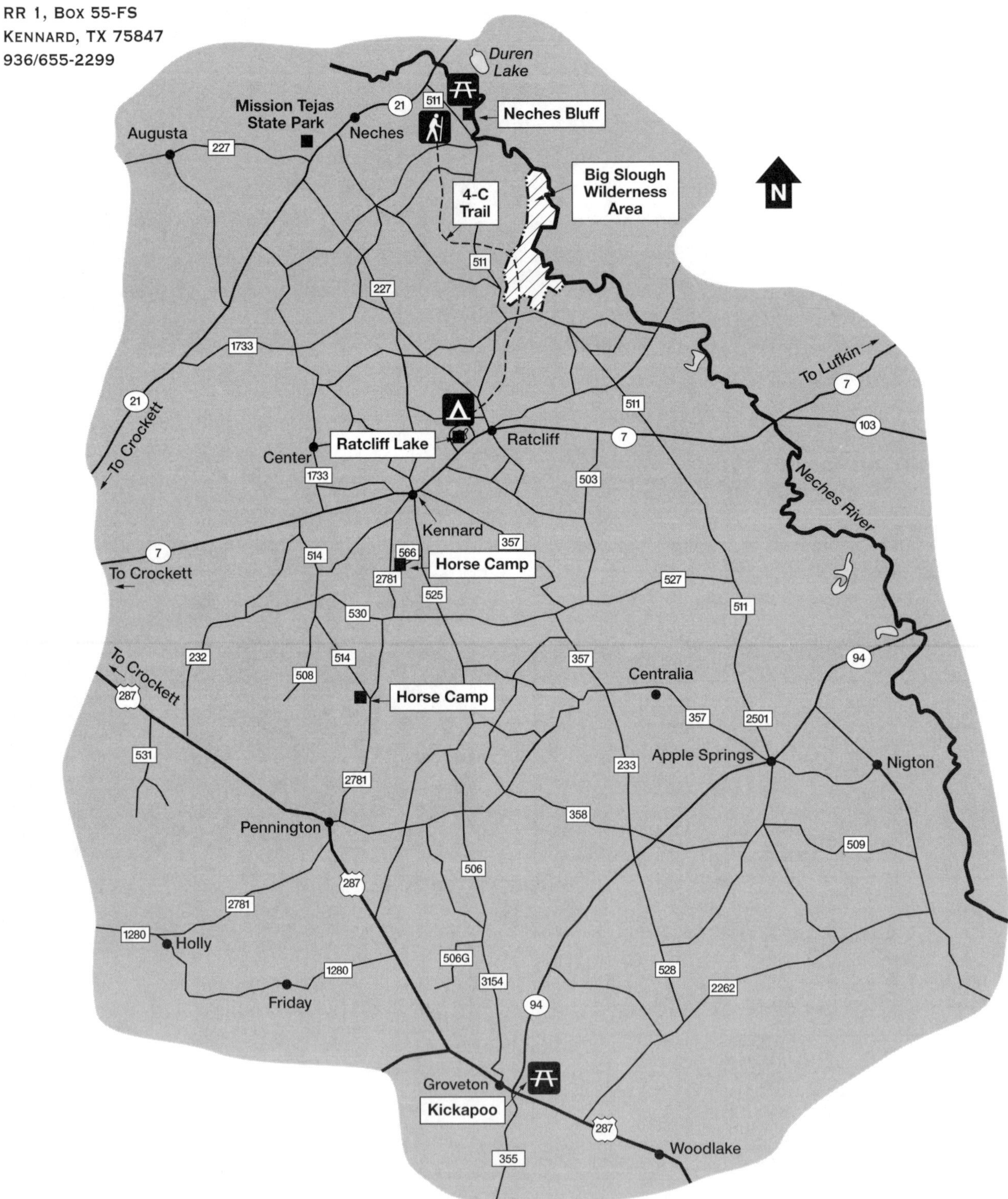

LOCATION

Davy Crockett National Forest is located in Houston and Trinity counties and has 160,647 acres. The Big Slough Wilderness Area is located along the Neches River 6 miles north of Ratcliff off FSR 511; it consists of about 3,639 acres of river bottomland and upland flats and contains 7 specific ecotypes.

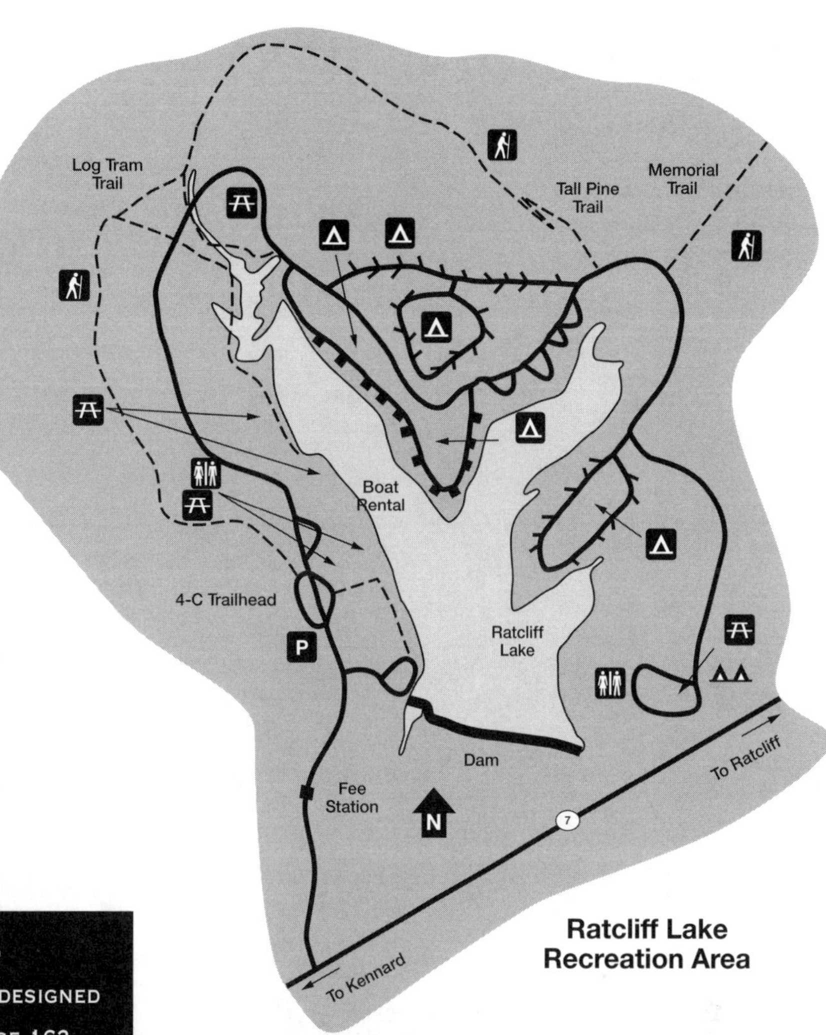

The 54-mile **Piney Creek Horse Trail** is located south of SH 7 near Kennard; it has 5 loops. The trail is primitive; its path follows Forest Service roads, tram roads, pipeline right-of-way, game trails, and highways. Trailhead parking areas are at the main access points. Camping is permitted anywhere along the trail and at two horse camps. There is a $10/vehicle charge for use of the horse trail.

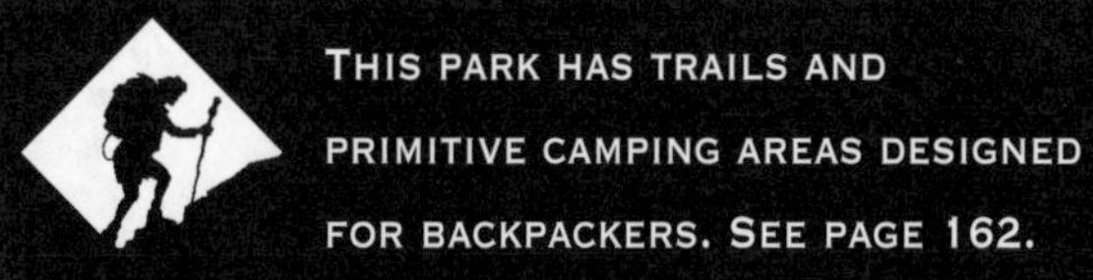

THIS PARK HAS TRAILS AND PRIMITIVE CAMPING AREAS DESIGNED FOR BACKPACKERS. SEE PAGE 162.

Gay Ippolito, U.S. Forest Service

The lake at Ratcliff can best be described as tranquil, peaceful, quiet, and calm ... a beautiful spot to pitch a tent!

HIKING/NATURE TRAILS AND LOCATIONS

- **Ratcliff Lake Recreation Area:** On TX 7 approximately 20 miles east of Crockett and 25 miles west of Lufkin. There is a ¾-mile accessible trail, as well as a 1½-mile "Tall Pine" hiking trail. The 20-mile 4-C Hiking Trail originates at the parking lot near the concession stand and ends at the Neches Bluff Overlook.
- **Neches Bluff Overlook:** Take TX 21 northeast from Crockett for 25 miles, then turn right (east) on FSR 511 for 1 mile, then turn left (north) and follow entrance road for 1 mile. The Neches Bluff Overlook is the site of a trailhead for the 4-C Hiking Trail.
- **Four-C Hiking Trail:** The 20-mile hiking and backpacking trail begins at Ratcliff Lake Recreation Area and ends at the Neches Bluff Overlook. See pages 162–166 for details.

Fort Parker State Park

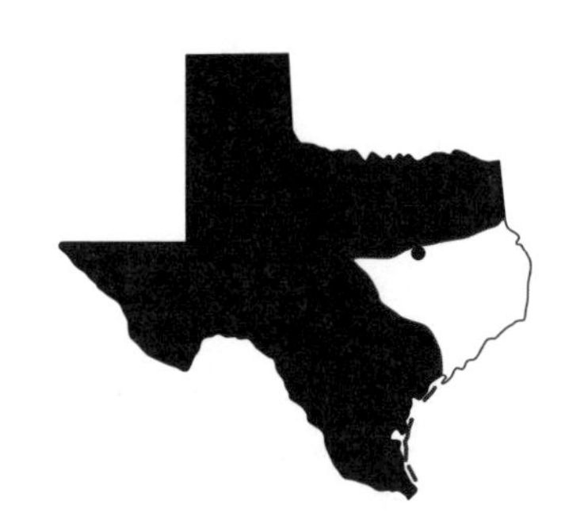

FOR INFORMATION

Fort Parker State Park
194 Park Rd. 28
Mexia, TX 76667
254/562-5751

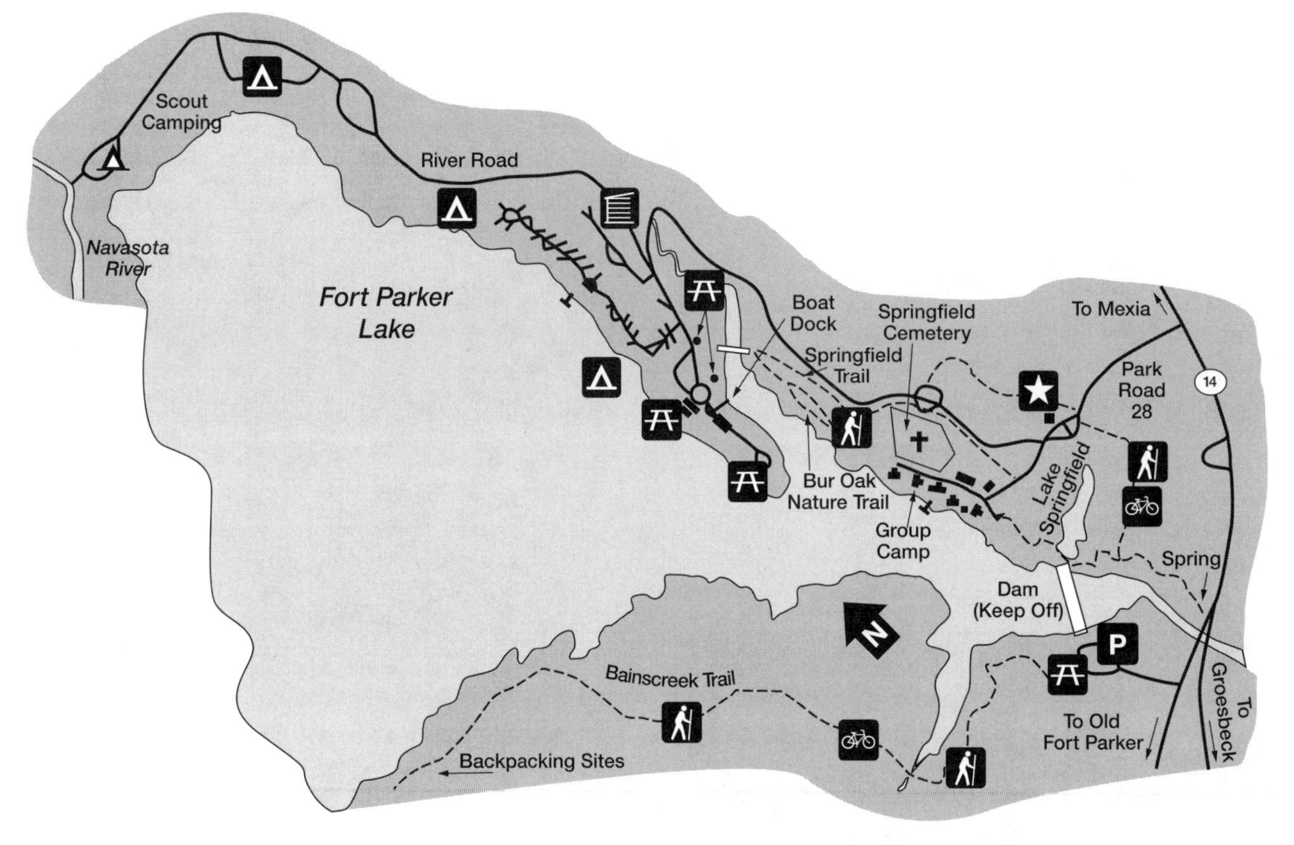

LOCATION

Fort Parker State Park is located 7 miles south of Mexia and 6 miles north of Groesbeck, off TX 14; the entrance is on Park Road 28. The park consists of the 724-acre Fort Parker Lake and 735 acres of gently rolling oak woodlands surrounding the lake.

TRAIL NOTES

Thickly wooded areas provide recreation opportunities for hikers, bikers, and other outdoor enthusiasts. The park has 2 miles of mountain bike trails as well as hiking trails. A 1-mile hiking trail is located between the dam on the Navasota River and a footbridge near the picnic area. Hikers can also enjoy the area near the banks of the Navasota River in the vicinity of the wilderness camping area.

These bikers are taking a break and deciding where to venture next.

Galveston Island State Park

FOR INFORMATION

Galveston Island State Park
14901 FM 3005
Galveston, TX 77554
409/737-1222

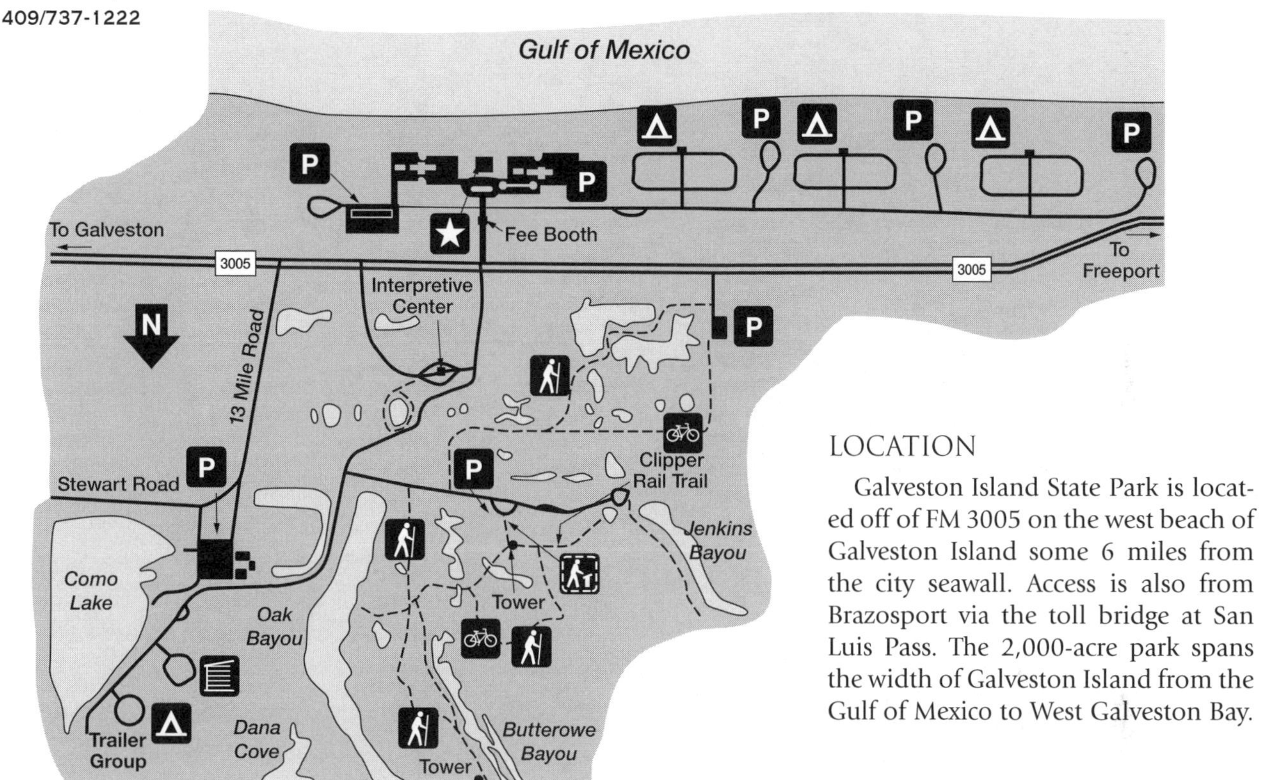

LOCATION

Galveston Island State Park is located off of FM 3005 on the west beach of Galveston Island some 6 miles from the city seawall. Access is also from Brazosport via the toll bridge at San Luis Pass. The 2,000-acre park spans the width of Galveston Island from the Gulf of Mexico to West Galveston Bay.

The gulls are ever ready for those who just can't resist tossing bits of bread.

TRAIL NOTES

The 4-mile nature trail at Galveston Island State Park is one of the most unique in the state, providing interpretation of the various transitional ecological zones that comprise the park. The trail begins in the salt meadows and enters the marsh, where the uplands and the sea merge, forming brackish saltwater ponds. Freshwater ponds are located in the meadows. The trail terminates with an observation point that overlooks the surf and sea. Special features of the trail are bird blinds for photography and a thousand-foot boardwalk over the marsh. From the trail a visitor has a panoramic view of the bay, including a chance to see a live oyster reef and a small bird nesting island just offshore.

Mountain bikes are allowed on any of the trails that are firm; they should not be ridden on marshy trails.

GRANGER LAKE/ COMANCHE BLUFF TRAIL

FOR INFORMATION

GRANGER PROJECT OFFICE
RR 1, BOX 172
GRANGER, TX 76530-9712
512/859-2668

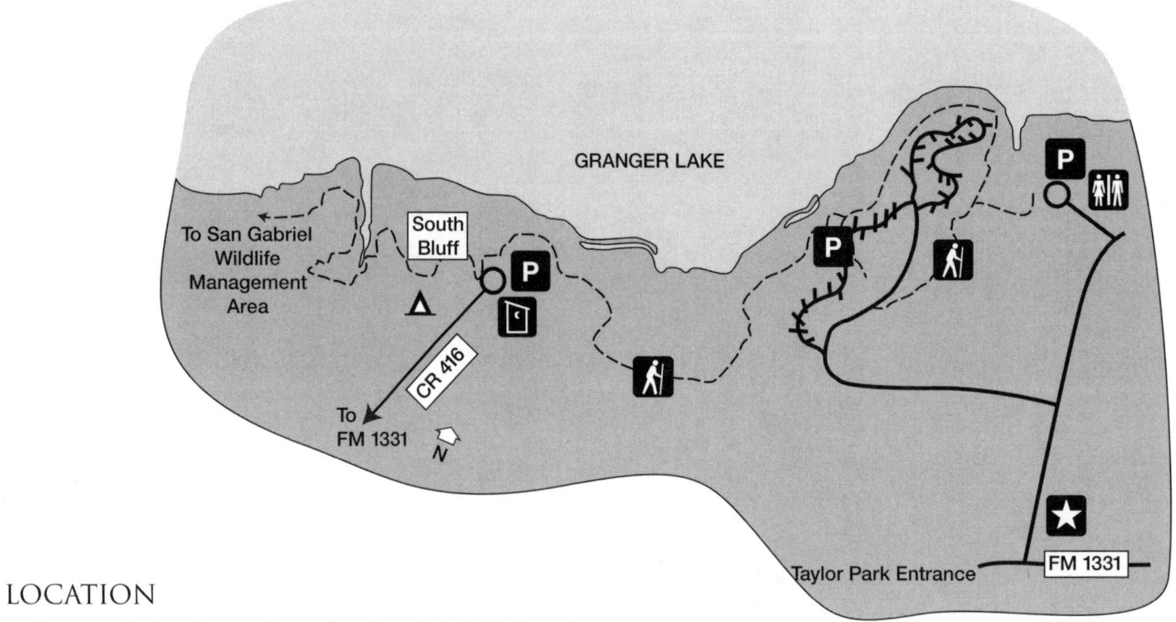

LOCATION

Granger Lake, located on the San Gabriel River, is east of TX 95 between Granger and Taylor. Access to Taylor Park, the location of the Comanche Bluff Trail, is via FM 1331.

TRAIL NOTES

A 3-mile hiking trail traverses a bluff in Taylor Park at Granger Lake; an interpretive brochure is available. Granger Lake is uniquely situated in the center of the Central Texas Blackland Prairie. The trail extends to the west into the San Gabriel Wildlife Management Area; however, the trail is not as developed as in the Taylor Park area. All hikers must be off the trail by dark unless registered in the primitive or developed camping areas in Taylor Park. Horses and motorized vehicles are not permitted.

The South Bluff primitive camping area, a walk-in tenting area in west Taylor Park, is designed for individuals and small non-organized groups. No more than 30 persons will be registered into the camping area at any one time. Individual group size is limited to 10. All campers are required to register with the Taylor Park gate attendant prior to entering the camping area, and to check out upon departure. Campsites are available on a first-come, first-served basis. Drinking water must be carried to the campground and can be obtained at the time of registration. Lake water is not recommended for drinking purposes. Fires are allowed within the designated fire pits only. The use of portable cooking stoves is encouraged. Chemical toilets are provided.

Houston Arboretum & Nature Center

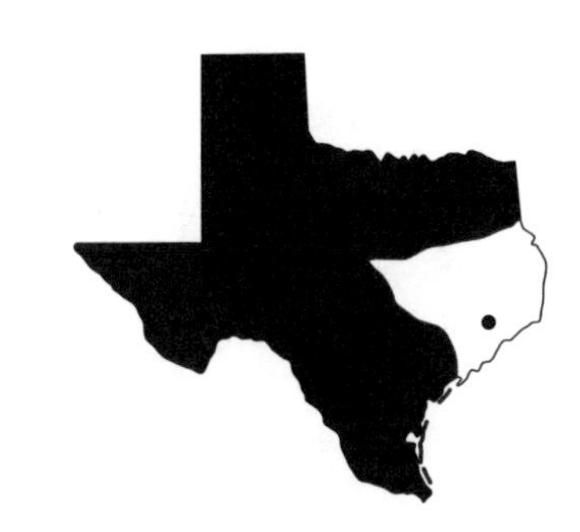

FOR INFORMATION

Houston Arboretum & Nature Center
4501 Woodway Dr.
Houston, TX 77024-7708
713/681-8433
www.houstonarboretum.org

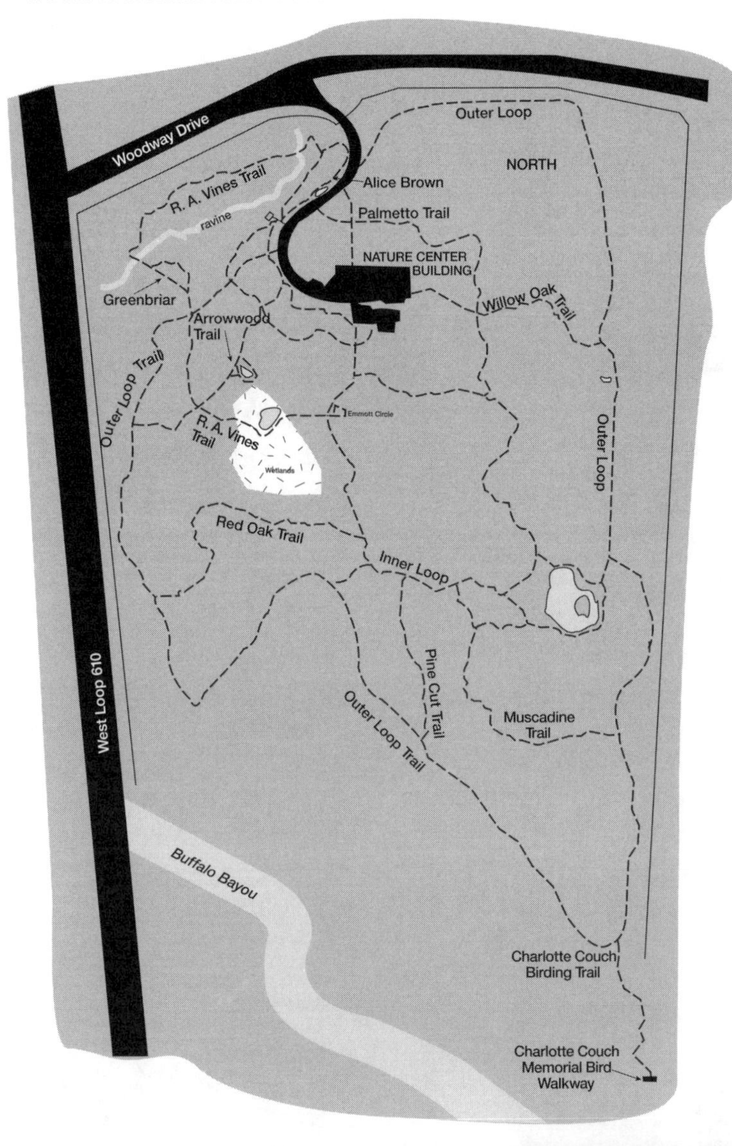

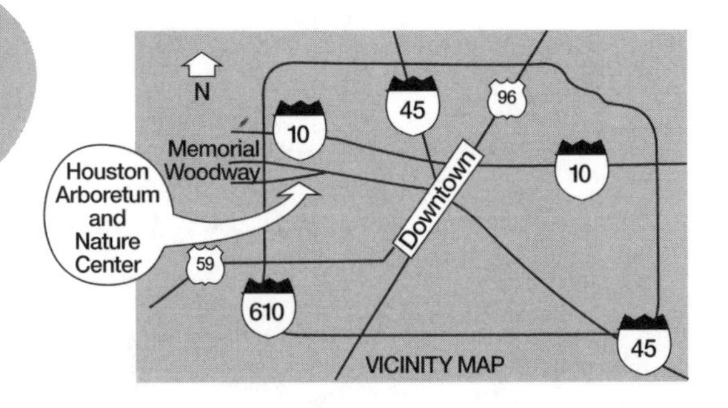

TRAIL NOTES

The Houston Arboretum & Nature Center, a non-profit 155-acre nature and wildlife sanctuary, is a hidden gem nestled quietly in the heart of bustling downtown Houston. Over five miles of nature trails roam through forest, meadow, and wetland areas that are home to over 300 native species of trees, shrubs, ferns, mosses, and wildflowers and a large variety of local wildlife. Other attractions include three bird observation decks, five ponds, and the indoor Discovery Room, which houses interactive educational exhibits including aquariums, touch screens, a 15-foot model tree, and microscopes with video monitor displays. Admission is free; donations are appreciated. The grounds are open daily from 8:30 a.m. to 6 p.m.

Over five miles of nature trails roam through this 155-acre nature and wildlife sanctuary.

Huntsville State Park

FOR INFORMATION

Huntsville State Park
P.O. Box 508
Huntsville, TX 77342-0508
936/295-5644

LOCATION

Huntsville State Park is located 8 miles south of Huntsville on I-45 and southwest on Park Road 40. The 2,083-acre park includes the 210-acre man-made lake, Lake Raven.

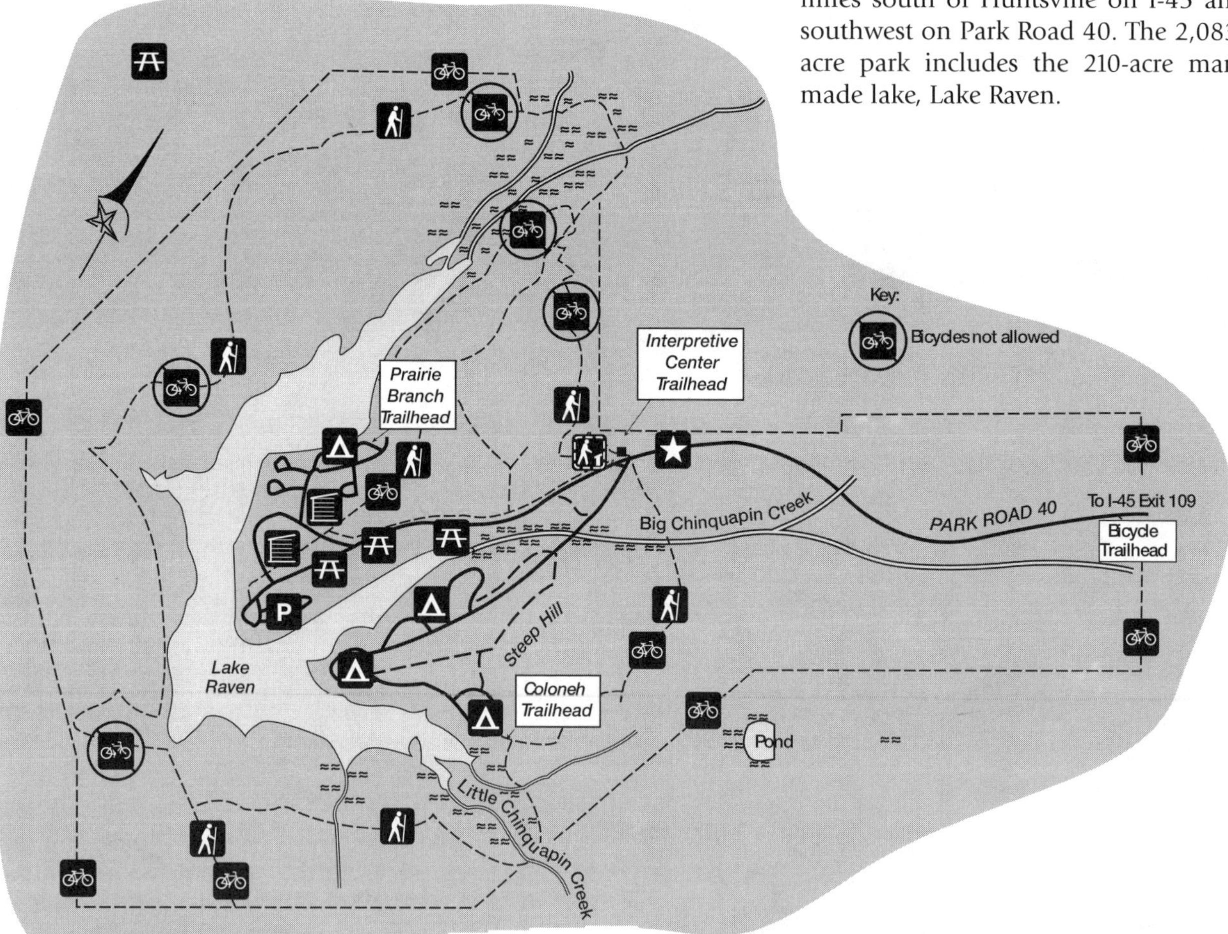

TRAIL NOTES

There are more than 11 miles of hiking and bicycle trails in Huntsville State Park. The 7.7-mile hiking trail that encircles the lake takes approximately 3½ hours to complete; part of the trail is shared with bicycles. Bicycle trails include both surfaced trails and unsurfaced trails. During wet conditions and immediately after rain, unpaved trails are closed to bicycles. Guided trail rides are available though Lake Raven Stables (936/295-1985). Late March and early April is the best time to see flowering dogwood and eastern redbud in bloom.

This young biker is well prepared to ride on either the paved trails or the unpaved trails.

LAKE BASTROP
SOUTH SHORE PARK

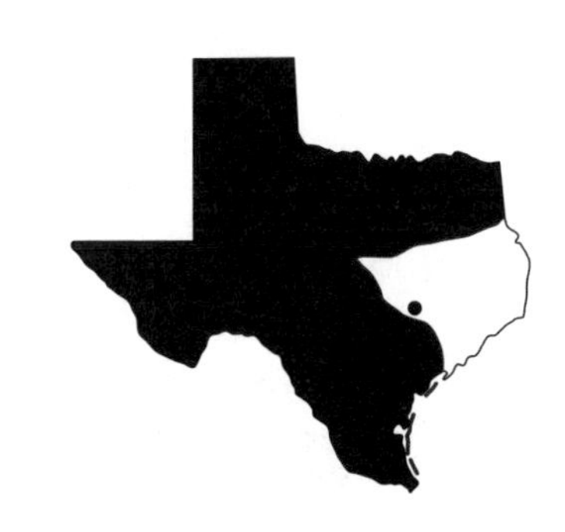

FOR INFORMATION

LCRA SOUTH AND NORTH SHORE PARK
P.O. BOX 761
BASTROP, TX 78602
512/303-7666

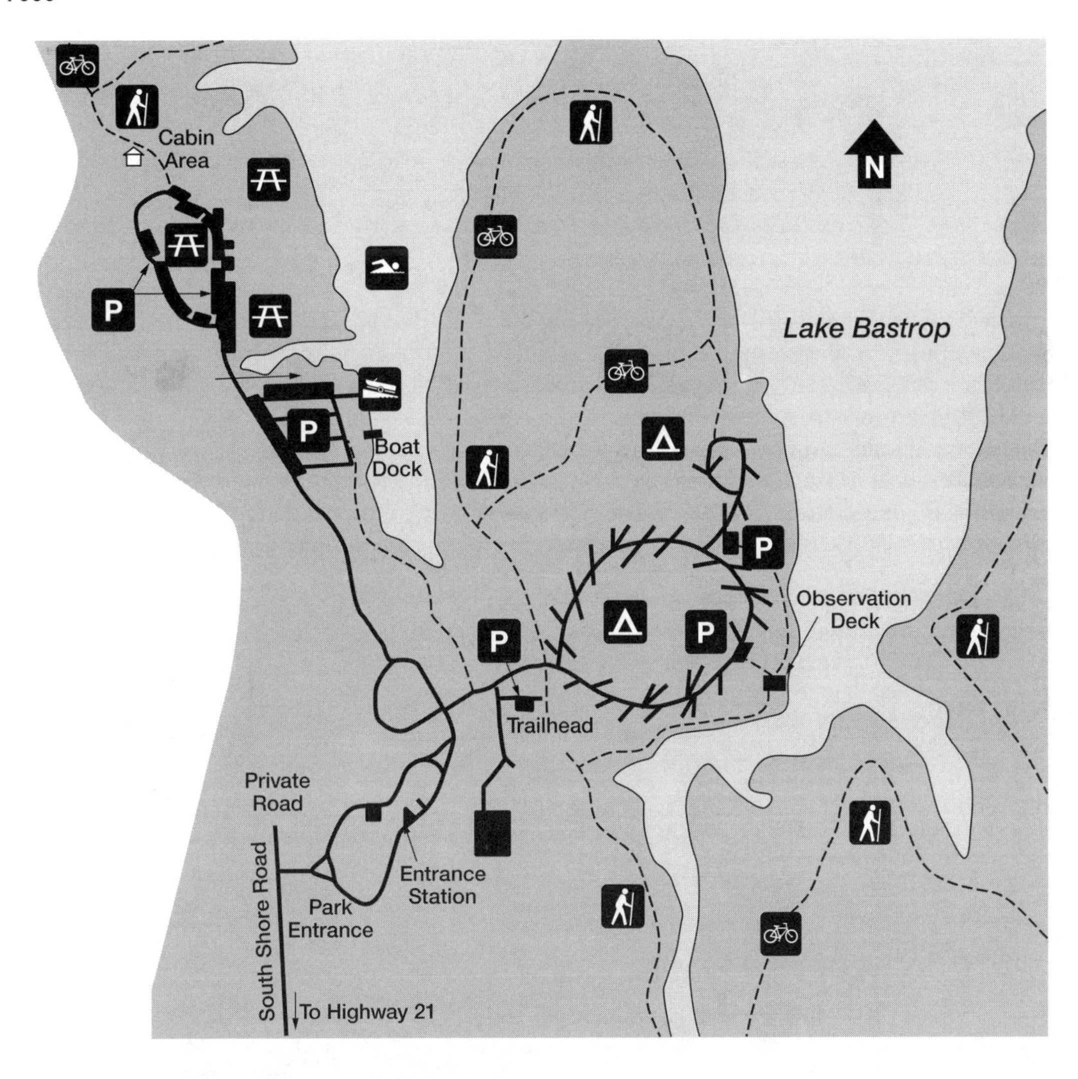

TRAIL NOTES

South Shore Park has 3½ miles of hiking/mountain bike trails. One trailhead is from the day-use area; another is adjacent to the campground located on a peninsula. Surrounded by woodlands, Lake Bastrop is nestled between the "Lost Pines" and Post Oak Savannah regions. Lost Pines is an "island" of loblolly pines created by an ancient upheaval in the earth's crust that placed these trees 80 miles west of Texas' main pine tree belt.

LOCATION

Lake Bastrop is located about 3 miles northeast of Bastrop. To reach the South Shore Park, take South Shore Road north from TX 21. This 906-acre lake was built by the Lower Colorado River Authority as a cooling pond for the Sim Gideon Power Plant. The constant mix of warm and cool water has created a fisherman's paradise. This park is operated by the Lower Colorado River Authority.

LAKE HOUSTON STATE PARK

FOR INFORMATION

LAKE HOUSTON STATE PARK
22031 BAPTIST ENCAMPMENT RD.
NEW CANEY, TX 77357-7731
281/354-6881

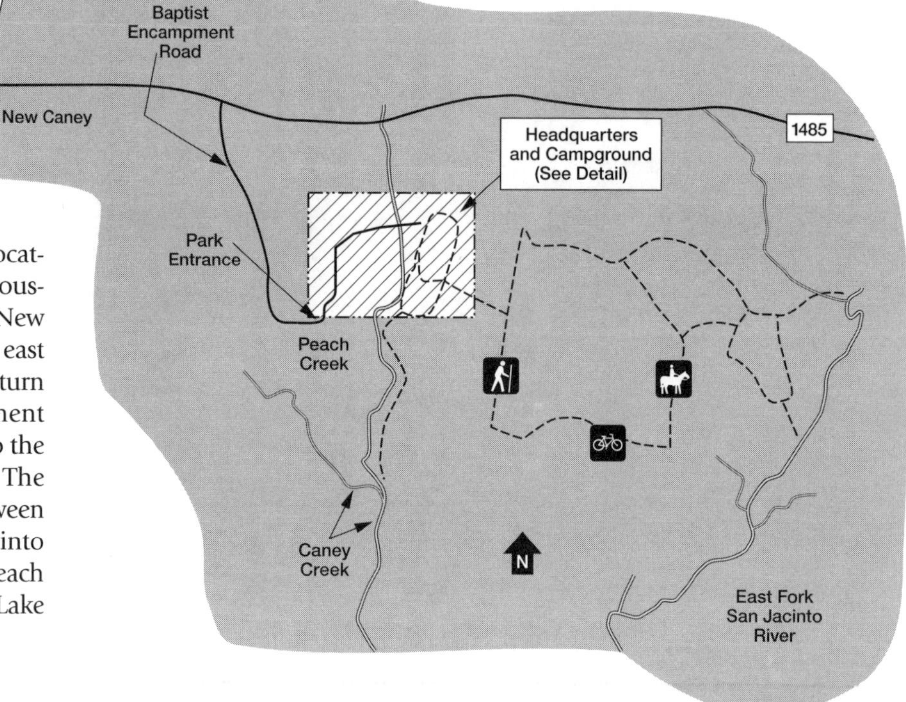

LOCATION

Lake Houston State Park is located about 30 miles north of Houston; take US 59 north to the New Caney and FM 1485 exit. Go east on FM 1485 about 2 miles, turn right on Baptist Encampment Road, and go about 1½ miles to the park entrance on the left. The 4,920-acre park lies tucked between the East Fork of the San Jacinto River and New Caney and Peach creeks; there is no access to Lake Houston at this time.

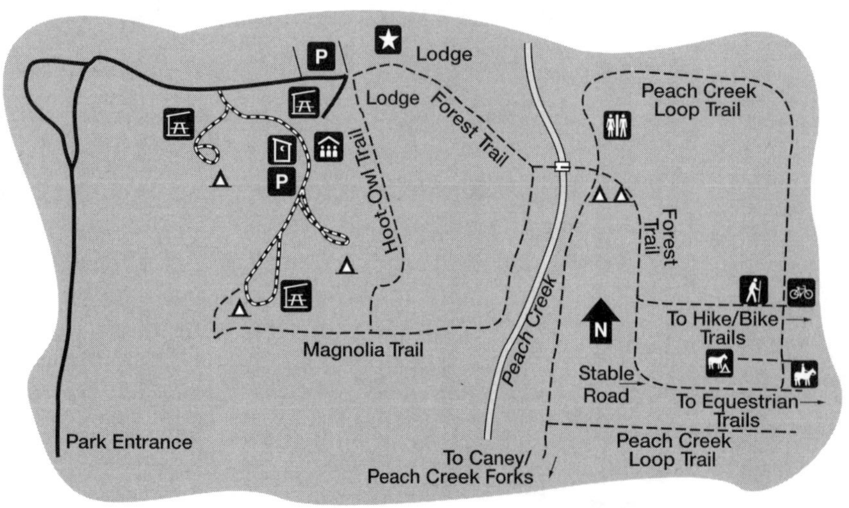

Headquarters and Campground Detail

TRAIL NOTES

Twelve miles of hiking and biking trails are available. Mountain bikes are allowed on all of the trails; this trail follows the slope of one of the many smaller creeks for a short distance and then meanders through various terrain, flora, and fauna. Sections of the hike and bike trails are widened and well developed while other parts of the trail simply follow small streams, small valleys, and slopes that are a part of the terrain.

This area was once the site of Peach Creek Girl Scout Camp with stables and a riding arena. They will be renovated for future use.

Lake Livingston State Park

For Information

Lake Livingston State Park
300 State Park Rd. 65
Livingston, TX 77351
936/365-2201

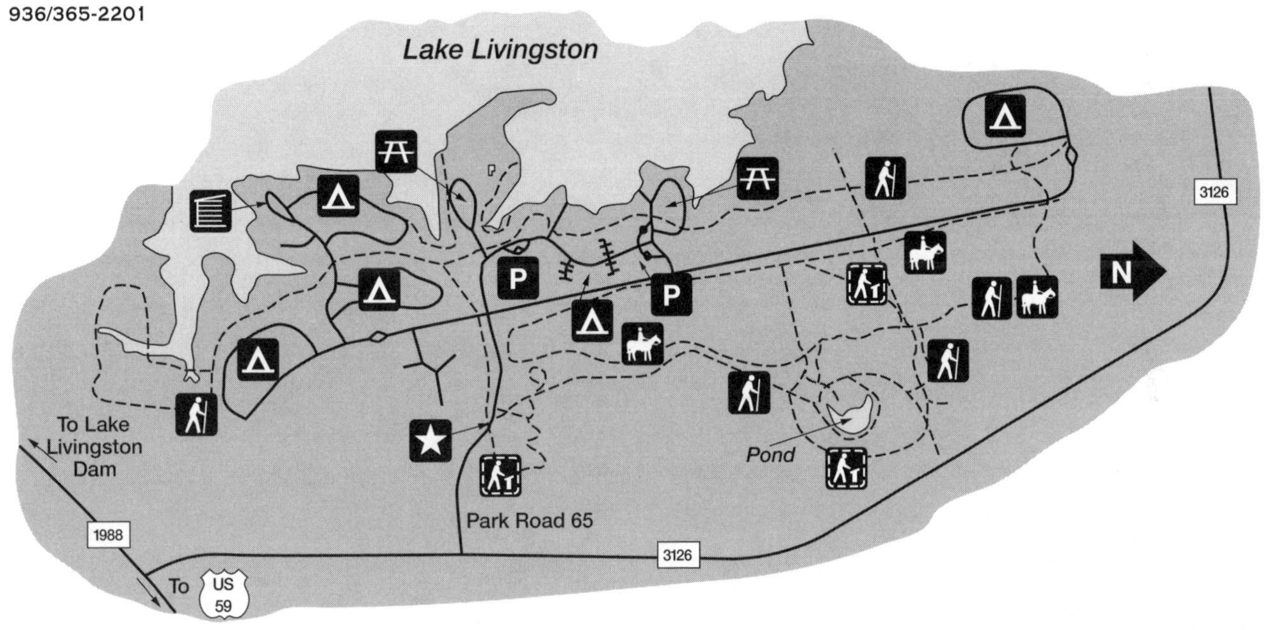

Location

Lake Livingston State Park is located on the east shore of Lake Livingston with a total acreage of 635. The park is 1 mile south of Livingston off of US 59, 4 miles west on FM 1988, and ½ mile north on FM 3126.

Trail Notes

There are 5 miles of hiking/biking trails in the park; some are surfaced. The Oak Flat Nature Trail, a ⅓-mile interpretive trail, begins at the headquarters and loops through a relatively undisturbed bottomland hardwood area, returning to the trailhead. The 84,800-acre reservoir and the approximately 2½ miles of park shoreline provide opportunities for additional hiking. A 2½-mile guided trail ride is available through Lake Livingston Stables. Phone: 409/967-5032.

These hikers have found a good vantage point to bird-watch along the shoreline trail.

Lake Somerville State Park and Trailway

Birch Creek Unit

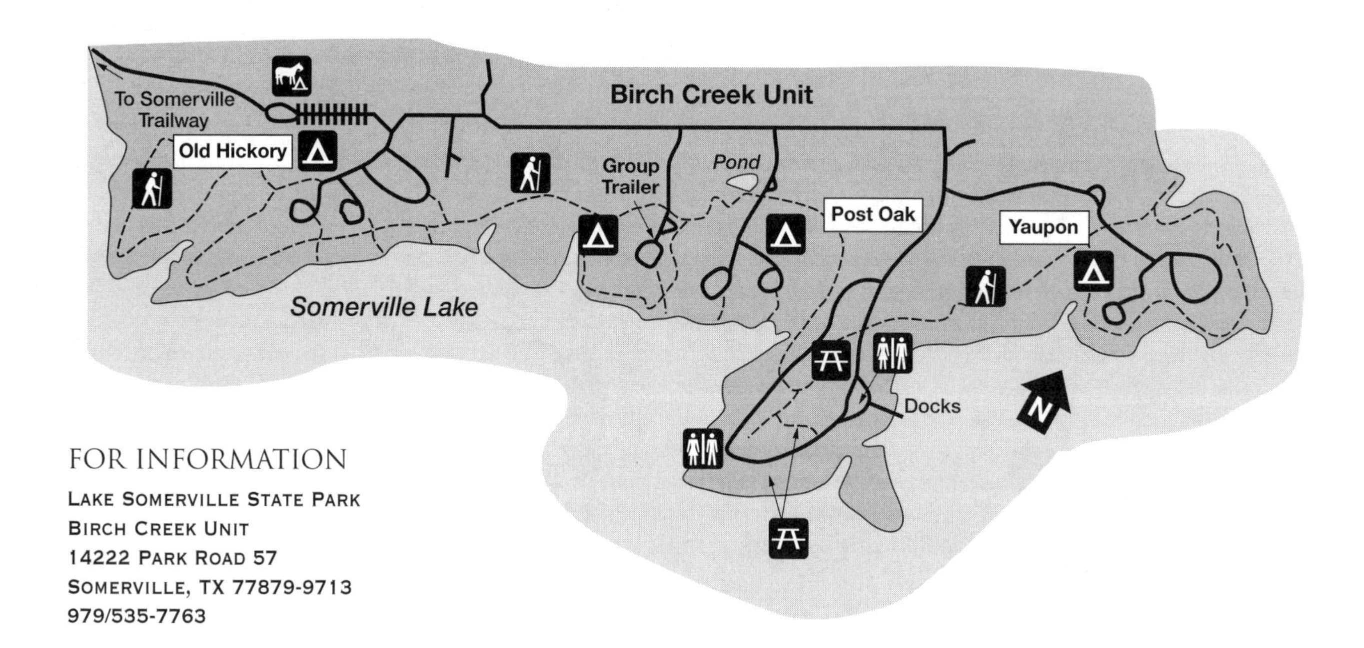

For Information

Lake Somerville State Park
Birch Creek Unit
14222 Park Road 57
Somerville, TX 77879-9713
979/535-7763

Location

The Birch Creek Unit of Lake Somerville State Park is located on the north shore of Somerville Lake and contains 2,365 acres. From TX 36, northwest of Somerville, travel 7.6 miles west on FM 60 to Park Road 57, then south for 4.3 miles to the park entrance.

Trail Notes

The Birch Creek Unit has 5 miles of hiking/nature trails, while the Nails Creek Unit has 3 miles of trails. The Lake Somerville Trailway with 13 miles of hiking trails connects the two units. Hikers, bikers, and equestrians are permitted on the trailway. Six primitive campgrounds with approximately 100 campsites are located along the trailway. See page 186 for details.

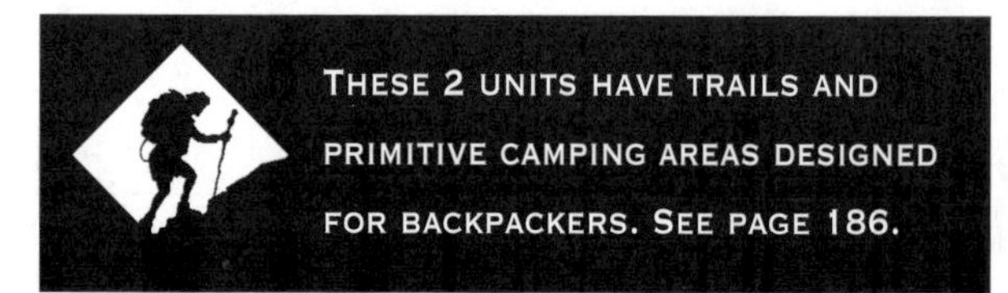

On a brisk spring day, these campers are enjoying a stroll through the day-use area at the Birch Creek Unit.

Nails Creek Unit

FOR INFORMATION

LAKE SOMERVILLE STATE PARK
NAILS CREEK UNIT
6280 FM 180
LEDBETTER, TX 78946-7036
979/289-2392

LOCATION

The Nails Creek Unit of Lake Somerville State Park is located on the south shore of Somerville Lake and contains 300 acres. From US 290 in Burton travel FM 1697 northwest, then right on FM 180 to the park. Or, from US 290 between Giddings and Ledbetter, travel northeast on FM 180 directly to the park.

Horseback riders at the Nails Creek Unit prepare for a ride on a portion of the 13-mile Lake Somerville State Trailway.

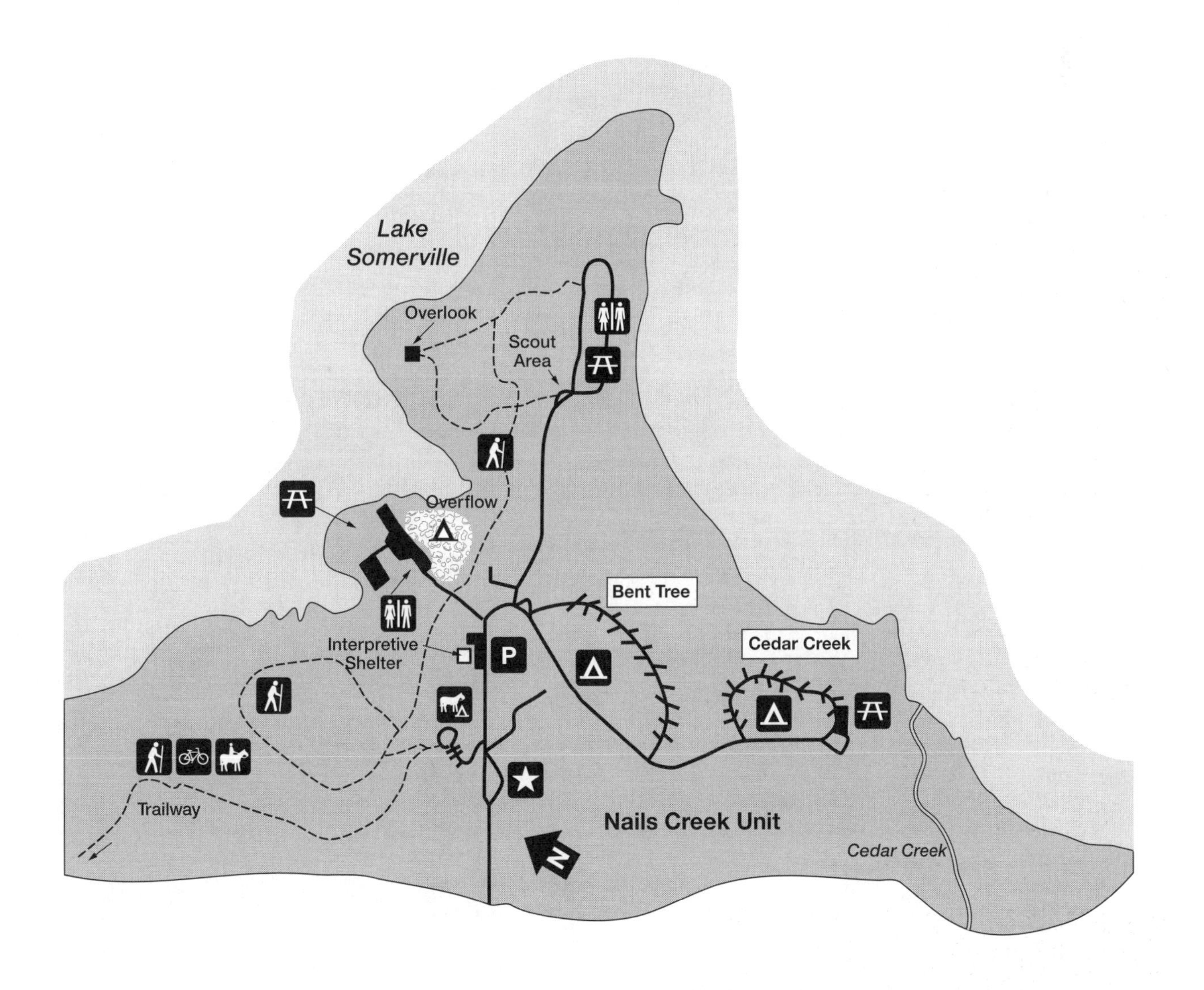

Martin Dies, Jr. State Park

For Information

Martin Dies, Jr. State Park
RR 4, Box 274
Jasper, TX 75951
409/384-5231

Location

Martin Dies, Jr. State Park can be reached by traveling 9 miles west from Jasper on US 190 to Park Road 48, or 15 miles east from Woodville on US 90 to Park Road 48. Located on the shore of B.A. Steinhagen Lake, the 705-acre park includes 3 separate units: Cherokee, Walnut Ridge, and Hen House Ridge.

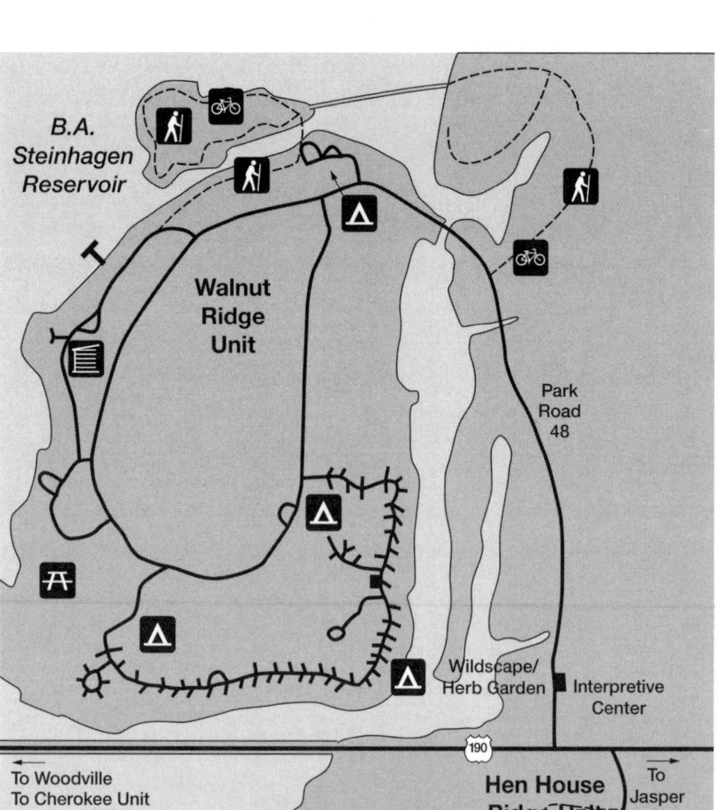

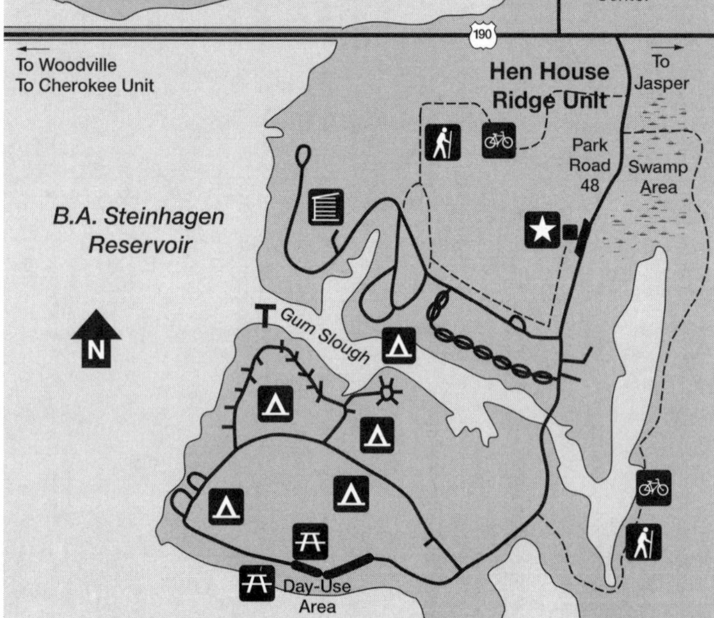

Trail Notes

Walnut Ridge Unit has a 1-mile loop trail that encircles a small island that is accessible via a wooden bridge. A footbridge leads to this same island. The bridge serves as a wildlife viewing area. Hen House Ridge Unit has two trails. A 1.6-mile trail to the east of Park Road 48 parallels a slough and swamp area as it heads north. It crosses the park road and heads west and then south to the camping area located on the north of Gum Slough. All of the trails are designated for hiking and mountain biking.

Gum Slough, located east of Park Road 48 in the Hen House Ridge Unit, presents a serene beauty each spring.

McKinney Roughs Nature Park

FOR INFORMATION

McKinney Roughs Nature Park
1884 State Highway 71
Cedar Creek, TX 78612
512/303-5073
For recorded trail information
800/766-5272, ext. 7427

LOCATION

McKinney Roughs Nature Park is located on SH 71, 13.2 miles east of Austin-Bergstrom International Airport and 8.4 miles west of Bastrop. The entrance includes a windmill and a rock wall. This 1,100-acre preserve, where four unique ecosystems come together, has been developed as a nature park and learning center. Hundreds of species of mammals, birds, amphibians, and reptiles live here. The park is open from 8 a.m. to 5 p.m., Monday through Saturday, and noon to 5 p.m. on Sunday, and is closed on major holidays.

TRAIL NOTES

A total of 14.6 miles of hiking and equestrian trails meander through approximately 1,100 acres of McKinney Roughs. The trail system is a combination of previously existing ranch roads and newly constructed trails. The system includes a self-guided nature trail, equestrian trails, and hiking trails. Some parts of the trail system are accessible for disabled visitors.

Motorized vehicles and bicycles are prohibited. Although hikers may use both equestrian and hiking trails, equestrians must stay on the equestrian trails and off of trails designated for hikers only.

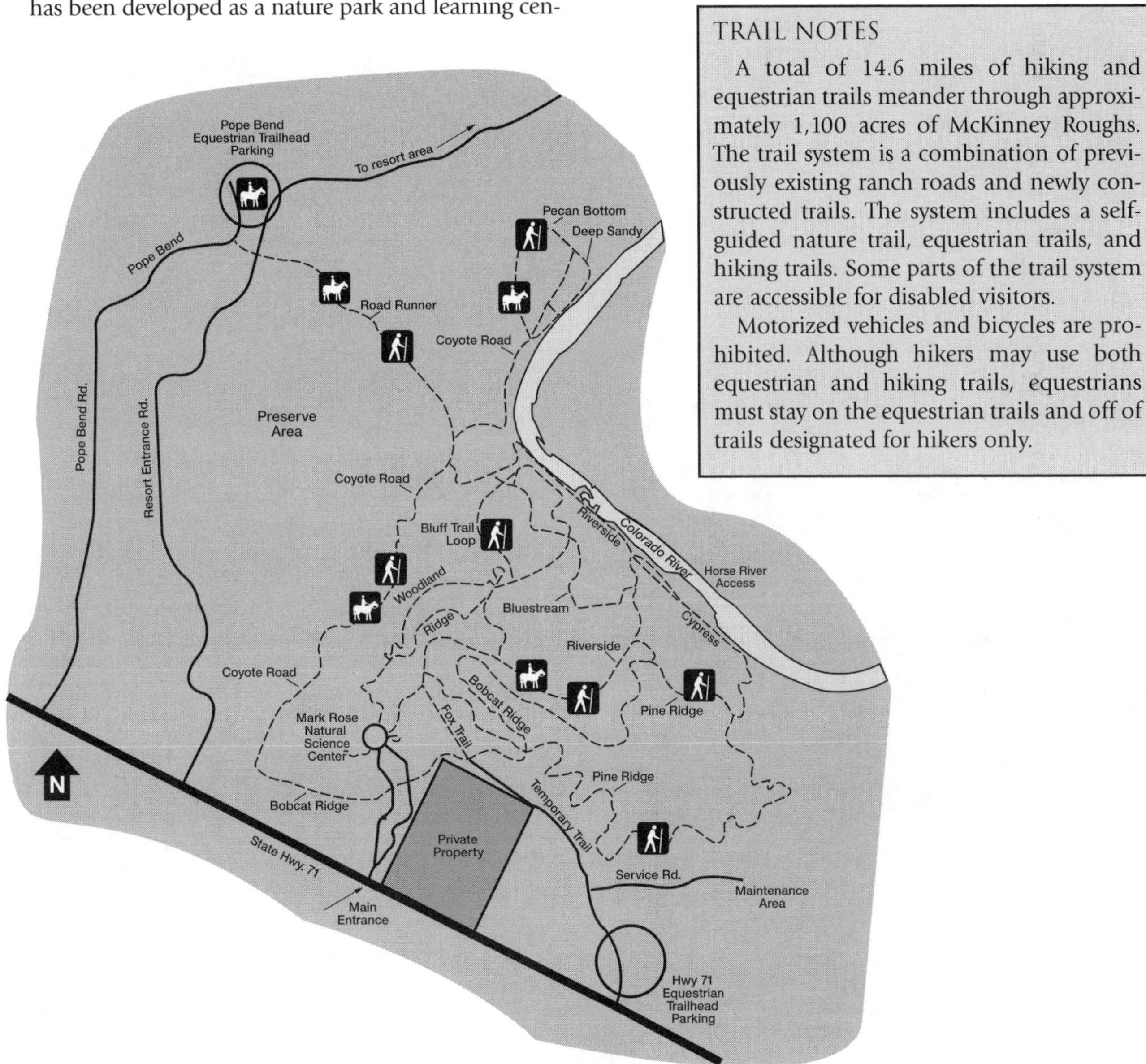

REGION 2

MISSION TEJAS STATE PARK

FOR INFORMATION

MISSION TEJAS STATE PARK
RR 2, BOX 108
GRAPELAND, TX 75844
936/687-2394

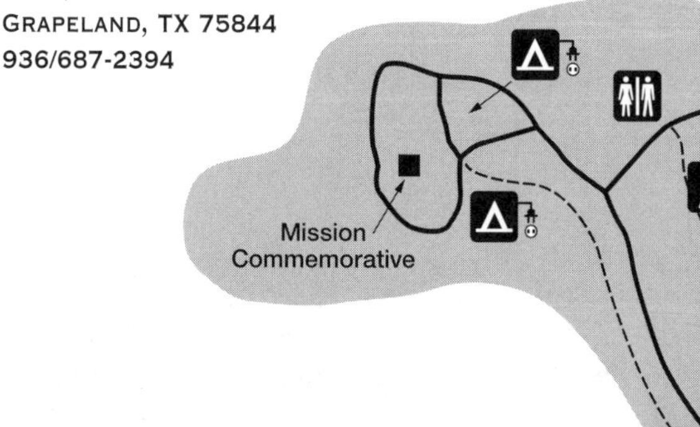

LOCATION

Mission Tejas State Park is located approximately 21 miles northeast of Crockett and 12 miles southwest of Alto on TX 21 (the old San Antonio Road). The entrance to the park is near Weches, where Park Road 44 intersects with TX 21. The 669-acre park is named for Mission San Francisco de los Tejas, the first Spanish mission in the province of Texas.

Texas Parks and Wildlife Department

TRAIL NOTES

There are several loop hiking trails and a nature trail at the park that total 4 miles. The Tejas Timber Nature Trail, although a relatively short trail, is well constructed and maintained; it encircles a picturesque 2-acre pond. The terrain along the hiking trails is gently rolling to hilly. The dominant vegetation is pine with numerous hardwoods, such as oaks, hickory, sweet gum, redbud, and dogwood. A loop trail off of the main hiking trail provides access to the Rice family log home and a historic marker.

In 1934, the Civilian Conservation Corps built this structure to commemorate Mission San Francisco de los Tejas, the first Spanish mission in the province of Texas. It is one of two historic structures at this state park.

Mother Neff State Park

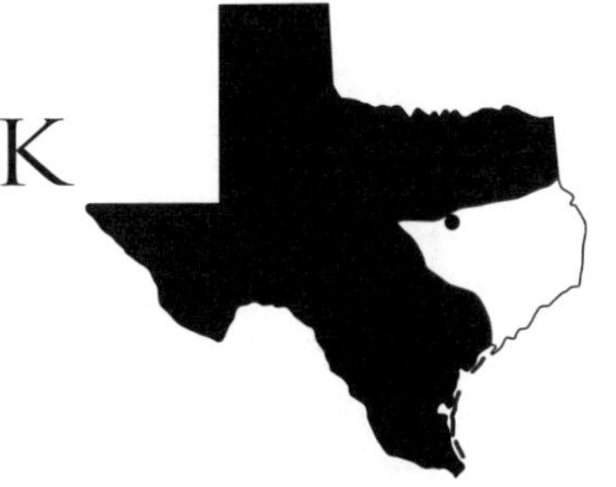

For Information

Mother Neff State Park
1680 Texas 236 Hwy.
Moody, TX 76557
254/853-2389

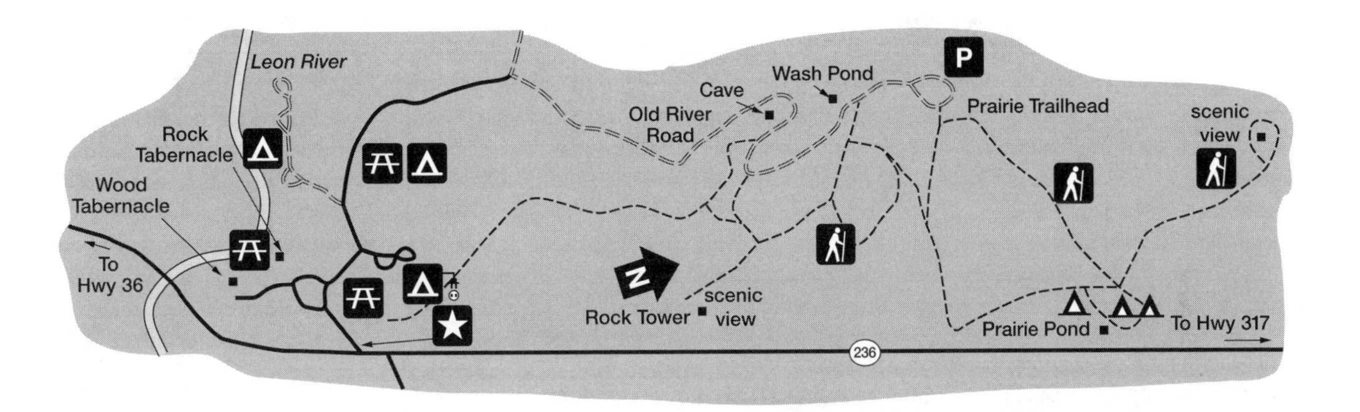

Location

Mother Neff State Park, the oldest park in the Texas State Park System, is adjacent to the Leon River. The 259-acre park is 15 miles northwest of Temple on TX 36, then 5 miles north on TX 236.

Trail Notes

The park has 2¾ miles of hiking trails. One trail winds through a cedar-oak woodland and leads to a round water tower built of native stone. Stone stairs, safeguarded by an iron handrail, lead to the top. This platform affords a beautiful view of the surrounding countryside. The trail to the tower forks and leads off to a beautiful pond, which may have been used by Indians and pioneer women to wash clothes.

The bottomlands of about 50 acres contain huge pecan, cottonwood, sycamore, and several species of oak trees, including the National Champion Texas Oak. Another point of interest at the park is the Tonkawa Indian Cave—a rock shelter in a deep ravine that was once used by the Tonkawas as a campsite and also for burials.

One of the outstanding features of Mother Neff State Park is its magnificent pecan, cottonwood, sycamore, and oak trees.

SABINE NATIONAL FOREST

FOR INFORMATION

SABINE NATIONAL FOREST
(201 SOUTH PALM)
P.O. BOX 227
HEMPHILL, TX 75948
409/787-3870 OR 2791
TOLL FREE: 866/235-1750

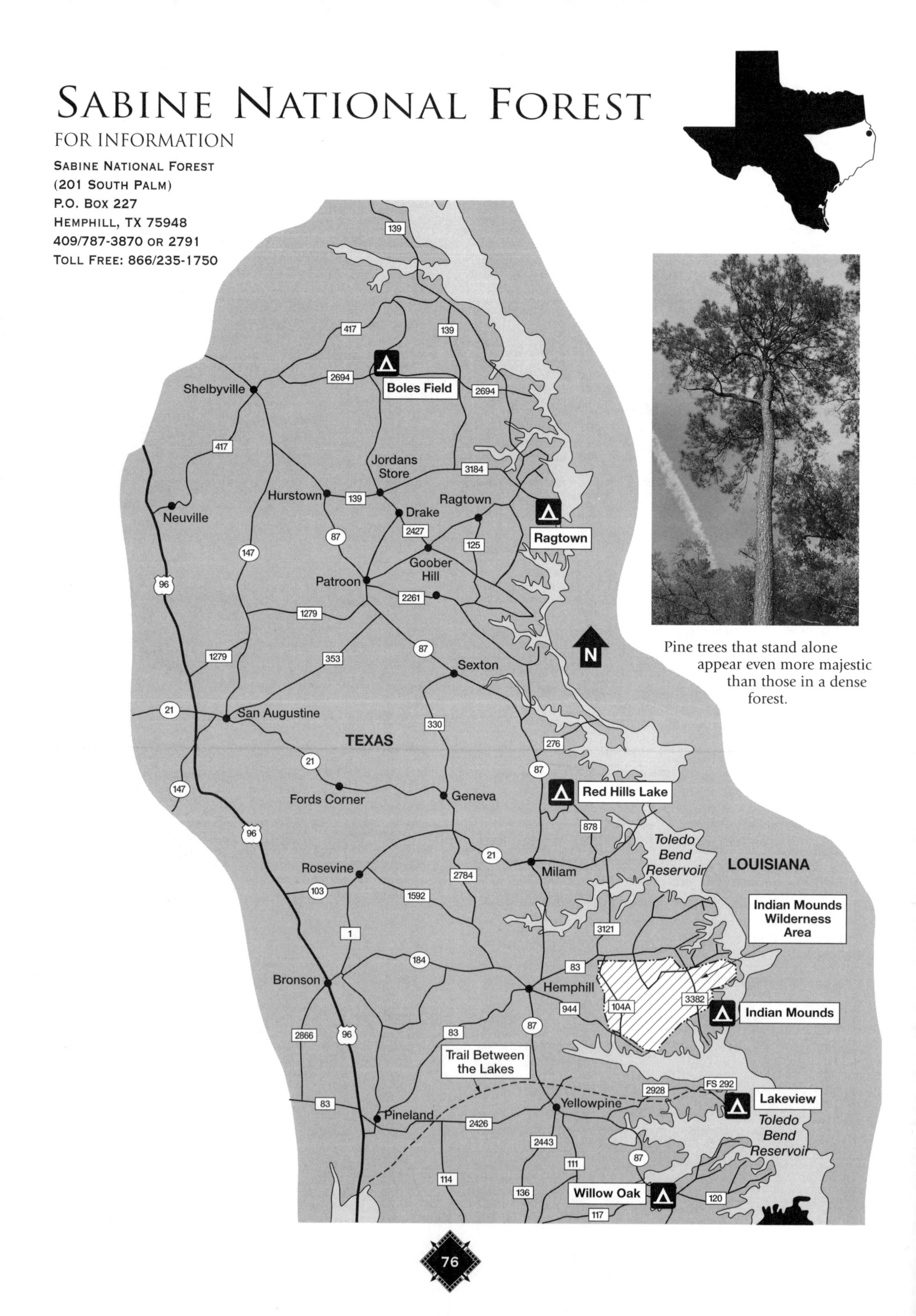

Pine trees that stand alone appear even more majestic than those in a dense forest.

LOCATION

Sabine National Forest is located in Jasper, Sabine, San Augustine, Newton, and Shelby counties and has 160,806 acres. The 12,369-acre Indian Mounds Wilderness Area is located on the Toledo Bend Reservoir on the national forest near the Indian Mounds Recreation Area. Hiking and horseback riding are allowed in wilderness areas; bicycles and other wheeled vehicles are prohibited.

Hiking and backpacking are permitted anywhere in the national forests in Texas and primitive camping is allowed anywhere unless otherwise posted. A recent restriction is that camping within the boundaries of red-cockaded woodpecker colonies in the national forests in Texas is prohibited. Boundaries are identified by trees with green markings and/or signs. In the Sabine National Forest there are developed trails at Ragtown Recreation Area and at Red Hills Lake Recreation Area. Hiking is a popular activity at the Indian Mounds Wilderness Area, which is adjacent to the Indian Mounds Recreation Area, although few trails are marked. A longer hiking trail, with opportunities for primitive camping, is the 28-mile Trail Between the Lakes. It extends from Lakeview Recreation Area on Toledo Bend Reservoir to TX 96 within sight of the easternmost point of Sam Rayburn Reservoir.

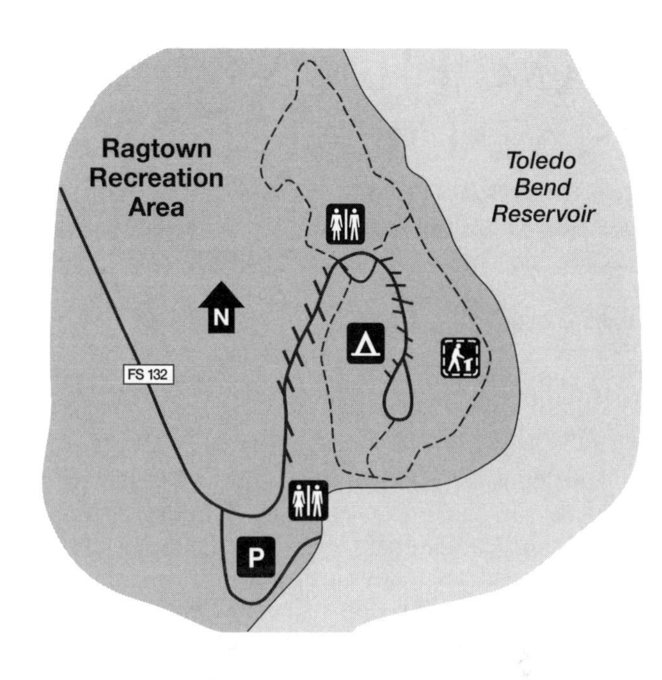

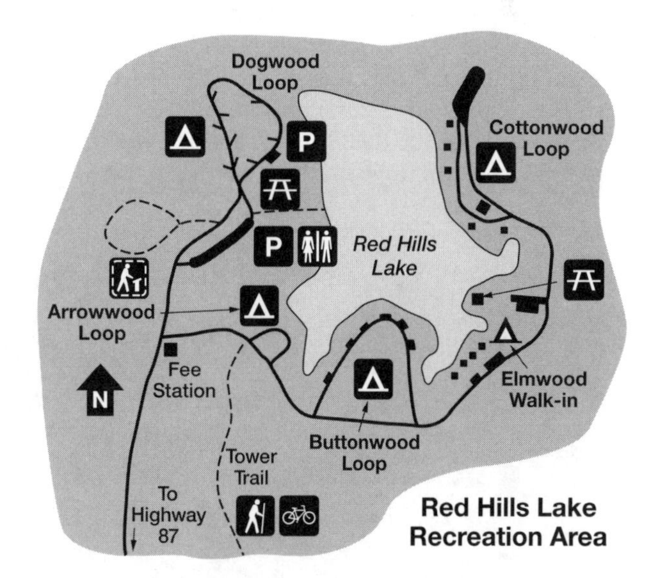

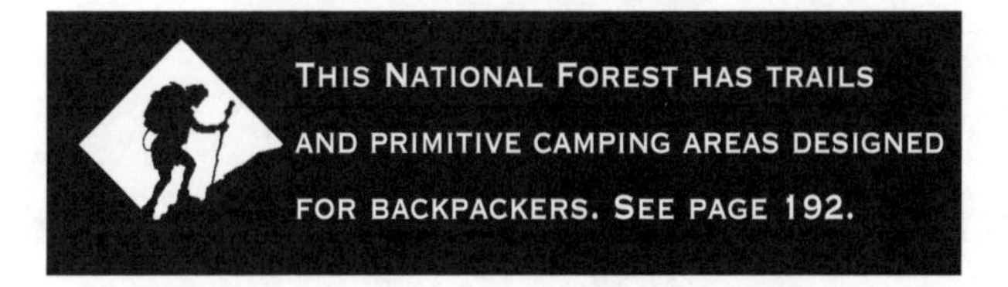

HIKING/NATURE TRAILS AND LOCATIONS

- ▲ **Indian Mounds Recreation Area:** Take FM 83 east from Hemphill 8 miles, turn right (south) on FM 3382 for 4 miles, then turn left (east) on FSR 130 for 1 mile. Short trails lead from the campground to the mounds.
- ▲ **Lakeview Recreation Area:** Take TX 87 south of Hemphill for 9 miles. Turn left on FM 2928 for 3 miles, follow signs, and continue on gravel road for 4 miles. The campground is a trailhead to the 28-mile Trail Between the Lakes.
- ▲ **Ragtown Recreation Area:** Take TX 87 southeast from Center for 11 miles, turn left (east) on FM 139 for 6½ miles, then bear right on FM 3184, and travel 4 miles to entrance. The 1-mile Mother Nature's Hiking Trail loops around the campground, winding through woodlands of magnificent oak and beech trees and along the lakeshore.
- ▲ **Red Hills Lake Recreation Area:** Take TX 87 north from Milam for 2½ miles. This area has a ½-mile scenic trail to the Chambers Hill lookout tower as well as a short nature trail.

Sam Houston National Forest

For Information

Sam Houston National Forest
394 FM 1375 West
New Waverly, TX 77358
409/344-6205

Location

Sam Houston National Forest, located in Montgomery, San Jacinto, and Walker counties, is the largest of the 4 national forests; it contains 163,037 acres. The forest extends northwest from Cleveland, is east and south of Huntsville, and encompasses about half of the northern portion of Lake Conroe. The 3,855-acre Little Lake Creek Wilderness Area is on the Sam Houston National Forest and the 129-mile Lone Star Hiking Trail traverses its entire width.

Hiking and camping are permitted anywhere in the national forests in Texas unless otherwise posted. During deer season when hunters abound in the forest, hikers use the trails at their own risk. The 129-mile Lone Star Hiking Trail passes through Winters Bayou Scenic Area, Big Creek Scenic Area, Double Lake Recreation Area, Stubblefield Lake Recreation Area, and the Little Lake Creek Wilderness. A multi-use trail system (dirt bike, equestrian, and mountain bike) consists of approximately 80 miles of marked trails divided into 3 separate series of loops adjacent to the 3 recreation areas at the north end of Lake Conroe. Trail maps for the 3 sections (East Lake Section, West Lake Section, and Northwest Section) are available at the New Waverly office or on the website for the National Forest. (See resources in the Appendix, page 203.)

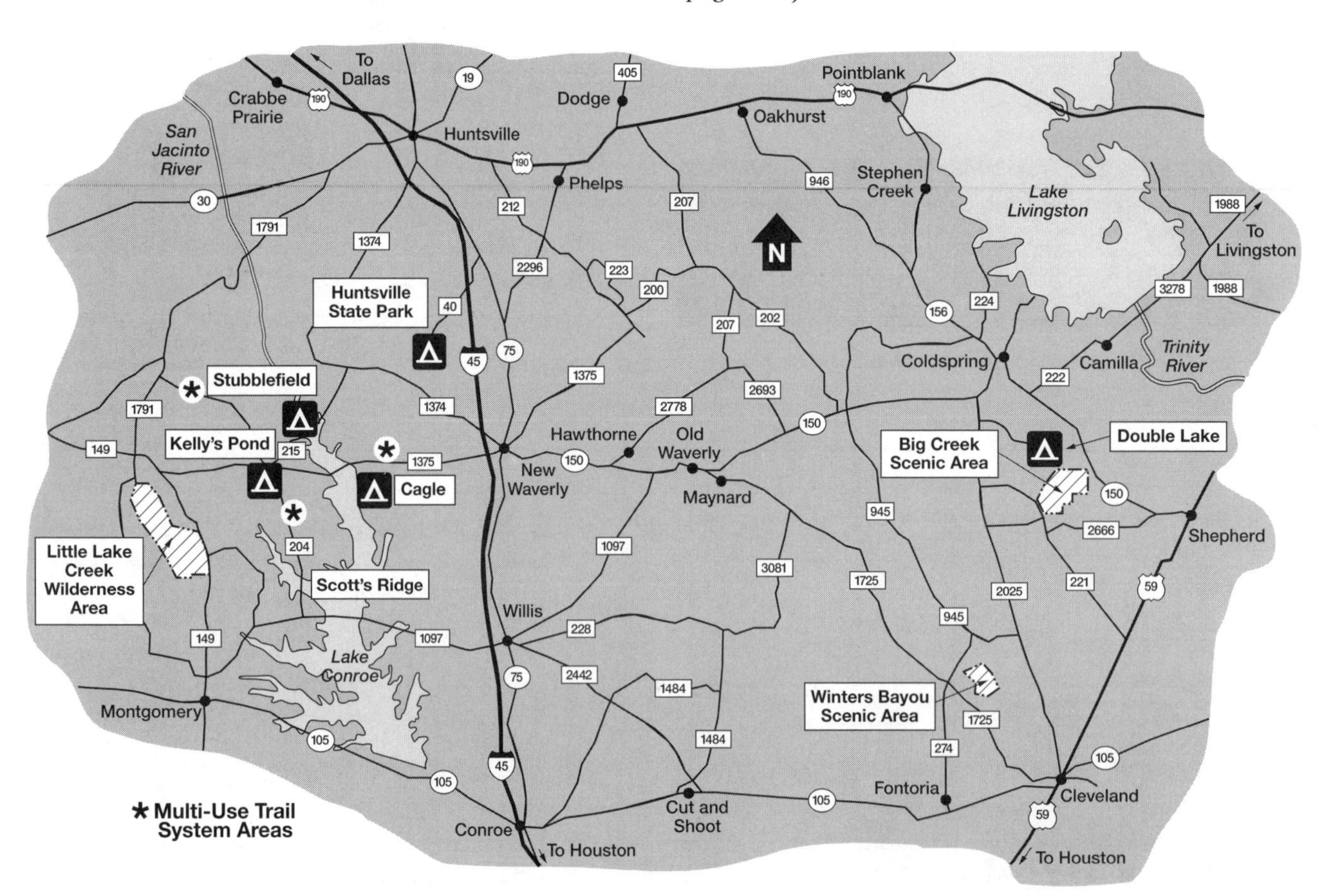

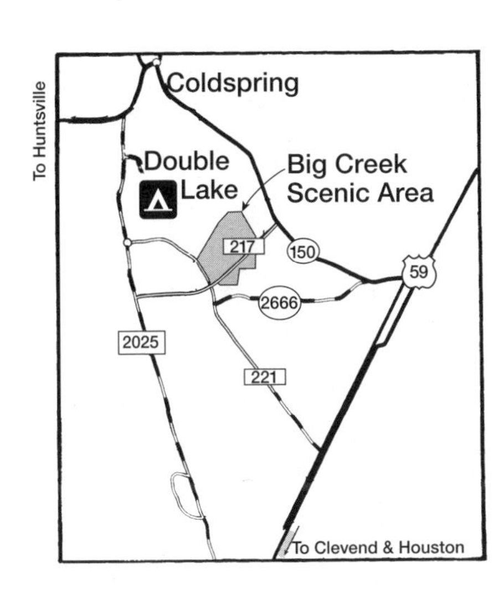

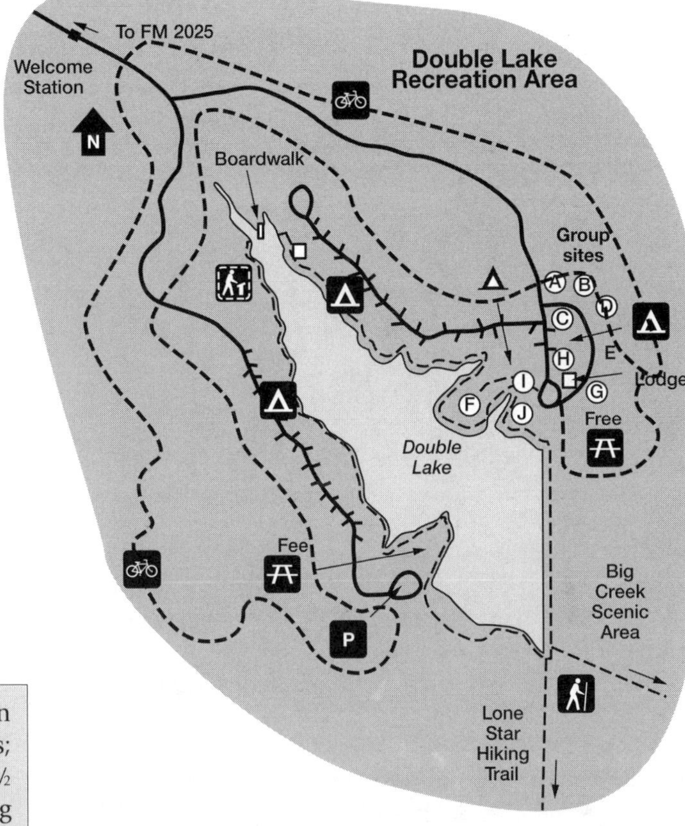

▲ **Double Lake Recreation Area:** From US 59 in Cleveland, take FM 2025 north for 17 miles; turn right on FSR 210 (entrance road) for 1½ miles. There are many opportunities for hiking and bicycling at Double Lake. The Lakeshore Nature Trail crosses the dam from the swimming and day-use area and follows the shoreline. The 5-mile trail leading to the Big Creek Scenic Area has its trailhead at the southeast corner of Double Lake near the swimming area and the 129-mile Lone Star Hiking Trail goes in both directions from near this point.

The Double Lake Mountain Bike Trail is about 8 miles in length. The trail offers a challenge for the experienced rider but is also one that the novice can complete. The trail is maintained by the Houston Area Mountain Bike Riders Association (HAMBRA) and the USDA, Forest Service; it is a year-round facility and even rideable shortly after light-to-medium rainfall.

▲ **Big Creek Scenic Area:** Take TX 150 northwest from Shepherd for 6 miles; turn left (southwest) on FSR 217 for 3 miles; or, if coming north from Cleveland on FM 2025, turn east on FSR 217 and then go 3 miles.

From the parking lot there are 3 loop trails ranging from ¾ to 2 miles in length. The 129-mile Lone Star Hiking Trail passes through the Big Creek Scenic Area from the south going to Double Lake Recreation Area. The trail from the scenic area parking lot to Double Lake is 5 miles.

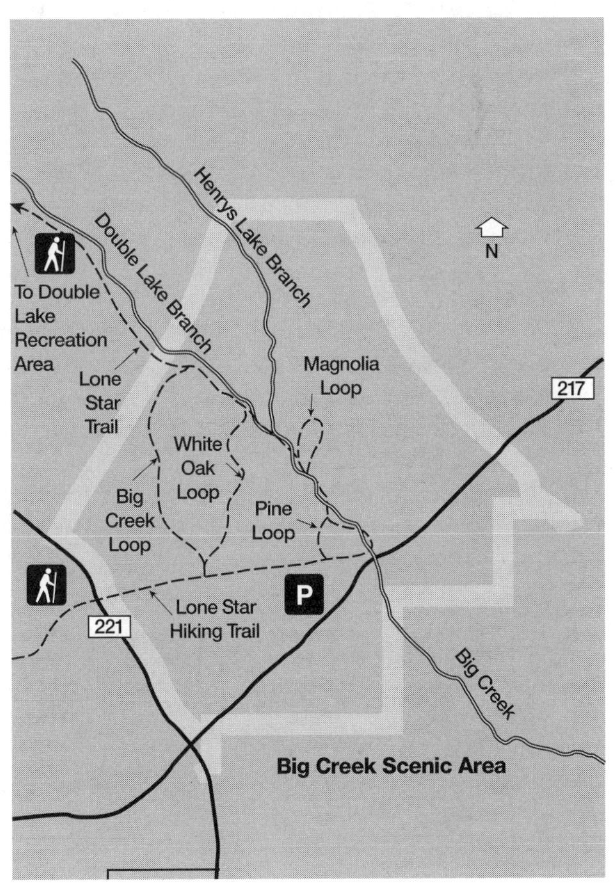

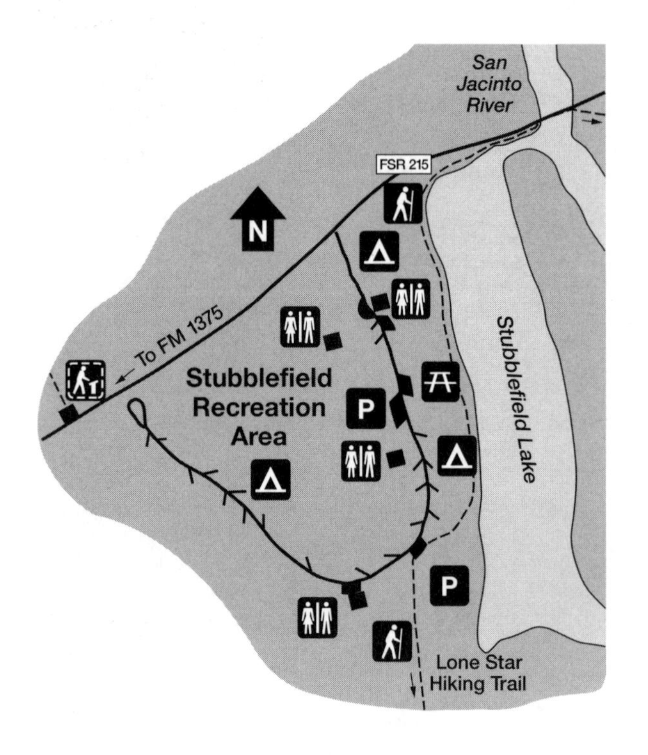

The 5-mile hiking trail from Double Lake to the Big Creek Scenic Area has numerous stream crossings.

▲ **Stubblefield Lake Recreation Area:** From I-45, take FM 1375 west from New Waverly for 10 miles; turn right (north) on FSR 215 for 3 miles. This area provides access to the 129-mile Lone Star Hiking Trail, as well as to some nearby logging roads that are suitable for hiking. Just north of the campground, adjacent to FSR 215, is a 1.1-mile loop trail with interpretive markers. Interpretive leaflets are available at the information board located at the trailhead and parking area along FSR 215.

▲ **Cagle Recreation Area:** From I-45, take FM 1375 west from New Waverly for 8 miles; turn left at sign. A 2-mile hiking trail surrounds the camping loops. The southernmost mile of the trail is paved.

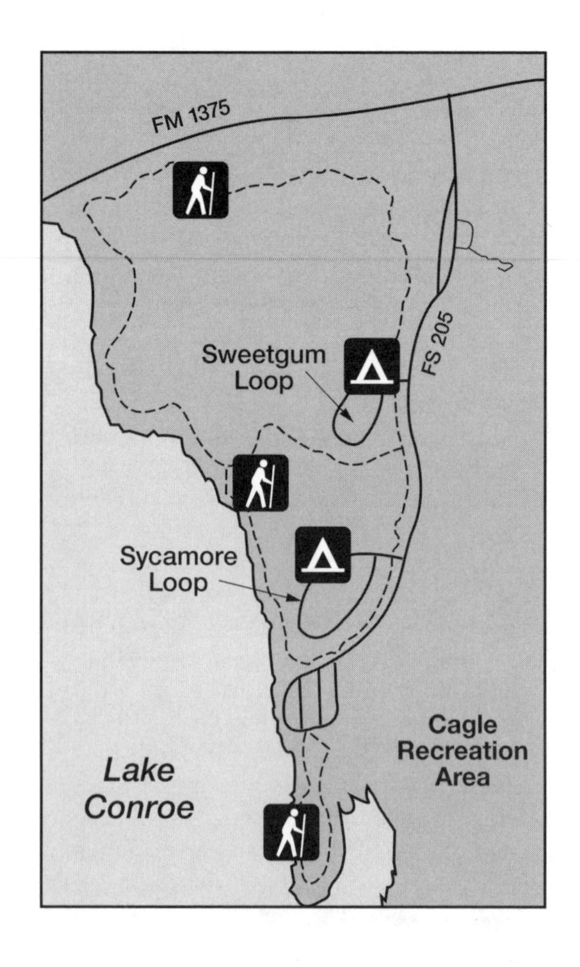

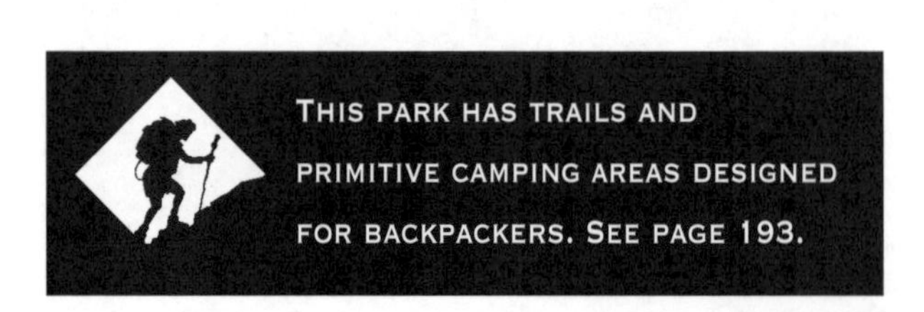

SEA RIM STATE PARK

FOR INFORMATION

SEA RIM STATE PARK
P.O. BOX 1066
SABINE PASS, TX 77655
409/971-2559

LOCATION

Sea Rim State Park is located 10 miles west of Sabine Pass on TX 87; the highway between Sea Rim and High Island is closed, so the *only access* to the park is from the east. The park consists of 4,141 acres of gulf coast beach and marshland. TX 87 separates the park into 2 distinct areas: south of the highway lies the D. Roy Harrington Beach Unit and north of the highway is the Marshlands Unit, which comprises the greater portion.

TEXAS HIGHWAYS Magazine

Canoeing is a great way to explore the boat trails in the Marshlands Unit.

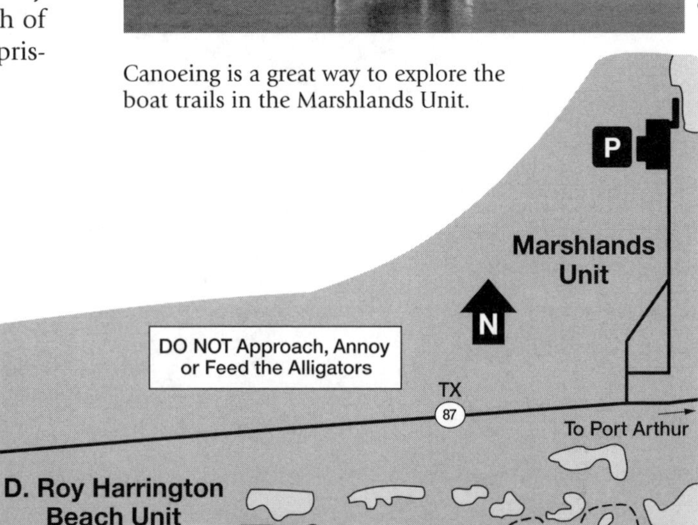

TRAIL NOTES

The Gambusia Trail is a ¾-mile boardwalk nature trail located on the eastern edge of the Beach Unit. The boardwalk, elevated 2 feet above the marshy surface, is provided for the park visitor to easily see the marsh. Three rest stops are provided for wildlife observation. Numbered posts along the trail correspond to numbers in a trail booklet available at the visitor center. The Willow Pond Trail, a ¼-mile elevated boardwalk on the park's western edge is a popular spot for birdwatching.

The Beach Unit has 5.2 miles of shoreline; 3 miles of it are sandy beach, suitable for pleasure walking, with small, picturesque sand dunes that separate the beach from the marshlands. Mountain bikers can ride on the beach.

North of TX 87 is the Marshlands Unit. Facilities include camping/observation platforms and boat trails through the marsh. The trails are ideal for canoe, kayak, and pirogue; maps are available. Canoes and paddleboats are for rent at the Marshland Unit. Airboat tours of the marsh are also available.

Stephen F. Austin State Park

FOR INFORMATION

Stephen F. Austin State Park
Box 125
San Felipe, TX 77473-0125
409/885-3613

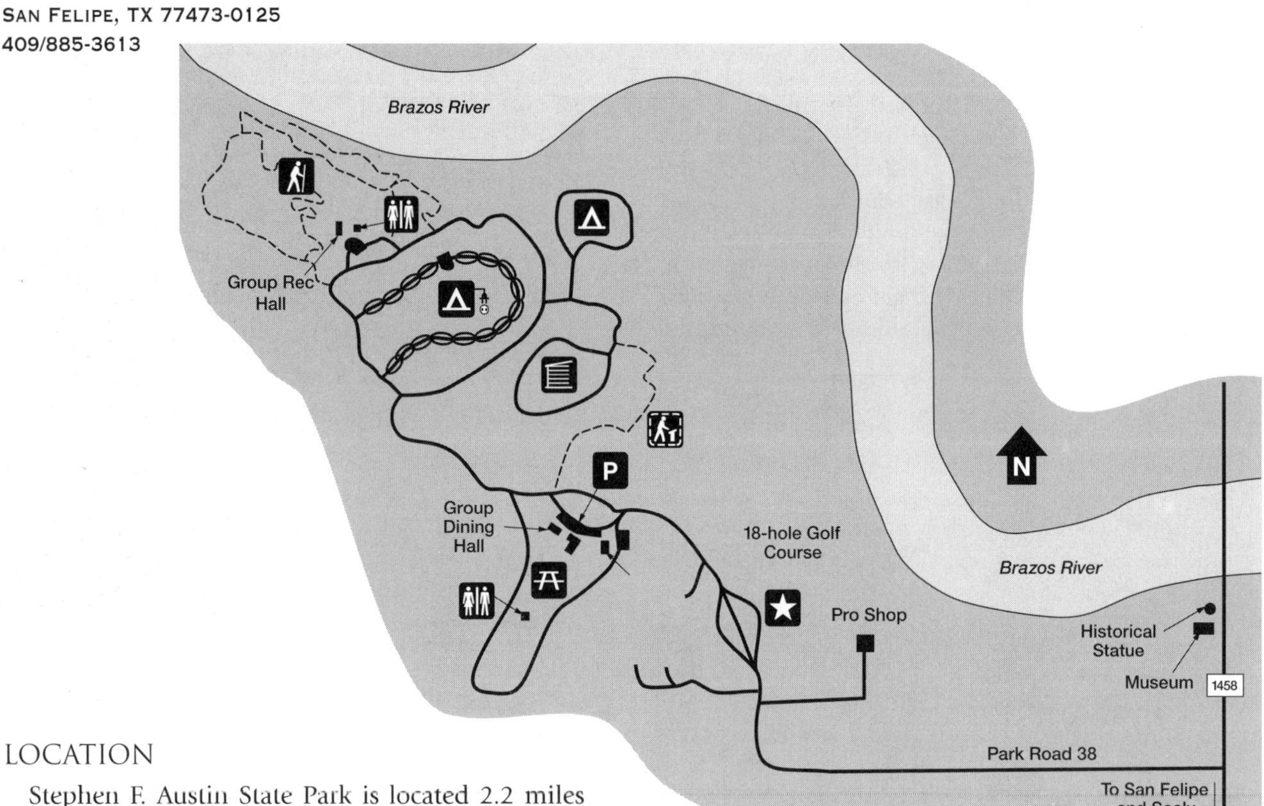

LOCATION

Stephen F. Austin State Park is located 2.2 miles north of San Felipe off of FM 1458 from I-10 on Park Road 38. The 663-acre park is on the Brazos River.

Gay Ippolito, U.S. Forest Service

This park is located in an area known for its beautiful bluebonnets each spring.

TRAIL NOTES

The densely forested park is bordered to the north by the Brazos River. Five hiking trails are located west of the camping area that provides full hookups. One of these trails leads to the Brazos River. The underdeveloped areas of the park permit primitive hiking and river fishing. A nature trail runs from the picnic area to the screened shelter area. Named after the "Father of Texas," the park is located in the historic town site of San Felipe de Austin. Twelve acres of the park are set aside in honor of the area's past.

Texas Forestry Association's Woodland Trails

FOR INFORMATION

Texas Forestry Association
Box 1488
Lufkin, TX 75902-1488
936/632-TREE

TRAIL NOTES

Some of the state's most unique forest scenery can be found on the Texas Woodland Trails, a series of pathways carefully selected by the Texas Forestry Association for walking and visual enjoyment of nature's handiwork. Founded in 1914, the Texas Forestry Association is one of the oldest conservation organizations in the state.

TFA Woodland Trails are located throughout East Texas. They vary in length and nature. Some are suitable for picnicking. Some are best noted for history. Some may best afford only a leisurely woodland stroll. The maps displayed here indicate approximate areas to access trails. Park areas and trails are subject to change. Trails are well marked, but are subject to reroutes.

The Texas Forestry Association's Woodland Trails vary in nature and length. Most trails are well marked, but are subject to reroutes.

ANGELINA COLLEGE FOREST FITNESS TRAIL

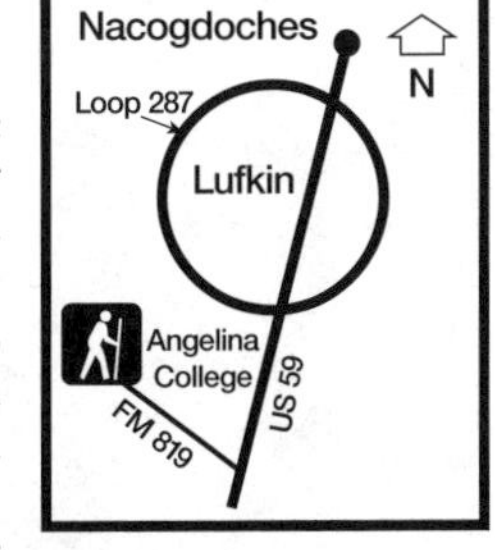

This overall 1-mile loop can be used as a fitness/walking trail or can be enjoyed at a slower pace as an arboretum where more than 50 different native trees and plants are identified. The trail begins on the hill behind the Angelina College Activity Center (in Lufkin, TX) and descends to Hurricane Creek on the undeveloped west side of the campus.

BIG PINES TRAIL

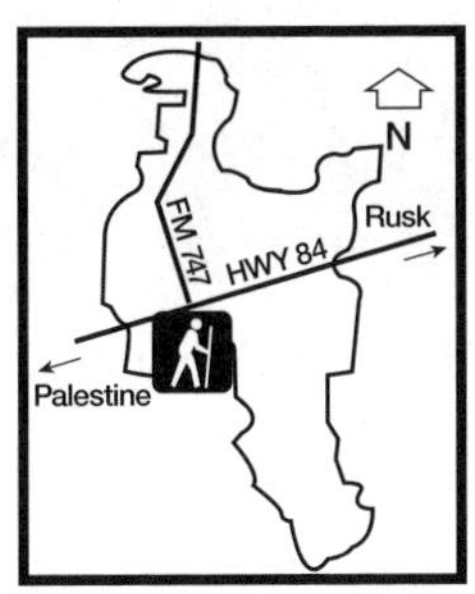

Located in the I. D. Fairchild State Forest on Hwy. 84, seven miles west of the town of Rusk, this trail is 10 miles in length. It crosses the Texas State Railroad. The trail is accessible from Hwy. 84 and the small park in the State Forest. It is marked with plastic white diamond markers.

CANYON RIM TRAIL

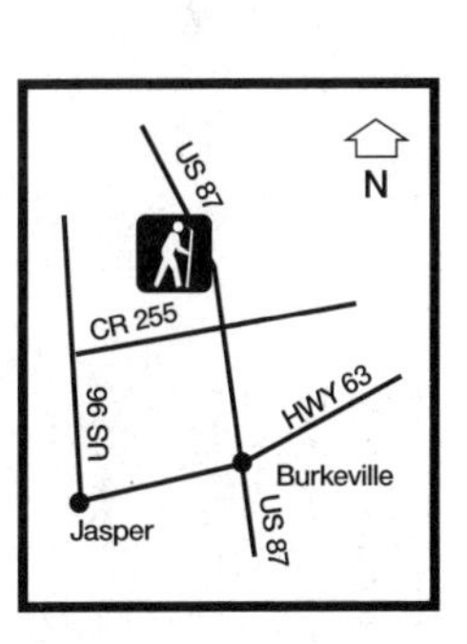

This 0.9-mile trail winds along the canyon's rim and is locatd in a pocket off U.S. Highway 87, north of Burkeville. Owned by International Paper Co., the area includes evidence of an old logging road last used by mule and ox-drawn wagons 75 years ago. Various tree species and points of interest are identified, and rest stops are provided to make the trail enjoyable for everyone.

DOGWOOD TRAIL

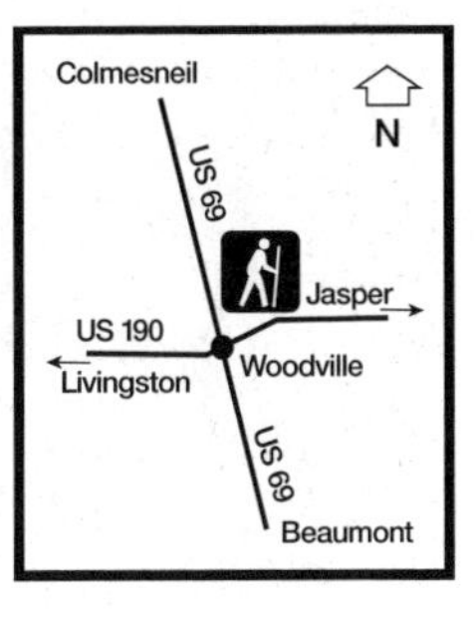

The Dogwood Trail, 1.5 miles in length, is true to its name; there are an abundance of dogwood blossoms during early spring. The trail, which consists of two loops, begins on Dogwood Drive located 3 miles east of Woodville just off U.S. Highway 190. It winds along the banks of Theuvenin Creek; spring is the best time to walk this short hiking trail to see the dogwoods in bloom.

Texas Forestry Association's Woodland Trails (continued)

GRIFF ROSS TRAIL

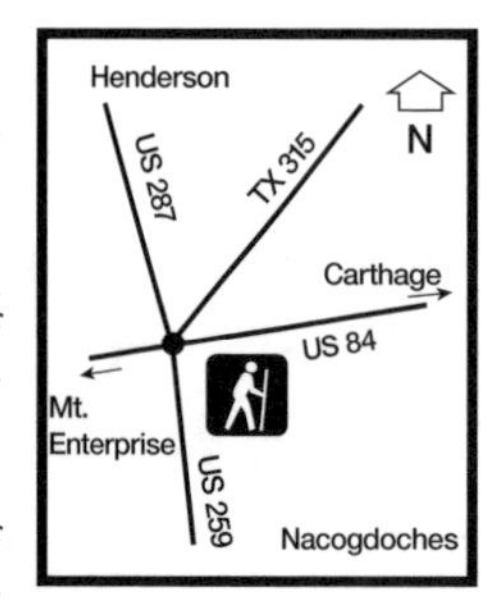

For a quiet, woodland walk, visit the Griff Ross Trail. This 0.75-mile loop follows the gentle slope of a wooded hill to the edge of a forest stream. It is located on 16.2 acres of land donated to the Texas Forestry Association in memory of Dr. and Mrs. Griff Ross. The trail is found 2.2 miles east of Mt. Enterprise off U.S. Highway 84. No picnicking or camping allowed.

HORSE-SUGAR TRAIL

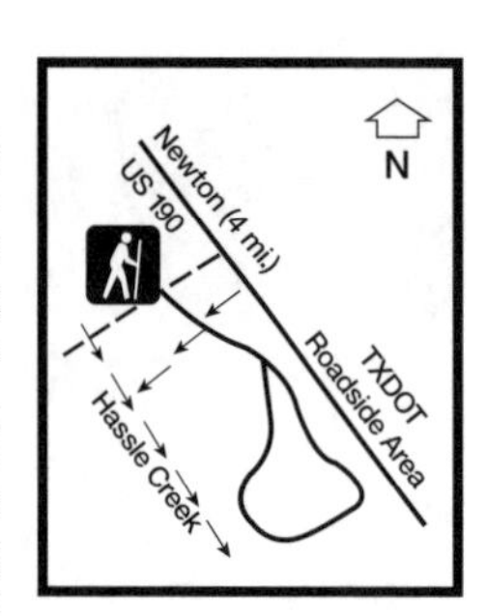

The Horse-Sugar Trail was first opened in 1970. The 0.5-mile trail is located approximately 4 miles southeast of Newton, Texas, along Hwy. 190, directly across from a roadside park. In the early 1900s, steam engines were used to skid and haul virgin logs to the sawmills along these logging tramways. The scenic trail offers more than 30 species of trees and shrubs along with the State Champion Sweet Leaf (Horse-Sugar).

LONGLEAF PINE TRAIL

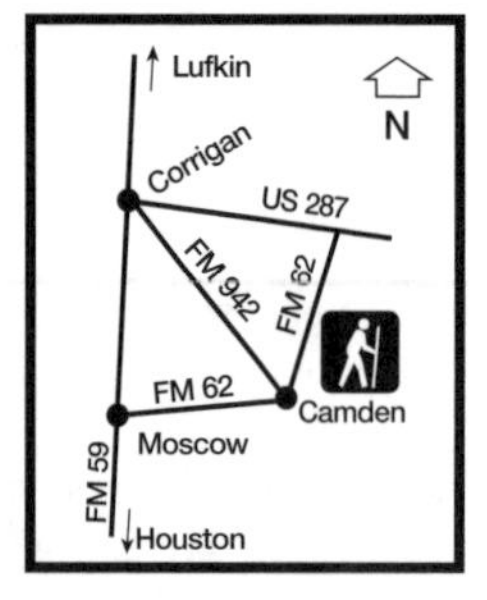

This 2.0-mile loop is located 3 miles east of Camden on FM 62 in Polk County. The Longleaf Trail leads through one of several stands of virgin pine timber still standing in East Texas. Many of the longleaf pine trees along this trail are more than 100 years old, and they stand today the same as they stood at the turn of the century—big, tall, majestic. By appointment only 936/639-5018.

STEPHEN F. AUSTIN INTERPRETIVE TRAIL

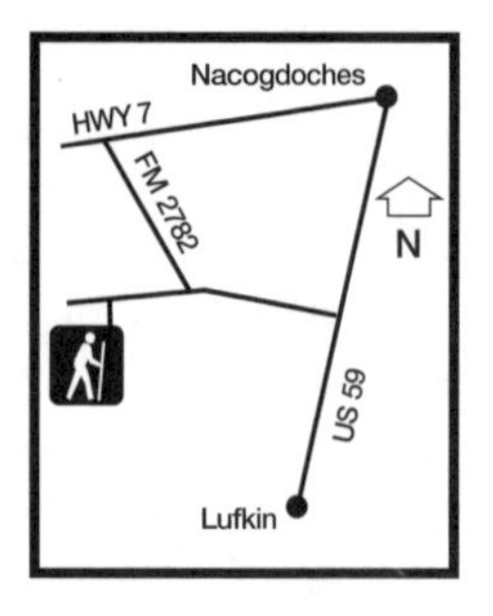

This unique trail system is located on the Stephen F. Austin Experimental Forest (part of the Angelina National Forest). The Forest entrance is approximately 2.5 miles from both U.S. 59 and Hwy. 7 via FM 2782, halfway between Lufkin and Nacogdoches. Jack Creek Loop (0.9 miles) offers universal accessibility through a beautiful hardwood-pine forest. The Management Loop (2.1 miles) features demonstrations of forest and wildlife management practices.

TEXAS FORESTRY MUSEUM URBAN WILDSCAPE TRAIL

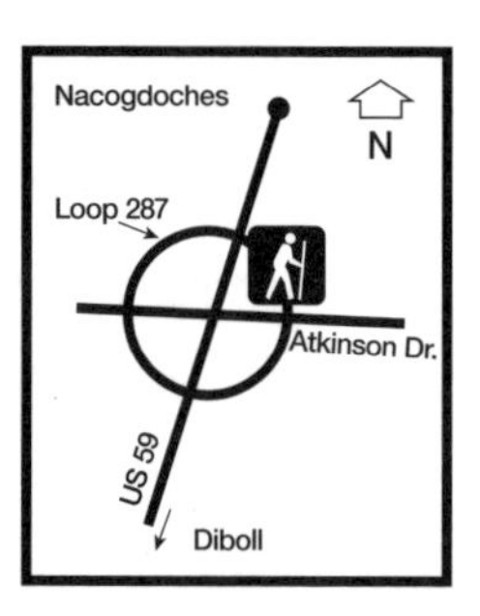

The trail is located just inside Loop 287, in Lufkin, at 1905 Atkinson Drive (Hwy. 103 East), behind the Texas Forestry Museum. The trail takes you through 3.5 acres of mixed pine-hardwood forest common in East Texas. Native species are identified along the trail; an interpretive brochure is available inside the Texas Forestry Museum. The barrier-free portion of the trail is 0.12 miles and is located at the trailhead. The remainder of the trail is broken into two chip-lined loops, totalling 0.58 miles. The trail contains 3 bridges, an outdoor classroom, bird blind, bat house, several birdhouses, and bird feeders.

WILD AZALEA CANYONS TRAIL

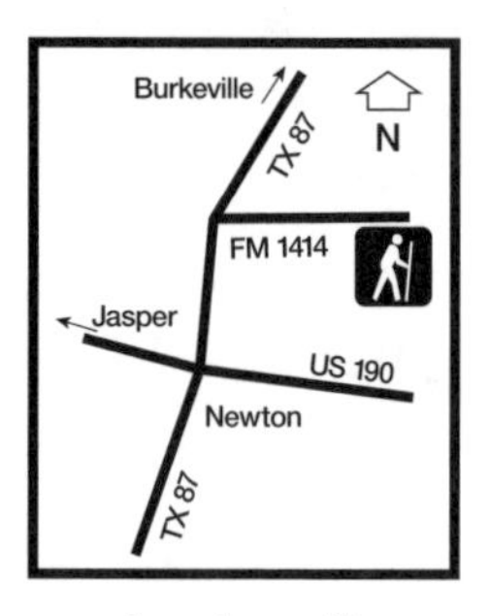

There are several short hiking paths in this trail, which is found 4.4 miles north of Newton on Texas Highway 87, then 6.7 miles east on FM 1414. Hikers must cover another 1.8 miles of unpaved road to reach the trail entrance. Once you reach the trail, you are inside a pocket wilderness of longleaf pines, rock cliffs, and wild azaleas that bloom on the edges of intermittent branches and fill the air with a strong, sweet aroma each spring. It is open during March and April only.

The Wild Azalea Canyons Trail is inside a pocket wilderness of longleaf pines, rock cliffs, and wild azaleas; it is open only during March and April.

Village Creek State Park

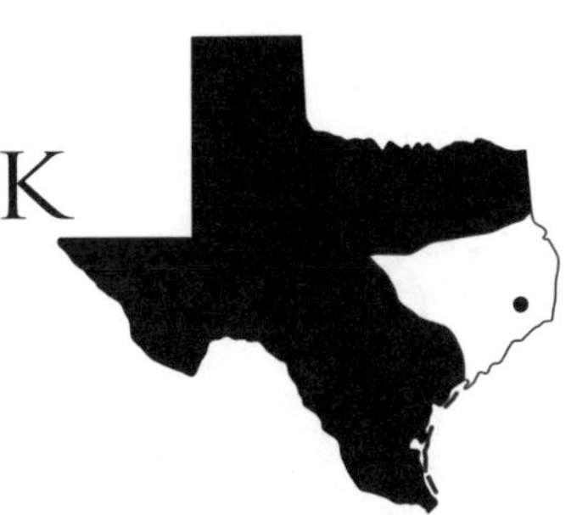

FOR INFORMATION

VILLAGE CREEK STATE PARK
P.O. BOX 8575
LUMBERTON, TX 77657
409/755-7322

TRAIL NOTES

There are 8 miles of trails at Village Creek State Park including the 1¼-mile Village Slough Nature Trail. Mountain bikers are allowed on all of the trails. These trails provide access to Big Thicket scenery—the dense bottomland forest, baygalls (miniature swamps), larger cypress swamps, water-tupelo swamps, and the wild and unspoiled Village Creek. Village Creek is one of the few remaining streams in East Texas that have no dams, and because this area of Texas receives some 60 inches of rain per year, floods are prevalent along Village Creek, with severe overflows occurring every 3 to 4 years.

The creek is renowned as a float stream. Canoeists have several options for using the park for float trips. They can put in upstream from the park at any of 3 road crossings, or they can put in at the park and take out downstream on the Neches River in the Big Thicket Preserve.

LOCATION

Village Creek State Park is located off US 69/96/287 in Lumberton on Alma Drive. From Beaumont, take US 69/96/287 to Mitchell Road, turn east on Mitchell Road, then immediately north on Village Creek Parkway for about 2 miles, then east on Alma Drive, cross the railroad tracks, and veer to left, and park entrance will be on the left. The 1,050-acre park is located on Village Creek, a 63-mile long renowned float stream that rises near the Alabama-Coushatta Indian Reservation and flows southeast to a junction with the Neches River.

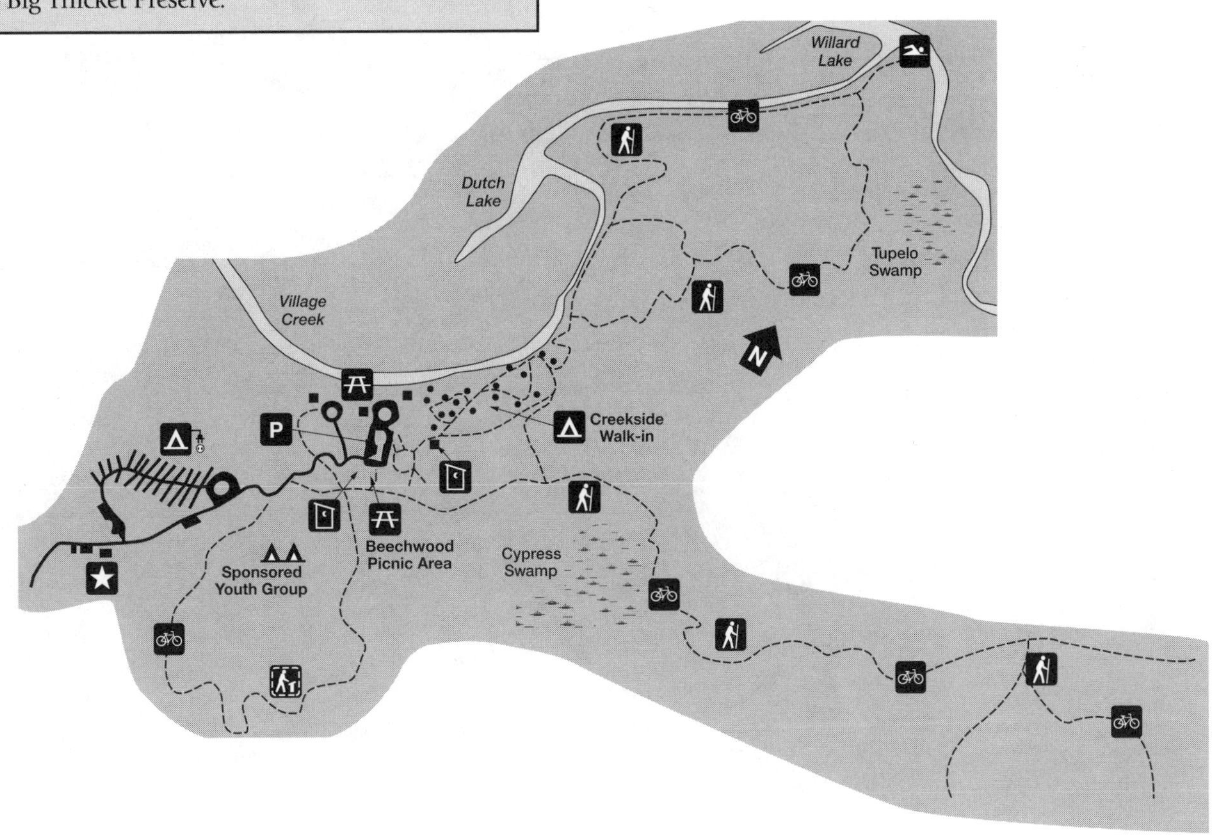

Washington-on-the-Brazos State Historic Site

For Information
Washington-on-the-Brazos State Historic Site
P.O. Box 305
Washington, TX 77880-0305
936/878-2214

LOCATION

From Bennham, take SH 105 East 14 miles and turn right on FM 912, 5 miles to Washington-on-the-Brazos State Historic Site, or, from Navasota, take SH 105 West 7 miles, and turn left on FM 1155. The capital of the Republic of Texas was located at this site from 1842–1845, but when Texas entered the Union in 1846, Austin became the capital of the state. In 1899 a monument was erected to commemorate the signing of the Texas Declaration of Independence; a state park came into being in 1916 and a replica of Independence Hall was built. The 293-acre park is located on the bank of the Brazos River where it joins the Navasota River; it is a day-use-only park. Facilities include Independence Hall, Barrington Living History Farm, Visitor Center, and the State of the Republic Museum.

TRAIL NOTES

Park visitors can walk the trails and learn about the natural beauties of the park. One trail takes you through lush woods consisting of sycamores and a variety of oaks, then to a beaver pond where you can get a glimpse of what a beaver's life is like by studying its environment. In the spring one trail provides an opportunity to view one of Texas' more famous sights—a field of bluebonnets. Other trails lead to historical sites in the park and one trail follows the river and leads to the picnic area.

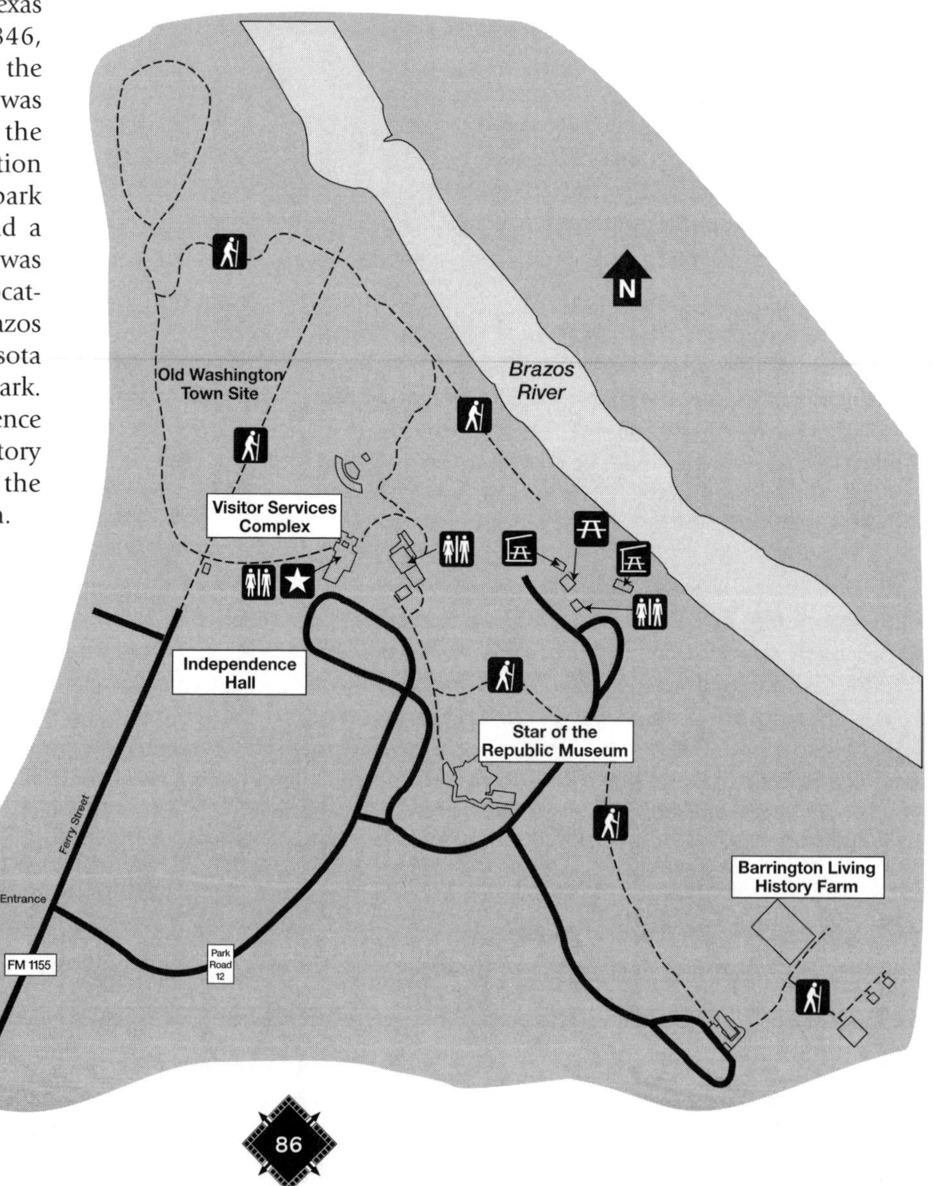

Other Trails in Region 2

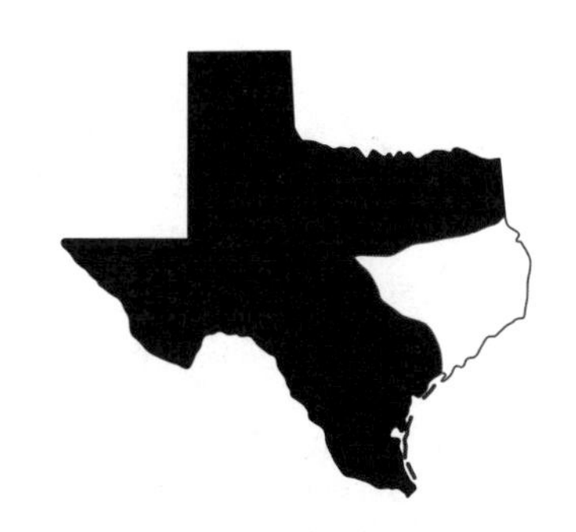

ALTO **Caddoan Mounds SHS**

▲ 0.7-mile self-guided trail tour around the mounds and village area provides an informative and thought-provoking look at the most sophisticated prehistoric Indian culture in Texas.

Caddoan Mounds State Historic Site
RR 2, Box 85C
Alto, TX 75925
936/858-3218

B. A. STEINHAGEN LAKE **Magnolia Ridge Park**

▲ 2-mile nature trail located across from campsite #21. Travel north of FM 92 from US 190 to reach the park.

Town Bluff Dam/B. A. Steinhagen Lake
890 FM 92
Woodville, TX 75979-9509
409/429-3491

BELTON **Belton Lake Trails**

▲ 2-mile bike trail at Temple Park
▲ 2-mile hiking trail at Cedar Ridge
▲ 2-mile fitness trail at Belton Lakeview
▲ 10 miles of nature trails at Miller Springs Nature Area

Belton Lake
3740 FM 1670
Belton, TX 76513-9503
254/939-2461

BELTON **Stillhouse Hollow Lake Trails**

▲ 15-mile multi-use trail with corral & water trough for horses at Dana Peak Park.

▲ 5 miles of hiking trails at the Chalk Ridge Falls Environmental Learning Center located below Stillhouse Hollow Lake Dam.

Stillhouse Hollow Dam
3740 FM 1670
Belton, TX 76513-9503
254/939-2461

BRAZORIA **San Bernard NWR**

▲ Wildlife viewing from 3 hikes: Bobcat Woods Trail, an accessible boardwalk and trail along Cocklebur Slough; 0.8-mile Scissor-tail Trail through a brush habitat; and 1.5-mile Cowtrap Trail, along a man-made levee.

San Bernard National Wildlife Refuge Complex
6801 CR 306
Brazoria, TX 77422
979/964-3639

CENTERVILLE **Fort Boggy State Park**

▲ There are 2 trails at this new state park: a 1-mile trail that loops around the 15-acre lake and a 2-mile hike/bike trail. This 1,847-acre park is presently operated as a day-use park and is open Wednesday through Sunday.

Fort Boggy State Park
4494 Hwy. 75 South
Centerville, TX 75833
903/344-1116

COLLEGE STATION **Greenways & Trails**

▲ An extensive trail system is planned for College Station Trail users. Trails presently exist in Bee Creek Park (0.26 mile), Central Park (0.72 mile), Lemontree Park (0.45 mile), and Lick Creek Park (3.5 miles). Lick Creek is a 515-acre wilderness park with trails for hiking, biking, and equestrian use.

▲ The D. A. "Andy" Anderson Arboretum, with native species and bridges on the trail, is located on Anderson Street.

City of College Station
Greenways Project Manager
P.O. Box 9960
College Station, TX 77842
979/764-3844

CONROE **Jones State Forest**

▲ 1-mile Sweetleaf Nature Trail has 60 numbered points and is a trail of interpretive forestry located in the northwest corner of the forest along Rice Branch; trail guide is available at office. Located in the 1,725-acre Jones State Forest about 5 miles southwest of Conroe and 2.4 miles west of I-45 along FM 1288. During the week, pick up a key to the nature trail at the office on FM 1288. A red-cockaded woodpecker viewing area is also north of FM 1288; hiking and horseback riding are permitted south of FM 1288.

Texas Forest Service
1328 FM 1288
Conroe, TX 77384
936/273-2261

FREEPORT **Brazoria NWR**

▲ The Big Slough Boardwalk and Trail leads to an obser-vaton platform. Main loop is 0.6 mile long; other loops run 0.1, 0.25, and 0.5 miles; starts at Visitor Information Pavillion. Middle Bayou Trail follows 2 miles along an abandoned railroad right-of-way parallel to CR 227. An Auto Route runs 7.5 miles through the recreation area.

Brazoria National Wildlife Refuge
4430 Trammel
Freeport, TX 77541
979/239-3915

HOUSTON

▲ The Houston Audubon Society operates the Edith L. Moore Nature Sanctuary at Wilchester and Memorial

Drive. Trails are located along Rummel Creek on 17 acres of scenic woodland. The sanctuary is open from dawn until dusk. For information on educational programs, contact the Houston Audubon Society. Their headquarters are located in the log cabin on the sanctuary. Phone: 713/932-1639.

HOUSTON **Hike & Bike Trails**

▲ More than 95 miles of trails for walking, hiking, jogging, and biking are available at the parks in Houston; 83 parks have trails less than a mile long; 11 have trails longer than 1 mile. Four of the longest trails are:

7.39 miles—Cullen Park (19008 Selinsky)
2.90 miles—Memorial Park (6501 Memorial Dr.)
2.85 miles—Herman Park (6001 Fannin)
2.81 miles—Herman Brown Park (400 Mercury Dr.)

Trails are also located along 9 bayous. Four of the longest trails are:

12.5 miles—Brays Bayou
4.8 miles—White Oak Bayou
4.5 miles—Buffalo Bayou
2.5 miles—Sims Bayou

Houston Parks and Recreation Department
2999 S. Wayside
Houston, TX 77023
713/845-1000

KOUNTZE **Roy E. Larsen Sandyland Sanctuary**

▲ 6 miles of nature trails; a self-guiding interpretive trail guide for an 0.8-mile section. The sanctuary borders Village Creek on the west, FM 418 on the north, and SH 327 on the south; it has been designated as a site on the Great Texas Coastal Birding Trail. Trailhead is off of SH 327. Guided tours for groups available. Phone the Pineywoods office: 409/385-0445

The Nature Conservancy of Texas
P.O. Box 1440
San Antonio, TX 78295
210/224-8774

LA GRANGE **Oak Thicket & Park Prairie Parks**

▲ A 3-mile hike/bike trail connects Oak Thicket and Park Prairie. Oak Thicket Park also has a bird and nature trail.

Lake Fayette Parks
P.O. Box 1248
La Grange, TX 78945
979/249-3504

LA PORTE **San Jacinto Battleground SHS**

▲ An interpretive trail starts at the parking lot on the north side of the San Jacinto Monument. The prairie portion of the trail extends 700 feet to the edge of the marsh. At the marsh, a 510-foot boardwalk trail crosses both dense marsh vegetation and the open water of the tidal channel. The trail is fully accessible.

San Jacinto Battleground State Historic Site
3523 Highway 134
La Porte, TX 77571
281/479-2431

MEXIA **Confederate Reunion Grounds**

▲ ¼-mile trail on the Confederate Reunion Grounds along the oak-shaded paths that border the Navasota River and cross Jack's Creek on 2 scenic footbridges.

Confederate Reunion Grounds State Historic Site
c/o Fort Parker State Park
194 Park Road 28
Mexia, TX 76667
254/562-5751

RUSK **Jim Hogg City Historical Park**

▲ 1½ miles of a combination nature/hiking trail with a spur trail to the old site of an old iron ore mine. The park features a structure representative of early pioneer homes in the area and the Hogg family cemetery.

Jim Hogg City Historical Park
RR 5, Box 80
Rusk, TX 75785
903/683-4850

WACO **Cameron Park Trails**

▲ Cameron Park's 450 acres has varying types of terrain with over 20 miles of trails for casual hikers to mountain bike extremists. Two major tributaries, the Bosque and Brazos, join at the park's border. Trails are color coded to indicate 4 levels of difficulty for bikers, from beginner to advanced rider. Cameron Park, with its limestone cliffs that tower above the riverbank, is renowned for its trail system; maps are available.

City of Waco
Parks and Recreation
P.O. Box 2570
Waco, TX 76702
254/750-8080

WEST COLUMBIA **Varner Hogg Plantation SHS**

▲ A walking tour of the 66-acre Varner Hogg Plantation State Historic Site includes the Hogg Mansion Museum and an entire complex of more than a dozen buildings and areas. The park is located northeast of West Columbia and is accessible via FM 2852; a tour fee is charged.

Varner Hogg Plantation State Historic Site
1702 N. 13th St.
West Columbia, TX 77486
979/345-4656

Region 3

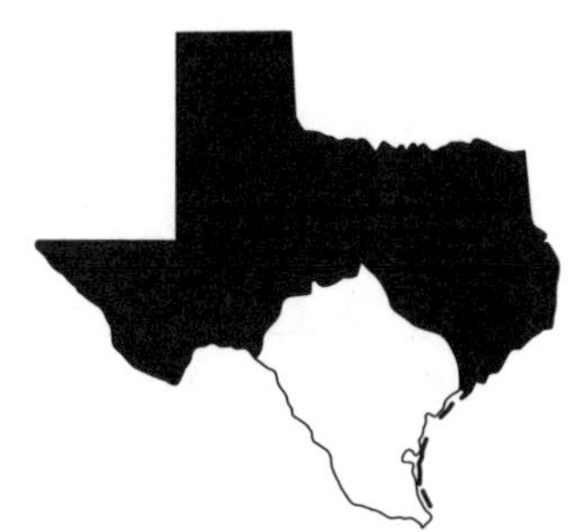

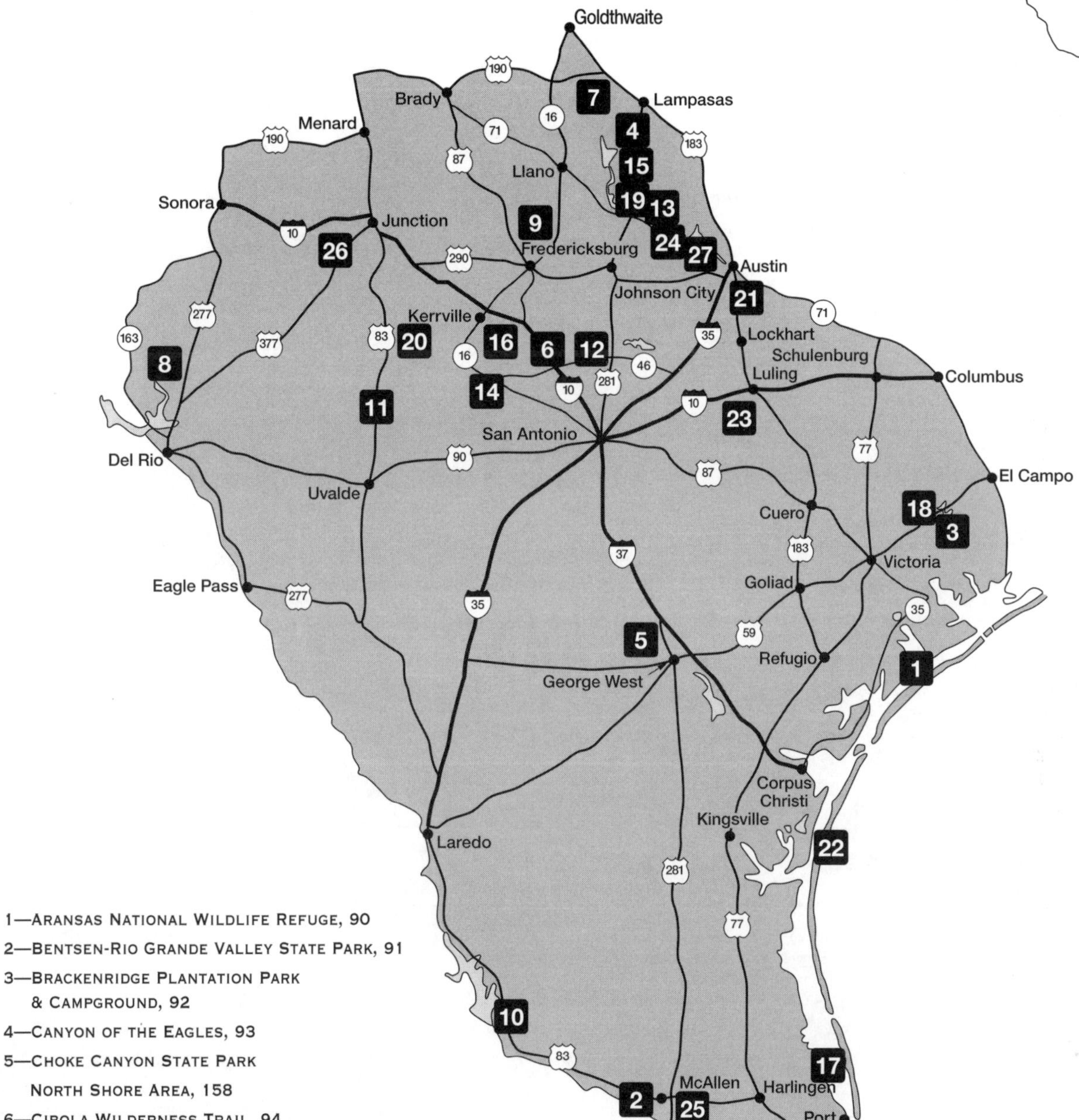
Goldthwaite
Brady
Lampasas
Menard
Llano
Sonora
Junction
Fredericksburg
Austin
Johnson City
Kerrville
Lockhart
Schulenburg
Luling
Columbus
San Antonio
Del Rio
Uvalde
El Campo
Cuero
Victoria
Eagle Pass
Goliad
Refugio
George West
Corpus Christi
Kingsville
Laredo
McAllen
Harlingen
Port Isabel
Brownsville
1
2
3
4
5
6
7
8
9
10
11
12
13
14
15
16
17
18
19
20
21
22
23
24
25
26
27

Aransas National Wildlife Refuge

FOR INFORMATION

Aransas National Wildlife Refuge
P.O. Box 100
Austwell, TX 77950
512/286-3559

LOCATION

The refuge entrance and visitor center are located 7 miles southeast of Austwell at the end of FM 2040. Austwell may be reached by either FM 774 or TX 239 off of TX 35 near Tivoli. The 70,504-acre refuge occupies Blackjack Peninsula, named for its scattered blackjack oaks, and is administered by the U.S. Fish and Wildlife Service.

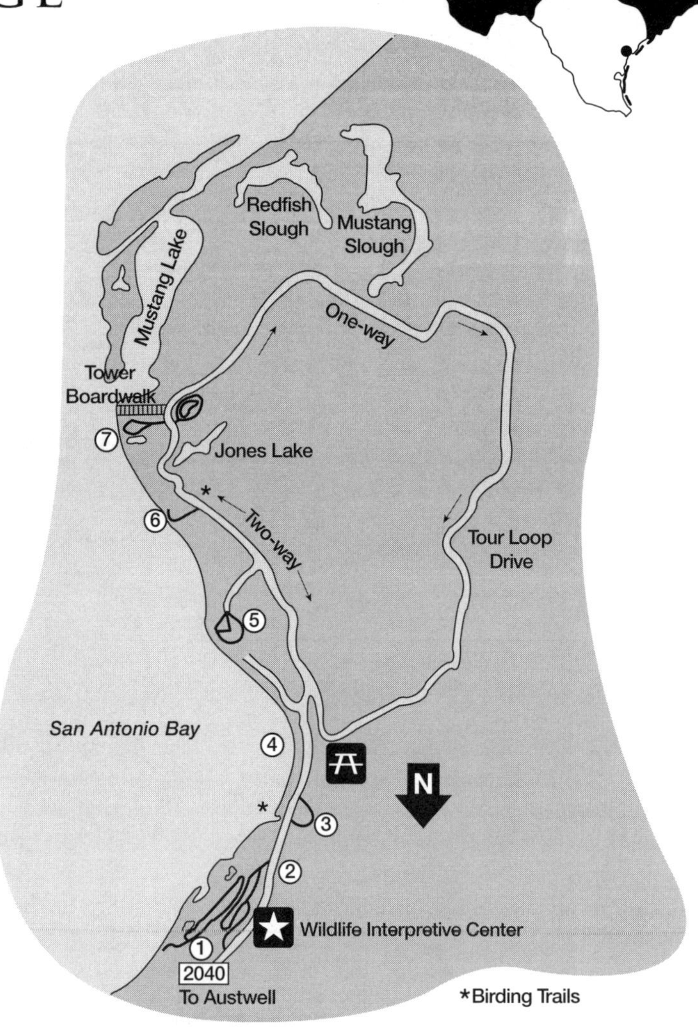

TRAIL NOTES

The trails within the refuge consist of 7 separate trails totaling 4.1 miles. These trails constitute an excellent means for nature study and wildlife observation. Of particular importance is the fact that the endangered whooping crane may often be viewed from the 40-foot observation tower during the winter and early spring. The trail numbers appearing on the map correspond to the following trails that are located along the 16-mile paved tour road:

1. *Rail Trail,* near the visitor center, is a 0.3-mile hiking trail.
2. *Heron Flats Trail* is a 1.4-mile nature trail that goes through an area of saltwater pools containing small sea animals and attracting numerous species of waterfowl that feed in the pools.
3. *Bird Trail #1* is a 0.1-mile trail through red bay and oak thickets.
4. *Bay Overlook* has a 0.1-mile trail.
5. *Dagger Point Trail* is a 0.9-mile hiking trail where the development of the dunes, their ponds, and the plant cover can be seen.
6. *Bird Trail #2* is a 0.6-mile trail through a grassland and oak forest lining the bay.
7. *Big Tree Trail* is a 0.7-mile hiking trail near the observation tower and is a favorite birding spot, especially during spring and fall migrations. The observation tower is 4.5 miles from the entrance.

The refuge opens at sunrise and closes at sunset. Registration is required. The Wildlife Interpretive Center is open daily from 8:30 a.m. to 4:30 p.m. Visitors should be prepared for mosquitoes, especially during the summer and fall. An entry fee is charged.

Bentsen-Rio Grande Valley State Park/ World Birding Center

FOR INFORMATION

BENTSEN-RIO GRANDE VALLEY STATE PARK/WORLD BIRDING CENTER
2800 S. BENTSEN PALM DRIVE
MISSION, TX 78572
956/585-1107

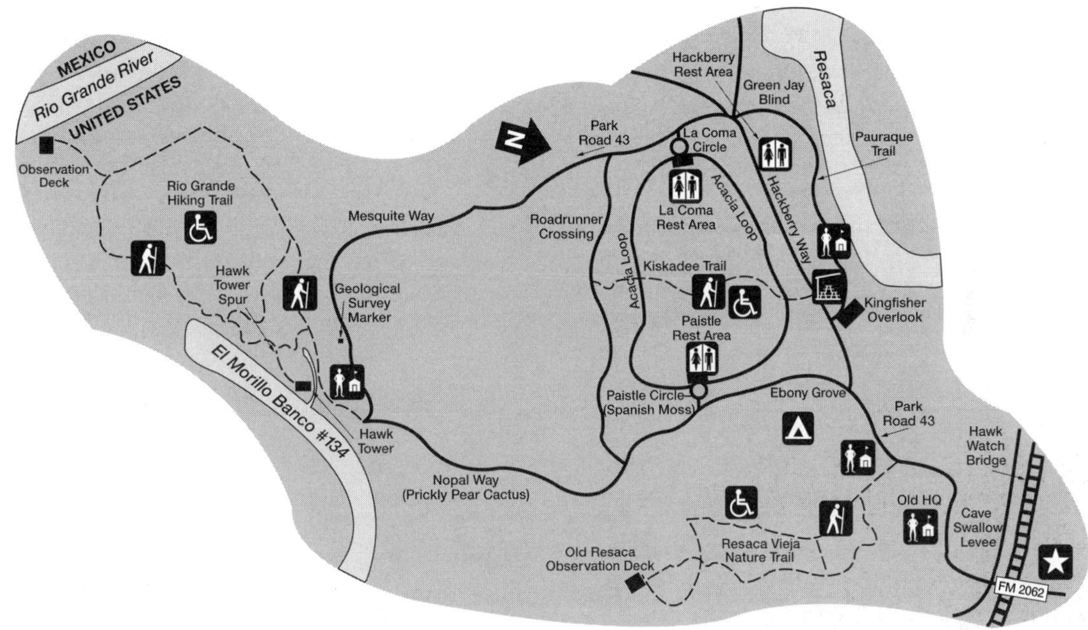

LOCATION

The park is located about 6 miles southwest of Mission. Take West Expressway 83 to Bentsen Palm Drive (FM 2062). Travel south on Bentsen Palm Drive and enter the World Birding Center Headquarters on Park Road 43.

TRAIL NOTES

The park has 2 trails: a 1.2-mile round-trip nature trail that takes you through the wilderness, and the other, a 1.8-mile round-trip hiking trail that takes you to the Rio Grande River. Both trails are interpreted, containing numerous informational stops, which correspond to a brochure. The 2 trails, 2 birding blinds and hawk tower are wheelchair accessible. The park also has 2 paved loops for pedestrians, bicycles and tram rides. The park is known across the nation as a treasure trove of "Valley Specialties"—those birds found nowhere else in the U.S. but deepest South Texas. Professional park naturalists conduct daily, on-site bird-watching and wildlife tours from December through March.

Serious bird-watchers flock to Bentsen-Rio Grande Valley State Park.

BRACKENRIDGE PLANTATION PARK & CAMPGROUND

FOR INFORMATION

BRACKENRIDGE PLANTATION PARK & CAMPGROUND
891 BRACKENRIDGE PKWY.
EDNA, TX 77957
361/782-5456
WWW.BRACKENRIDGEPARK.COM

LOCATION

Brackenridge Plantation Campground & Marina is located east of Edna on the western shore of Lake Texana. Take TX 111 south from US 59 in Edna and travel about 7 miles; the campground is to the right before reaching the Lake Texana bridge. Lake Texana is a 11,000-acre reservoir that extends 18 miles up the Navidad River from Palmetto Bend Dam, and has 125 miles of shoreline. The campground and marina are owned by the Lavaca-Navidad River Authority.

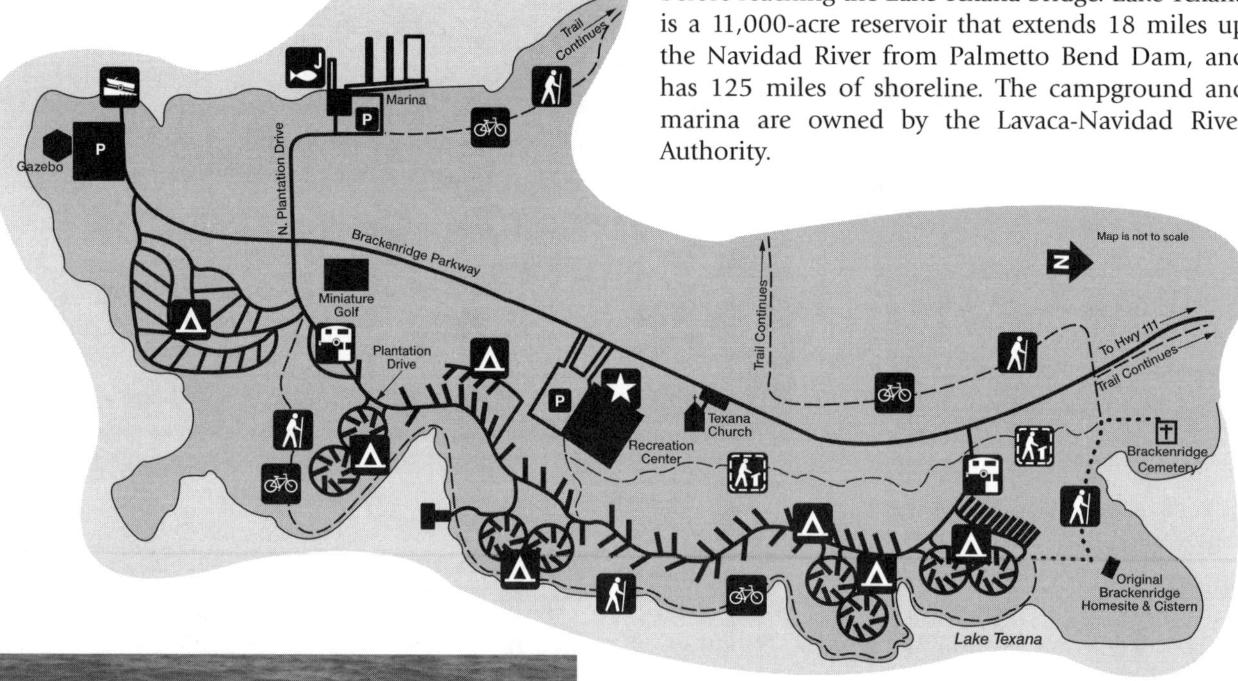

TRAIL NOTES

The park has 3 trails: a 5-mile hike and bike trail that meanders through the park, along the shoreline and nature areas; a nature trail that leads to the Brackenridge Cemetery from the Recreation Center; and a short historic trail that leads to the original Brackenridge Homesite & Cistern. Lake Texana is a great place for viewing and photographing wildlife; it is one of the sites on the Great Texas Coastal Birding Trail to observe birds at an intersection of two major migration flyways.

Located on the western shore of Lake Texana, this park has a campground and a marina.

CANYON OF THE EAGLES

FOR INFORMATION

CANYON OF THE EAGLES
16942 RR 2341
BURNET, TX 78611
512/334-2070
1-800-977-0081
WWW.CANYONOFTHEEAGLES.COM

LOCATION

Canyon of the Eagles is a 940-acre nature park located northwest of Burnet on the shores of Lake Buchanan. From Burnet, travel west on SH 29, turn right on RR 2341 and travel 15 miles to the park entrance. The park is recognized internationally as a habitat for endangered wildlife, including the American bald eagle, black-capped vireo and golden-cheeked warbler. The LCRA owns the Nature Park and developed the camping areas and many of the recreation facilities. However, Presidian Destinations developed the lodge, conference center, and dining facilities and also operates the park and its facilities.

TRAIL NOTES

The park has approximately 14 miles of trails. A 38-page booklet entitled *Guide to the Hiking Trails at Canyon of the Eagles Nature Park* is a must for the hiker; it describes the 5 major hiking trails and their connecting routes. Numbered posts, which correspond to the junction numbers on the map, are located at each trail junction. Hikers should be aware that some trails are closed during the year for endangered and threatened species.

The western two-thirds of the park consists of low-elevation landforms shaped by years of Colorado River meandering. The eastern third of the park includes the steep limestone slopes of the Edwards Plateau. The dominant vegetation type in the park is live oak and juniper woodland with scattered grassland openings.

REGION 3

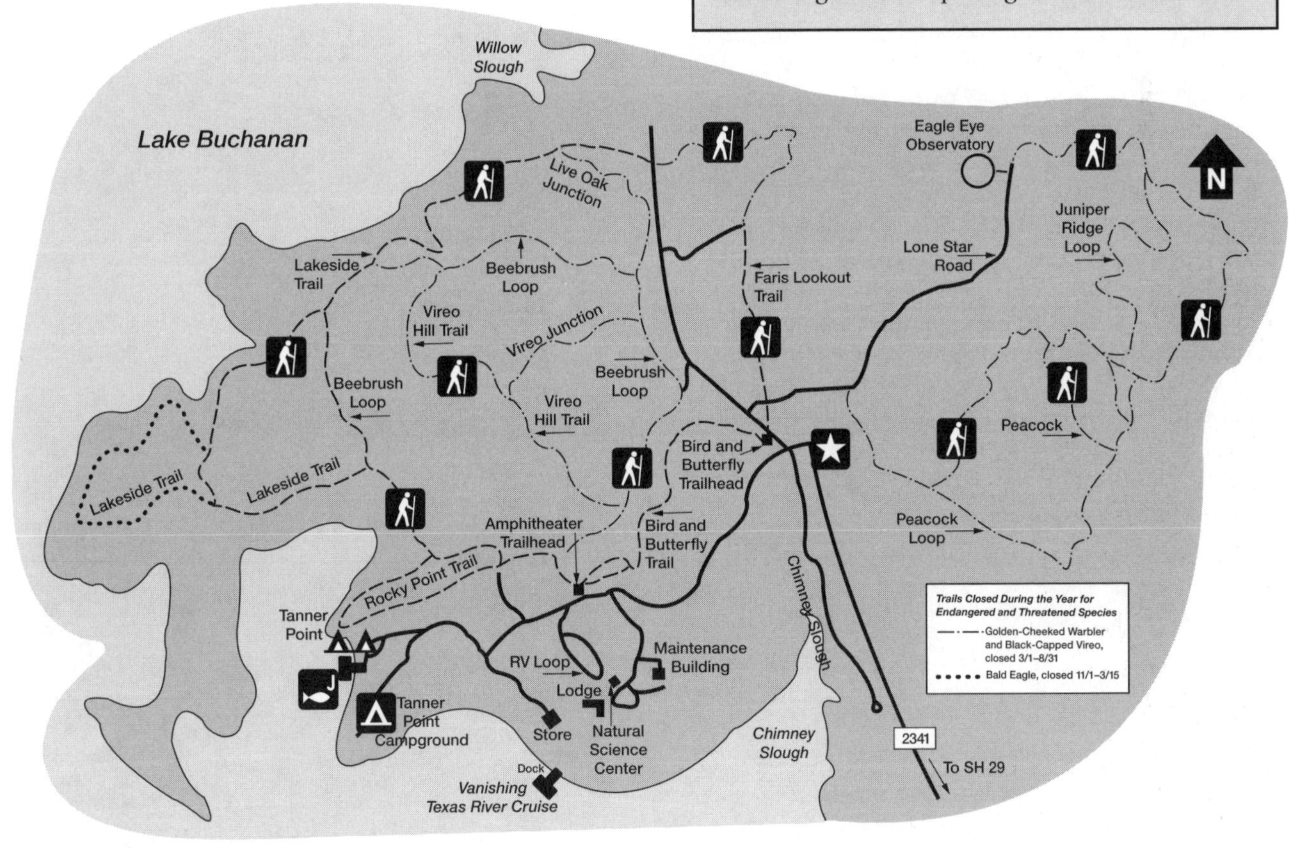

Cibolo Nature Center

FOR INFORMATION

Cibolo Nature Center
P.O. Box 9
Boerne, TX 78006
830/249-4616

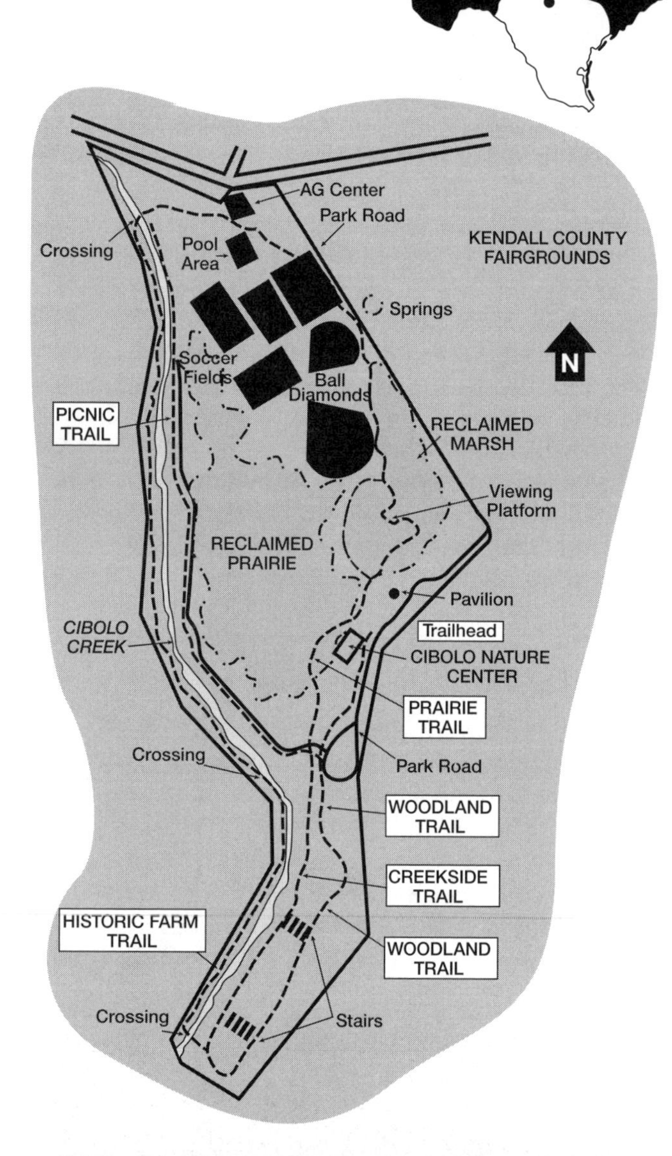

LOCATION

The Cibolo Nature Center is located on the southern portion of Boerne City Park; the northern end of the park has a swimming pool, soccer and baseball fields, and an agricultural center. To reach the park, travel east on TX 46 from downtown Boerne for about a mile, turn right on a paved road and travel about one-half mile, while following the signs. The trail travels from grassland to creekbed, and from marshland to woodland, demonstrating a broad cross section of the habitats, animal life and flora native to the Hill Country. The native prairie, marsh, and cypress-lined Cibolo Creek are a nature lover's paradise and an important classroom for local students.

TRAIL NOTES

The Cibolo Nature Center covers 100 acres and has several trails: ¼-mile Prairie Trail; 1-mile Historic Farm Trail; ⅓-mile Creekside Trail; ½-mile Woodland Trail; ⅔-mile Picnic Trail; and the ½-mile Marsh Loop. Trail maps are available at the trailhead and at the Cibolo Nature Center. Several trails can be combined to create a longer hike; they lead through the marsh on boardwalks and through the prairie on marked trails with informative brochures on the plants, flowers, and grasses. In 1993, the Cibolo Nature Center was opened. Monthly educational programs, sponsored by the Friends of the Cibolo Wilderness, teach about such topics as snakes, birds of prey, and wildflower identification. Visitors also are encouraged to walk through the center and browse through displays and resource materials.

If you want to learn more about this lizard, plan to attend one of the Nature Center's monthly educational programs.

Enchanted Rock State Natural Area

FOR INFORMATION

ENCHANTED ROCK STATE NATURAL AREA
16710 RANCH ROAD 965
FREDERICKSBURG, TX 78624
325/247-3903

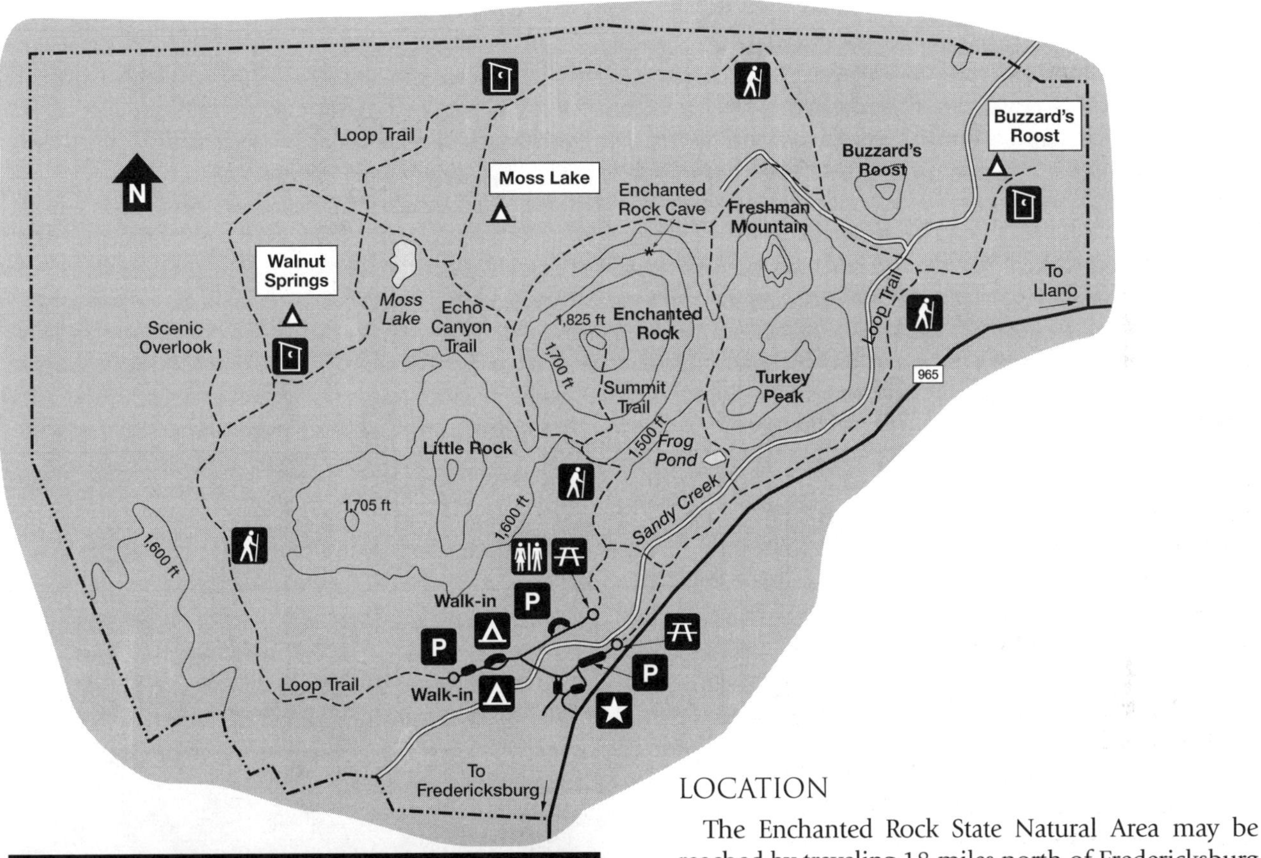

THIS PARK HAS TRAILS AND PRIMITIVE CAMPING AREAS DESIGNED FOR BACKPACKERS. SEE PAGE 169.

LOCATION

The Enchanted Rock State Natural Area may be reached by traveling 18 miles north of Fredericksburg on RR 965 or by traveling south from Llano on TX 16 for 14 miles and then west on RR 965 for 8 miles. The 1,643-acres are dominated by massive dome-shaped hills of pinkish granite.

TRAIL NOTES

There are approximately 7 miles of hiking trails for park visitors to enjoy. Bicycles are not permitted on trails. Most park visitors hike the Summit Trail to the crest; this trail of moderate difficulty climbs 425 feet in 6/10 of a mile. Don't let the climb intimidate you—remember, you may terminate your hike at any point along the trail; the view will always be magnificent. Serious hikers and backpackers like to explore the 4-mile Loop Trail that circumvents the granite domes. For those who wish to camp in the backcountry, 3 primitive camping areas are accessed by the Loop Trail. See page 169 for details.

The 1,000-ft.-long Enchanted Rock Fissure, with its entrance located on top of the dome is of geological interest; visitors exploring it should use CAUTION. This talus fissure contains over 20 entrances with tight passages; wet, slippery surfaces; numerous steep inclines; and hazardous vertical drops. Passage through the cave requires some skill and climbing ability. To ensure safety, carry at least one light source, preferably two, and wear loose, protective clothing, and proper footwear.

Falcon State Park

For Information

Falcon State Park
P.O. Box 2
Falcon Heights, TX 78545
956/848-5327

Location

Located on the Texas-Mexico border, Falcon State Park may be reached by traveling 15 miles northwest of Roma on US 83, FM 2098 and Park Road 46. The 572-acre park is on the eastern shore of the 87,210-acre Falcon Reservoir on the Rio Grande River.

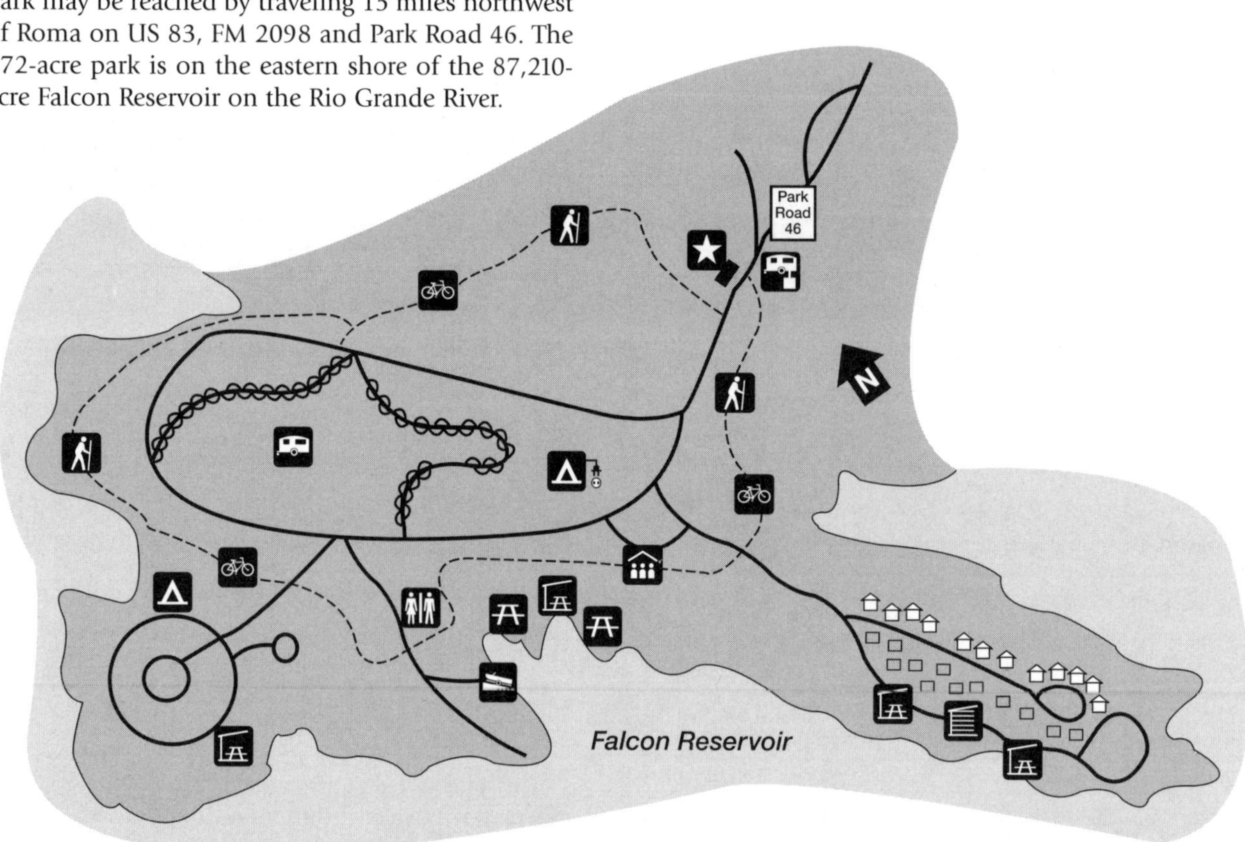

This state park has a boat ramp and dock, as well as a fish cleaning facility.

Trail Notes

The 3-mile trail at Falcon Lake State Park is a hike and bike trail; it begins and ends at the Park Headquarters. The first mile is a nature trail and has the flora/fauna marked. The trail starts with a downhill ride/hike and ends with an uphill ride/hike; it is a winding trail with rolling terrain and a few sandstone outcrops. There are thorn scrub brush and shrubs on both sides and a few benches along the way for resting. An abundance of wildlife can be seen and heard along the trail. This trail is best suited for hiking and slow bicycle traffic.

Garner State Park

FOR INFORMATION

Garner State Park
HCR #70, Box 599
Concan, TX 78838
830/232-6132

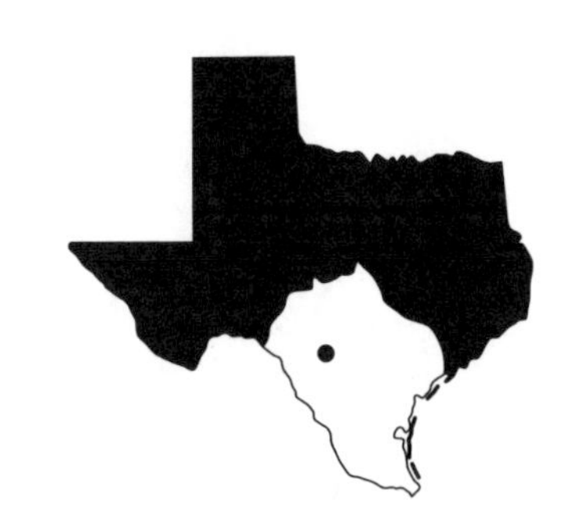

Huge bald cypress border the clear, spring-fed waters of the Frio River as it flows through Garner State Park.

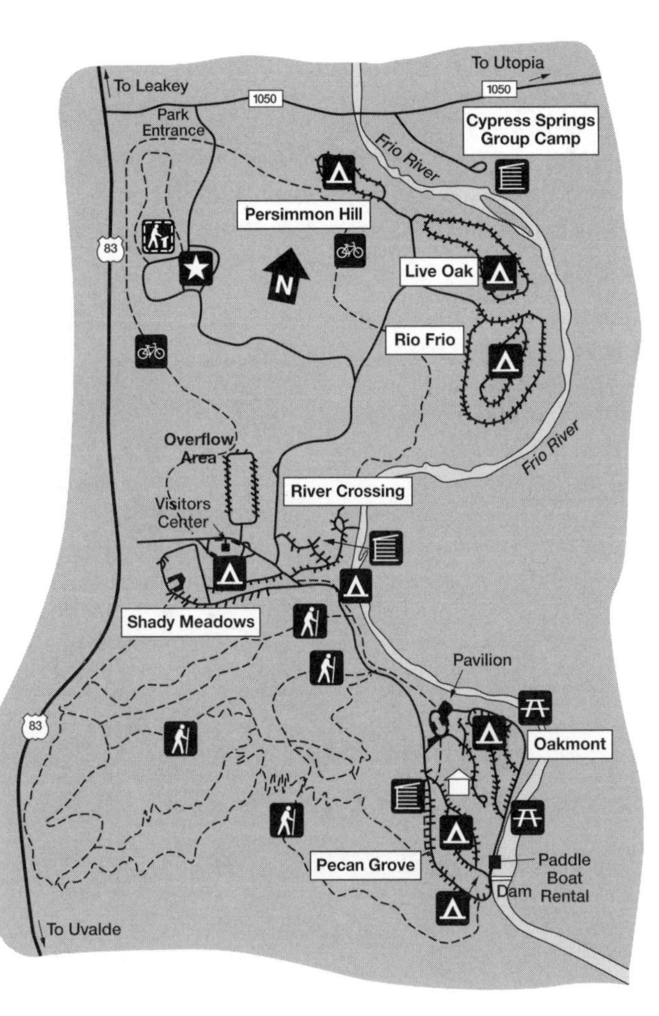

TRAIL NOTES

There are numerous opportunities for hiking at Garner State Park, including a ¼-mile nature trail adjacent to the park office near the entrance, and 6.7 miles of hiking trails in the southwest portion of the park. A trail map is available that displays the west loop trail and the east loop trail. The map shows the contour of the land as well as the mileage between the various trail junctions. A paved hike/bike trail connects the main concession pavilion with the Shady Meadows Camping Area. Foot trails exist along the river and others connect the north and south camping areas.

LOCATION

Garner State Park is located 31 miles north of Uvalde, 7 miles north of Concan, and 10 miles south of Leakey on US 83. The Frio River, with its clear, spring-fed waters and shade from huge bald cypress, borders the east boundary of this 1,420-acre park. The park is named for John Nance Garner, former vice president of the United States who lived in nearby Uvalde, and was constructed in the late 1930s by the Civilian Conservation Corps.

Guadalupe River State Park

For Information

Guadalupe River State Park
3350 Park Rd. 31
Spring Branch, TX 78070
830/438-2656

Location

Bisected by the clear, flowing waters of the Guadalupe River, this state park comprises a 1,938-acre segment of the Texas Hill Country noted for its ruggedness and scenic beauty. The 3-mile road to the park (Park Road 31) can be reached by traveling 13 miles east of Boerne on TX 46, or 8 miles west of the US 281 intersection with TX 46.

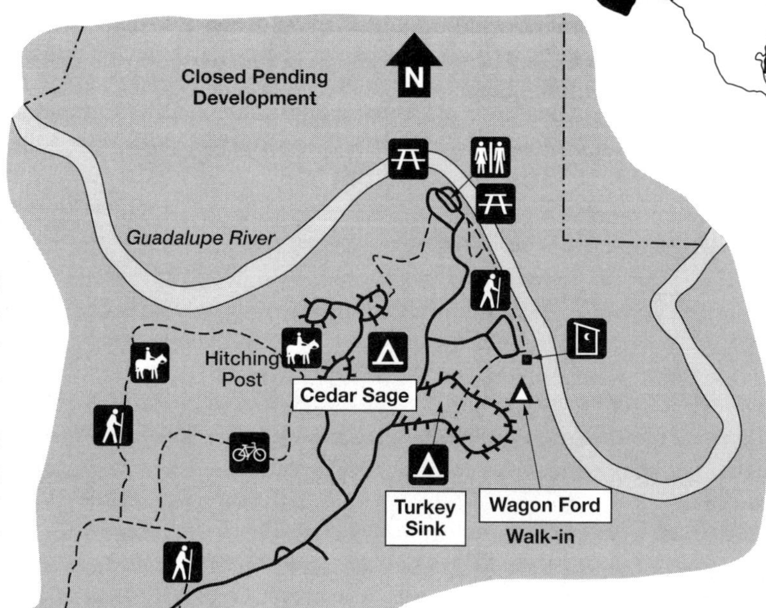

Trail Notes

The park has about 8 miles of hiking trails; one trail follows the riverbank, leads from the picnic area to the tent camping area, and connects the walk-in tent site area with the multi-use camping area. Bicycles are not allowed on this trail. Another longer trail accommodates hikers, bikers, and equestrians. The Guadalupe River, with banks lined by huge bald cypress trees, is the park's most outstanding natural feature.

Honey Creek State Natural Area

Entrance to the 2,293-acre Honey Creek State Natural Area is through Guadalupe River State Park. The diverse geology, flora, and fauna make Honey Creek a special place for all visitors. Guided nature walks are scheduled almost every Saturday morning at 9:00 a.m. The tour lasts about 2 hours; reservations are not required. Tours are conducted by volunteer members of the Friends of Guadalupe; there is no fee but donations are encouraged. Please confirm the tour schedule with Guadalupe River State Park. In addition, a variety of guided tours are offered on Saturdays that are specific to birds, wildflowers, geology, photography, etc. Some of these tours may require a reservation.

The location of this park allows river paddlers to begin or end their trip here, or to have a lay-over.

Hamilton Pool Park

FOR INFORMATION

Travis County Parks
c/o Travis County Public Improvements and Transportation Dept.
Box 1748
Austin, TX 78767
512/473-9437 (County Parks information)
512/264-2740 (Hamilton Pool information)

LOCATION

Hamilton Pool Park is located about 30 miles west of Austin on FM 3238. From the TX 71/US 290 junction southwest of Austin, take TX 71 about 8½ miles to FM 3238 (Hamilton Pool Road), turn left and travel about 13 miles to the park. The entrance to the 232-acre park is on the right. The park is managed as a natural area (preserve) with emphasis on habitat protection and restoration, environmental education for public and private groups, and ongoing research; it offers limited, day-use only, recreational opportunities such as picnicking, hiking, swimming and nature study.

TRAIL NOTES

The well-marked hiking trail leads from the parking lot to Hamilton Creek. At the creek, the trail to the right goes to the pool and the trail to the left follows the creek downstream to the Pedernales River. Bald cypress trees, lush, diverse plant communities, and a variety of wildlife species occupy the grotto and downstream areas. The hike from the parking lot to the pool is about ¼ mile round-trip; the hike along the creek from the pool to the river is about ¾ mile, or 1½ miles round-trip from the parking lot.

Swimming in the pool is allowed only when the water quality meets safe standards.

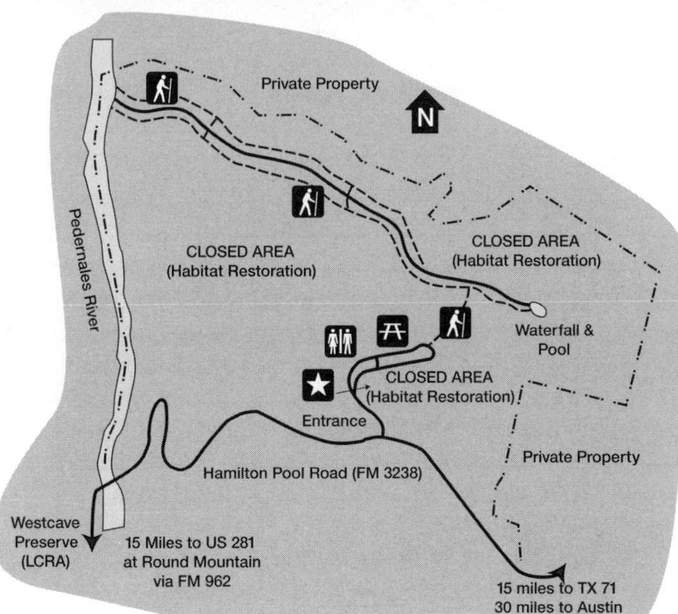

ABOUT THE PARK

The park's pool and grotto were formed when the dome of an underground river collapsed thousands of years ago. Outstanding features of the park include a 50-foot waterfall, swimming hole and nature trails along the creek. Swimming is allowed only when the water quality meets safe standards. Water quality is monitored regularly. Updated information is posted at the entrance booth and provided on the park's telephone recorder message (512/264-2740). The parking lot is sized for 75 cars, and when all spaces are taken, the park will close temporarily. Drinking water or concessions are not available in the park; chemical toilets are provided. Pets are prohibited.

Hours of operation are 9 a.m. to 6 p.m. daily. Travis County parks are closed on Thanksgiving Day, Christmas Day and New Year's Day. A per-vehicle entrance fee is charged.

INKS LAKE STATE PARK

FOR INFORMATION

INKS LAKE STATE PARK
3630 PARK ROAD 4 WEST
BURNET, TX 78611
512/793-2223

LOCATION

Inks Lake State Park is located between Burnet and Llano off of TX 29 three miles south on Park Road 4. Also accessible from US 281 between Burnet and Marble Falls via Park Road 4 west. The 1,200-acre park borders 803-acre Inks Lake, created by a dam on the Colorado River.

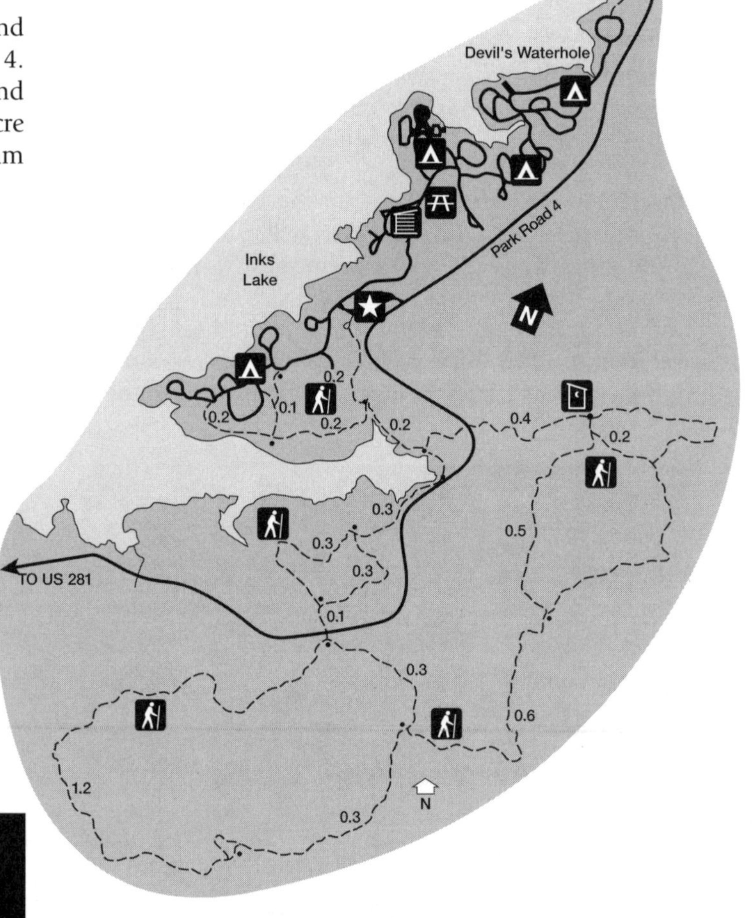

These hikers are on the trail to the Devil's Waterhole.

THIS PARK HAS TRAILS AND PRIMITIVE CAMPING AREAS DESIGNED FOR BACKPACKERS.

TRAIL NOTES

Inks Lake State Park has 7½ miles of hiking trails amid the rugged pink granite outcroppings, cedar and oak woodlands, and grasslands. The Inks Lake area is considered one of the most beautiful in Texas because of its scenic diversity and wealth of minerals, water, and wildlife. Two short trails include a scenic trail along the constant-level lake of clear blue water and a trail that leads to the Devil's Waterhole from the camping area at the northernmost area of the park.

The 7½-mile network of trails south and east of the lake and Park Road 4 were probably planned with the serious hiker and backpacker in mind. Several loops exist so hikers can choose a section that suits their stamina. A walk-in primitive camping area is located on one of the loop trails; a primitive toilet is nearby. This camping area is about 1 mile from park headquarters or about ½ mile from Park Road 4. Backpackers, desiring a longer trek than this, could begin their trip at a more distant trailhead. Because this primitive camping area is located so near a trailhead, and because the trails used by backpackers are identical to those used by hikers, the Inks Lake State Park trail map is not duplicated in the Backpacking Trails section.

KERRVILLE-SCHREINER PARK

FOR INFORMATION

KERRVILLE-SCHREINER PARK
2385 BANDERA HIGHWAY
KERRVILLE, TX 78028
830/257-5392
WWW.KERRPARK@KERRVILLE.ORG

LOCATION

Kerrville-Schreiner Park is located on the south edge of Kerrville on TX 173 via TX 16 or via Loop 534 off of TX 16 just south of I-10. The 517-acre park is adjacent to the shores of Flat Rock Lake on the Guadalupe River, and is managed by the city of Kerrville.

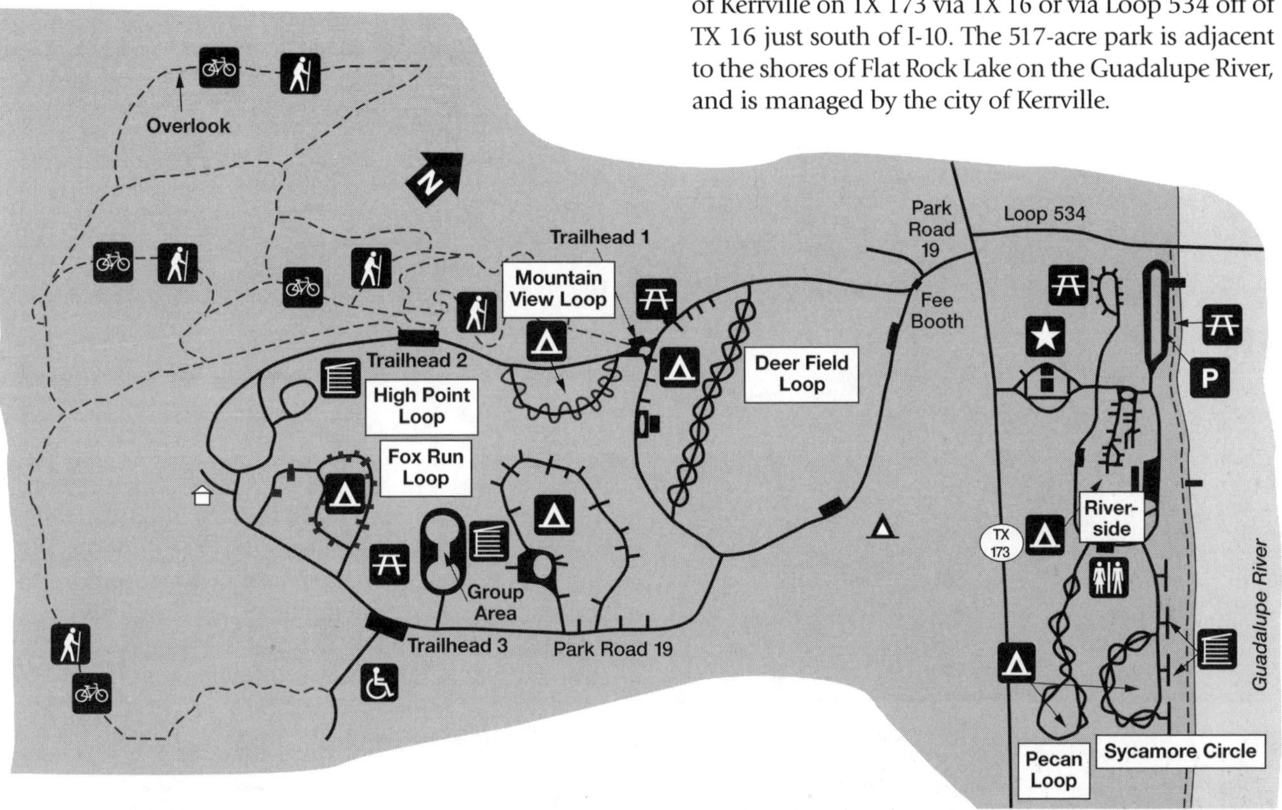

TRAIL NOTES

The park has a network of 7.7 miles of hiking trails; all of them can be used for mountain biking. Many of the trails are color coded: the Blue Trail is 3.2 miles, the Orange Trail is 2 miles, and the Yellow Trail is 0.9 mile in length. There are 3 trailheads. Trail users should pick up a map from the park office; it shows which trails are closed for restoration.

Many of the trails at Kerrville-Schreiner Park are color coded to assist hikers in making the right choice at a trail junction.

LAGUNA ATASCOSA NATIONAL WILDLIFE REFUGE

FOR INFORMATION

LAGUNA ATASCOSA NATIONAL WILDLIFE REFUGE
P.O. BOX 450
RIO HONDO, TX 78583
956/748-3607

LOCATION

Laguna Atascosa is now 88,808 acres in size and contains three main units: 45,616-acre Laguna Atascosa Unit, 19,910-acre Bahia Grande Unit, and 23,282-acre South Padre Island Unit. Only the Laguna Atascosa and South Padre Island Units are open to public access during daylight hours. There are no developed trails on the South Padre Island Unit; however, the public may hike along the beach front, in the dunes, or behind the dunes. Camping and motorized vehicles are allowed on the beach front only, but not in or behind the dunes. To reach the Laguna Atascosa Unit from Harlingen, travel through Rio Hondo on FM 106 and from Brownsville travel north on FM 1847 through Los Fresnos.

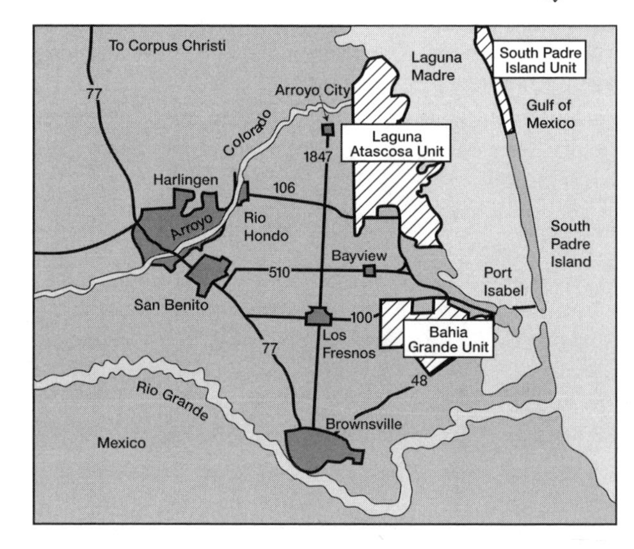

VICINITY MAP

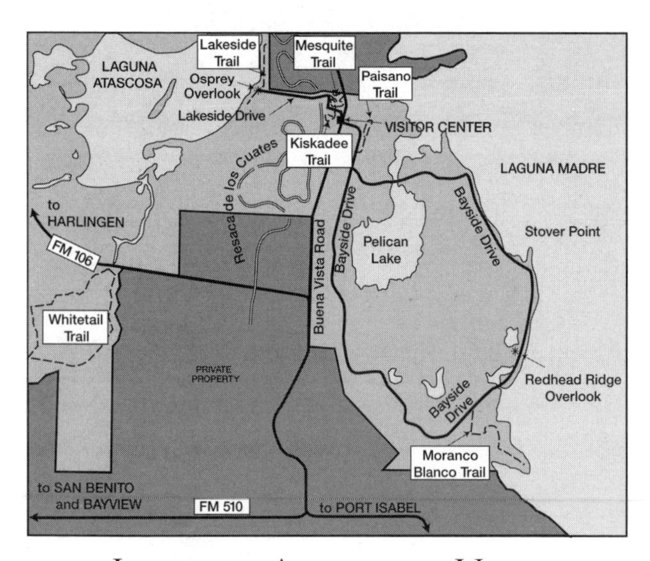

LAGUNA ATASCOSA UNIT

TRAIL NOTES

There are six self-guided trails, totaling 9¾ miles. A trail leaflet is available.

- ▲ **Kiskadee Trail** is a ¼-mile trail that starts between the Visitor Center and the refuge office building.
- ▲ **Mesquite Trail** is a 1½-mile double-loop trail that is west of the visitor center parking lot and runs north of Lakeside Drive.
- ▲ **Lakeside Trail** is 1½ miles in length including two side trails. The trailhead is 1½ miles west of the visitor center at Osprey Overlook.
- ▲ **Paisano Trail** is a 1-mile loop on a blacktop road with the trailhead located on Bayside Drive 1 mile from the visitor center.
- ▲ **Whitetrail Trail** is 4 miles in length. The trailhead is south of FM 106 near the west entrance.
- ▲ **Moranco Blanco Trail** is a 1.5-mile trail located off of Bayside Wildlife Drive in the southeasterly part of this unit past the Redhead Ridge Overlook.

There are two auto tours: the **Bayside Drive** is a 15-mile one-way loop that winds past the Laguna Madre, while the 1.5-mile **Lakeside Drive** goes to the Osprey Overlook to view the Laguna Atascosa. The refuge tour roads are open from sunrise to sunset. An entrance fee is charged. The Visitor Center is open October through April.

Bicycles are allowed on both wildlife drives (Lakeside and Bayside) and on all service roads, but not on any of the walking trails except the 4-mile Whitetail Trail. Off-road bikes with tire sealant are recommended for riding on unpaved service roads and Whitetail Trail.

Lake Texana State Park

FOR INFORMATION

Lake Texana State Park
46 Park Rd. 1
Edna, TX 77957-0760
512/782-5718

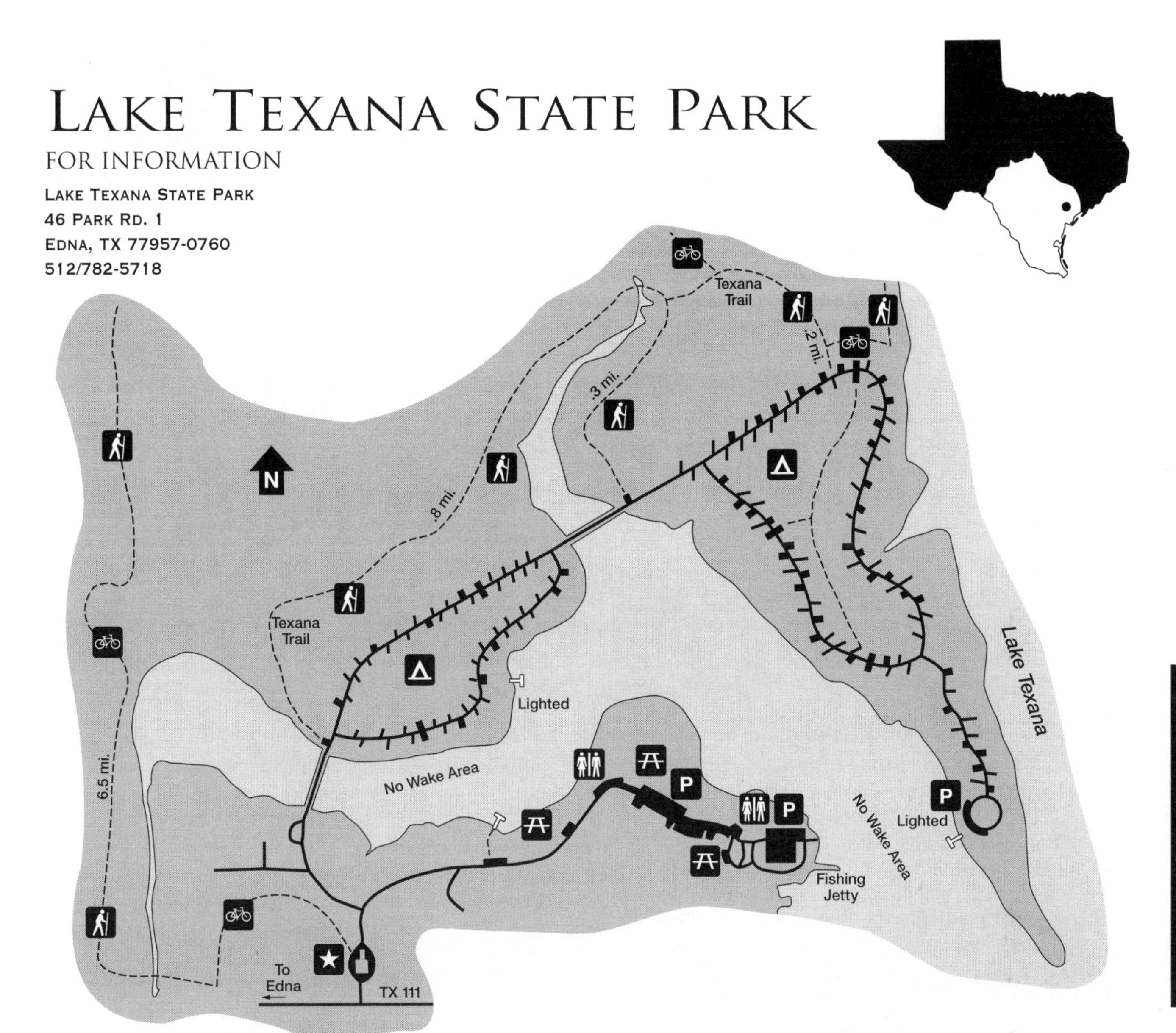

REGION 3

LOCATION

This 575-acre state park is located on the west side of 11,000-acre Lake Texana; the lake backs up water from the Navidad River for 18 miles, and has 125 miles of shoreline. The park entrance is 6½ miles east of Edna off of TX 111.

TRAIL NOTES

Lake Texana State Park has almost 8 miles of hiking/biking trails, including a section of trail of granite gravel surface accessible to the handicapped. Most of park land consists of mixed oak and pecan woodlands associated with the Navidad River. Alligators are found in the park coves and should not be approached or fed.

In addition to the designated bike trails, campers also enjoy cycling on the paved roads.

Longhorn Cavern State Park

FOR INFORMATION

Longhorn Cavern State Park
P.O. Box 732
Burnet, TX 78611
1-877/441-CAVE (Toll free)
830/598-CAVE

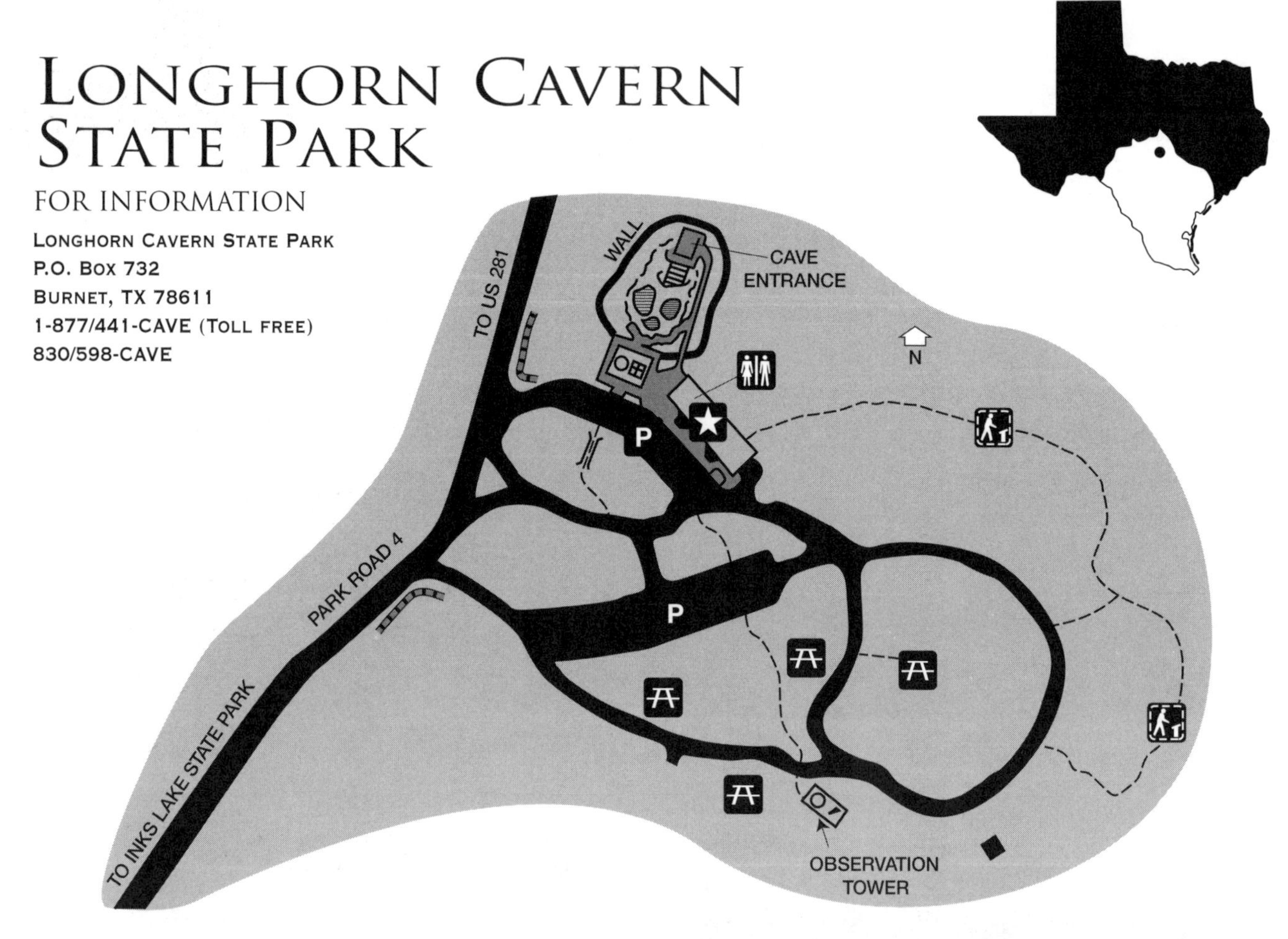

LOCATION

Longhorn Cavern State Park is located southwest of Burnet on Park Road 4 via US 281, 6 miles south of Burnet, or via TX 29, 6 miles west of Burnet. The park covers 639 acres of scenic and rugged Hill Country in the heart of the Highland Lakes.

TRAIL NOTES

The tour into the cavern is a 1¼-mile round-trip and takes about 1 hour 25 minutes. Always a comfortable 64°F, the cavern offers a level and easy walk through one of the most unique caverns of the world. Phone for a recorded message on tour hours. Tours are available daily except Christmas Eve and Christmas Day.

Two other trails are available to park visitors: a ½-mile nature trail with an interpretive brochure and a 1-mile hiking trail. (Note: The hiking trail is not drawn to scale on this map; the location is correct but the distance depicted is misleading. The hiking trail is twice as long as the nature trail.)

TEXAS HIGHWAYS Magazine

Longhorn Cavern was acquired in 1932 from private owners and dedicated a state park. In 1971, it was dedicated as a natural landmark.

Lost Maples State Natural Area

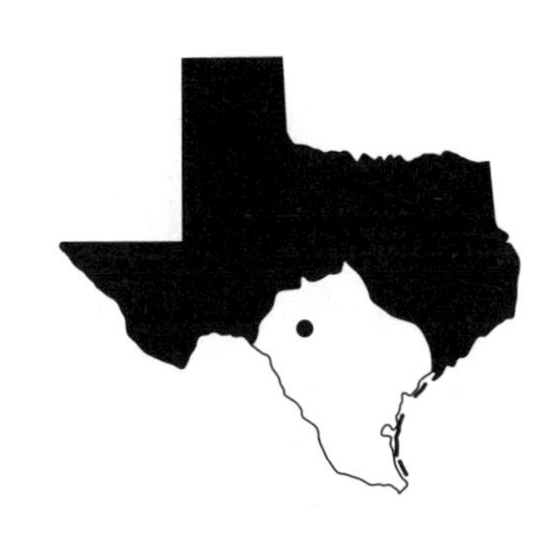

FOR INFORMATION

Lost Maples State Natural Area
37221 FM 187
Vanderpool, TX 78885
830/966-3413

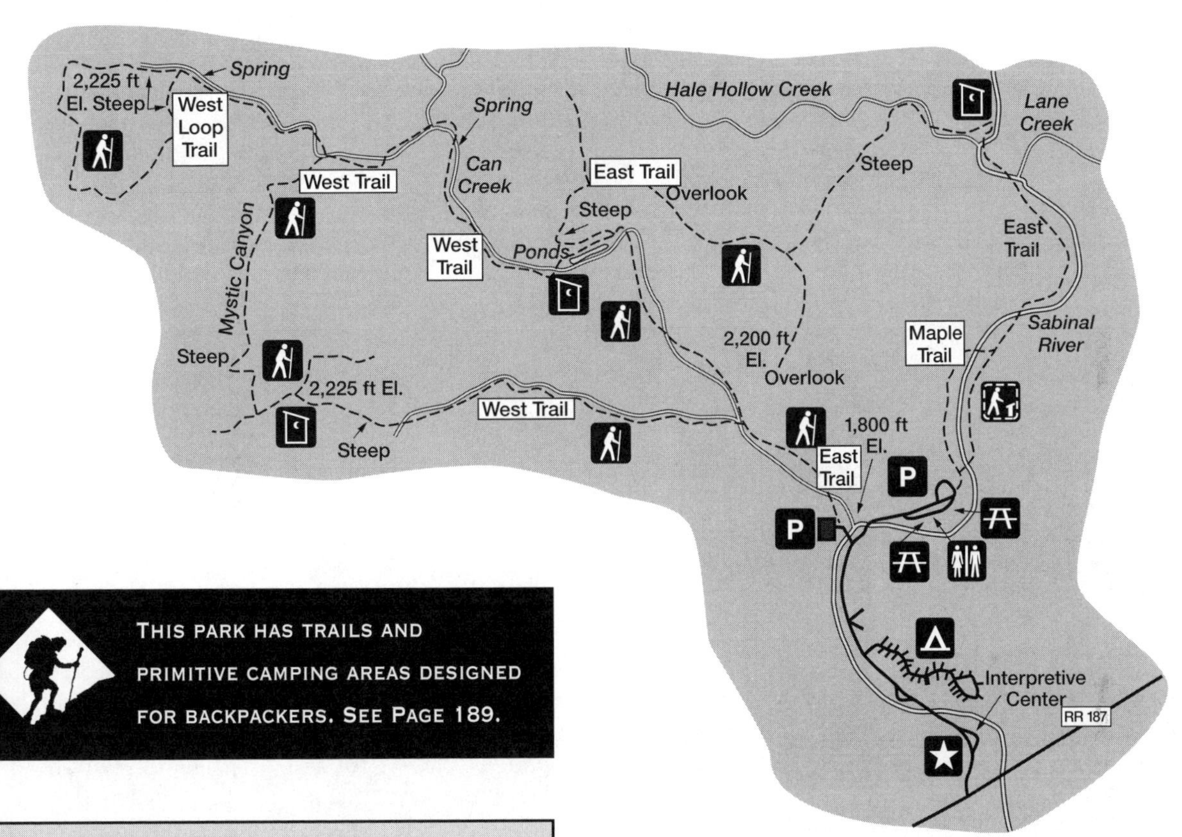

THIS PARK HAS TRAILS AND PRIMITIVE CAMPING AREAS DESIGNED FOR BACKPACKERS. SEE PAGE 189.

TRAIL NOTES

The bigtooth maples, or canyon maples, are the outstanding feature of Lost Maples State Natural Area. These maples may turn in mid-fall (October–November) and can yield spectacular displays of fall color. Conditions must be just right and should not be expected every year. There is a day-use area with 24 picnic sites, parking spaces, and a restroom. Parking in the park is limited to 250 spaces.

There are 10½ miles of hiking trails. The Maple Trail, the shortest of the 4 trails, is a developed nature trail that follows the Sabinal River for 4/10 of a mile and begins at the trailhead parking near the day-use area. The maple groves along this trail are the easiest to see. The other 3 trails are more strenuous, but can be enjoyed as day hikes; 8 primitive campsites for backpackers are located along these trails. See page 189 for details.

LOCATION

Lost Maples State Natural Area is located 4 miles north of Vanderpool on RR 187 in Bandera County. If traveling from Kerrville, take TX 39 west from Kerrville through Ingram and Hunt. About 20 miles southwest of Hunt, turn onto RR 187 and proceed southward toward Vanderpool. If traveling from Bandera, take TX 16 west out of Bandera for 3 miles and turn southward onto RR 470 through Tarpley. Seventeen miles out of Tarpley take RR 187 to the right through Vanderpool. Total acreage of the park is 2,174.

McKinney Falls State Park

FOR INFORMATION

McKinney Falls State Park
5808 McKinney Falls Parkway
Austin, TX 78744
512/243-1643

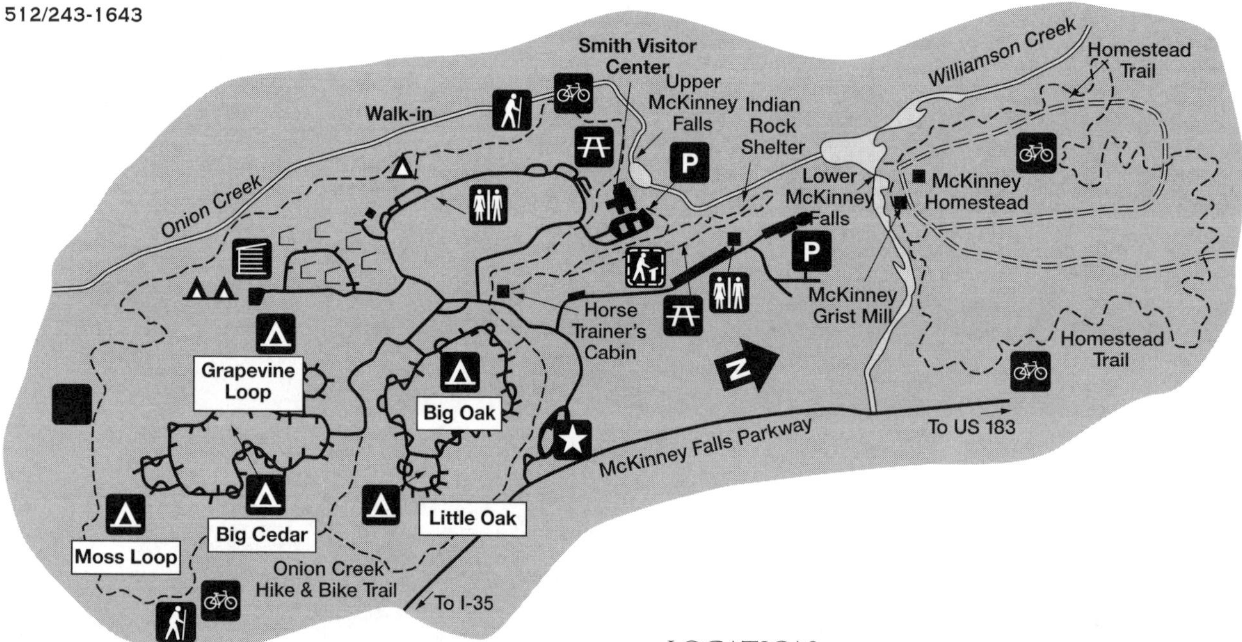

LOCATION

This state park is located about 13 miles southeast of the state capitol in Austin; it is east of I-35, south of Ben White Blvd. and west of US 183. The 744-acre park is named for the waterfall on Onion Creek. From the east, the park may be reached from US 183, either via traveling south on McKinney Falls Parkway, or via traveling west for 2 miles on Scenic Loop Road. From the west, the park may be reached off of I-35 by taking East William Cannon Drive (exit 228) to McKinney Falls Parkway.

This picturesque bridge is located on the ¾-mile Smith Rockshelter interpretive trail that parallels Onion Creek.

TRAIL NOTES

A variety of trails are available at McKinney Falls: the ¾-mile Smith Rockshelter interpretive trail, a 3.2-mile hike and bike trail, and the 3-mile Homestead Mountain Bike Trail. The interpretive trail has a booklet available. The mountain bike trail is located in the northern portion of the park with foot access through the McKinney Falls area. Onion Creek winds through the park for 1.7 miles and is characterized by long quiet pools lined with bald cypress, occasional rapids, and two beautiful waterfalls.

PADRE ISLAND NATIONAL SEASHORE

FOR INFORMATION

PADRE ISLAND NATIONAL SEASHORE
(20420 PARK RD. 22)
P.O. BOX 181300
CORPUS CHRISTI, TX 78480-1300
361/949-8068 (VISITOR CENTER)
361/949-8171 (HEADQUARTERS)
361/949-8175 (FOR RECORDED MESSAGE ON TIDES, WEATHER, BEACH CONDITIONS, ETC.)

LOCATION

Stretching for 113 miles along the Texas Gulf Coast from Corpus Christi on the north almost to Mexico on the south, this barrier island ranges in width from a few hundred yards to about 3 miles. The National Seashore encompasses the undeveloped central part of the island and is one of the longest stretches of primitive, undeveloped ocean beach in the United States. Access to the park is from the north end. There are two approaches: The first leads over a causeway from Corpus Christi (TX 358) to North Padre Island and then via Park Road 22; the other leads from Port Aransas down Mustang Island via TX 361. The visitor center is approximately 10 miles south of the junction of Park Road 22 and TX 361.

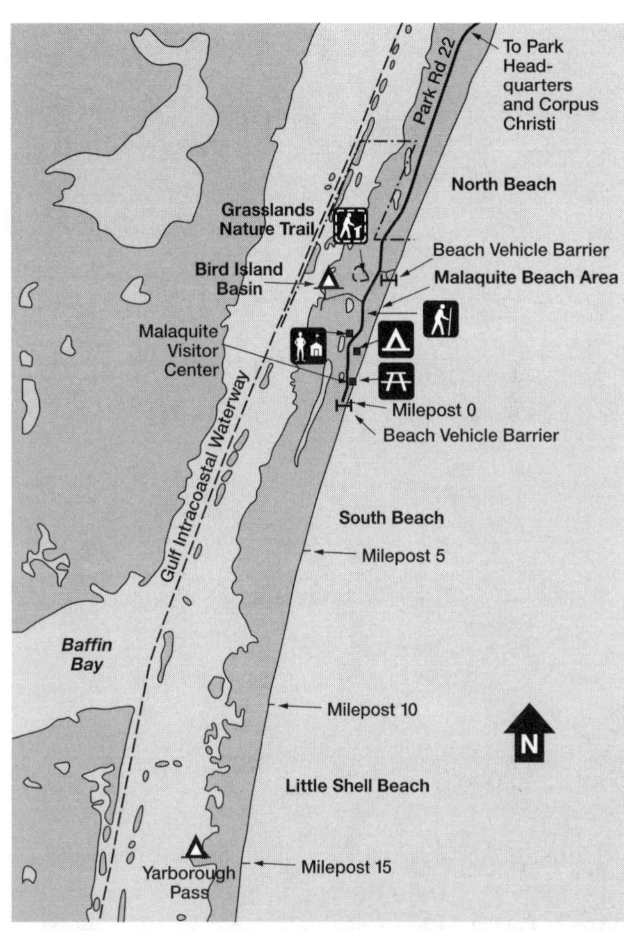

TRAIL NOTES

The Grasslands Nature Trail, a ¾-mile loop walk, provides an opportunity to explore the grassland environment and actually see the various stages of plant succession. Pamphlets, available at the start of the trail, explain features as you walk along. Numbered paragraphs relate to numbered stakes along the trail to help you gain a better understanding of this unique environment.

The 4½-mile stretch of beach between the north access road and the southern end of Malaquite Beach is closed to all motor vehicular traffic. This stretch of beach has been set aside for pedestrians. There is no marked hiking trail but this is an excellent hiking area on the beach along the water's edge.

Very few things in life are more enjoyable than walking barefoot along the beach while the waves roll in.

BACKPACKING IS PERMITTED AT PADRE ISLAND NATIONAL SEASHORE. SEE PAGE 190.

REGION 3

Palmetto State Park

FOR INFORMATION

Palmetto State Park
78 Park Road 11 South
Gonzales, TX 78629-5180
830/672-3266

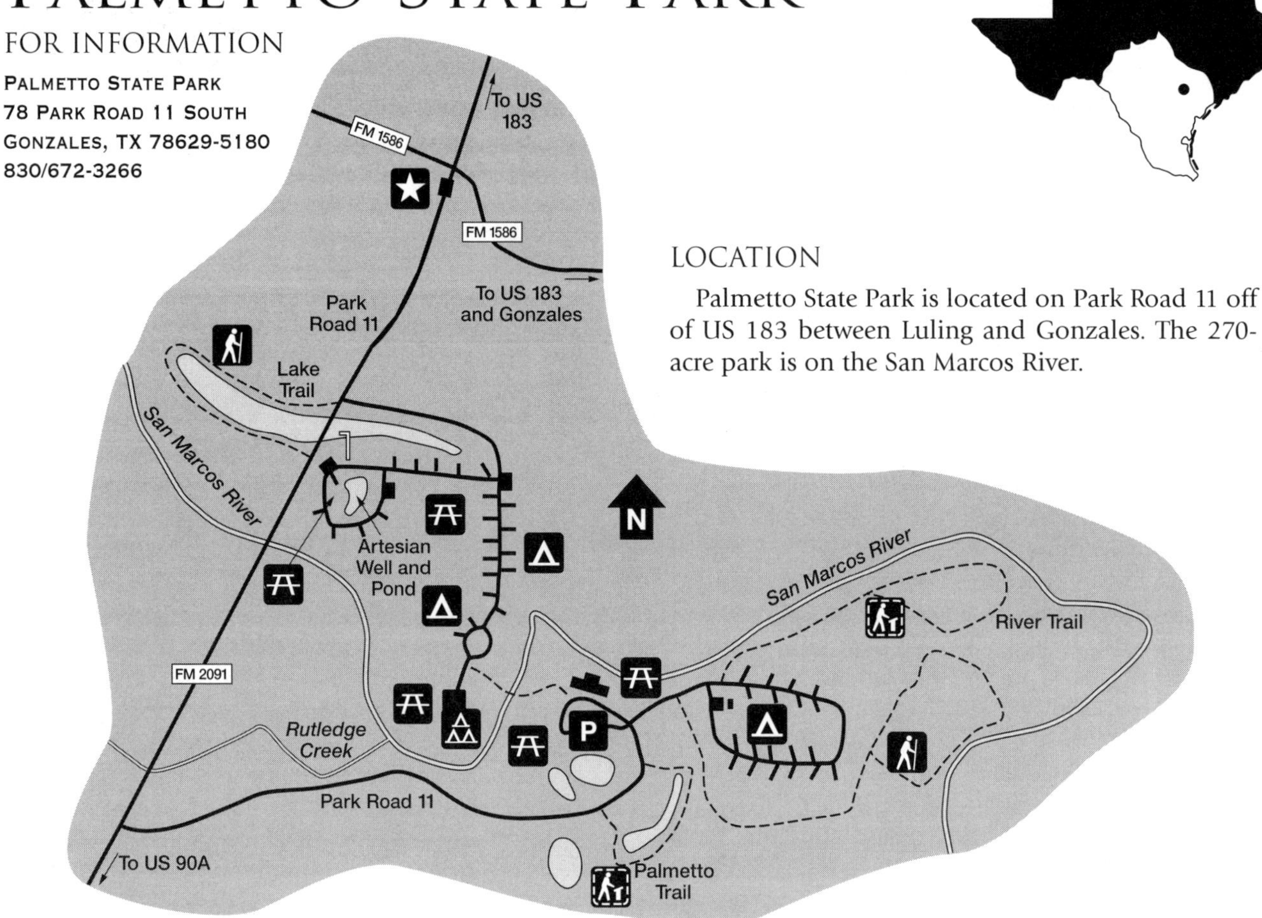

LOCATION

Palmetto State Park is located on Park Road 11 off of US 183 between Luling and Gonzales. The 270-acre park is on the San Marcos River.

TRAIL NOTES

The park has 2 nature trails and 2 hiking trails that total nearly 3 miles: the ⅓-mile Palmetto Trail, the ⅔-mile River Trail, the ⅔-mile Lake Trail, and a 1¼-mile hiking trail. The trails are canopied with trees covered in Spanish moss and vines, while the ground is thick with palmetto and other low-growing shrubs. Brochures available at park headquarters describe features along the trails so that visitors can better understand and enjoy the natural features of the park. Palmetto State Park and the immediate vicinity have been recognized for years as one of the birding hot spots of Texas. Approximately 240 species of birds have been observed in and around the park.

The ⅓-mile Palmetto Trail closely resembles a tropical botanical garden; during the rainy season it even resembles a rain forest.

Pedernales Falls State Park

FOR INFORMATION

Pedernales Falls State Park
2585 Park Rd. 6026
Johnson City, TX 78636
830/868-7304

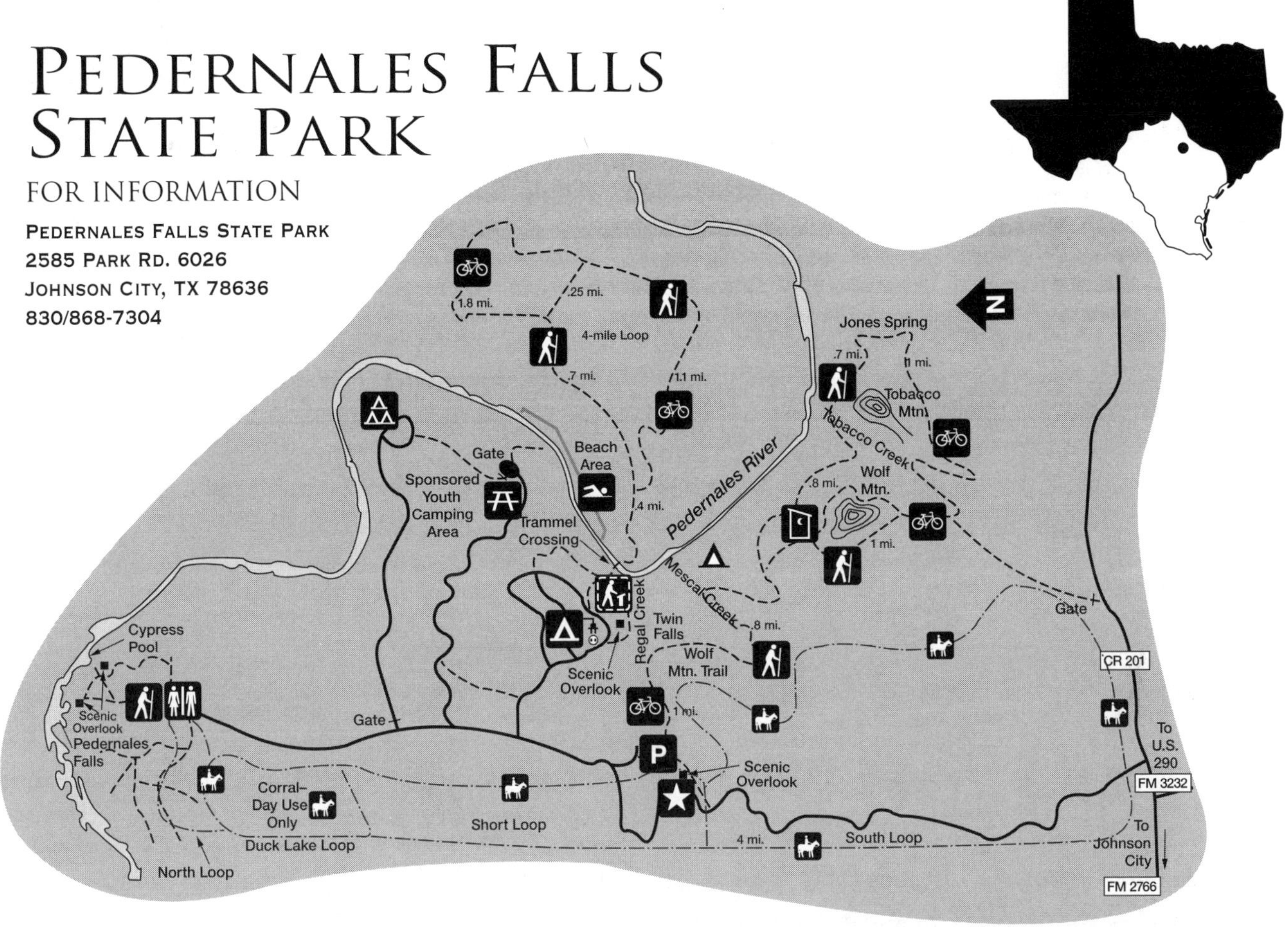

LOCATION

Pedernales Falls State Park may be reached by traveling 9 miles east of Johnson City on FM 2766, or by traveling west of Austin for 32 miles on US 290, then north on FM 3232 for 6 miles. The 5,211-acre park stretches along both banks of the Pedernales River for 6 miles and for an additional 3 miles along the south side of a rugged and picturesque gorge known as the Pedernales Falls.

The falls may be viewed from a scenic overlook, but most folks enjoy a closer look.

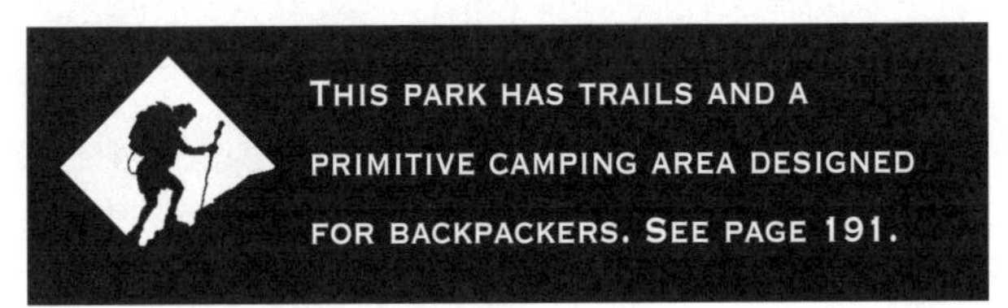

This park has trails and a primitive camping area designed for backpackers. See page 191.

TRAIL NOTES

The falls are the park's main attraction and may be viewed from a scenic overlook at the north end of the park; a wide, well-maintained trail leads from the parking lot to the overlook. In this area, the elevation of the river drops about 50 feet over a distance of 3,000 feet. Swimming, tubing, and wading are not permitted 1 mile upstream and 2 miles downstream from the scenic overlook.

Trails lead to the river from the parking lots at the camping area, picnic area, and swimming area; trails have also been created from foot traffic along the river in these areas. A nature trail makes a 1.4-mile loop adjacent to the campground; a viewing platform overlooking twin falls is located along this trail. The 7½-mile loop, known as Wolf Mountain Trail, is popular amoung serious hikers, mountain bikers, and backpackers. Trails are also available across the river for hikers and bikers; the location known as Trammel Crossing is usually the most shallow area to wade across. Hikers and bikers have a total of about 20 miles of trails available for this use. The trailhead for a 10-mile equestrian trail is the corral west of the park road to the overlook; this trail is designated for horses only.

Santa Ana National Wildlife Refuge

For Information

SANTA ANA NATIONAL WILDLIFE REFUGE
RR 2, BOX 202A
ALAMO, TEXAS 78516
956/787-3079

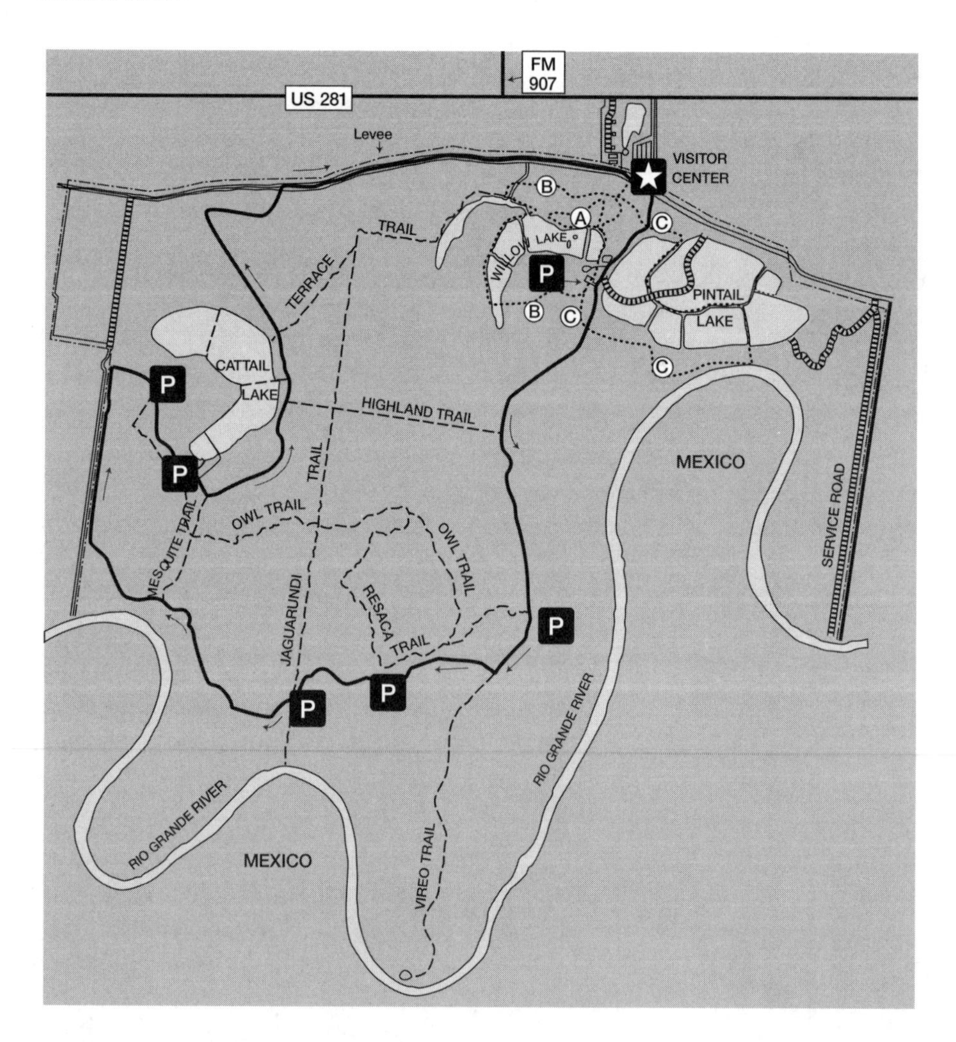

Location

Santa Ana National Wildlife Refuge is located adjacent to the Rio Grande River 13 miles from McAllen. From US 83 at Alamo, drive 7½ miles south on FM 907 to US 281. Turn east for ¼ mile on US 281 to the refuge entrance. The 2,088-acre refuge is located along the banks of the lower Rio Grande River.

DISTANCES:	MILES
REFUGE DRIVE	7.0
WILDLIFE TRAILS	
A SANTA ANA (HANDICAPPED ACCESS TRAIL)	.5
B SANTA ANA'S COMMUNITIES	1.6
C WILDLIFE MANAGEMENT	2.0
OTHER TRAILS	
CATTAIL LAKE	1.5
HIGHLAND	.6
JAGUARUNDI	1.4
MESQUITE	.3
OWL	2.0
RESACA	1.0
TERRACE	.8
VIREO	.9

Trail Notes

The trails within Santa Ana National Wildlife Refuge provide an excellent means to explore a remnant of subtropical forest, where many plants and animals are found that are seldom seen anywhere else in the United States. There are 11 interconnecting foot trails totaling 12.6 miles, as well as 7 miles of auto trail.

Foot access on the Refuge is permitted from sunrise to sunset. Proper clothing and insect repellant are helpful. Summer months are extremely hot and humid. Picnicking on the Refuge is prohibited due to problems created for wildlife.

The 7-mile wildlife drive is open from 9 a.m. to 4 p.m. Saturday and Sunday from May through November. A 60-passenger interpretive tram is in operation from Thanksgiving to the end of April, 7 days a week. Bicycles are welcomed on the wildlife drive daily from sunrise to sunset.

The Visitor Center is open 8 a.m. to 4 p.m. except Thanksgiving, Christmas, and New Year's. An entry fee is charged except on the first Sunday of each month.

SOUTH LLANO RIVER STATE PARK

FOR INFORMATION

SOUTH LLANO RIVER STATE PARK
1927 PARK ROAD 73
JUNCTION, TX 76849-9502
325/446-3994

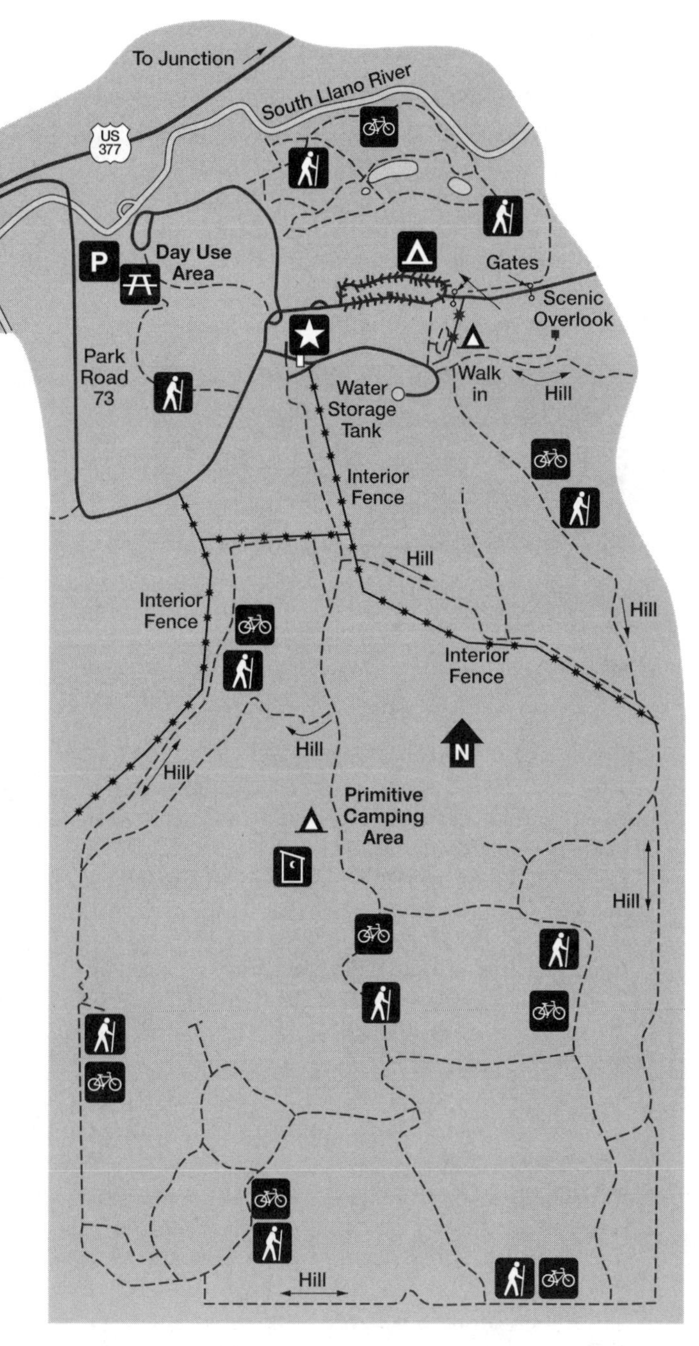

LOCATION

South Llano River State Park and the adjoining Walter Buck State Wildlife Management Area are located 5 miles south of Junction off US 377 on Park Road 73. The winding South Llano River forms the northern park boundary with 1½ miles of river frontage. The park and wildlife management area encompass 2,657 acres. The park is open year-round, except when wildlife management activities dictate closure of part of the park.

TRAIL NOTES

The riverbottom section of the park contains about 2 miles of hiking and biking trails; these are easy trails under the shade of hundreds of large pecan trees. However, this area closes to park visitors from October 1 through March each year. The Wildlife Management Area that joins the park has about 18 miles of trails for hiking and biking. These "trails" are old roads that are well-marked and well-defined; many are rather rough, making them a real challenge for bikers. This area of the park also closes to park visitors when public hunting is in season or when research projects are in progress. The closed dates change from year to year and even from week to week during various hunting seasons. When planning a trip to the park that involves hiking in the Wildlife Management Area, phone the park ahead of time for current information.

There are 6 walk-in camping sites located 30–70 yards from the parking area. Water is available and each site includes a picnic table and fire grill. This area is limited to 4 persons per site.

Wild Basin Wilderness Preserve

For Information

Wild Basin Wilderness Preserve
805 N. Capital of Texas Hwy.
Austin, TX 78711
512/327-7622

Location

The entrance to Wild Basin is on Loop 360, 1¼ miles north of Bee Cave Road, or 3¼ miles south of the bridge on Lake Austin. This 227-acre tract of beautiful Austin Hill Country is ideally situated on Bee Creek on the Balcones escarpment at a point where three major ecologic zones meet.

This preserve is a safe haven for wildlife.

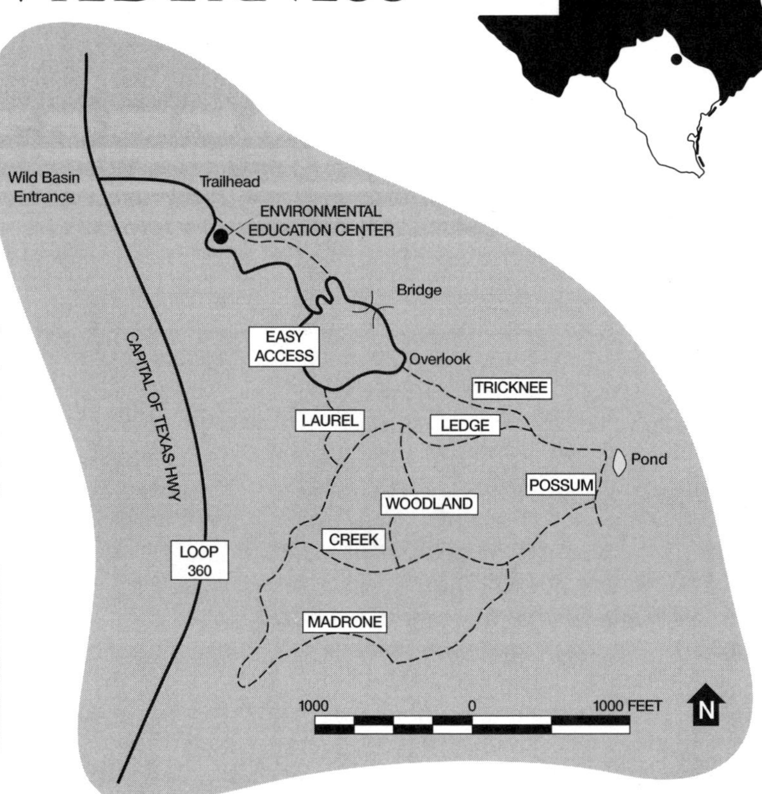

Trail Notes

Wild Basin is home to several endangered species of plants, animals, and birds as well as hundreds of commonly found species. The area has been set aside for the preservation of its natural resources through active management, education and research. About 2½ miles of trails pass through woodland, grassland, and stream-side habitats. The trails include:

- ▲ **Easy Access**—designed for mobility impaired and ideal for a less strenuous walk; benches every 300 feet, no steep inclines. This natural trail changes with the weather; call about accessibility.
- ▲ **Laurel**—named for the Texas mountain laurels found along a portion of this trail; steep incline down to Ledge.
- ▲ **Tricknee**—steep and rocky from the overlook to the intersection of Ledge and Possum trails.
- ▲ **Ledge**—level and wide through a grassland in the center of the preserve. Intersects with Laurel to the waterfall on the Preserve's southwest corner.
- ▲ **Possum**—winding through Spanish oaks and ash junipers, connects with Creek in the Cedar Elm Grove.
- ▲ **Creek**—follows Bee Creek, crossing it twice over stepping stones; features waterfall and plunge pool.
- ▲ **Woodland**—cool, shady, and winding, along a wet weather creek; seldom traveled and private.
- ▲ **Madrone**—a restricted area accessible only by special guided tour to see the unique madrone trees.

Trails maps are available in the office. *Foot traffic only,* no bikes or motorized vehicles, except wheelchairs and strollers on the Easy Access Trail.

Wild Basin is open every day from sunup to sunset. Entrance fees are not collected, but donations are accepted; it is supported largely by contributions of individuals who become members of Wild Basin because of their interest in protecting unique and scenic areas. The environmental education center provides classroom space for students and continuing education programs; it also has a small gift shop. Guided tours are offered every Saturday from 10 to 11:30 a.m. and Sunday from 1 to 2:30 p.m. Tours cover a wide range of interesting topics for all ages, such as birding and animal tracking; geology; wildflowers and native plants; reptiles and amphibians; insects; hiking for exercise; and moonlight and stargazing. These programs are led by trained volunteer guides and are $3 for adults and $1 for children ages 5–12. Phone 512/327-7622 for more details.

Cathy Murphy

TEXAS HIGHWAYS Magazine

Phil Gavenda

◤In Big Bend, this plant is called the Century Plant; in Mexico it is also known as agave, maguey, and mescal.

▲Unless they live in the Texas Panhandle, most Texans never see Palo Duro Canyon State Park in the snowy season.

◀Close up views of El Capitan (8,085 feet) and Guadalupe Peak (8,749 feet) from the El Capitan Trail. Guadalupe Peak, on the right, is the highest mountain in Texas.

Mickey Little

▲Sunset at Inks Lake . . . one of the six lakes in the Highland Lakes that stair-step up the Colorado River from Austin.

◀The Maple Trail is a developed nature trail at Lost Maples that follows the Sabinal River for 4/10 of a mile.

▼A proud fisherman displays his catch of the day.

Mickey Little

Texas Parks & Wildlife Dept. © 2004

Texas Parks & Wildlife Dept. © 2004

▲Bicycling at Hill Country State Natural Area can present a few challenges.

Mickey Little

▲Springtime in East Texas is almost synonymous with flowering dogwood trees.

▼Prickly pear and yucca thrive in the same terrain as the Texas bluebonnet.

Mickey Little

Texas Parks & Wildlife Dept. © 2004

TEXAS HIGHWAYS Magazine

▲The 3.8-mile round-trip hike to Mule Ears starts at on overlook along Big Bend's Ross Maxwell Scenic Drive.

◀The bigtooth maples, or canyon maples, can yield spectacular displays of fall color.

▼The hiking trail at the Walnut Ridge Unit of Martin Dies, Jr. State Park crosses this bridge.

Mickey Little

Mickey Little

▲The urge to toss bits of bread to the seagulls is irresistible.

▼Time-lapse photography of Big Bend's Casa Grande Peak from the Basin campground yields awesome results.

Phil Gavenda

TEXAS HIGHWAYS Magazine

▼A impressive view of Guadalupe Peak and El Capitan from the Williams Ranch side of Guadalupe Mountains National Park.

Mickey Little

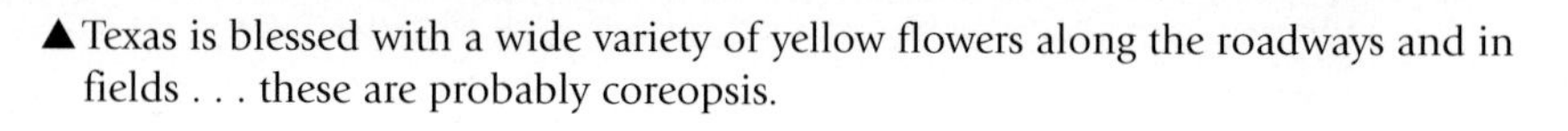

▲Texas is blessed with a wide variety of yellow flowers along the roadways and in fields . . . these are probably coreopsis.

Mickey Little

▲Everyone—even non-Texans—knows that the bluebonnet is the state flower of Texas.

▼Fishing at sunset on an East Texas lake.

TEXAS HIGHWAYS Magazine

TEXAS HIGHWAYS Magazine

Texas Parks & Wildlife Dept. © 2004

Mickey Little

◤Camping at Ratcliff Recreation Area in the Davy Crockett National Forest.

▲Honey Creek is a special place; access to this protected natural area is through Guadalupe River State Park.

◀This field of flowers is predominately Gaillardia—commonly known as firewheel or Indian blanket.

Phil Gavenda

▲Juniper Canyon is visible from the Lost Mine Trail in Big Bend National Park. On a clear day, Mexico can be seen near the horizon.

Mickey Little

▼Several hiking trails at Lake Livingston State Park have bridge crossings.

TEXAS HIGHWAYS Magazine

▼Horses provide a dry means of crossing a stream.

OTHER TRAILS IN REGION 3

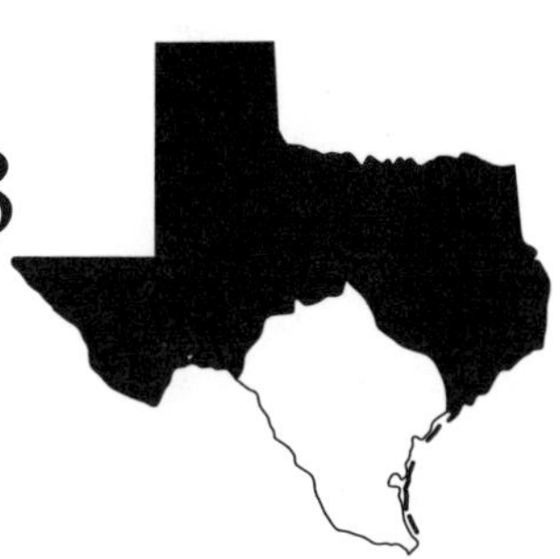

AUSTIN **Hike & Bike Trails**

▲ Austin Parks and Recreation oversees over 190 parks, 11 preserves, and 24 greenbelts that run along scenic creeks. Over 56 parks and greenbelts offer trails for walking, hiking, and biking; 20 of them have trails over a mile long. Some of the longest trails are:

11.2 miles—Walnut Creek Park (secondary)
10.1 miles—Town Lake Hike & Bike Trail
9.13 miles—Emma Long Metro Park (bike course)
7.5 miles—Barton Creek Greenbelt
5.26 miles—Walnut Creek Park (main)
4.62 miles—Shoal Creek Greenbelt & Pease Park
3.73 miles—Mary Moore Searight Park
3.43 miles—Lower Bull Creek Greenbelt & District Park

City of Austin
Parks and Recreation Department
Box 1088
Austin, TX 78767-8833
512/974-6700

AUSTIN **National Wildflower Research Center**

▲ Follow the Seed Court Trail to the 23 Display Gardens; stroll along the ¼-mile Forest Trail and the ¼-mile Meadow Trail. Then view the unique gardens and grounds from the Observation Tower and Cistern. Picnic areas are available.

National Wildflower Research Center
4801 LaCrosse Avenue
Austin, TX 78739
512/292-4100

BLANCO **Blanco State Park**

▲ An unimproved 0.7-mile hiking trail on an old road along the southeast side of the river in Blanco State Park.

Blanco State Park
P.O. Box 493
Blanco, TX 78606
830/833-4333

CALLIHAM **Choke Canyon State Park**

▲ There are approx. 2 miles of hiking trails at the Calliham Unit. A 1-mile portion of the trail has bird feeders.

Choke Canyon State Park
Calliham Unit
P.O. Box 2
Calliham, TX 78007
361/786-3868

Founded in 1982 by Lady Bird Johnson and the late Helen Hayes, the National Wildflower Research Center is dedicated to protecting and preserving North America's native plants and natural landscapes.

CANYON LAKE **Canyon Lake**

▲ Canyon Park has a 1.1-mile hiking trail and a 3½-mile equestrian trail; Guadalupe Park has an 0.8-mile interpretive trail.

Canyon Lake
601 C.O.E. Road
Canyon Lake, TX 78133-4112
839/964-3341

CASTROVILLE **Landmark Inn State Historic Site**

▲ 0.6-mile nature trail along the lower terraces of the Medina River form the Landmark Inn State Historic Site, where milling equipment and mill structures may be viewed.

Landmark Inn State Historic Site
402 Florence Street
Castroville, TX 78009
830/931-2133

CORPUS CHRISTI

▲ 2-mile multi-use seawall sidewalk on Shoreline Drive.

▲ 1.3-mile hiking and bicycle trail at West Guth Park.

▲ 1-mile Natural Wildlife Trail at Oso Creek.

▲ Developed trails at South Guth Park, St. Andrews Park, and Swantner Park.

▲ Birding trail at Blucher Park.

▲ 0.6-mile bicycle path at Cole Park.

▲ 5-mile bike trail at Oso Creek Parkway.

▲ 0.8-mile hiking and bicycle trail at Hans A. Suter Wildlife Area.

▲ 17-mile hike/bike Bay Trail has been planned from the Central Business District to the Texas A&M-Corpus Christi campus, Naval Air Station, and the abandoned U.S. Navy Railroad trestle in the Flour Bluff area.

Park and Recreation Department
P.O. Box 9277
Corpus Christi, TX 78469-9277
361/880-3461

DEL RIO **Amistad National Recreation Area**

▲ A self-guided nature trail is located at the Pecos River Overlook and has 17 stations; descriptive literature is available. There is also a nature trail at Diablo East.

Amistad National Recreation Area
HCR 3, Box 5J
Del Rio, TX 78840
830/775-7491

FORT MCKAVETT **Fort McKavett SHS**

▲ ¼-mile self-guided hiking trail from the parking area at Fort McKavett State Historic Site to a lime kiln, rock quarry, and "Government Springs."

Fort McKavett State Historic Site
P.O. Box 68
Fort McKavett, TX 76841
325/396-2358

FREDERICKSBURG **Admiral Nimitz SHS—National Museum of the Pacific War**

▲ 3 acres of World War II artifacts, tanks, guns, and large relics are features at the "History Walk of the Pacific War." A brochure assists with identification of numbered artifacts. Many of the items on display were actually used in combat in the Pacific.

▲ A short walk along the Memorial Wall and through the Garden of Peace, a gift from the people of Japan out of respect for Admiral Nimitz. A leaflet about the garden is available at the front desk.

Admiral Nimitz Museum State Historic Site—
National Museum of the Pacific War
P.O. Box 777
Fredericksburg, TX 78624
830/997-4379

GOLIAD **Angel of Goliad Trail**

▲ A 2½-mile hike/bike trail follows the banks of the San Antonio River from South Market Street near the Courthouse Square to the burial site of Colonel Fannin. The trail passes through Goliad State Park, crosses the river, goes past the restored Presidio La Bahia and the Angel of Goliad monument and circles the Fannin Monument. A portion of the trail is an interpretive trail.

Goliad Chamber of Commerce
361/645-3752

GOLIAD **Goliad State Park**

▲ A ⅓-mile nature trail named for the Aranama Indians who were living here when the Spaniards first arrived.

▲ A 1-mile hiking trail along the bank of the San Antonio River.

Goliad State Park
108 Park Road 6
Goliad, TX 77963-3206
361/645-3405

JOHNSON CITY **Lyndon B. Johnson National Historical Park**

▲ ¼-mile walking trail from the visitor center in the Lyndon B. Johnson National Historical Park to the Exhibit Center and the Sam Ealy Johnson Log House in the Johnson Settlement. The trail is also accessible from a parking area on US 290, just 3 blocks west of the caution signal light.

Lyndon B. Johnson National Historical Park
P.O. Box 329
Johnson City, TX 78636
830/868-7128

LA GRANGE **Monument Hill/Kreische Brewery State Historic Sites**

▲ Two trails; a ½-mile interpretive trail that begins at headquarters takes the visitor to a scenic bluff overlook trail that offers a good view of the brewery ruins; a ½-mile nature trail is east of the headquarters.

Monument Hill/Kreische Brewery State Historic Sites
414 State Loop 92
La Grange, TX 78945-5733
979/968-5658

PORT ARANSAS **Mustang Island State Park**

▲ 5 miles of beach hiking and biking at Mustang Island State Park located between Port Aransas and Corpus Christi.

Mustang Island State Park
P.O. Box 326
Port Aransas, TX 78373
361/749-5246

PORT O'CONNOR **Matagorda Island State Park**

▲ Over 80 miles of beach, roadways and mowed pathways on Matagorda Island for hiking and bicycling; motorized vehicles are not permitted. There are no concessions, no electricity, no telephone, and no drinking water on the island. All visitor access to the island is by chartered or private boat. Round-trip ferry is available through a concessionaire. There are some concessions on the ferry. Island guided tours are available. Contact the park office in Port O'Connor for maps and other information. The ferry office is located at 418 S. 16th St., Bldg. B.

Matagorda Island State Park
P.O. Box 117
Port O'Connor, TX 77982
361/983-2215

ROCKPORT **Goose Island State Park**

▲ A ¾-mile nature trail is located in the northwest area of the campground. A paved hike and bike path leads across the bridge to the camping area on the island.

Goose Island State Park
202 S. Palmetto St.
Rockport, TX 78382
361/729-2858

ROUND MOUNTAIN **Westcave Preserve**

▲ 1-mile round-trip hike at Westcave Preserve into two very different ecosystems: upper half is grassland savannah with stands of ash juniper and live oak; lower half is a lush green canyon grotto with waterfall and giant cypress trees. Tours are scheduled every Saturday and Sunday at 10 a.m., noon, 2 p.m., and 4 p.m. No reservations are taken, and tours are limited to the first 30 visitors. Picnic tables available, no pets allowed, no drinking water available. Come early and enjoy the new Warren Skaaren Environmental Learning Center. Entry fee is charged. The preserve is west of Austin on Hamilton Pool Road (FM 3238) off of SH 71 at Bee Cave, ½ mile past Hammett's Crossing on the Pedernales River.

Westcave Preserve
24814 Hamilton Pool Rd.
Round Mountain, TX 78663
830/825-3442

SAN ANTONIO **Government Canyon State Natural Area**

▲ Government Canyon State Natural Area, a recent acquisition of the Texas Parks and Wildlife Department that totals more than 8,200 acres, is located in northwest Bexar County near Helotes, TX. Construction of the State Natural Area facilities began in late 2003 and should be completed and opened to the public by late 2005. When completed a trail system totaling more than 40 miles will be provided for hiking, biking, and equestrian activities. There will also be both walk-in and backcountry (primitive) tent camping sites available. Directions: From the intersection of Loop 1604 and FM 471 (Culebra Road), travel west 3½ miles to Galm Road. Turn right on Galm Road and travel 1.6 miles; entrance with signs on the left. ***Currently Government Canyon SNA is NOT open to the public pending completion of development.***

Government Canyon State Natural Area
12861 Galm Road
San Antonio, TX 78254
210/688-9055

SAN ANTONIO **Park Trails**

▲ There are 47 parks in San Antonio that offer trails for walking, hiking, jogging, and biking; they total 53 miles. Six of the longest trails are:

7.2 miles—Mission Parkway (100 Mission Road)
6.4 miles—Eisenhower Park (19399 N.W. Military Hwy.)
4.5 miles—O. P. Schnabel Park (9606 Bandera)
4.4 miles—Friedrich Park (21480 Milsa Road)
3.8 miles—Leon Creek Greenway (12160 Blanco Road)
3.0 miles—McAllister Park (13102 Jones Maltsberger)

San Antonio Parks and Recreation Department
P.O. Box 839966
San Antonio, TX 78283
210/207-2879

SAN ANTONIO **San Antonio Missions NHP**

▲ 7.1-mile Mission Hike/Bike Trail is a paved trail that winds through an impressive concentration of eighteenth-century Spanish colonial architecture nestled along the historic banks of the San Antonio River, linking the 5 missions that were established by Spanish padres.

▲ ⅓-mile loop trail, the San Juan Woodlands Trail, is located at Mission San Juan; it showcases the flora and fauna of the San Antonio River riparian environment.

San Antonio Missions National Historical Park
2202 Roosevelt Avenue
San Antonio, TX 78210-4919
210/932-1001

SPRING BRANCH **Honey Creek State Natural Area**

▲ 1-mile guided hikes and 2-mile guided hikes are available at Honey Creek State Natural Area most Saturdays at 9 a.m. Tour emphasis varies: native grass identification, wildflower and native plant tour, and cultural, biological, and geological history of the Hill Country. There is no fee but donations are encouraged. Access to Honey Creek is through Guadalupe River State Park.

Honey Creek State Natural Area
c/o Guadalupe River State Park
3350 Park Road 31
Spring Branch, TX 78070
830/438-2656

STONEWALL **Lyndon B. Johnson State Park and Historic Site**

▲ A 1.2-mile interpretive nature trail winds past wildlife enclosures stocked with bison, white-tailed deer, and longhorn cattle and the Sauer-Beckmann Farmstead, a Living History Farm.

Lyndon B. Johnson State Park and Historic Site
P.O. Box 238
Stonewall, TX 78671
830/644-2252

VICTORIA **Coleto Creek Reservoir**

▲ ½-mile self-guided nature trail that includes both a wetland site and a prairie/wooded area.

▲ 1-mile hiking trail along the shore of the Coleto Creek Reservoir. The terrain is flat to gently rolling; dominant vegetation is oak, upland grasses, mesquite and huisache.

Coleto Creek Reservoir & Park
365 Coleto Park Rd.
Victoria, TX 77905
361/575-6366

The Sauer-Beckmann Farmstead at the LBJ State Historic Site is a Living History Farm. Life is presented as it was in 1918. Tours of the complex last approximately an hour.

REGION 4

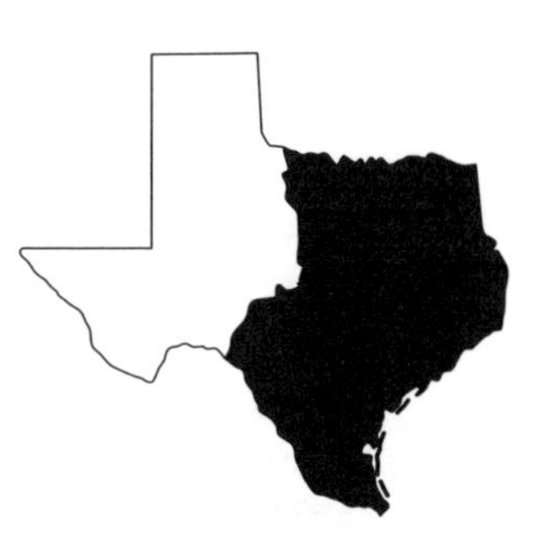

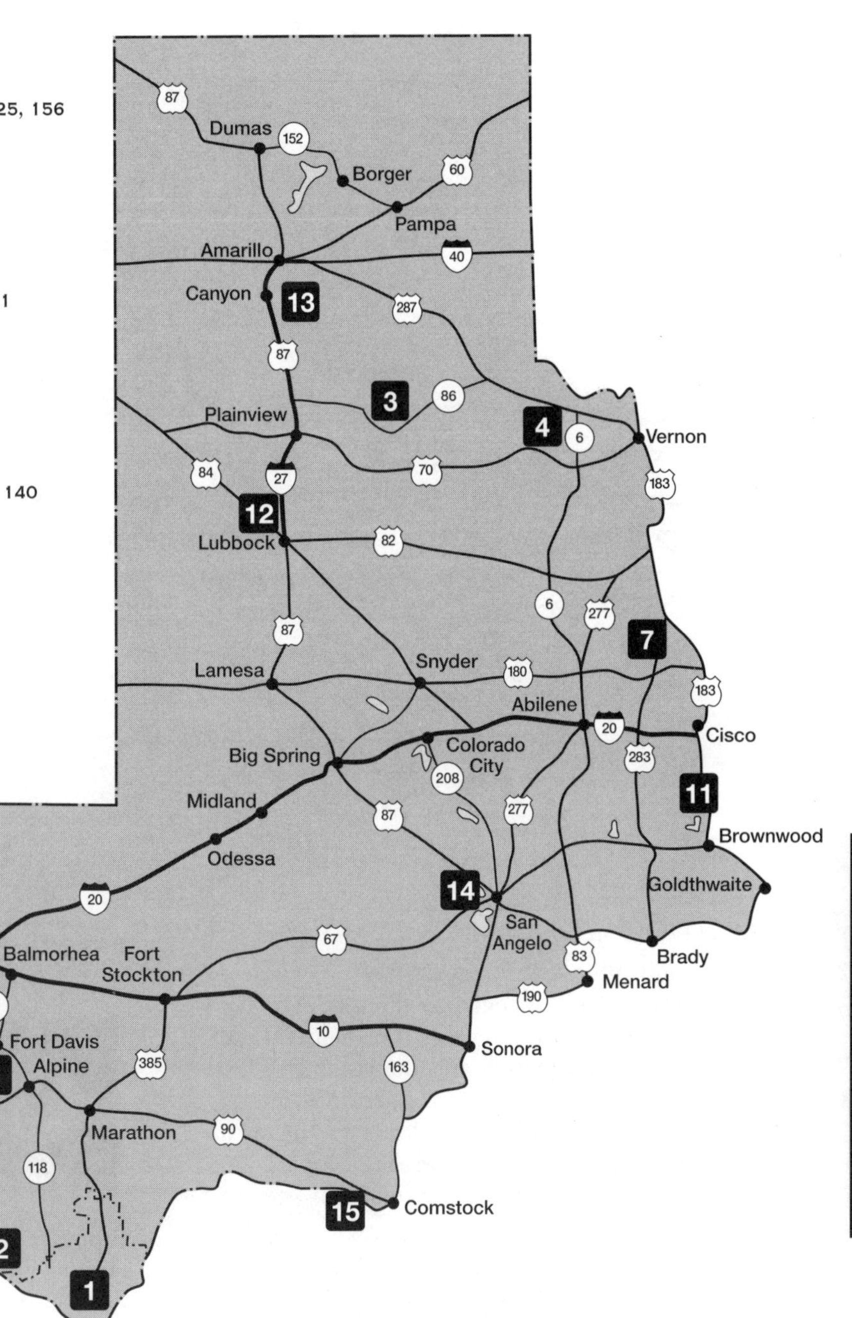

REGION 4

Big Bend National Park

FOR INFORMATION

Big Bend National Park
P.O. Box 129
Big Bend National Park, TX 79834-0129
432/477-2251 Visitor Center/Park Headquarters

LOCATION

Big Bend National Park encompasses a vast area of 801,163 acres and is edged on three sides by the "big bend" of the Rio Grande, the international boundary between Mexico and the United States. US 385 leads from Marathon to the north entrance; TX 118 from Alpine leads to the west entrance; and RR 170, from Presidio, joins TX 118 at Study Butte before the west entrance.

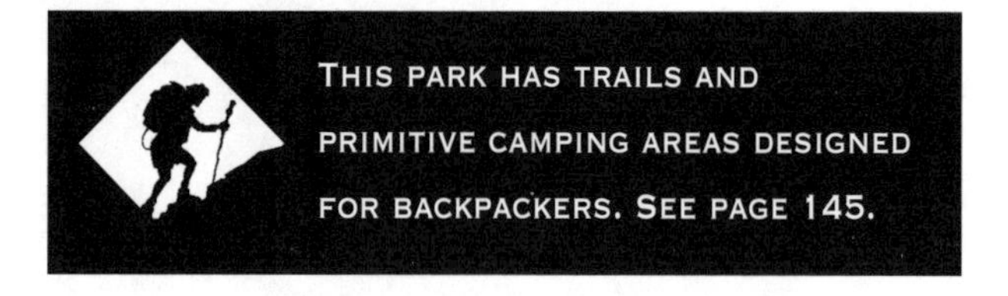

ABOUT THE PARK

The park can be thought of as having 3 natural divisions: the river, the desert, and the mountains. The Rio Grande River, often referred to as a linear oasis, defines the park's southern boundary for 107 miles. The park is 97% Chihuahuan Desert; the Chisos Mountains interrupt it as a green island in a desert sea. At 4,500 feet the first trees begin to appear; higher up in the drainages you see masses of trees—junipers, small oak trees, and pinyon pines.

Winter is nippy in the mountains and comfortably warm during the day in the lowlands. Once or twice a year snow falls in the mountains. Spring weather arrives early with a slow succession of blooms beginning in late February and reaching the mountains' heights in May. Some desert plants bloom throughout the year.

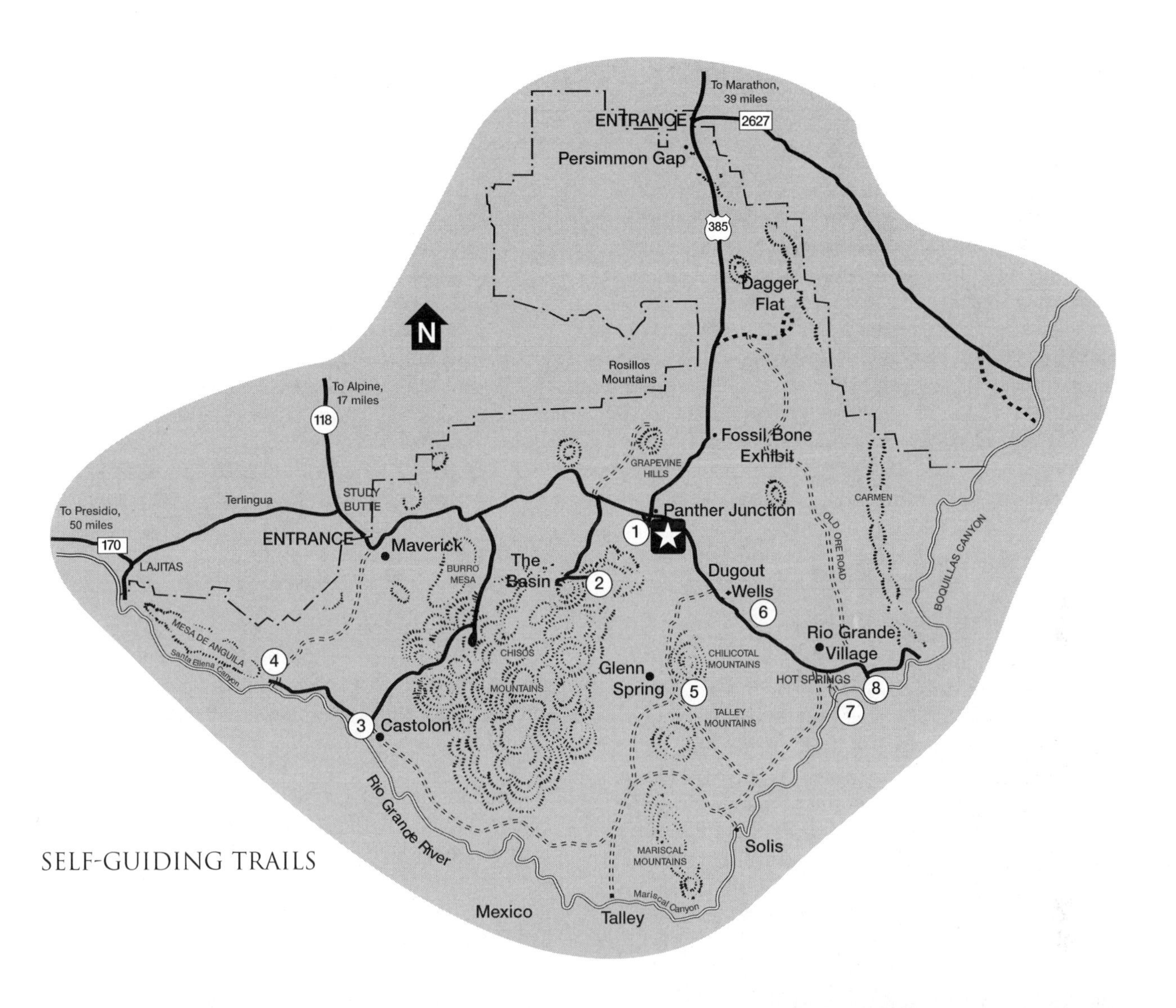

SELF-GUIDING TRAILS

HIKER'S LEGEND

Easy Walking—Trail developed and well defined. Easy grades. All ages. Street shoes or sneakers okay.

Medium Difficulty—Trail sometimes poorly defined. Can include steep grades and/or long distances. Not recommended for those with heart trouble or other physical problems. Hiking boots recommended.

Strenuous Day Hike—For experienced, conditioned hikers only. Rough trails and longer distances. Sturdy hiking boots are a necessity.

Strenuous, Backpackers only—Knowledge of map reading, compass usage, and desert conditions are required. Experienced backpackers only.

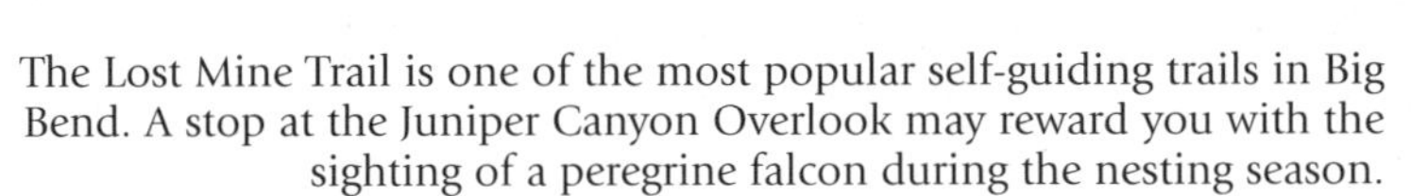
The Lost Mine Trail is one of the most popular self-guiding trails in Big Bend. A stop at the Juniper Canyon Overlook may reward you with the sighting of a peregrine falcon during the nesting season.

TRAIL NOTES

Trails at Big Bend National Park are classified as self-guiding trails, developed trails, and primitive routes. The descriptions of trails in this section are for the self-guiding trails and all of the developed trails other than those of the High Chisos Complex. For information on the developed trails in the High Chisos Complex and the primitive routes, please refer to pages 145–152 in the backpacking section of this book. Those day-hikers in good physical condition will, no doubt, enjoy exploring some of these trails.

The descriptions of the trails that appear in this section are abbreviated from the publication entitled *Hiker's Guide to Trails of Big Bend National Park* published by the Big Bend Natural History Association in cooperation with the National Park Service. Permission has been granted to cite this material.

Desert hiking is one of Big Bend's most rewarding experiences, but such exploring requires special precautions:

1. Protect yourself from the sun. Wear a hat, long pants, and a long-sleeved shirt.
2. Don't rely on springs, no matter what the map says. Carry plenty of water and drink often, even if you don't feel thirsty.
3. Travel as the animals do, in the morning or evening, rather than during the heat of the day.
4. Watch the weather. Even distant rain can cause flash floods where you are.

SELF-GUIDING TRAILS

All walks in this section have short leaflets or interpretive signs to introduce you to special features along the trail. Although most are short and easy, don't forget to take along a canteen of water in summer.

No. 1—Panther Path (Easy walking; fifty-yard loop trail) Fifteen minutes spent on this level trail at the visitor center will acquaint you with many cacti and other common plants that inhabit the Chihuahuan Desert.

No. 2—Lost Mine Trail (Medium difficulty; 4.8 miles round-trip.) Beginning at Panther Pass on the Basin Road, this trail starts at 5600′ elevation and leads upward along the northern slope of Casa Grande to a promontory high on the ridge separating Pine and Juniper Canyons.

If you have limited time, hike only to the Juniper Canyon Overlook , 1 mile from the trailhead, for one of the finest views in the park.

TEXAS HIGHWAYS Magazine

An abundance of colorful flowers make hiking in the Basin even more enjoyable.

No. 3—Castolon Historic Compound (Easy walking; ¼ mile.) Most of the buildings in this historic settlement were originally built as part of a cavalry encampment during the days of Pancho Villa's border raids.

No. 4—Santa Elena Canyon Trail (Easy walking; 1.7 miles round-trip.) The trail begins at the end of the Ross Maxwell Scenic Drive, and is one of the prettiest short walks in the park. Once across the creek, the trail climbs a flight of concrete steps, then slopes gradually down to the river's edge inside the canyon. This is one of the narrowest places in the 7-mile long Santa Elena Canyon.

No. 5—Glenn Spring (Easy walking; ½ mile.) This old settlement is available only by primitive dirt road. Check with a ranger about road conditions before you go. No trail, but the leaflet contains a map to guide you through the vanished settlement.

No. 6—Chihuahuan Desert Nature Trail (Easy walking; 0.5 miles round-trip.) Located 5.9 miles east of Panther Junction at Dugout Wells, this easy trail winds through typical shrub desert habitat and serves as an excellent introduction to the vast Chihuahuan Desert.

No. 7—Hot Springs Historic Walk (Easy walking; 2 miles round-trip.) Located at the end of a 2-mile improved dirt road, this interesting walk is a must for history buffs and nature lovers alike.

No. 8—Rio Grande Village Nature Trail (Easy walking; 0.4-mile loop trail.) Beginning in the southeastern corner of the Rio Grande Village Campground, this trail passes through the dense, jungle-like vegetation of the river floodplain, then climbs abruptly into the arid desert environment. A high promontory provides panoramic views along the Rio Grande and south into Mexico.

DEVELOPED TRAILS

The trails listed in this section are all well-defined and easy to follow. They serve as excellent introductory hikes for newcomers to Big Bend. If the trail starts on a primitive road, be sure to check road conditions before starting.

No. 9—Tuff Canyon (Easy walking; ¾-mile round-trip.) Tuff Canyon is located west of the Ross Maxwell Scenic Drive, 5 miles south of the Mule Ears Overlook spur road. The trail begins on your left as you face Tuff Canyon from the parking area and leads you to the bottom of Tuff Canyon.

No. 10—Burro Spring Trail (Easy walking; 2.2 miles round-trip.) The trail starts along the spur road leading to the Burro Mesa Pour-off parking area (see Hike No. 11). This easy-to-follow desert trail leads to an overlook above one of the better springs in this part of the park.

No. 11—Burro Mesa Pour-Off (Easy walking; 1 mile round-trip.) The trail begins at the parking area below Sotol Vista along the Ross Maxwell Scenic Drive, at the end of the paved Burro Mesa spur road. The pour-off is at the head of the narrow box canyon to the right, and can be reached by a trail that is delightful even in summer, since it is shaded most of the day.

No. 12—Grapevine Hills Trail (Easy walking; 2.2 miles round-trip.) Beginning 6 miles down the Grapevine Hills improved dirt road, this trail leads into the heart of Grapevine Hills, following a sandy wash through massive granite boulders to a low pass at the south end of the drainage. A picturesque "window" of boulders can be found by following a series of metal stakes for 100 yards to the right of the pass.

No. 13—Pine Canyon Trail (Medium difficulty; 2.0 miles round-trip.) The trail begins at the end of the Pine Canyon primitive road. The trail continues up the canyon and winds through a heavily wooded section where Mexican pinyon, junipers, oaks, ponderosa pine, Texas madrone, bigtooth maple, and Emory and Graves oaks are common. The trail ends at the base of a 200-foot cliff that becomes a delightful waterfall after heavy rainstorms.

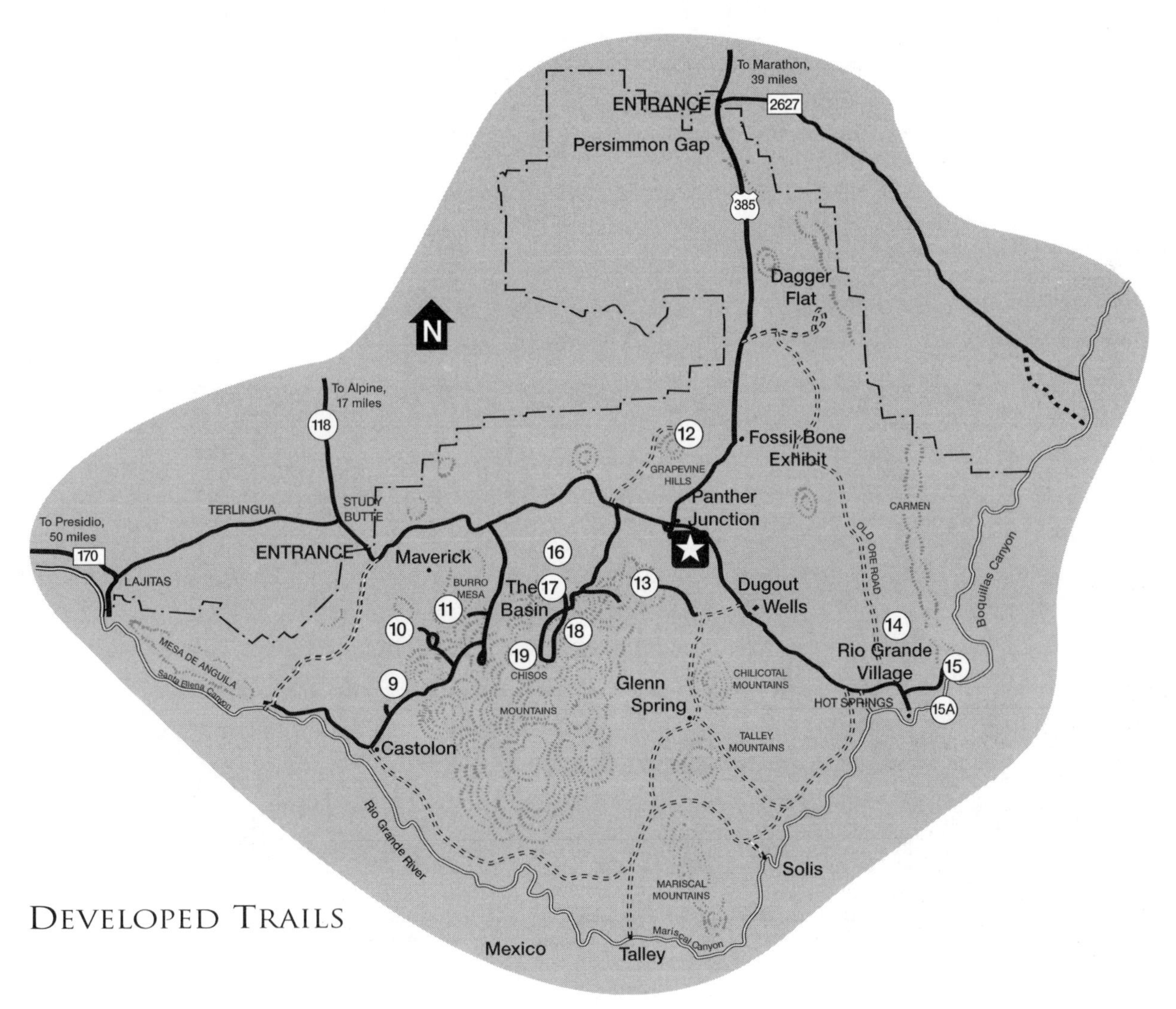

DEVELOPED TRAILS

REGION 4

No. 14—Ernst Tinaja (Easy walking; 1 mile round-trip.) The trail begins at the end of the Ernst Tinaja spur road, which leaves the Old Ore Road about 5 miles from its southern end. Both are primitive dirt roads. Check with a ranger on their condition before attempting to drive these roads. Walk up the canyon to the huge, natural tinaja (Spanish for "big earthen jar") that is carved into the massive limestone cliffs.

No. 15—Boquillas Canyon Trail (Easy walking; 1.4 miles round-trip.) Starting from a parking area at the end of the Boquillas Canyon spur road, the trail climbs over a low hill and drops down to the river near a group of Indian bedrock mortar holes. Just past this point is a huge sand slide formed by down-canyon winds that pile loose sand against the canyon wall on the Texas side, below a shallow cave.

No. 15A—Hot Springs Canyon Trail (Medium difficulty; 6.0 miles round-trip.) This 3.0 mile one-way trail connects the Daniels Ranch area at Rio Grande Village with the Hot Springs Historic Area. There is no shade so avoid it during the summer heat. A sign at Daniels Ranch marks the trailhead. The trail winds up the side of a limestone cliff before leveling out along the top of Hot Springs Canyon. Steep cliffs prevent access to the river itself.

No. 16—The Window Trail (Medium difficulty; 5.2 miles round-trip.) The trail starts at the Basin Trailhead, but can also be picked up from the Basin Campground, in which case the distance is 4 miles round-trip. The trail passes through an area of open chaparral vegetation before dropping into Oak Creek Canyon and following it to where it narrows down to only 20 feet at the base of the Window. This is where the drainage from the basin pours out into lower Oak Creek.

No. 17—Window View Trail (Easy walking; 0.3 miles.) The trail begins at the Chisos Basin Trailhead and circles the low hill to the west. Benches have been placed at several places along the trail. A stroll on this trail is excellent in the evening. The setting sun through the Window is uniquely Big Bend.

No. 18—Chisos Basin Loop Trail (Easy walking; 1.6 miles round-trip.) This route starts at the Basin Trailhead and follows the Laguna Meadow trail for ¾ mile before branching off to the left. It reaches a promontory overlooking the upper Chisos Basin, then heads back toward the Basin via the Boot Springs (Pinnacles) Trail.

No. 19—High Chisos Complex. This section includes all of the Chisos Mountain trails between the Basin Trailhead and the South Rim, and Juniper and Blue Creek Canyons as well (see pages 145–152). These high country trails are some of the park's most attractive hikes. During summer, the Chisos highlands provide a cool retreat from the warmer lowlands.

These hikers, at the Tuff Canyon trailhead, read the information on the interpretive display. Notice Santa Elena Canyon on the horizon; that will be their next destination.

Big Bend Ranch State Park

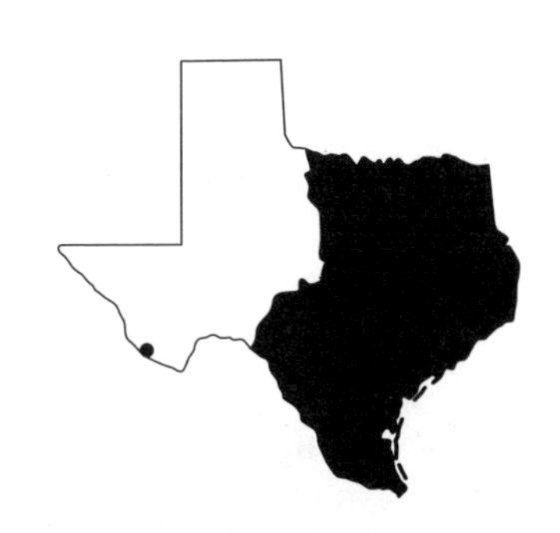

FOR INFORMATION

BIG BEND RANCH STATE PARK COMPLEX
P.O. BOX 2319
PRESIDIO, TX 79845
432/229-3416

BIG BEND RANCH STATE PARK
SAUCEDA
432/358-4444

BARTON WARNOCK EDUCATION CENTER
432/424-3327

FORT LEATON STATE HISTORIC SITE
432/229-3613

LOCATION

Big Bend Ranch State Park lies both south and north of RR 170 between Lajitas and Redford. RR 170, called "El Camino del Rio," parallels the Rio Grande River and offers one of the most scenic drives in Texas.

Some of the rapids on the portion of the Rio Grande that flows through the state park boundaries are quite challenging.

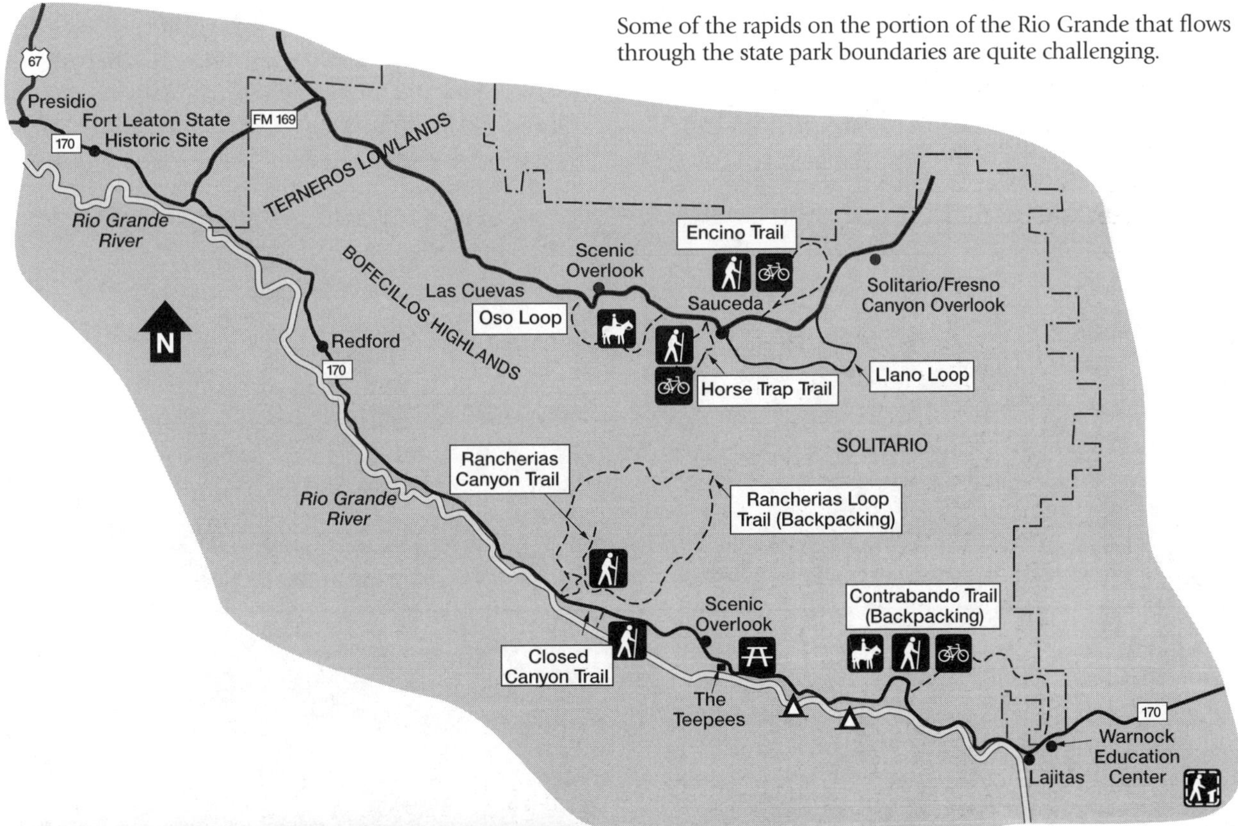

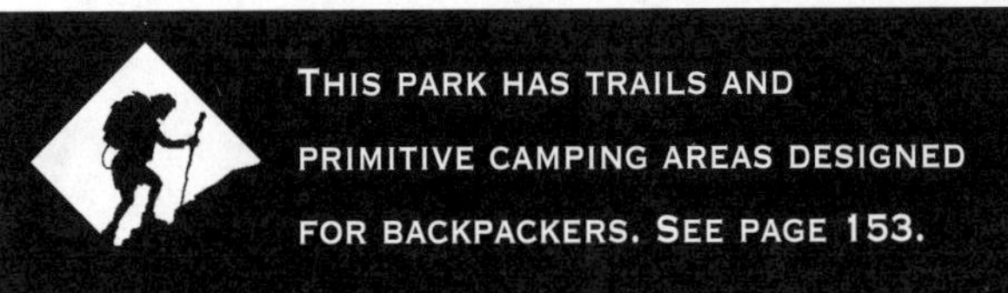
THIS PARK HAS TRAILS AND PRIMITIVE CAMPING AREAS DESIGNED FOR BACKPACKERS. SEE PAGE 153.

REGION 4

LOCATION

Big Bend Ranch State Park is located just west of Big Bend National Park. The 299,623-acre park lies both south and north of FM 170, which parallels the Rio Grande River for 23 miles between Lajitas and Redford. FM 170, called "El Camino del Rio," offers one of the most spectacular drives in Texas. Contact points for the Big Bend Ranch State Park Complex include Fort Leaton State Historic Site, which is 4 miles southeast of Presidio on FM 170 (River Road), and Barton Warnock Education Center, located just east of Lajitas on FM 170.

To enter the interior, visitors must contact either the Big Bend complex office or Fort Leaton or the Warnock Center to obtain permits, pay fees, and *receive instructions for vehicular access into the interior of the park.* The interior is reached by traveling east on FM 170 from Fort Leaton for about 4 miles, and turning left onto a dirt road called Casa Piedra Road (FM 169). When the road forks, turn right where the sign says Big Bend Ranch and follow the main road to the locked entrance gate. It is 28 miles from the turnoff on FM 170 to Sauceda, the old ranch headquarters. An additional 7 miles to the Solitario viewpoint are open to visitors; high-clearance vehicles are recommended.

TRAIL NOTES

A self-guided 2½-acre botanical garden at the Warnock Center allows visitors to walk among the characteristic plants of the Chihuahuan Desert. The center is open every day from 8 a.m. to 5 p.m.; an admission fee is charged for the museum and gardens. Two trails, suitable for day-hikes, are the Closed Canyon Trail (1.4 miles round-trip) and the Rancherias Canyon Trail (9.8 miles round-trip). Both trails are in the Colorado Canyon area west of Lajitas with access from FM 170; both trails are entirely in a canyon bottom so *hikers should be aware of the potential for flash floods.* Also accessible from FM 170, are 3 primitive camping areas that have river access, and 2 primitive camping areas for groups.

Three short hiking trails and 2 longer hike/bike trails are located off the gravel road into the park interior. Ten primitive drive-in backcountry camping areas are located along this 35-mile interior road; a high-clearance vehicle is needed. Mountain bikes are permitted on 26+ miles of trails. Get details from the park ranger for the location of each of these activities when you get your permit to enter the interior.

Texas Highways Magazine

With over 399,000 acres of Chihuahuan Desert wilderness, Big Bend Ranch State Park embraces some of the most remote and rugged terrain in the Southwest. It encompasses two mountain ranges containing ancient extinct volcanoes, precipitous canyons, and waterfalls.

CAPROCK CANYONS STATE PARK AND TRAILWAY

FOR INFORMATION

CAPROCK CANYONS STATE PARK AND TRAILWAY
P.O. BOX 204
QUITAQUE, TX 79255
806/455-1492

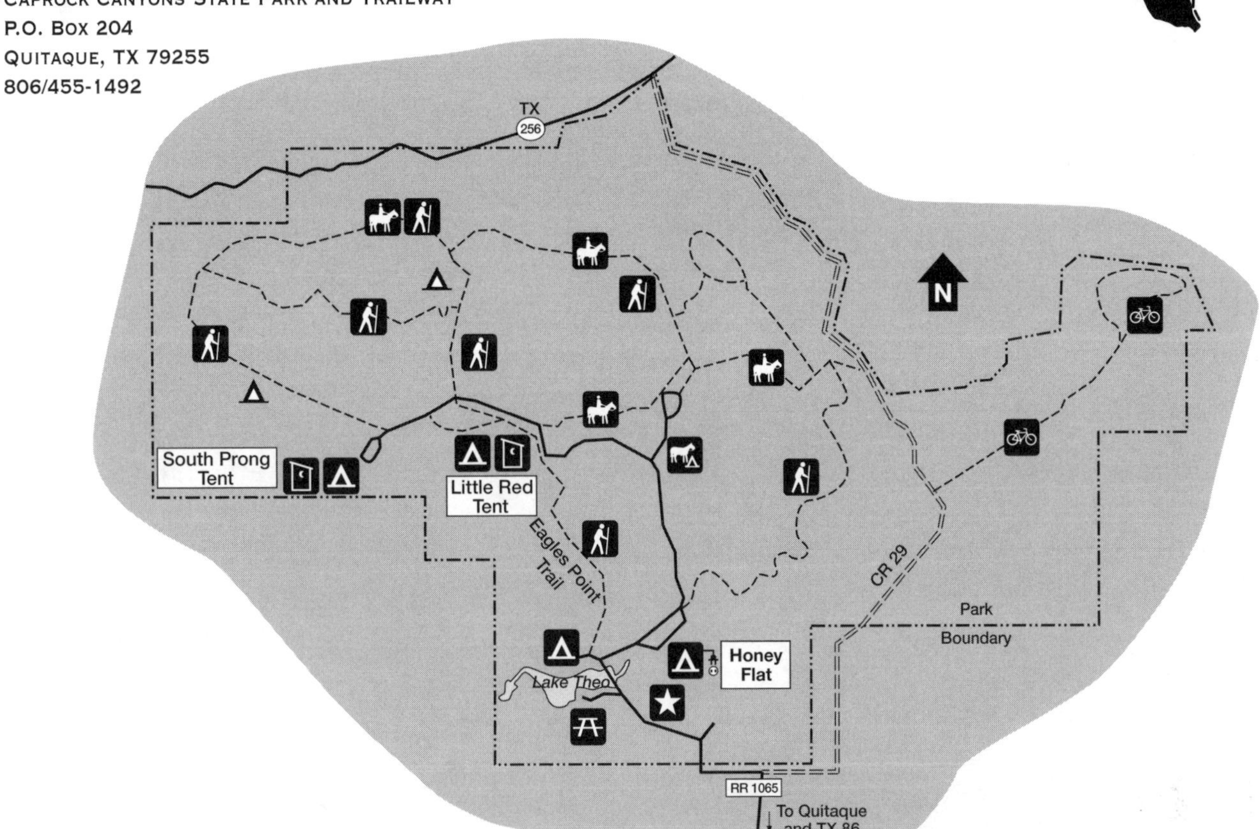

LOCATION

Caprock Canyons State Park and Trailway is located 3 miles north of the town of Quitaque (pronounced "kít-uh-kwa"). Although bordered on the north by TX 256, the park entrance is on the south and most easily accessible by traveling north through Quitaque on RR 1065. Quitaque is on TX 86, which runs east from I-27/US 87 at Tulia and west from US 287 at Estelline. Lake Theo, a 120-acre lake, is a feature attraction. The 15,160-acre park is named for the scenic and rugged escarpment that separates the tablelands of the Southern High Plains from the breaks and rolling plains to the east.

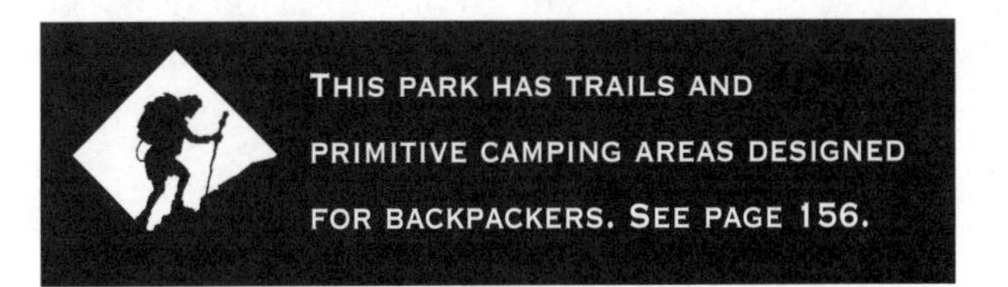

THIS PARK HAS TRAILS AND PRIMITIVE CAMPING AREAS DESIGNED FOR BACKPACKERS. SEE PAGE 156.

TRAIL NOTES

A riding area in excess of 5,000 acres and over 28 miles of hiking and riding trails are available throughout the park. Also, an 8-mile mountain bike trail, located on the eastern portion of the park, is accessible from County Road 29. Many park visitors hike the 2-mile Eagles Point Trail from the day-use area at Lake Theo to a scenic overlook along the park road just north of Eagles Point. Backpackers and other serious hikers explore the four other hiking trails located in the northwest part of the park. Two primitive camping areas for backpackers, and one equestrian primitive camping area are provided in the backcountry. A hike or ride of approximately one mile is required to reach each of these areas. See pages 156–157 for details.

Copper Breaks State Park

FOR INFORMATION

COPPER BREAKS STATE PARK
777 PARK RD. 62
QUANAH, TX 79252-7679
940/839-4331

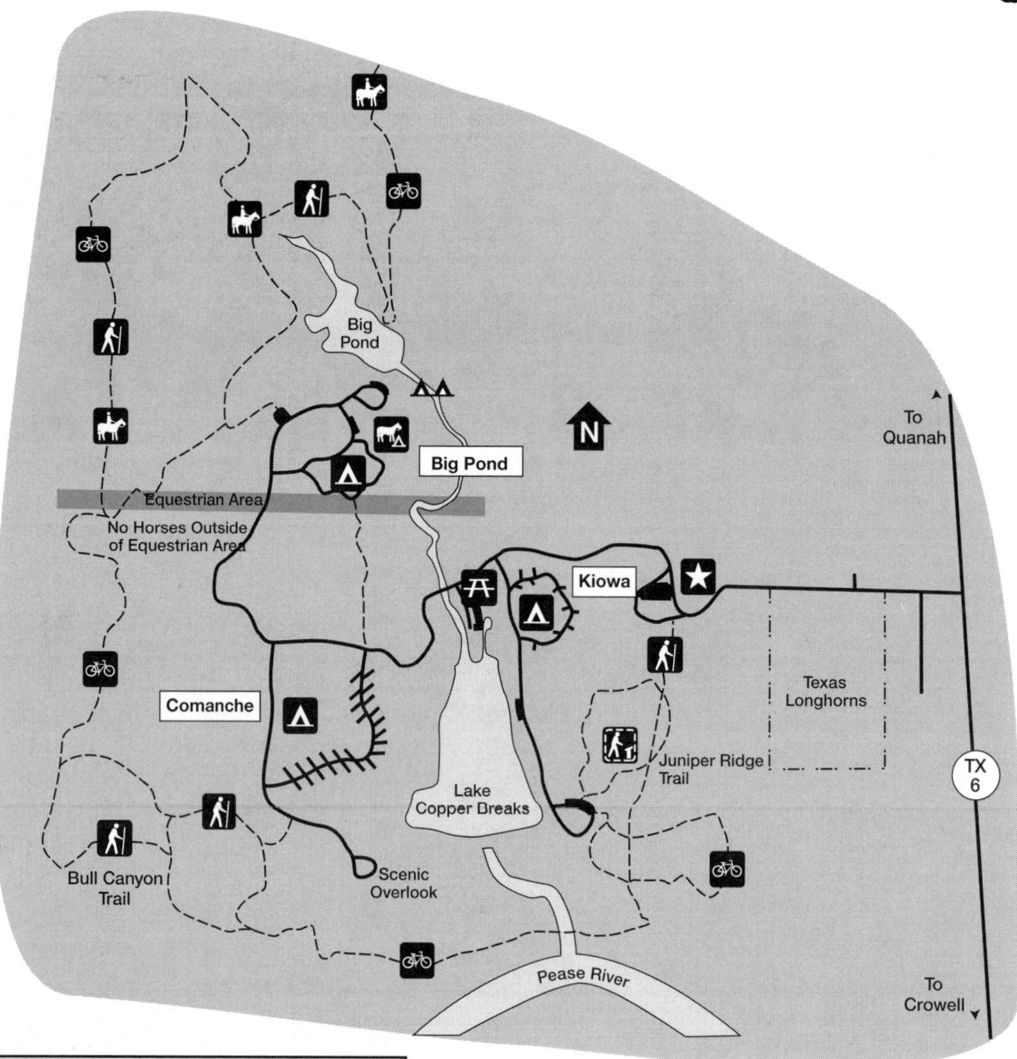

TRAIL NOTES

A self-guided nature trail about ½-mile in length, passes through some of the many natural features of the park. Equestrian trails, that total 9½ miles, and facilities for equestrian campers, are located in the northern part of the park. Hikers and mountain bikers may also use these horse trails. An extensive trail system has recently been opened at Copper Breaks for hikers and mountain bikers. The trail extends south from the equestrian trail, joins the Bull Canyon double-loop trail, continues east and then heads north to the park office. This trail is accessible from 4 park locations.

LOCATION

Copper Breaks State Park is located 13 miles south of Quanah or 11 miles north of Crowell on TX 6. The south boundary of the park is formed by the Pease River, a tributary of the Red River. Total acreage is 1,899 with 70 acres in lakes and ponds.

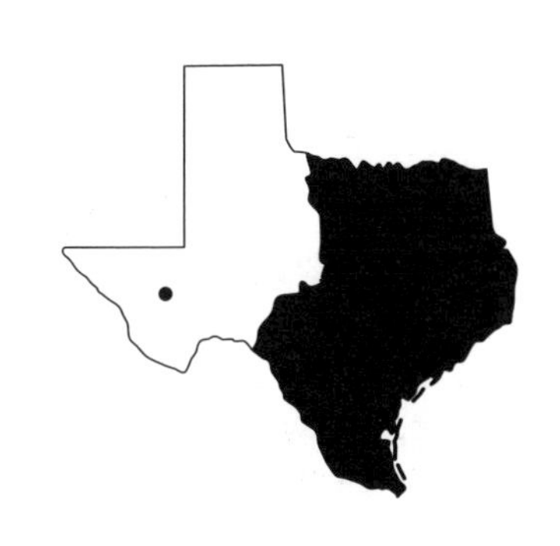

Davis Mountains State Park

FOR INFORMATION

Davis Mountains State Park
P.O. Box 1707
Fort Davis, TX 79734
432/426-3337

LOCATION

Davis Mountain State Park is located 4 miles northwest of Fort Davis; from just north of Fort Davis on TX 17, go west on TX 118 to Park Road 3. The park contains 2,709 acres and is adjacent to Fort Davis National Historical Site. The park is located in the rolling foothills of the scenic mile-high Davis Mountains, the most extensive mountain range in Texas.

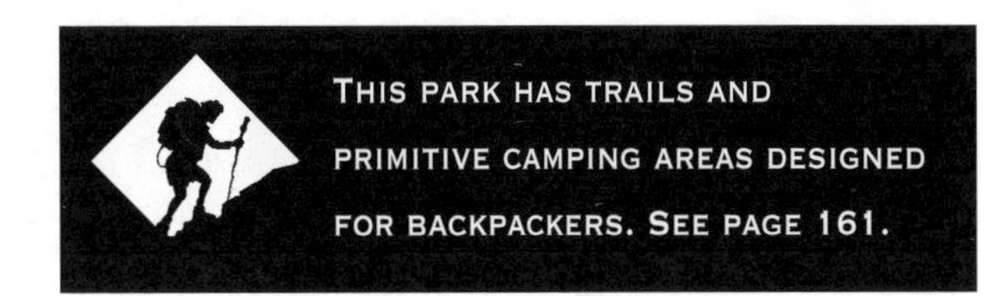

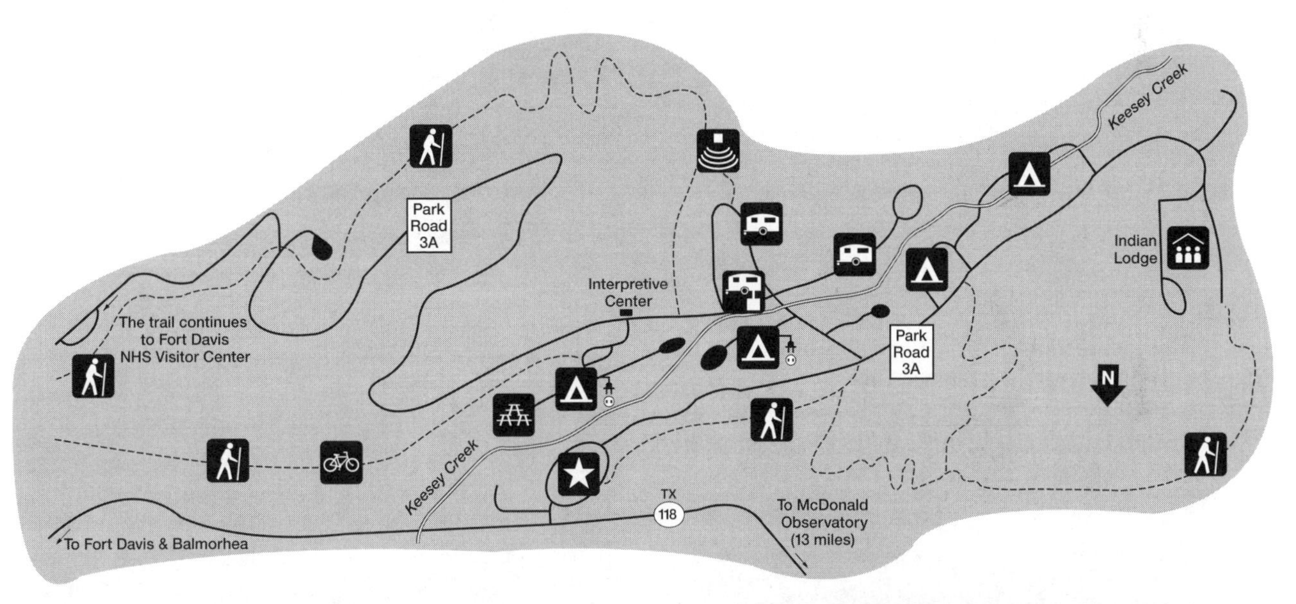

TRAIL NOTES

The 4½-mile hiking trail follows the ridge in the park, from the interpretive center, past two scenic overlooks, then connects up with the trail at Fort Davis National Historical Site. Numerous scenic views provide sweeping panoramas of the vast countryside. Other trails include a 3½-mile mountain bike trail and a 3-mile scenic hiking trail.

The northern half of the park, north of TX 118, has been designated the Limpia Canyon Primitive Area. Currently, it includes 6½ miles of backcountry hiking/equestrian trails with six primitive campsites. See page 161 for details.

The Indian Lodge, visible from the 4 ½-mile hiking trail that follows the ridge, is a Southwestern adobe lodge with original handcrafted interiors dating from its 1930s construction by the CCC.

FORT DAVIS NATIONAL HISTORIC SITE

FOR INFORMATION

FORT DAVIS NATIONAL HISTORIC SITE
P.O. BOX 1379
FORT DAVIS, TX 79734
432/426-3224

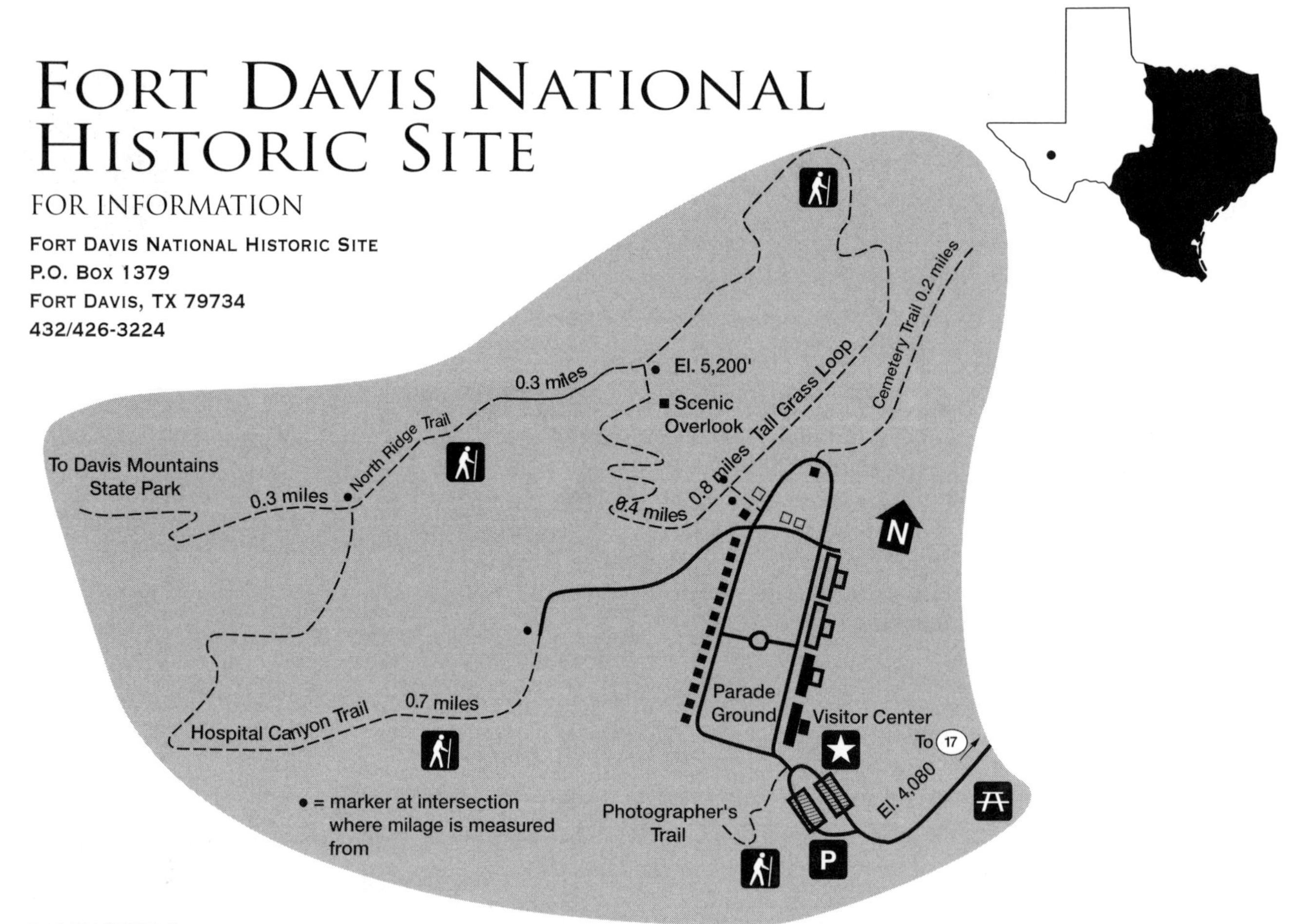

LOCATION

Fort Davis National Historic Site is on the northern edge of the town of Fort Davis. From I-10 on the north or US 90 on the south, the site can be reached by TX 17/118. Fort Davis guarded the travelers on the Trans-Pecos section of the San Antonio-El Paso route from 1854–1891.

High above the restored officers quarters of the national historic site is the location of the ridge trail that connects the hiking trail from Davis Mountains State Park with the Fort Davis trail.

TRAIL NOTES

Backdropped by rugged peaks, Fort Davis is located on a small, flat plain in the high country of the Davis Mountains. Predominant vegetation is desert-types, consisting of cacti, sotol, yucca, and sagebrush.

The Fort Davis National Historic Site trail is actually an interconnecting system of several smaller trails, totaling approximately 3 miles, providing access within the historic site and to Davis Mountains State Park. Hospital Canyon Trail and Cemetery Trail lead from the main fort complex to areas of historic interest. The Tall Grass Nature Trail leads from the fort to a higher elevation and a scenic overlook. The North Ridge Trail connects with the trail in Davis Mountains State Park. These interconnecting trails provide a unique scenic and historic tour to this once all-important frontier army post.

The visitor center and museum are open daily and audio programs, a 15 minute video, and a self-guiding tour of the entire site are among the year-round services provided. A cottonwood grove with a picnic area is located at the site.

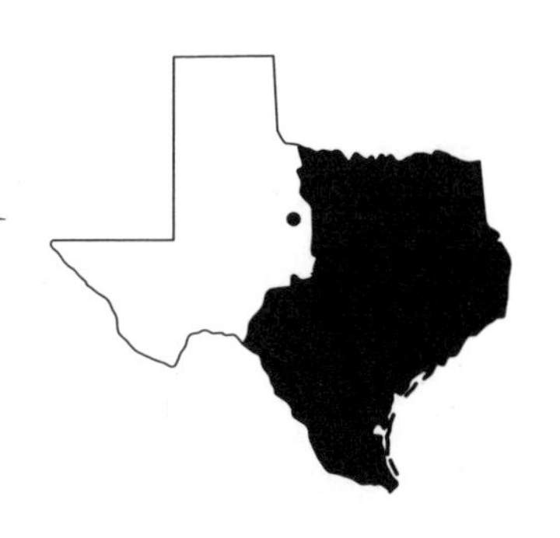

FORT GRIFFIN STATE PARK & HISTORIC SITE

FOR INFORMATION

FORT GRIFFIN STATE PARK & HISTORIC SITE
1701 NORTH U.S. HWY 283
ALBANY, TX 76430
325/762-3592

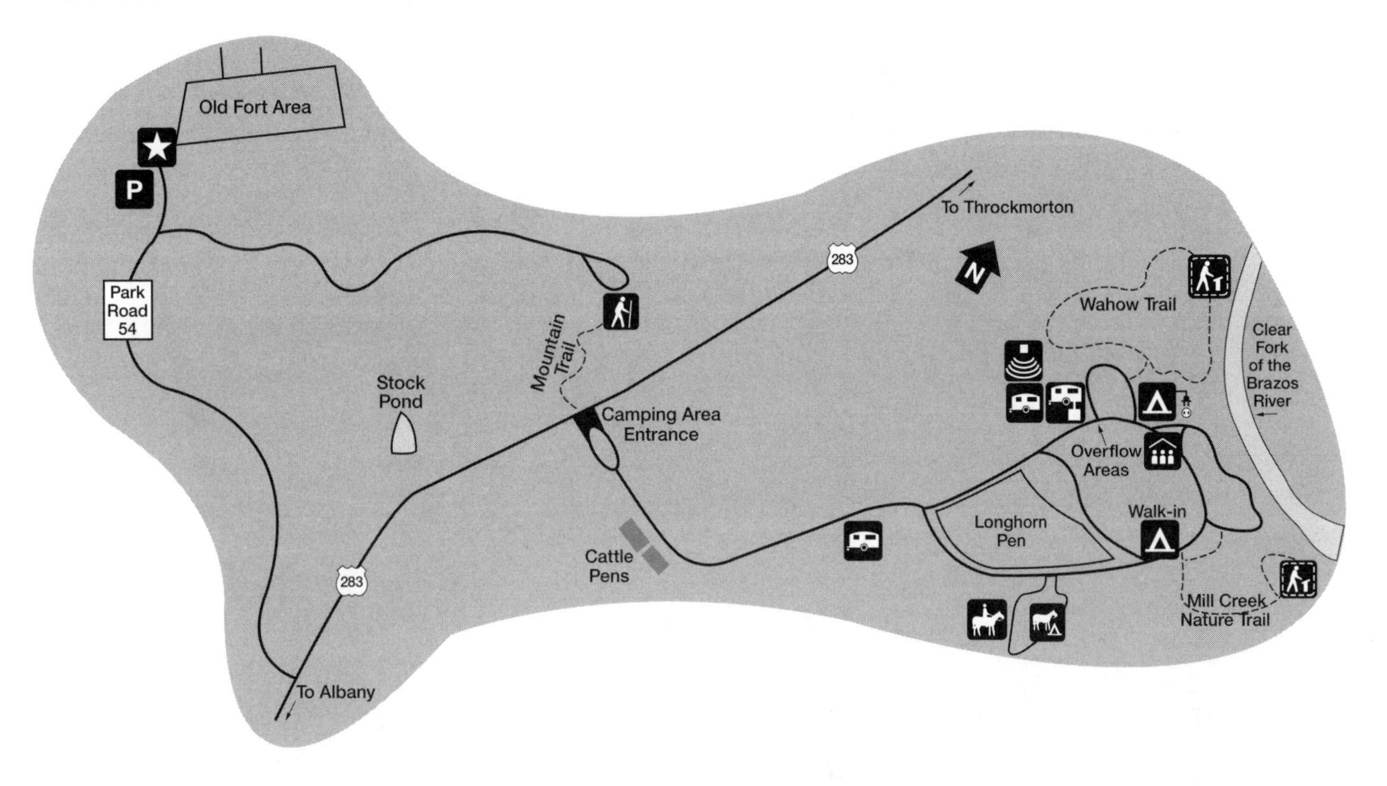

LOCATION

Fort Griffin State Park is located 15 miles north of Albany, on US 283. Fort Griffin was one of the best-known frontier installations and assumed an important role in providing protection for settlers and travelers. The 506-acre current-day Fort Griffin features the stabilized ruins of the fort buildings and the official state of Texas Longhorn Herd. A large number of the historic range animals can be seen in pastures within the park. Regimental reenactments are done periodically. Each June brings 6 performances of the Fandangle—a musical pageant that presents all major elements of the Clear Fork country in the 1870s and 1880s, including pioneer settlers, Indians, cowboys, military men of the fort, and longhorns. Call for details.

TRAIL NOTES

Hiking opportunities are plentiful at Fort Griffin. They include a ¼-mile river walk along the scenic Clear Fork of the Brazos River and 2 nature trails in the camping area that total 2 miles; trail guides are available. The park road adjacent to the camping area that encircles the Longhorn cattle provides a 1½-mile hike, and the historic walk through the remains of the frontier military post is about 1 mile. There is also an area for equestrian use, as well as undeveloped areas of the park that may be used for hiking; see a member of the park staff for locations. The park brochure advises visitors to *bring insect repellent, especially for ticks from March through November.*

FRANKLIN MOUNTAINS STATE PARK

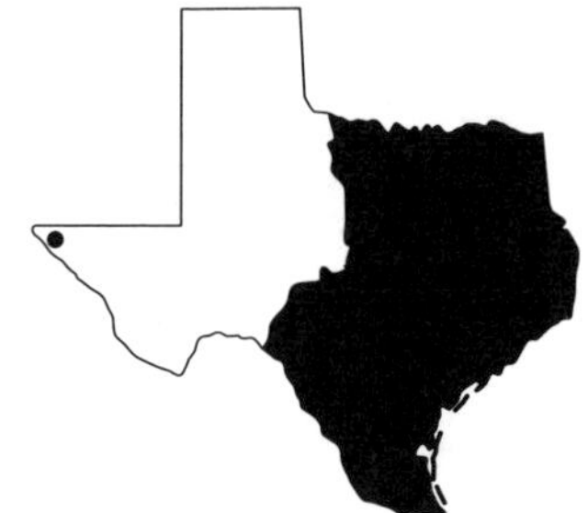

FOR INFORMATION

FRANKLIN MOUNTAINS STATE PARK
1331 MCKELLIGON CANYON RD.
EL PASO, TX 79930
915/566-6441

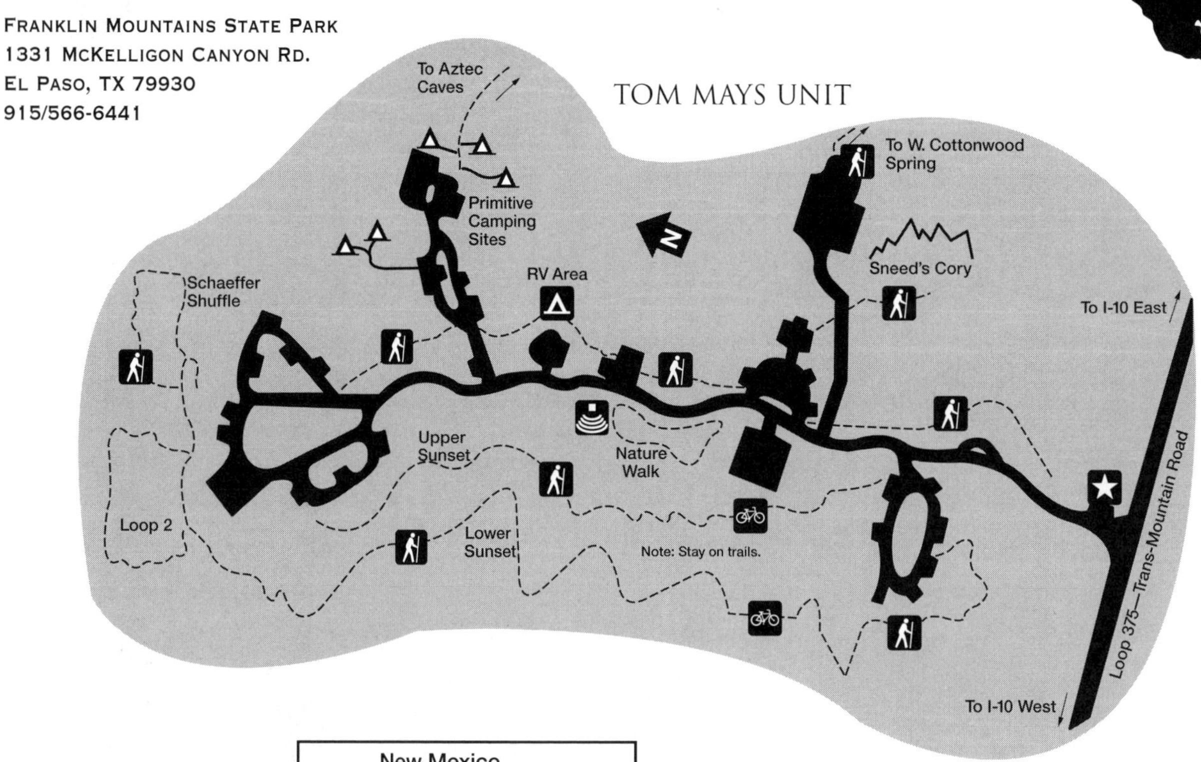

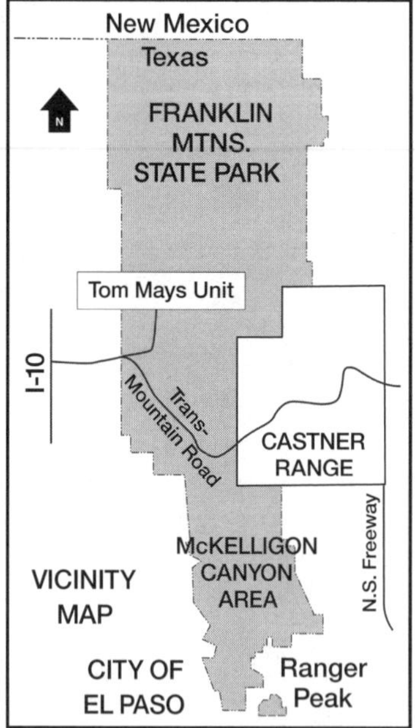

LOCATION

This state park is located completely within the city limits of El Paso; it is the largest urban wilderness park in the nation. The 24,050-acre park, with about 45 miles of boundary, includes an entire Chihuahuan Desert mountain range soaring to an elevation of 7,192 feet at the summit of North Franklin Peak, some 3,000 feet above the city of El Paso. State Loop 375 (Trans-Mountain Road) traverses the park. To reach the park entrance from the east, travel north on US 84 from I-10, then left on Loop 375. From the west, the park entrance is located 3.8 miles east of I-10. Take the Canutillo/Trans-Mountain Road and travel toward the mountains on Loop 375.

TRAIL NOTES

Many hiking trails are currently accessible off of Loop 375/Trans-Mountain Road. Work is underway for a trail network that will ultimately offer a 118-mile network. All 118 miles will be open to hiking, 51 miles will be open to hiking and mountain biking, and 22 miles will be open for multi-use—hiking, mountain bikes, and horseback riding. Hikers are urged to wear appropriate clothing and footwear to guard against agave spines, cacti, thornbushes, insects, and an unexpected rattlesnake. Carry plenty of water, as well as snacks, for a long hike. Potentially, any hike in the Franklin Mountains can be dangerous, so always take extra precautions.

To obtain up-to-date information on the location and status of the trails at this stage of the park's development, contact the park headquarters at Canutillo.

Guadalupe Mountains National Park

FOR INFORMATION

GUADALUPE MOUNTAINS NATIONAL PARK
HC60, BOX 400
SALT FLAT, TX 79847-9400
915/828-3251

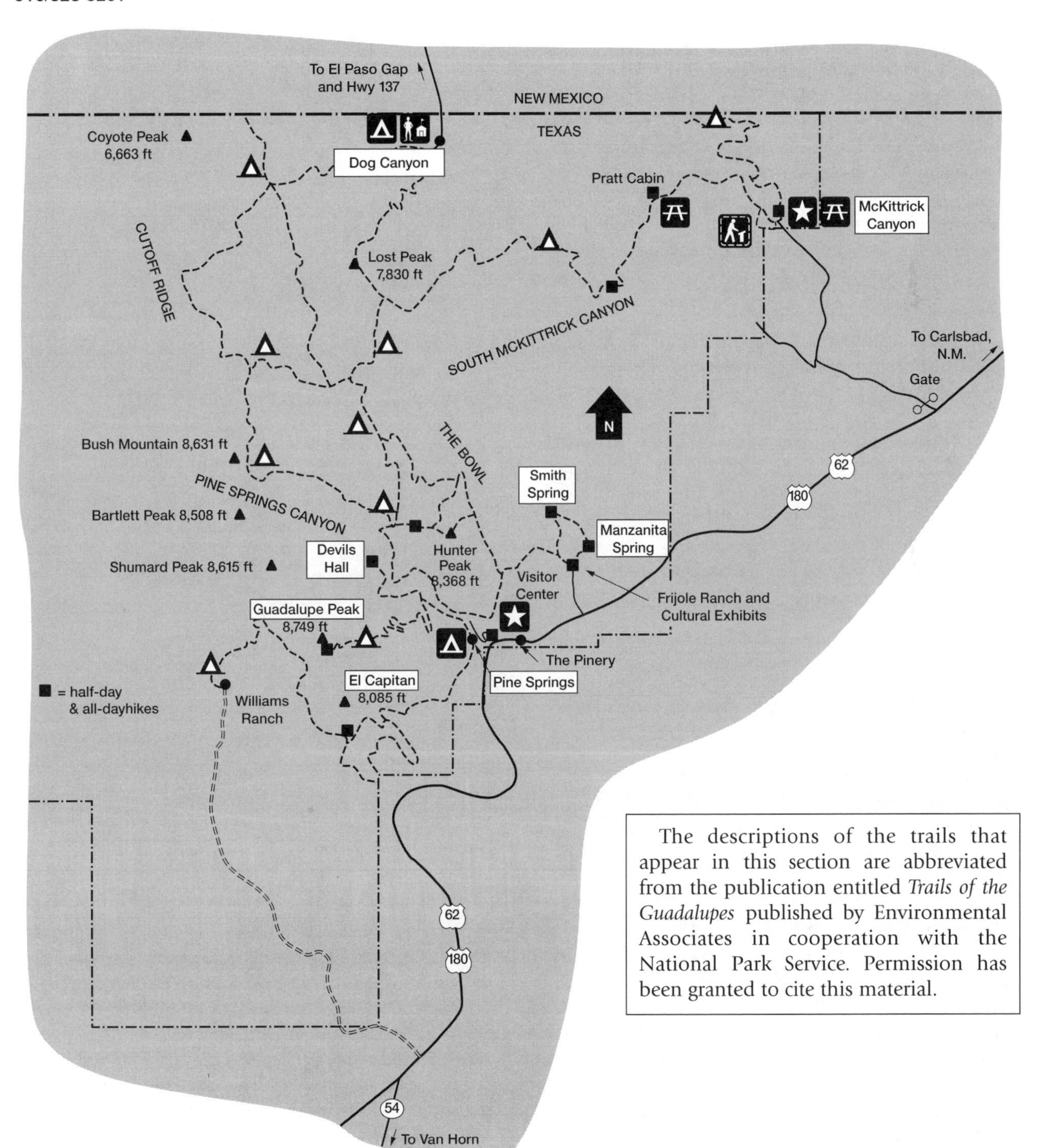

The descriptions of the trails that appear in this section are abbreviated from the publication entitled *Trails of the Guadalupes* published by Environmental Associates in cooperation with the National Park Service. Permission has been granted to cite this material.

LOCATIONS

Headquarters Visitor Center—On US 62/180, 55 miles southwest of Carlsbad, New Mexico, and 110 miles east of El Paso, Texas. Open daily 8:00 a.m. to 4:30 p.m. (MST) in winter; 8:00 a.m. to 6:00 p.m. in summer.

Pine Springs Campground—¼ mile west of the Headquarters Visitor Center. Drinking water, flush toilets, and picnic tables available.

Dog Canyon Campground—in the northern part of the park near the New Mexico border, 70 miles from Carlsbad, NM, via US 285 and NM 137. Drinking water, flush toilets, and picnic tables available.

McKittrick Canyon Visitor Center—7 miles northeast of Headquarters Visitor Center on US 62/180 to McKittrick Canyon turnoff; another 5 miles northwest to end of road. Interpretive exhibits, drinking water, flush toilets, and picnic area available.

ABOUT THE PARK

The Guadalupe Mountains stand like an island in the desert, silent sentinels watching over the most extensive fossil reef complex known to man. The mountain range resembles a massive wedge—rising in Texas, its arms reach northward into New Mexico. At its "V" stands El Capitan, a 2,000-foot sheer cliff. The mountains and canyons shelter a unique remnant of forest plants and animals, which have struggled for survival since the end of the ice ages, about 10,000 years ago.

The 88,416-acre park lies astride these mountains' most scenic, rugged portions. Here, the highest point in Texas, 8,749-foot Guadalupe Peak, stands in sharp contrast with the park's lowest elevation, 3,650 feet at the base of the western escarpment. The 46,850-acre Guadalupe Mountains Wilderness Area is the largest designated wilderness area in Texas.

In the park you can explore desert lowlands, superb canyons, and forested mountains. You can study geology, visit historic sites, and see plants and animals uncommon to the surrounding semi-arid lowlands. Those who climb into the high country can enjoy outstanding views across the Salt Basin to the west, the Delaware Basin to the south and east, and the deeply cut canyons to the north.

TRAIL NOTES

The park contains more than 80 miles of rugged mountain trails. Three of the trails are considered half-day hikes (2–4 hours) and three other trails could be considered all-day hikes (8–10 hours). The other trails are best traveled by backpackers who plan to camp in the backcountry at the designated primitive campsites. Before venturing onto these trails, backpackers must make thorough preparations and check in at the Headquarters Visitor Center to obtain a free backcountry permit. They also should check in upon their return. See pages 171–181 for details of the trails and backcountry policies and safety suggestions.

El Capitan, with its 2,000-foot sheer cliff, appears to be the highest peak in the Guadalupe mountain range. It is an awesome sight indeed, but Guadalupe Peak, the highest peak in Texas, is located due north of El Capitan and is 679 feet higher.

HALF-DAY HIKES

McKittrick Canyon—Day use area. Highway entrance gate opens at 8:00 a.m., closes 4:30 p.m., Mountain Time (8 a.m. to 6 p.m. during summer). Drive to the Visitor Center at canyon mouth and hike 4.6 miles round-trip to Pratt Cabin or hike 6.8 miles round-trip to Grotto Picnic Area. Picnic tables are available at Pratt Lodge. Hunter Lodge is a short distance beyond the Grotto Picnic Area; the canyon area is restricted beyond this point. Striking fall colors late October, early November. An 0.8-mile nature trail is located at the Visitor Center. There are no restrooms or water available in the canyon.

Smith and Manzanita Springs—This loop trail begins from Frijole Historic Site, the original Rader house built around 1876; it was the first permanent dwelling in the park. This is the location of Frijole Spring. The trail passes by Manzanita Spring, then climbs very gradually to Smith Spring, a cool, well-watered spot surrounded by madrone, alligator juniper, and maple. Round-trip, 2.3 miles, 1½ hours.

Devils Hall—This trail leads to a section of narrow canyon walls in the dry streambed of Pine Canyon. The trail begins at the Pine Springs Campground and follows the Guadalupe Peak horse trail for about a mile, then drops to follow the rocky streambed itself. After another mile, the stair-step-like layers of rock called Hikers Staircase appear; just beyond are the steep walls of Devils Hall. Trail is 4.2-mile round-trip; allow 4 hours.

ALL-DAY HIKES

Guadalupe Peak—The trail from Pine Springs Campground to the highest point in Texas (8,749 feet) is a well-graded trail that climbs steadily for an elevation gain of about 3,000 feet before gaining the summit at 4.2 miles. A small monument is at the summit; it was erected by American Airlines in 1958, on the 100th anniversary of the completion of the first transcontinental mail route that went through Guadalupe Pass. From this point there are spectacular views of the entire surrounding area. Start early on this 8.4-mile round-trip hike and don't forget the snacks and water.

Hunter Peak/Bowl—Another very challenging all-day hike is the 8½-mile loop up the Tejas trail from Pine Springs Campground, along the ridge on the Bowl Trail to Hunter Peak, then down the Bear Canyon Trail. At the 8,368-foot summit of Hunter Peak, the hiker is able to see a great distance in every direction. The Bear Canyon Trail is extremely steep and switchbacks frequently as it descends among boulders; it is a section of the trail that requires plenty of time and energy. Many hikers prefer to return the way they came; doing so will add 1.1-mile to the hike. Start early and take plenty of snacks and water.

El Capitan Trail—This trail leads around the base of El Capitan and ends at the Old Williams Ranch House; the distance is 9.4 miles. Unless you have made arrangements for a friend to pick you up at the ranch, consider hiking only to the base of El Capitan for an 8.6-mile round-trip from the Pine Springs Campground. Good views of El Capitan are available from about 1½ miles on. The trail reaches an altitude of 6,362 feet just below the base with spectacular views of the cliffs above and the Williams Ranch region to the west.

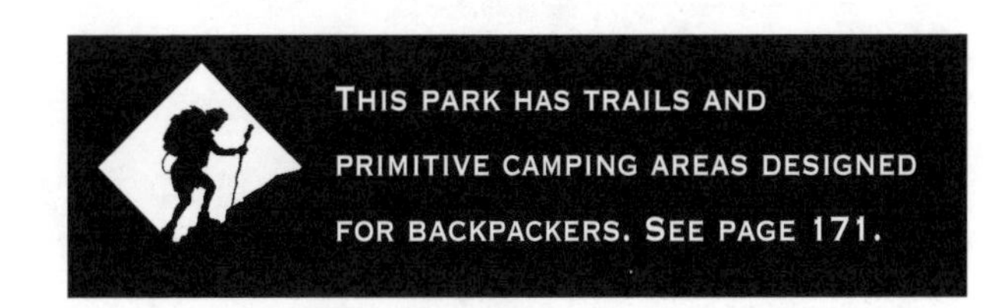

You'd be smiling too if you had just climbed Guadalupe Peak. This hiker started at the Pine Springs Campground and ascended about 3,000 feet before reaching the summit after 4.2 miles of hiking.

HUECO TANKS STATE HISTORIC SITE

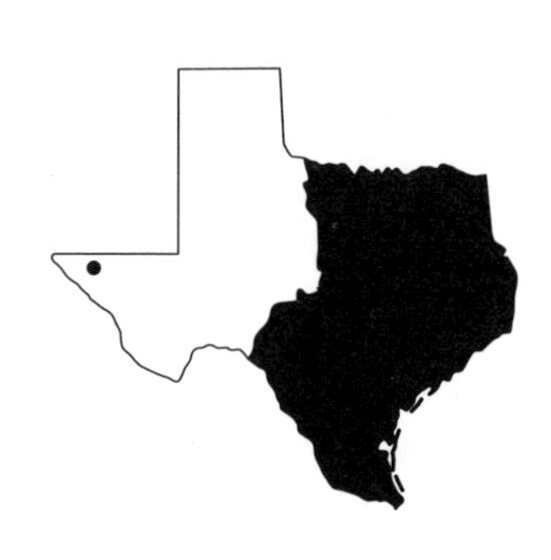

FOR INFORMATION

HUECO TANKS STATE HISTORIC SITE
6900 HUECO TANKS ROAD #1
EL PASO, TX 79938
915/857-1135
TOUR RESERVATIONS 915/849-6684

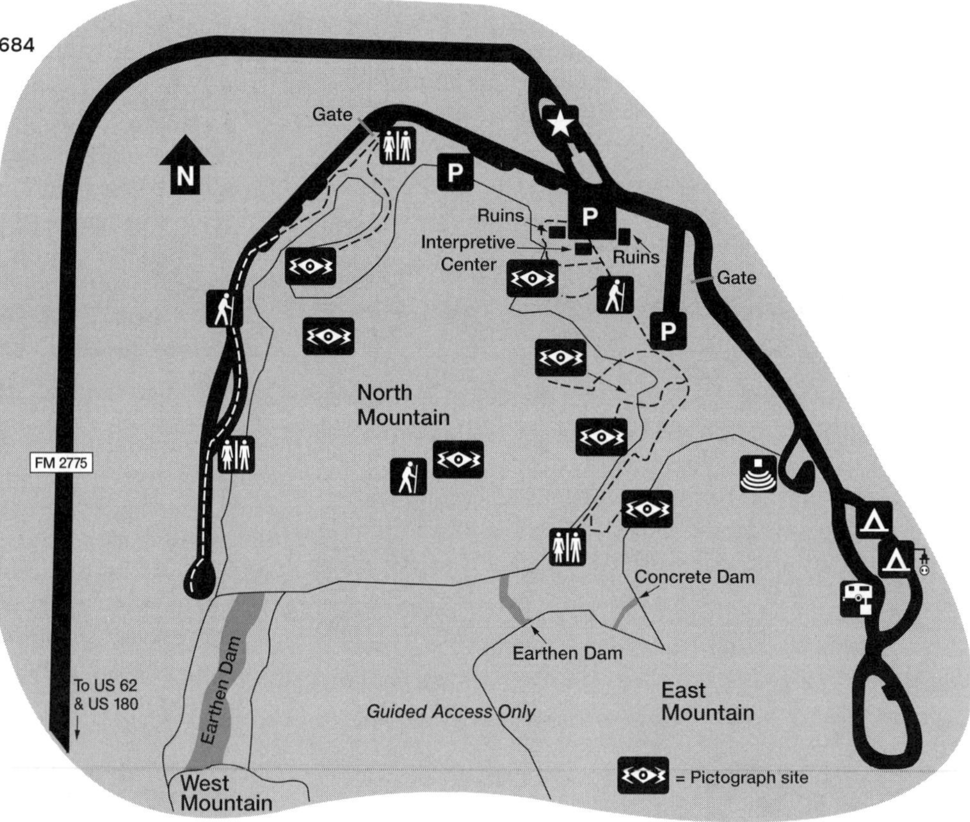

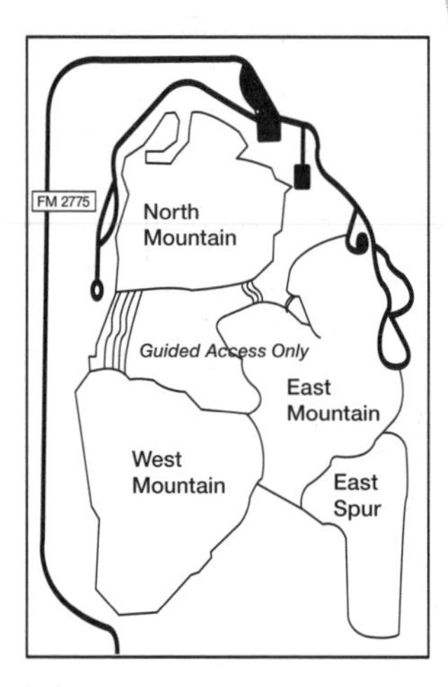

LOCATION

Hueco Tanks State Historic Site is located 32 miles east of El Paso off of US 62/180 on FM 2775. According to geologists, the three jumbled rock masses that make up most of this 860-acre park were formed about 34 million years ago. The weathering process left countless depressions in the rocks, called *huecos* in Spanish, that collect and hold rainwater.

TRAIL NOTES

Only the North Mountain section of the park is accessible without a guide. Reservations are recommended; limited access. For guided tours, contact the park. A 300-foot sheer cliff, a natural bridge, several small ponds, and many hidden valleys are only a few of the park's scenic attractions. The highest peaks in the area offer splendid views of the mountains and desert that surround the park.

Scattered throughout the rocks are the signs of earlier inhabitants. It has been estimated that there may be 3,000 pictographs (rock paintings) at Hueco Tanks, dating back perhaps several thousand years. Pictographs comprise the bulk of the Hueco Tanks rock art, with only a few petroglyphs (carved or chipped designs) to be found. The sheer rock faces are attracting increasing numbers of technical climbers, as well as scramblers. *Visitors are required to register and sign a liability release in the park office. Specific rules, regulations and closed area information are available there.*

Lake Brownwood State Park

FOR INFORMATION

LAKE BROWNWOOD STATE PARK
200 STATE PARK RD. 15
BROWNWOOD, TX 76801
325/784-5223

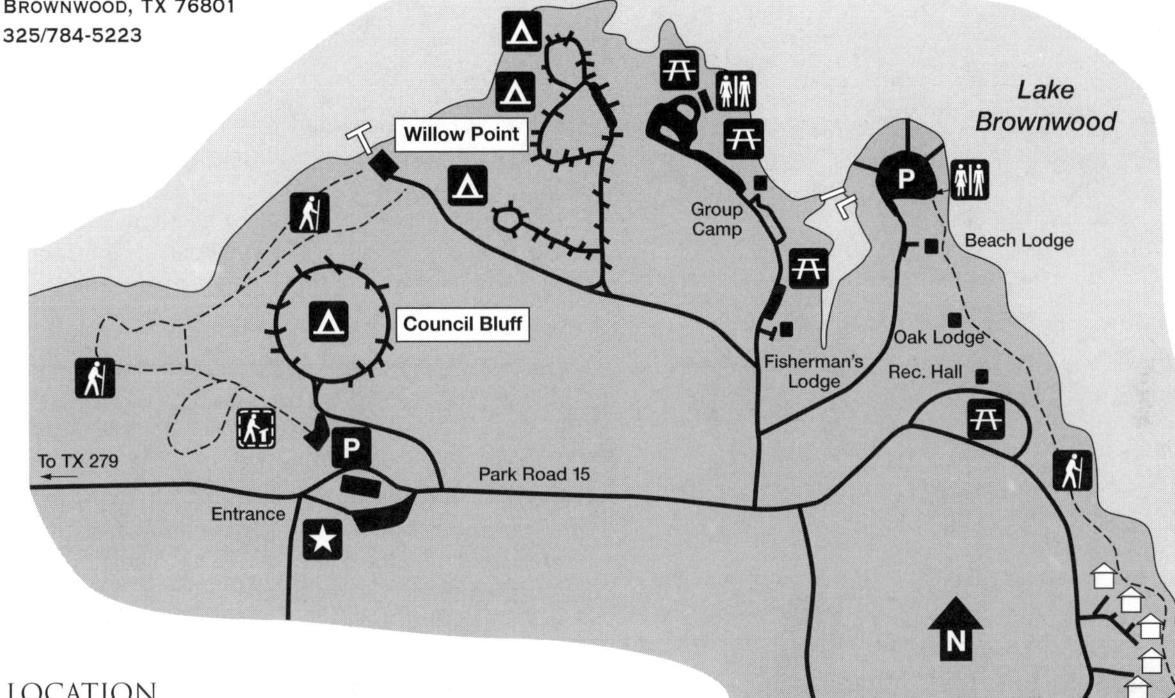

LOCATION

Lake Brownwood State Park is located 23 miles northwest of Brownwood via TX 279 and Park Road 15. The 538-acre park is located on the west shore of 7,300-acre Lake Brownwood.

The hiking trail in the western end of the park starts at the fishing pier.

TRAIL NOTES

Lake Brownwood State Park has several hiking trails that total 2½ miles and a ½-mile nature trail. One trail follows the shoreline between the Beach Lodge and the Comanche Trails camping area near the screened shelters. Another trail leads southwest from Willow Point camping area past the Council Bluff trailer area. This area has been designated as an observation area of native wildflowers; the trail has several loops and leads to the nature trail. One of the loop trails is handicap accessible; a parking area is nearby.

LUBBOCK LAKE LANDMARK

FOR INFORMATION

LUBBOCK LAKE LANDMARK
2401 LANDMARK DRIVE
LUBBOCK, TX 79415
806/742-1116
WWW.MUSEUM.TTU.EDU/LLL

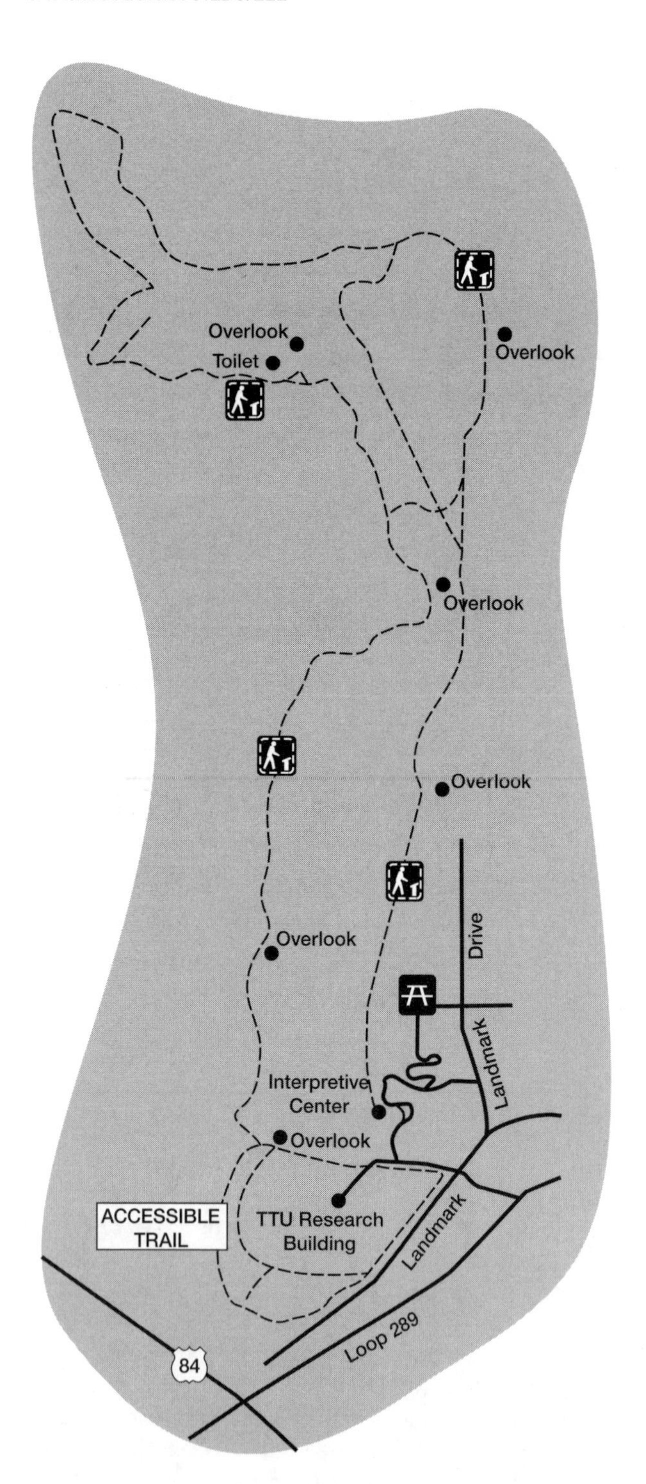

LOCATION

Lubbock Lake Landmark is located on the northwest edge of the city of Lubbock near the intersection of Loop 289 and US 84; it is accessible via marked exits on Loop 289 or by following signs at US 84. This 336-acre park, a day-use-only park, has an interpretive center, 2 hiking trails, and 3 picnic areas.

ABOUT THE PARK

The park is a unique archaeological and natural preserve administered by the Museum of Texas Tech University. Analysis of materials excavated when Lubbock Lake was created revealed that Lubbock Lake currently is the only known site in North America that contains deposits related to all the cultures known to have existed on the Southern Plains. The Robert A. Nash Interpretive Center houses museum exhibits, a children's educational center, an auditorium, gift shop, and administrative office. The park is open Tuesday through Saturday from 9 a.m. to 5 p.m. and on Sundays from 1 to 5 p.m.; guided tours are available by appointment. Ongoing excavation areas are available for viewing during the summer.

TRAIL NOTES

The park has 2 trails: a handicapped accessible ¾-mile archaeological trail and a 3-mile nature trail. The archaeological trail is a self-guided trail that leads around a 20-acre excavation area and provides numerous interpretive wayside exhibits. The longer trail meanders along the slopes and bed of Yellowhouse Draw, a dry, ancient river now covered with native vegetation. The trail has several shade shelters, overlooks, interpretive wayside exhibits and a chemical toilet.

PALO DURO CANYON STATE PARK

FOR INFORMATION

PALO DURO CANYON STATE PARK
11450 PARK RD. 5
CANYON, TX 79015
806/488-2227

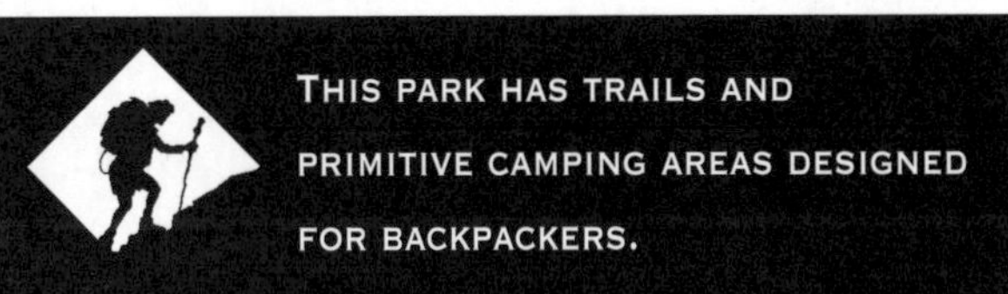

LOCATION

Palo Duro Canyon State Park is located about 12 miles east of Canyon on TX 217. From Amarillo, it is south on RR 1541, then 8 miles east on TX 217. The park road drops 600 feet as it winds from the interpretive center into the canyon. The Prairie Dog Town Fork of the Red River runs through this 18,438-acre park. This stream has carved out a rugged, scenic canyon to a depth of almost 800 feet and several miles in length. The predominant feature of the canyon is its magnificent, rugged scenery, which presents a constantly changing panorama of colors. The Pioneer Amphitheater, a 1,742-seat outdoor theater, is the site of summer performances of the outstanding musical drama "Texas Legacies."

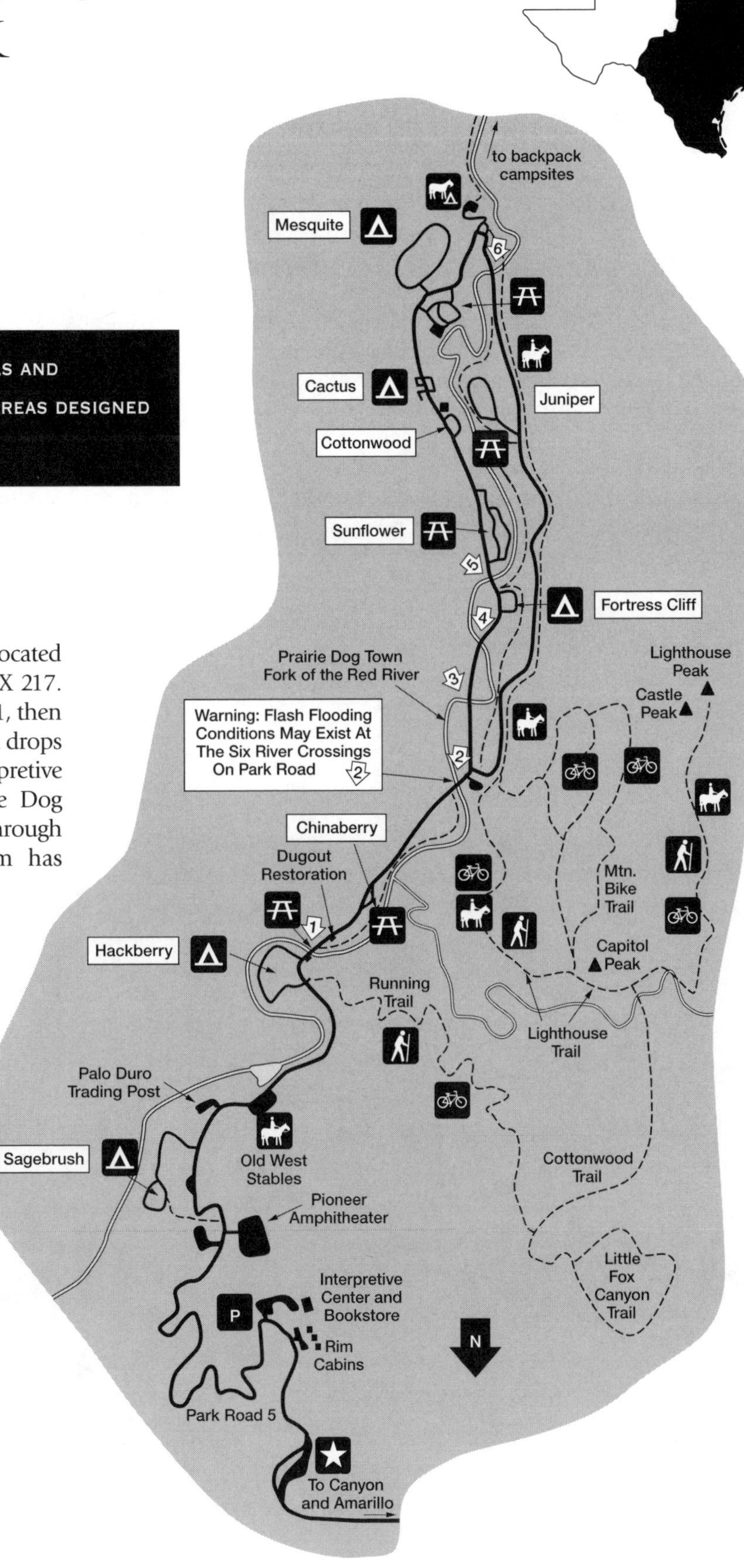

TRAIL NOTES

About 25 miles of trails exist within the canyon for hiking, biking, jogging, and horseback riding. The most popular trail for all trail users is the Lighthouse Trail. The lighthouse is a pillar of soft mudstone about 75 feet high capped by a layer of resistant sandstone. For hikers and bikers, it is a 6-mile round-trip to the Lighthouse formation. The Givens, Spicer, and Lowry Running Trail provides a 9-mile round-trip to the Lighthouse. For horseback riders using the Equestrian Trail from the staging area in the south end of the park, the trip to the Lighthouse is 12 miles round-trip.

18½ miles of trails are designated for mountain bikers; the Capitol Peak Mountain Bike Trail is for bikers only. Mountain bikes can be rented at the Old West Stables. Horses may be ridden on about 12½ miles of trails. Three trails are strictly for horses, and a third is for horses, hikers, and bikers. The 4-mile round-trip Turnaround Trail is south of the designated equestrian campground. This campground has 2 large trailer-parking areas and 6 primitive campsites with a corral and water nearby.

Although not shown on the map, the park has a hike-in primitive area that is ½ to ¾ miles in. Containerized fuel must be used as ground fires are not permitted; water is available at the trailhead. Backpack campsites are located ½ to 2 miles in, with potable water at the trailhead and restrooms ¼ mile from the parking area. Contact the park office for information on these primitive camping areas.

These folks get their first panoramic view of the rugged scenery of the canyon; they notice how the hues of color change when a cloud blocks the rays of the sun.

San Angelo State Park

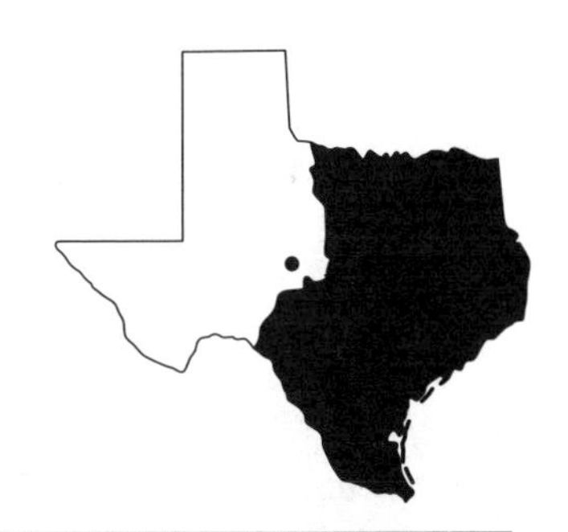

FOR INFORMATION

SAN ANGELO STATE PARK
3900-2 MERCEDES RD.
SAN ANGELO, TX 76901
325/949-4757

TRAIL NOTES

The park has over 50 miles of developed multi-use trails for hiking, mountain biking, and equestrian use, and a nature trail that is located west of the Chaparral Group Camp. There are numerous primitive campsites accessible by foot, mountain bike, and horseback along the trails that connect the south end of the park with the north end. These primitive campsites are used by backpackers more often than other users. Some of the trails in this section of the park are steep and rugged. Because the primitive campsites are not designated and because the trails used by backpackers are identical to those used by bikers and horseback riders, this park map is not duplicated in the Backpacking Trails section.

THIS PARK HAS TRAILS AND PRIMITIVE CAMPING AREAS DESIGNED FOR BACKPACKERS.

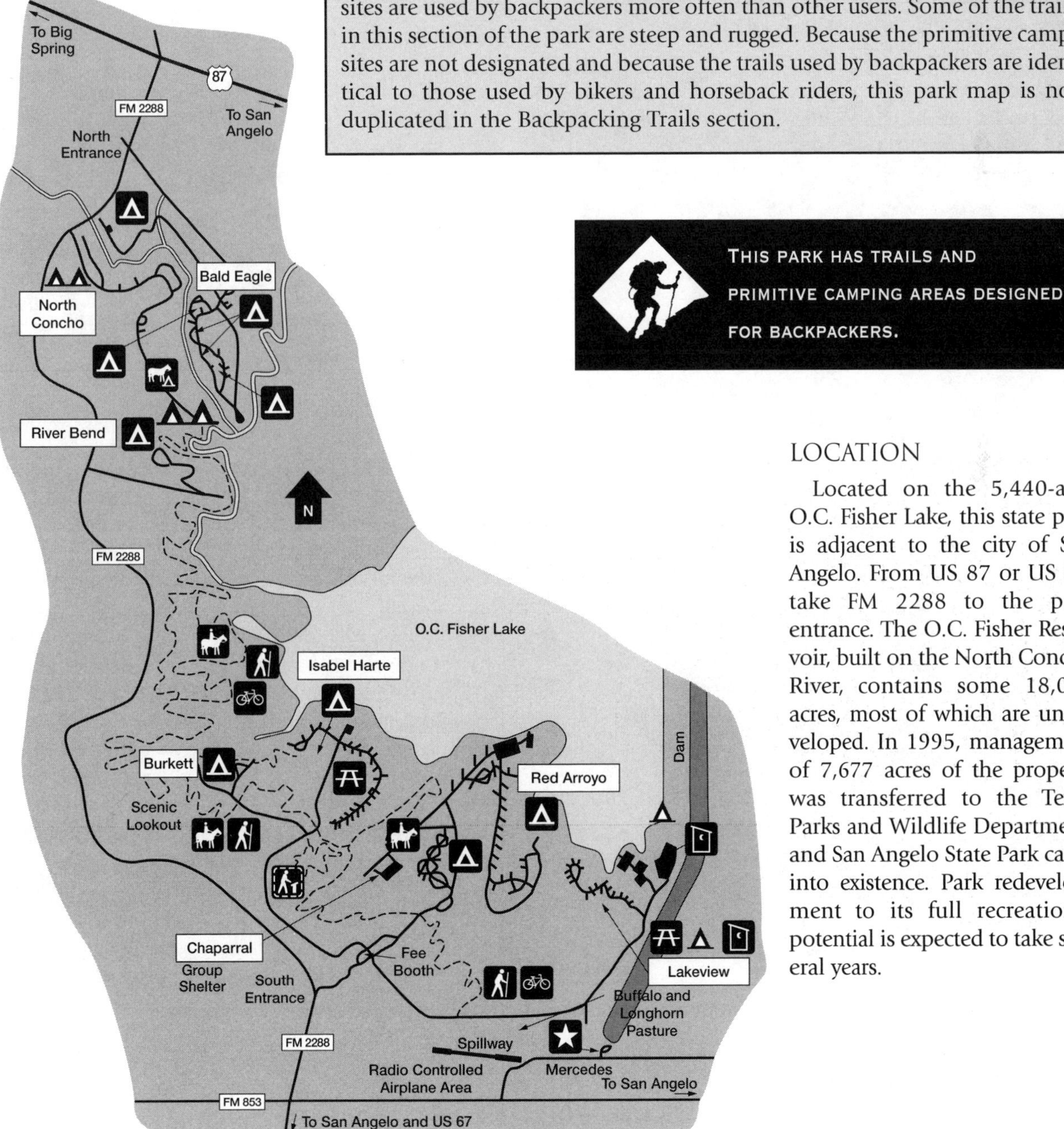

LOCATION

Located on the 5,440-acre O.C. Fisher Lake, this state park is adjacent to the city of San Angelo. From US 87 or US 67, take FM 2288 to the park entrance. The O.C. Fisher Reservoir, built on the North Concho River, contains some 18,000 acres, most of which are undeveloped. In 1995, management of 7,677 acres of the property was transferred to the Texas Parks and Wildlife Department, and San Angelo State Park came into existence. Park redevelopment to its full recreational potential is expected to take several years.

SEMINOLE CANYON STATE PARK & HISTORIC SITE

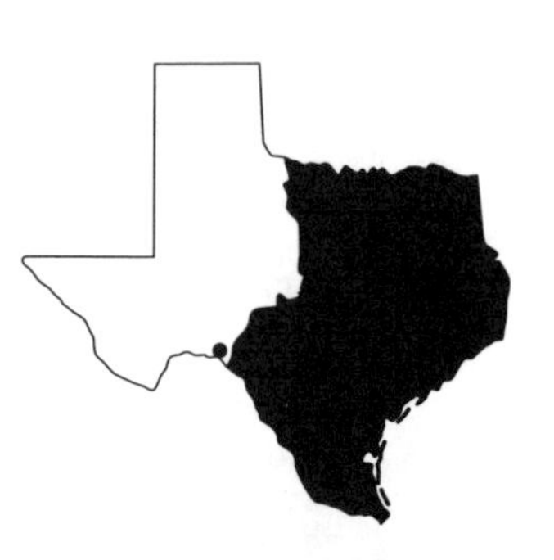

FOR INFORMATION

SEMINOLE CANYON STATE PARK & HISTORIC SITE
P.O. BOX 820
COMSTOCK, TX 78837
915/292-4464

LOCATION

Seminole Canyon State Park & Historic Site is located west of Comstock and east of Langtry off of US 90. From Comstock, travel 9 miles west to the park entrance; when approaching the park from the west, the entrance is just east of the high bridge across the Pecos River.

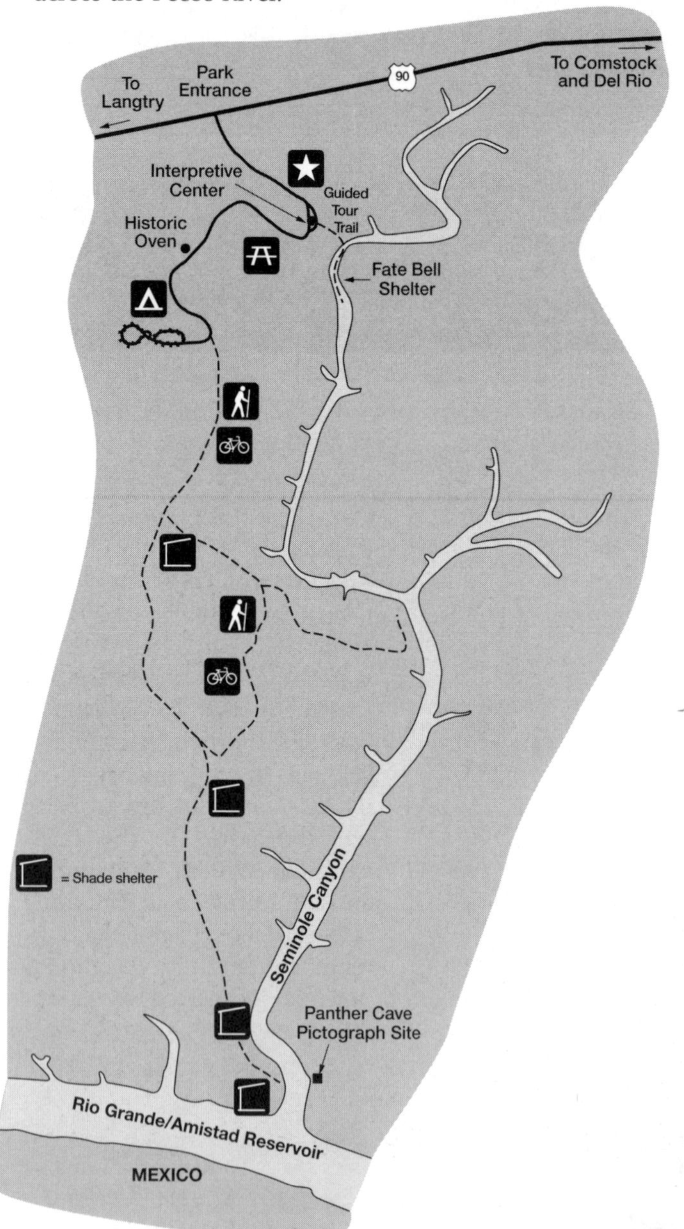

The Fate Bell Shelter is accessible only by a guided tour.

TRAIL NOTES

Fate Bell Shelter in Seminole Canyon contains some of North America's oldest pictographs believed to have been painted as long as 4,000 years ago; it is accessible only by guided tour. The regular tour schedule is Wednesday through Sunday, 10 a.m. and 3 p.m.; tours may be canceled during inclement weather. The visitor center contains exhibits and a life-size cave diorama that portrays daily activities of early man; the center is open 8 a.m. to 5 p.m. daily. The trail from the visitor center to the shelters, called the Canyon Trail, is 2 miles round-trip. Because some moderately strenuous hiking with many steep steps to climb is involved, persons planning to go on the tour should be in good physical condition.

The Rio Grande River Trail is a 6-mile round-trip hiking and mountain bike trail that begins at the camping area and ends at a shade shelter overlooking the Rio Grande, Seminole Canyon, Panther Cave, and Mexico. The trail follows an old ranch road and is not strenuous; there are 4 shade shelters along the trail. This trail is a day-use trail and overnight camping is not allowed. *Canyons are closed to hikers except for guided tours.*

Other Trails in Region 4

BIG SPRING **Big Spring State Park**

▲ ⅓-mile nature trail in Big Spring State Park that runs northwest from the Prairie Dog Town.

Big Spring State Park
#1 Scenic Drive
Big Spring, TX 79720
432/263-4931

COLEMAN **Hords Creek Lake**

▲ ⅔-mile self-guided nature trail, with a trail brochure available, on the north side of Hords Creek Lake near Lakeside Park.

Hords Creek Lake
230 Friendship Park Rd.
Coleman, TX 76834-9320
325/625-2322

EL PASO **Chamizal National Monument**

▲ The Cordova Island Trail is a 1.8-mile walking trail that encircles the 55-acre urban park. Views of the Franklin and Juarez Mountains, the El Paso downtown skyline and an international bridge can be seen from the trail.

Chamizal National Monument
800 South San Marcial Street
El Paso, TX 79905
915/532-7273

MONAHANS **Monahans Sandhills State Park**

▲ A self-guiding interpretive trail leads from the interpretive center of the Monahans Sandhills State Park and winds its way through the dunes. Hiking is also permitted in the pure sand that stretches for miles; horseback riding is also permitted in some areas of the park.

Monahans Sandhills State Park
P.O. Box 1738
Monahans, TX 79756
432/943-2092

TEXAS HIGHWAYS Magazine

A little known fact about Texas is that it has 91 mountains a mile or more high. All of them are in the Trans-Pecos region. For the outdoor enthusiast, the two most popular mountainous areas are Big Bend and the Guadalupe Mountains.

TEXAS HIGHWAYS Magazine

Hueco Tanks has become a popular rock climbing area in recent years. Two other state parks known for rock climbing opportunities are Enchanted Rock and Lake Mineral Wells.

MULESHOE **Muleshoe NWR**

▲ 1-mile nature trail near the campground and the refuge headquarters. Also a ¼-mile trail at Pauls Lake, 6 miles northeast of headquarters. The refuge roads may be traveled during daylight hours. Refuge office is 2¼ miles on a gravel road from SH 214.

Muleshoe National Wildlife Refuge
P.O. Box 549
Muleshoe, TX 79347
806/946-3341

PAMPA

▲ 3-mile walking and bicycle trail along the upper reaches of Red Deer Creek, a small tributary of the Canadian River that runs through the heart of Pampa.

▲ ¾-mile walking and bicycle trail that encircles the Old City Lake at Recreation Park.

Parks Department
P.O. Box 2499
Pampa, TX 79066-2499
806/669-5760, Ext. 3

SHEFFIELD **Fort Lancaster SHS**

▲ 125-yard nature trail located behind the picnic area at Fort Lancaster State Historic Site.

▲ ¾-mile self-guided trail around the ruins of old Fort Lancaster.

Fort Lancaster State Historic Site
P.O. Box 306
Sheffield, TX 79781
432/836-4391

TUSCOLA **Abilene State Park**

▲ 2 trails that total 1½ miles; a nature trail that follows Elm Creek, and Eagle Trail that has a side trail to a buffalo wallow before connecting to the Elm Creek Trail.

Abilene State Park
150 Park Road 32
Tuscola, TX 79562
325/572-3204

UMBARGER **Buffalo Lake NWR**

▲ Prairie Dog Town interpreted trail on FM 168, 2 miles south of FM 1714 intersection; Cottonwood Canyon birding trail follows the canyon walls through riparian habitats; drive the auto tour road to observe wildlife.

Buffalo Lake NWR
P.O. Box 179
Umbarger, TX 79091
806/499-3254

BACKPACKING TRAILS

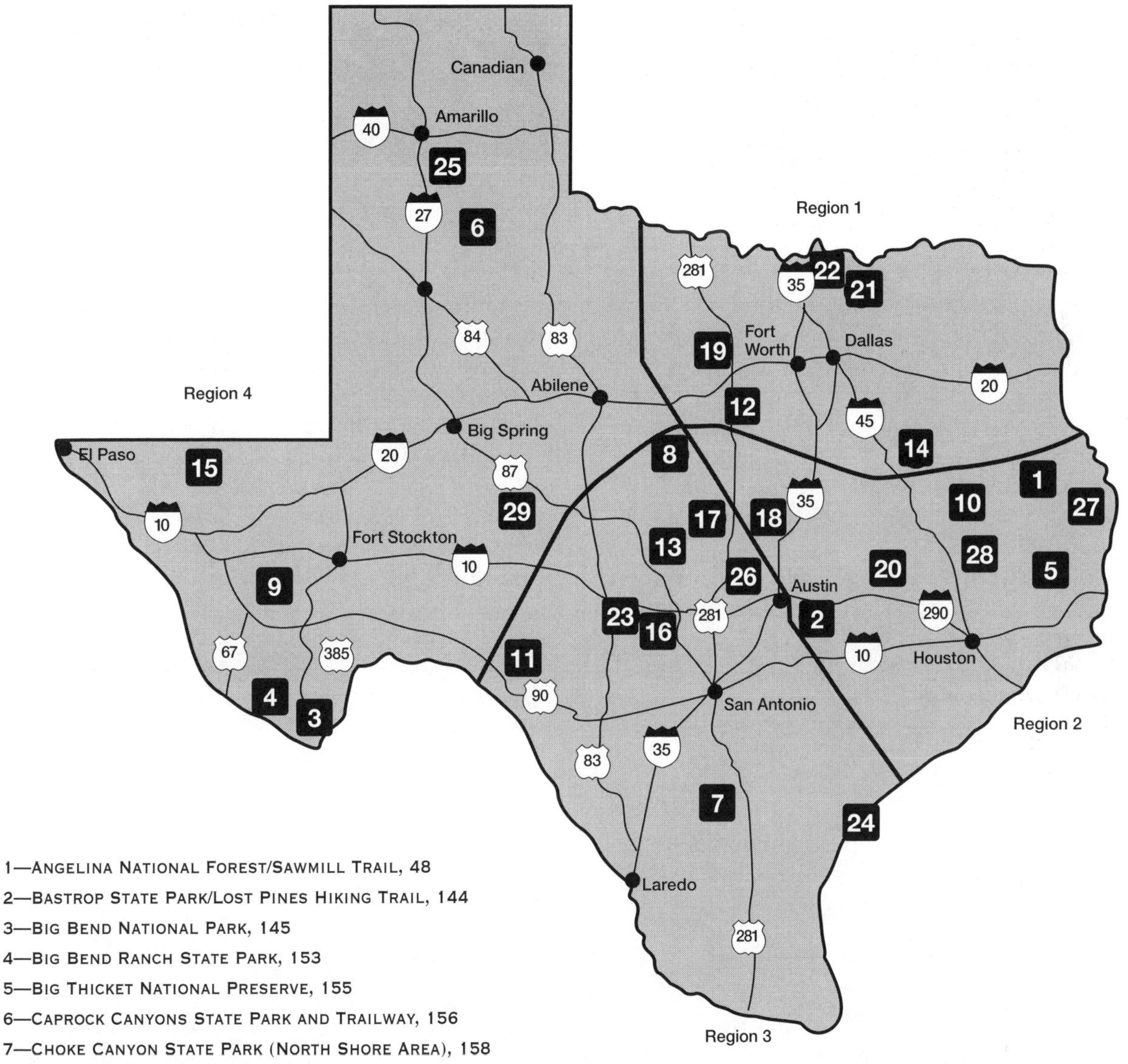

Bastrop State Park/ Lost Pines Hiking Trail

FOR INFORMATION

Bastrop State Park
P.O. Box 518
Bastrop, TX 78602-0518
512/321-2101

LOCATION

Bastrop State Park is located 1 mile east of Bastrop on TX 21 and is also accessible from the east by way of Buescher State Park along Park Road 1 or from TX 71. The 5,926-acre park includes a 10-acre lake.

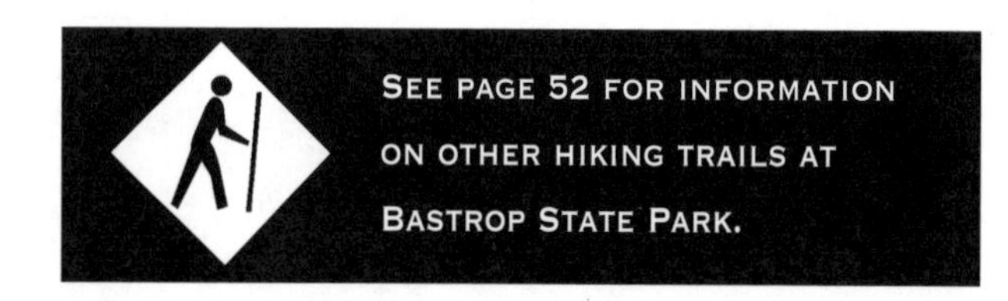
See page 52 for information on other hiking trails at Bastrop State Park.

TRAIL NOTES

This 8½-mile trail has been constructed primarily through the efforts of volunteers form the Texas Trails Association and the Sierra Club. The trail is intended to be a primitive footpath that offers the least intrusion into the natural beauty of the area. Regular fees apply to the use of this area for backpack camping. Overnight camping is permitted only in the area east of the primitive road (see map). Camp at least 50 feet from the trail and 100 feet from any open water.

There is no drinking water available along the trail. However, there is a faucet near the trailhead. You must carry water for all your drinking, cooking, and washing needs. Creek and pond water in this area is not suitable for consumption, even when boiled or treated. Do not wash dishes or bathe in the creeks or ponds. Campfires are not permitted in the area where primitive camping is allowed because of ground scarring and the possibility of wildfires. Cooking shall be done only on containerized fuel stoves. During severe droughts, stoves may be prohibited.

No toilet facilities are located adjacent to the trail. Alternative disposal of human waste should follow standard field disposal practice. The trail is marked with 2 × 4-inch aluminum markers attached to trees approximately at eye level. Standard wooden park signs are used to mark the major intersections. *Bicycles are not allowed on trails due to the highly erosive soils.*

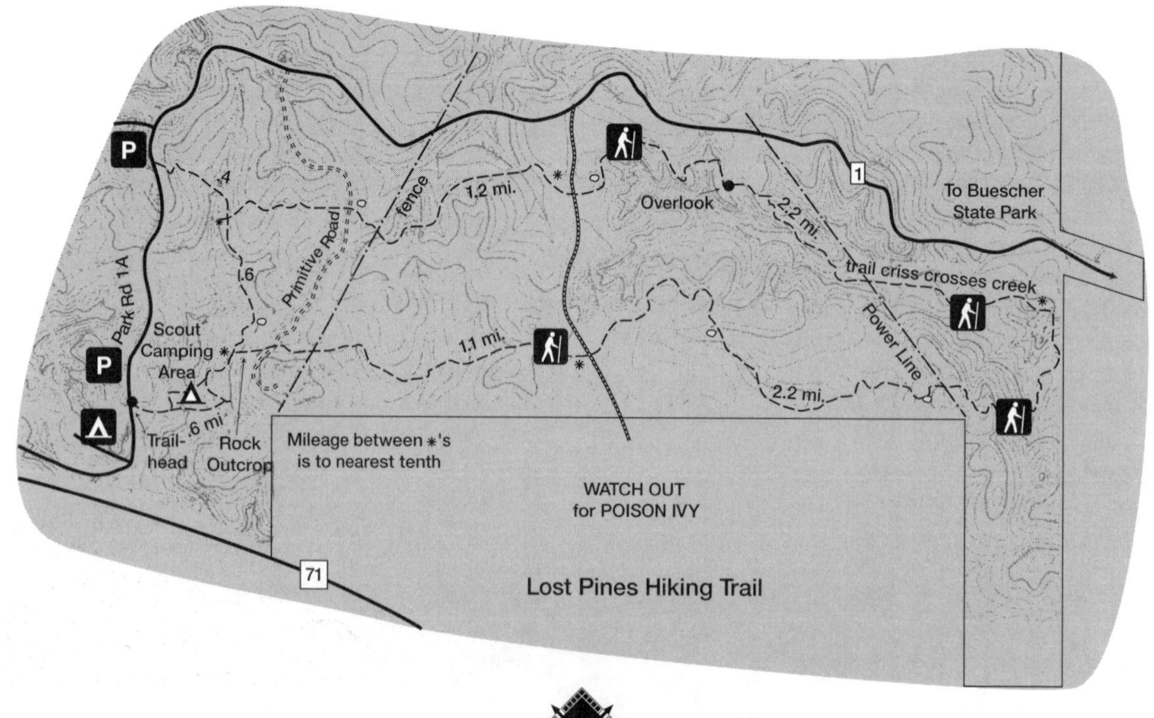

Big Bend National Park

FOR INFORMATION

Big Bend National Park
P.O. Box 129
Big Bend National Park, TX 79834-0129
432/477-2251 Visitor Center/Park Headquarters

LOCATION

Big Bend National Park is accessible off of US 90 at Marathon via US 385 (69 miles); from Alpine via TX 118 (108 miles); and from Marfa/Presidio via US 67 and FM 170 (156 miles). The park encompasses a vast area of 801,163 acres and is edged on three sides by the "big bend" of the Rio Grande, the international boundary between Mexico and the United States.

BACKPACKING IN BIG BEND NATIONAL PARK

The descriptions of the trails that appear in this section are abbreviated from the publication entitled *Hiker's Guide to Trails of Big Bend National Park* published by the Big Bend Natural History Association in cooperation with the National Park Service. Permission has been granted to cite this material as well as the following information on hiking hints and special conditions.

HIKING HINTS

▲ **Know Your Route.** If your hike takes you away from the maintained trails, you should carry a topographic map and a reliable compass, and KNOW HOW TO USE THEM. Inquire first about the condition of your route and of possible water resources. If you get lost, or hurt, stay in one place, conserve water, THINK! and signal for help. A whistle can save your life. Hikers everywhere recognize three blasts on a whistle as a distress call.

▲ **Inform Someone of Your Whereabouts.** If you are only going out for the day, let someone know where you are going and when you expect to return. Permits for overnight trips can be obtained at any ranger station. Park headquarters at Panther Junction is the best place to get complete information about how to safely use the park backcountry and to obtain a permit.

▲ **Be Prepared.** Plan to carry enough food and water to last until your return, plus a little extra. One gallon of water per person per day is recommended in summer, and slightly less in winter. Drink often, even if you don't feel thirsty. Springs in the desert are unreliable no matter what the map says. Travel as animals do, in the morning or evening, rather than during the heat of the day. Protect yourself from the sun by wearing a hat, long pants, and a long-sleeved shirt. Use sunscreen. Hiking boots, preferably with lug soles, provide important protection against rocks and sharp desert plants, as well as ankle support and increased traction for safety. Rattlesnakes are rare in winter and common in summer, especially at night. For your own safety, wear tough clothing and carry a first aid kit. Carry a flashlight after dark. Avoid narrow canyons when thunderstorms threaten because of flash floods. If lightning strikes, stay low, and avoid ridges or other high points.

SPECIAL CONDITIONS

1. *All overnight backpackers must obtain a free Backcountry Use Permit.* Permits are issued IN PERSON ONLY on a first-come, first-served basis no more than one day in advance. Permits for the high Chisos designated campsites are available at the Basin Ranger Station. The maximum group size is 15.
2. Campfire use is highly restricted.
3. Concerning litter—if you pack it in, YOU pack it out!
4. No smoking on trails when hiking. If you do smoke, remember that cigarette butts are litter. PACK THEM OUT!
5. Motorized vehicles are permitted on designated roads only.
6. Pets are not permitted on the trails or anywhere in the backcountry.
7. Leave all natural and historic features undisturbed, including wildlife, plants, rocks, artifacts, etc.
8. Camp at least 200 feet from any road, trail, historic structure, spring or other water source, and well out of and away from dry washes.
9. Do not use soap in springs or streams. Do not disturb springs.

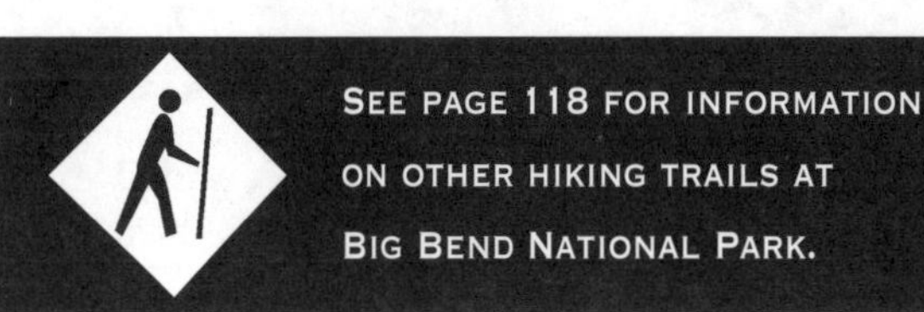
See page 118 for information on other hiking trails at Big Bend National Park.

10. Stay on the trails. Do not take shortcuts across switchbacks.
11. The use of firearms and metal detectors is prohibited.

FOR YOUR SAFETY

1. Do not rely on springs. Carry adequate water.
2. Do not climb rock faces. Rock throughout the park is very unstable.
3. Watch out for poisonous reptiles, but remember, they are protected too.
4. Do not camp or park your car in arroyos or dry creekbeds. Flash floods appear quickly after rainstorms.

HIGH CHISOS COMPLEX

This section includes all of the Chisos Mountain trails between the Basin Trailhead and the South Rim, and Juniper and Blue Creek Canyons as well. These high country trails are some of the park's most attractive hikes. During summer, the Chisos highlands provide a cool retreat from the warmer lowlands.

Carry plenty of water. Water is sometimes, though not always, available at Boot Spring, below the cabin. Check with a ranger when you get your permit. As at any exposed water source, treatment is recommended. Use only as much water as you absolutely need. Rains are few and far between in this country.

Experienced hikers *do not take shortcuts.* Switchbacks prevent trail erosion and make hiking easier. Don't defeat their purpose by cutting across them.

The trail to Mule Ear Peaks and Springs is a primitive route that starts at the Mule Ears Overlook parking area along the Ross Maxwell Scenic Road; it is marked in places with metal stakes.

HIKER'S LEGEND

Easy Walking—Trail developed and well defined. Easy grades. All ages. Street shoes or sneakers okay.

Medium Difficulty—Trail sometimes poorly defined. Can include steep grades and/or long distances. Not recommended for those with heart trouble or other physical problems. Hiking boots recommended.

Strenuous Day-Hike—For experienced, conditioned hikers only. Rough trails and longer distances. Sturdy hiking boots are a necessity.

Strenuous, Backpackers only—Knowledge of map reading, compass usage, and desert conditions are required. *Experienced* backpackers only.

Remember to take a camp stove. Use of campfires is highly restricted in the Park; open fires are not permitted at all in the Chisos Mountains. More detailed maps and information on all of these trails can be obtained at Park Headquarters or in the Basin. Topo maps: The Basin and Emory Peak.

▲ **No. 19A—South Rim** (Strenuous day-hike; 13–14.5 miles round-trip, depending on route.) The South Rim may be seen on a loop hike starting and ending at the Basin Trailhead. Hike up via the Boot Spring Trail (Pinnacles Trail) and down via Laguna Meadow, or vice versa. Any of these make good day hikes if you do not wish to make the entire trip to the South Rim. However, once you reach Boot Canyon or Laguna Meadow, you have gained much of the necessary elevation, and it is relatively easy to hike the rest of the way to the South Rim.

The shortest route to the South Rim is 6.5 miles from the Basin Trailhead via Laguna Meadow. You may return by the same trail, or you may circle the East Rim and hike out through Boot Canyon and the Boot Spring Trail. The full round-trip is 14.5 miles. You may wish to exclude the East Rim section and to return via the Boot Canyon "shortcut" trail to Boot Spring and to the Chisos Basin, a round-trip of 13 miles.

▲ **No. 19B—Pinnacles Trail** (Strenuous day-hike; 6.4 miles, one way, Basin Trailhead to the South Rim.) This trail is perhaps the prettier of the two trails going to the South Rim, but is the steeper of the two and is usually hiked south to north as the second half of the South Rim loop hike, allowing the hiker to cover it downhill. Caution must be used on the Pinnacles Trail, as it is steep and contains loose rubble.

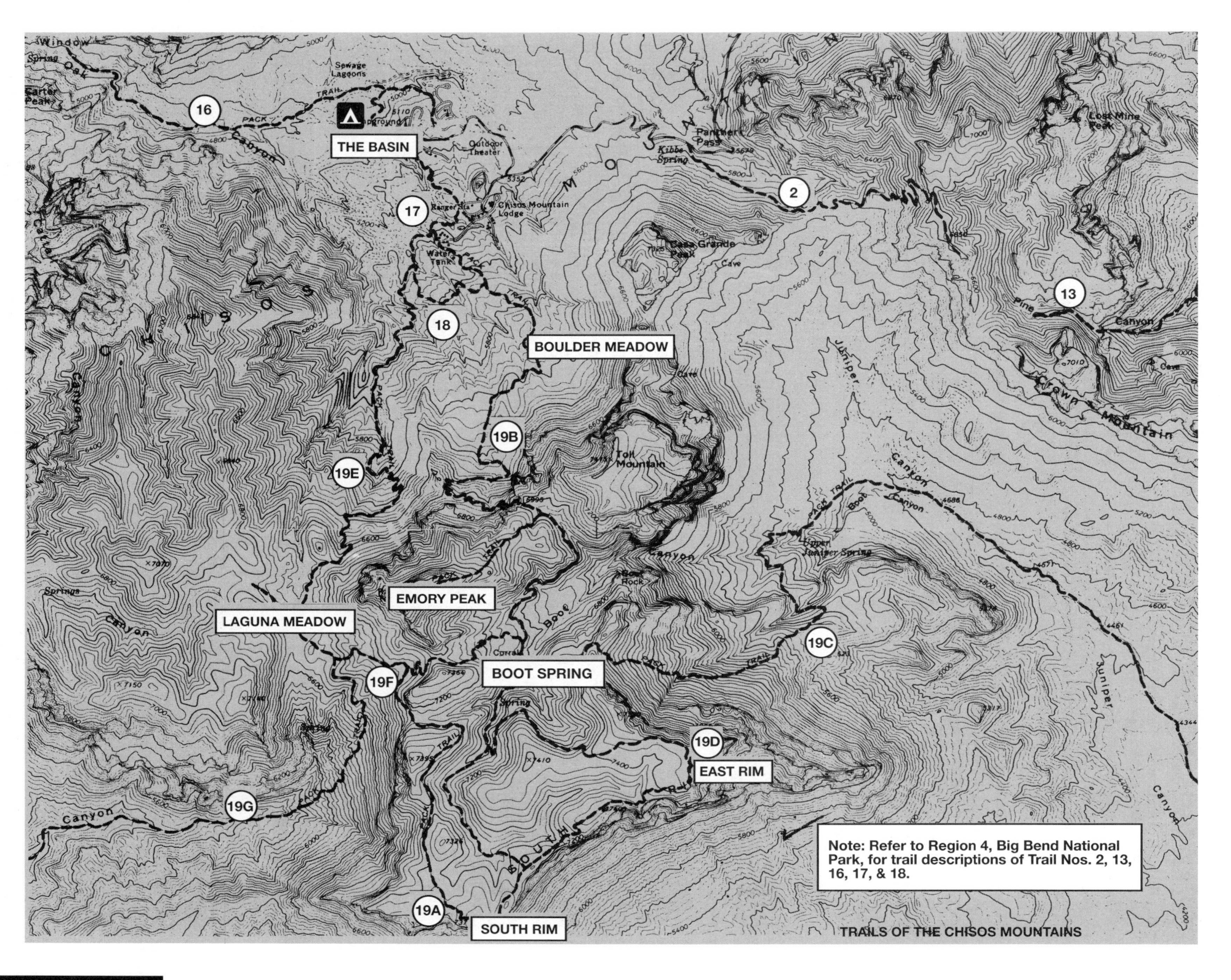

Note: Refer to Region 4, Big Bend National Park, for trail descriptions of Trail Nos. 2, 13, 16, 17, & 18.

TRAILS OF THE CHISOS MOUNTAINS

▲ **Boulder Meadow** (1.5 miles from the Basin Trailhead.) This meadow is a pretty, boulder-strewn flat at the base of Toll Mountain, and can be reached by an easy half-day round-trip hike through pinyon-juniper-oak woodlands.

▲ **Emory Peak** (4.5 miles from the Basin Trailhead.) The 1-mile trail to Emory Peak breaks to the right just over Pinnacles Pass, 3.5 miles from the Basin Trailhead. This spur trail leads to the highest point in Big Bend National Park—the summit of Emory Peak, elevation 7,835 feet. The last few feet require a scramble up a rock wall, but the view is superb in all directions.

▲ **Boot Spring** (4.5 miles from the Basin Trailhead.) The spring is located about the center of Boot Canyon; a little flat above the spring contains a cabin and corral. No camping is permitted in the vicinity of the spring or the cabin. The cabin is used by park service personnel who maintain and patrol the trails. The "Boot" is located at the pour-off of Boot Canyon into Juniper Canyon. This volcanic spire, shaped like an upside-down cowboy boot, has given the canyon its name.

▲ **No. 19C—Juniper Canyon Trail** (Medium difficulty; 4 miles one way from Boot Canyon to Juniper Canyon primitive road.) This side trail begins 0.2 mile beyond the Boot Springs cabin, 4.7 miles from the Basin Trailhead. It runs left off the Boot Springs Trail, climbs over a high pass, and descends to the end of the Juniper Canyon primitive road. Near the bottom of the hill, the trail passes Upper Juniper Spring. This spring is not dependable in dry years. The Juniper Canyon Trail and Road are part of the Outer Mountain Loop backpacking route. See Hike No. 28.

▲ **No. 19D—East Rim** (Medium difficulty; 3.3-mile loop from the Boot Spring Trail to the South Rim junction.) The East Rim can be reached by continuing up Boot Canyon behind the Juniper Canyon Trail junction to the East Rim Trail junction. The East Rim Trail bears to the left and follows a side canyon to the East Rim where there are several excellent overlooks into Juniper Canyon. The trail then runs south and west along the edge of the high Chisos rim to the South Rim.

▲ **No. 19E—Laguna Meadow Trail** (Strenuous day-hike; 6.5 miles one way, Basin Trailhead to the South Rim.) This is the usual route to the South Rim from the Basin, since the climb is more gradual than it is via the Pinnacles Trail.

▲ **Laguna Meadow** (3.5 miles from the Basin Trailhead.) An ancient marshy area or meadow, Laguna apparently was a popular camping place for Indians.

Ward Mountain primitive trail starts along the north side of Laguna Meadow and is about two miles in length. A small rock dam is located at the end of this hike.

Just past Laguna Meadow, the trail begins a climb in the direction of Emory Peak before intersecting the Colima Trail.

▲ **No. 19F—Colima Trail** The Colima Trail provides a 0.8-mile shortcut between the Laguna Meadow and Pinacles trails. As the trail descends into Boot Canyon, it passes a small stand of Douglas fir, another rare tree of the Chisos Mountains.

▲ **No. 19G—Blue Creek Trail** (Strenuous day-hike; 5.5 miles one way to the Blue Creek Ranch Overlook from the South Rim Trail junction.) This trail begins 0.2 mile south of Laguna Meadow and follows Blue Creek Canyon to the Blue Creek Ranch and the Castolon Road. The entire hike from the Basin Trailhead is 9 miles, and is especially enjoyable if you can leave a vehicle at the Blue Creek Ranch Overlook. This trail is one of the few that traverses so many plant zones.

The lower end of this route passes through some of the most colorful rock formations in the park. The myriad pinnacles and balanced rocks are collectively called Red Rocks Canyon, and can be reached by hiking up the Blue Creek Trail 2.5 miles from the Blue Creek Ranch Overlook.

PRIMITIVE ROUTES

There are vast wilderness areas in Big Bend National Park where few hikers enter; yet many areas contain an abundance of old roads and trails that were in use from the late 1800s until the park was established in the 1940s. Some of these routes are still quite visible, at least in a few places. Others are marked by occasional rock cairns, or metal stakes, or not at all. For any of these hikes, a 7.5-minute topographic map, a compass, knowledge of the desert, up-to-date information, proper gear, and common sense are necessary commodities.

No hike should be attempted without adequate water to last your first evening on the trail and get you back to your vehicle or starting point, should your destination be dry.

▲ **No. 20—Dog Canyon** (Medium difficulty; 5 miles round-trip; no water; topographic maps; Dagger Flat and Bone Spring.) This hike starts 5 miles south of Persimmon Gap, at the Dog Canyon Parking area. The best route on this hike is line of sight from the parking area to the canyon itself. The hike is relatively level, but is a true scorcher in warm weather. This hike is often done in conjunction with a visit to Devil's Den. See Hike No. 21.

▲ **No. 21—Devil's Den** (Medium difficulty; 5.6 miles round-trip; water variable; topographic maps: Dagger Flat and Bone Spring.) This route also starts from the Dog Canyon parking area. You can see the deep cut of Devil's Den in the north-facing slope between the northern end of Dagger Mountain and Dog Canyon. Follow Bone Spring Draw toward Dog Canyon to Nine Point Draw (check your 7.5-minute map), then to a wash that enters from the south. Follow this wash all the way to Devil's Den. You can hike part way up the canyon (about ½ mile when potholes are full) or along the western edge for the best photographic opportunities. See also Dog Canyon Hike No. 20.

▲ **No. 22—Ward Spring** (Medium difficulty; 3.6 miles round-trip; water usually available; topographic map: Emory Peak.) This hike starts from a parking area along the Ross Maxwell Scenic Road, 2.2 miles south of the Old Ranch. It is a pleasant hike that passes through part of the old Homer Wilson ranching properties on the western slope of the Chisos Mountains.

The route follows an old pipeline route, no longer visible, that carried water from Ward Spring to a stock tank north of the parking area. You can barely see the spring from the parking area.

▲ **No. 23—Top of Burro Mesa Pour-off** (Medium difficulty; 3.6 miles round-trip; no water; topographic map: Cerro Castellan.) The trail begins near the southern end of the Burro Mesa along the Ross Maxwell Scenic Road, 4.0 miles south of the Old Ranch, at a raised platform on the right side of the road. The route follows a dry wash downstream, through some very narrow rock gorges, to the lip of the pour-off.

▲ **No. 24—Chimneys Trail** (Medium difficulty; 4.8 miles round-trip; no water; topographic maps: Cerro Castellan and Castolon.) The trail starts from the Ross Maxwell Scenic Road 1.2 miles south of the Burro Mesa Pour-off spur road, and follows an old roadway to a series of "chimneys"—high rock outcrops that are visible to the west of Kit Mountain. The Chimneys have served as an important landmark for hundreds of years.

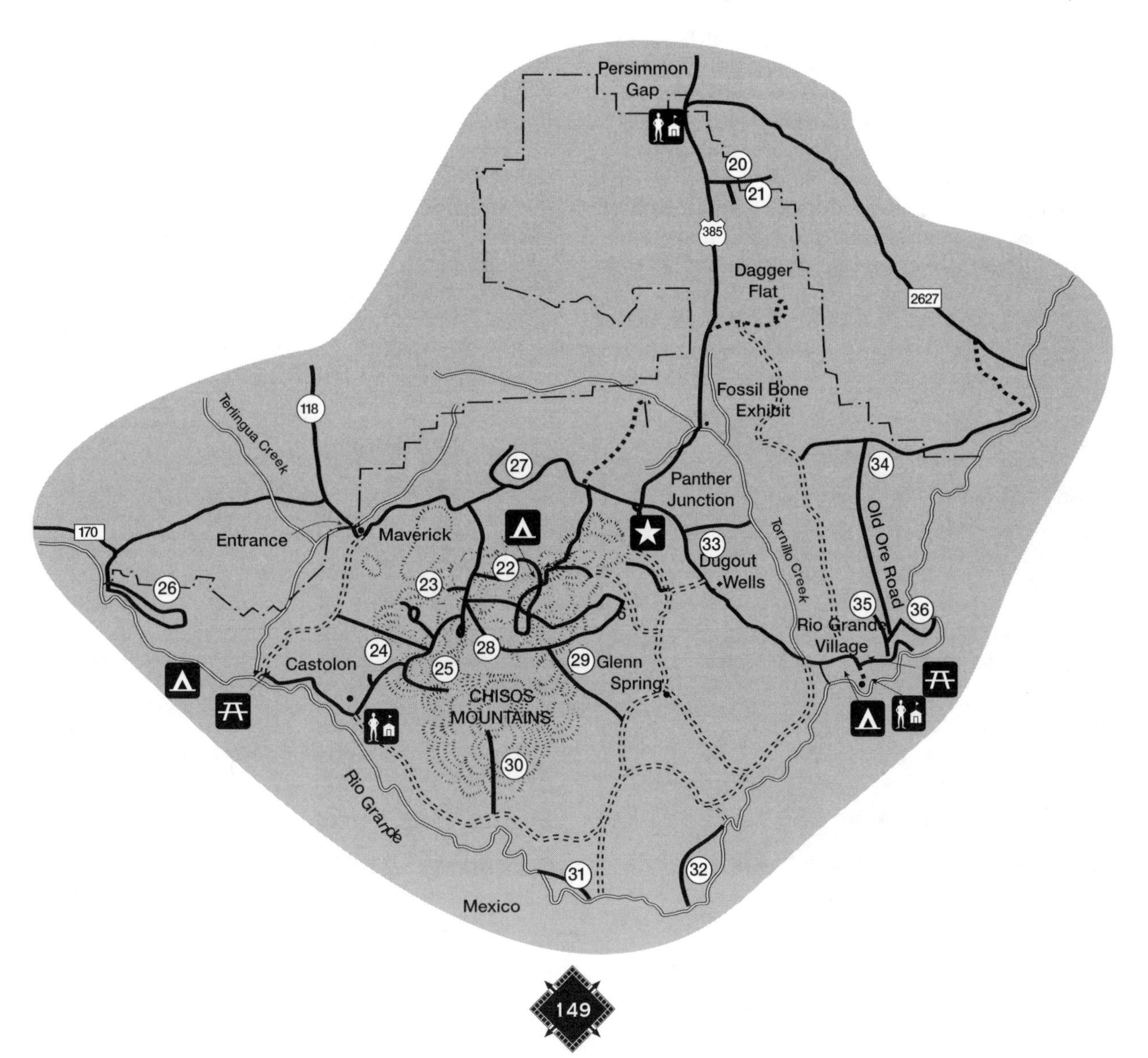

It is possible to continue to hike west for 4.6 miles, past Pena Spring, to a point just north of Luna's jacal on the Old Maverick Road. This hike can be a very pleasant 7-mile wintertime hike if transportation can be arranged on the opposite end.

▲ **No. 25—Mule Ear Spring** (Medium difficulty; 3.8 miles round-trip; water usually available; topographic map: Cerro Castellan.) This delightful trail starts at the Mule Ears Overlook parking area along the Ross Maxwell Scenic Road, and is marked in places with metal stakes. This primitive trail skirts the south slope of Trap Mountain, crossing several arroyos before reaching a wash that it follows almost to Mule Ear Spring.

The following trails are rated as either strenuous day-hike or strenuous backpacking.

▲ **No. 26—Mesa de Anguila Complex** (Strenuous, backpackers only; water variable; topographic maps: Lajitas and Mesa de Anguila.) There is a maze of trails on the mesa, most of which can be followed by using a detailed topographic map, preferably a 7.5-minute USGS quadrangle. Major routes on the west half of the Mesa are fairly well marked, and turnoffs to other routes are marked with rock cairns. All of them should be considered winter hikes. They travel through rough country and are suggested for the most adventuresome and competent backpackers only. You will need several days and much water.

▲ **No. 27—Slickrock Canyon** (Strenuous day-hike; 10 miles round-trip; no water; topographic maps: The Basin and Tule Mountain.) The route starts from the paved road, halfway between Croton Spring Road and Ross Maxwell Scenic Road junction, 8.3 miles west of the Basin Junction. It follows Oak Creek northwest and turns north into the drainage that passes along the south side of Slickrock Mountain. Or you may wish to leave Oak Creek after the first one-half mile and cut across the flats directly to Slickrock. The canyon is carved deep into the side of the mountain, and is very colorful early and late in the day.

▲ **No. 28—Outer Mountain Loop** (Strenuous, backpackers only; 33-mile loop; water available; topographic map: Emory Peak.) This is a triangular hike covering parts of the Pinnacles and Laguna Meadow trails, the Juniper Canyon Trail, and the Blue Creek Trail (all described in the High Chisos Complex section, Hike No. 19) and the Dodson Trail, described below.

You can start and end in the Chisos Basin, Juniper Canyon, or the Blue Creek Ranch Overlook. The trail can be traveled either clock-wise or counterclockwise. Either way will take you through a wide range of plant communities and scenery.

▲ **Dodson Trail** (11.5 miles) Although some sections of this trail are fairly easy to follow, others can be very confusing. It is advisable to carry a

These backpackers are on a trail in the Mesa de Anguila leading to the mouth of Santa Elena Canyon. As they look across the Rio Grande River into Mexico, they carefully check their map to determine their exact location. This is rugged country, and many of the trails are poorly marked.

7.5-minute map and consult it often. The eastern portion of the route (between Juniper Canyon road and the Dodson Place) is fairly easy to follow because of rock cairns that mark the way. An old fence line parallels your route for the first 4 miles. Keep the fence line to your left all the way to the Dodson Place, even though other trails appear to be crossing it.

The last segment of the hike, from the spring to the junction with the Elephant Tusk Trail, is the most difficult to follow. There are few rock cairns, and you can lose your way among the drainages. Pay close attention to your map.

Beyond the Elephant Tusk Trail, the route is again easier to find as it passes around the base of Carousel Mountain to the Blue Creek Ranch, and the junction with the Blue Creek Trail.

▲ **No. 29—Elephant Tusk, Fresno Creek** (Strenuous, backpackers only; 16 miles round-trip; water usually available; topographic maps: Glenn Spring and Emory Peak.) This hike can be made as a 16-mile loop trip. It is a poorly defined trail that starts from the Black Gap Road (not maintained), 5 miles from Glenn Spring and heads northwest toward the east side of Elephant Tusk. A metal stake adjacent to the roadway marks the start of the trail. A round-trip hike can be made by continuing on this trail beyond Elephant Tusk to a point just below Tortuga Mountain where you can turn back and follow Fresno Creek all the way back to the Black Gap Road.

▲ **No. 30—Dominguez Spring** (Strenuous day-hike and/or backpackers; 14 miles round-trip; water usually available; topographic maps: Reed Camp and Emory Peak.) This beautiful hike starts from the River Road, 23.0 miles from the west end. The trail follows an old roadway through open desert for 4.5 miles before entering the rugged canyons of the Sierra Quemada. The trail then follows a wash to the west and south of Dominguez Mountain. A small rock dam and rock house mark the spring site. Although the dam collapsed many years ago, the house is one of the best preserved rock houses in the park. It is possible to hike beyond the spring to join the Dodson Trail or turn west toward Mule Ear Spring and the overlook along the Ross Maxwell Scenic Road.

▲ **No. 31—Mariscal Canyon Rim** (Strenuous day-hike; 6.6 miles round-trip; no water; topographic map: Mariscal Mountain.) The hardest part of this hike is finding where it starts. Begin by hiking to the top of the bluff to the northeast, visible from the parking area at the end of the unimproved dirt road to Talley. The trail goes out around the end of the bluff toward the river before cutting back across some large, open flats and ascending the west side of Mariscal Mountain. The first 2 miles of this old burro trail are easy walking, but the next mile is very steep. The trail ends at a magnificent overlook high on the Mariscal Canyon rim. From the highest point of the rim, the river is nearly 1,500 feet below.

▲ **No. 32—Cross Canyon Trail** (Strenuous day-hike and/or backpackers only; 14 miles round-trip; no water; topographic maps: Solis and Mariscal Mountain.) This is the primitive route between Solis and Cross Canyon in Mariscal Canyon. It is poorly defined and is not shown on the 7.5-minute USGS quadrangle maps. A thorough knowledge of the country is a must for this hike.

▲ **No. 33—Banta Shut-In** (Strenuous day-hike and/or backpackers; 15 miles round-trip; water supply unreliable; topographic maps: Roy's Peak and Panther Junction.) One route starts from the K-Bar primitive campsite, located 4 miles southeast of Panther Junction. This hike is entirely within desert terrain that is very hot in summer. It involves a series of old roads that can be difficult to locate.

An easier, though longer, route begins at the Fossil Bone Exhibit 8 miles north of Park Headquarters toward Persimmon Gap. Park at the exhibit parking lot, drop down into the Tornillo drainage, and follow it all the way to the Shut-In. Round-trip distance along this route is close to 20 miles. Be alert for flash floods when taking this route.

▲ **No. 34—Strawhouse, Telephone Canyon Trails** (Strenuous, backpackers only; no water; topographic maps: Roy's Peak, Boquillas, Ernst Valley, and Sue Peaks.) There are many trails located in the Dead Horse Mountains. They are recommended for only the most experienced hikers who have thoroughly explored the other trails in the park and have acquired a good working knowledge of map and compass. The two most prominent trails, in addition to the Marufo Vega Trail (Hike No. 36), are the Strawhouse Trail and the Telephone Canyon Trail. They have been used for years as a route for Mexicans traveling from Boquillas and San Vicente to Adams' Ranch and beyond.

The Telephone Canyon Trail is approximately 20 miles in length. It starts along the Old Ore Road and runs east over the western ridges of the Dead Horse Mountains to join the Strawhouse Trail in Heath Canyon, then follows Heath Canyon to Adams' Ranch.

The Strawhouse Trail runs for approximately 14 miles between Heath Canyon and the Boquillas Canyon road, just below Boquillas Canyon Overlook (the same trailhead as the Ore Terminal and Marufo Vega Trails).

▲ **No. 35—Ore Terminal** (Strenuous day-hike; 8 miles round-trip; no water; topographic map: Boquillas.) The route begins in the wash just below the entrance to the Canyon Overlook near Boquillas Canyon. The entire route is within the open limestone hills below 3,000 feet elevation. This is a wintertime hike that is very uncomfortable in midsummer.

The Ore Terminal Trail was used to service the towers during the operation of the tramway from 1909 to 1919. The 6-mile tramway carried a total of 90 ore buckets of zinc, silver, and lead ore between Mexico's Corte Madera Mine and the Texas terminal.

▲ **No. 36—Marufo Vega Trail** (Strenuous day-hike and/or backpackers; 12 miles round-trip; no water; river water not potable; topographic maps: Boquillas and Ernst Valley.) It is 6 miles to the Rio Grande and about the same distance to a high promontory along a south fork of the main trail. The trail starts in the drainage below the Canyon Overlook. This route offers some good views of the river and Sierra del Carmen.

ADDITIONAL EXPLORING

Big Bend National Park contains countless canyons, arroyos, expanses of open desert and other vast trackless areas that can be explored at length by the experienced backpacker who has traveled the more developed routes already. If the trails listed here have merely whetted your appetite for more, consult with personnel on duty at Park Headquarters for additional ideas for backcountry exploring.

Maps. Topographic maps with scales of 1:24,000 and contour intervals of 40 feet are available from:

Big Bend Natural History Association
Big Bend National Park, TX 79834

or

Distribution Section
U.S. Geological Survey
Federal Center
Denver, CO 80225

This view of the Rio Grande River is from a nature trail on a high promontory a short distance from the Rio Grande Village campground. From this vantage point the views are fantastic—downriver is the Mexican village of Boquillas and Boquillas Canyon, and upriver are the Chisos Mountains beyond Hot Springs Canyon.

BIG BEND RANCH STATE PARK

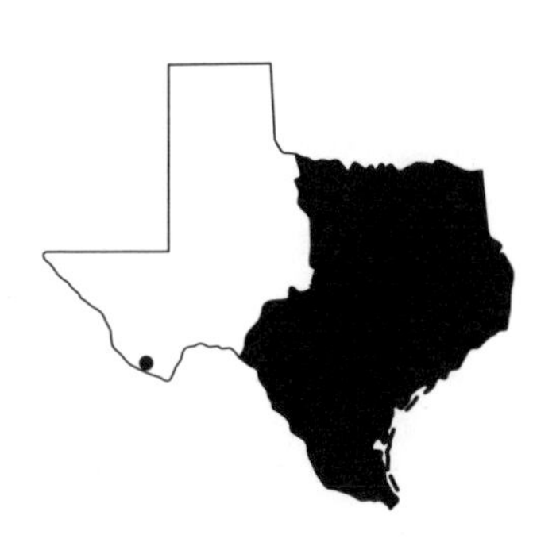

FOR INFORMATION

BIG BEND RANCH STATE PARK COMPLEX
P.O. BOX 2319
PRESIDIO, TX 79845
432/229-3416

BIG BEND RANCH STATE PARK
SAUCEDA
432/385-4444

LOCATION

Big Bend Ranch State Park is located just west of Big Bend National Park. The 299,623-acre park lies both south and north of FM 170, which parallels the Rio Grande River between Lajitas and Redford; it was purchased by the state of Texas in 1988. Previously used as ranch land, the park is often called "The Crown Jewel of the Texas State Parks System." Recreational activities are designed for low- or no-impact use.

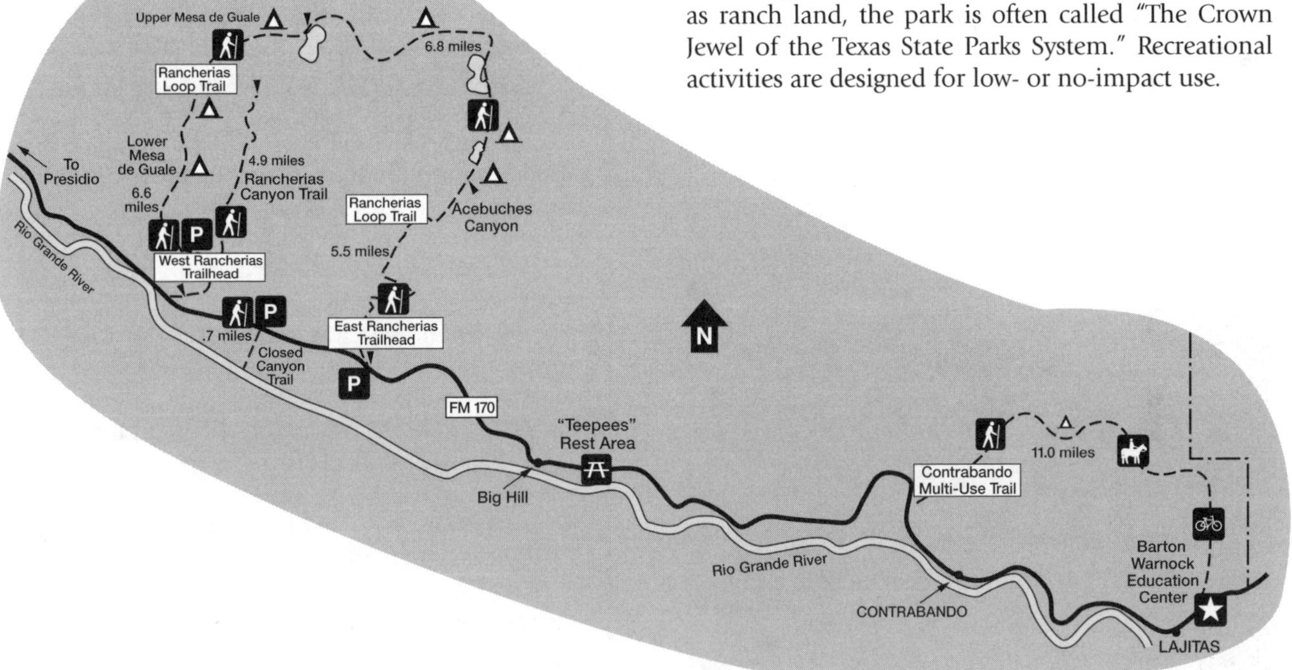

Texas Highways Magazine

BARTON WARNOCK ENVIRONMENTAL EDUCATION CENTER

After 3 years of renovation, the state's newest exhibit of the Big Bend region opened to the public in December, 1998. The museum, originally owned by the nonprofit Lajitas Foundation was purchased by the state in 1990. The adobe-and-red-tile museum complex is 1 mile east of Lajitas on FM 170 beneath a towering rock

Currently, there are 32 miles of trails at the Big Bend Ranch State Park that are designated for horses.

formation known as the Lajitas Mesa. The exhibit consists of a series of walk-through galleries exploring the geology and biology of the Chihuahuan Desert—the largest of the continent's four major deserts.

The center serves as a visitor information center for all public and private facilities within a 100-mile range of Lajitas. It also serves as the eastern gateway to the Big Bend Ranch State Park. Camping and river permits for the state park are available, as are permits for certain uses of the Big Bend National Park. The museum is open 7 days a week from 8 a.m. to 4:30 p.m. Admission price for adults is $3 and $1.50 for children, 6 to 12.

This renovation project also includes a new visitor center at the Sauceda complex in the interior of the Big Bend Ranch State Park, as well as new exhibits there depicting the park's ranch history and other improvements.

Day one of this 3-day trip required some serious rock scrambling when climbing out of Acebuches Canyon.

TRAIL NOTES

The **Rancherias Loop Trail** is about 19 miles long and is a suggested 3-day, 2-night trip into the canyon country of the Bofecillos Mountains. The east and west trailheads to this loop trail are along FM 170 west of Lajitas near the trailheads to the two-day-hike trails in Colorado Canyon. The trail system within the park is a complex of traditional routes, in combination with historic wagon road, and modern jeep roads. At times, a trail is no more than a "way" defined by the presence of springs or obvious points of passage. Unless the route is obvious, trails have been marked with rock cairns; cairns also direct you when 2 or more trails intersect. Because of the primitive nature of these trails, you must have a topographic map and compass and *know how to use them.*

A trail guide and map are available with backcountry information and guidelines. The guide describes the trail in 3 segments—from the east trailhead as well as from the west trailhead. Information regarding the approximate mileage, estimated walking time, and net elevation change proves valuable when planning a trip. Six backcountry camping areas along the loop trail are suggested on the map. Camping is prohibited within 300 feet of any spring or natural water source. Springs marked on the map are not reliable water sources; carry a minimum of 1 gallon of water per day, per person. There is no camping in the 3 critical management zones marked on the map. Obtain a backcountry permit.

The 11-mile **Contrabando Trail** is along an old jeep road and old horse trails and is for horses, hikers and bikers. There are more difficult trails off the main trunk. A primitive camping area is located midway along the trail. There are 2 trailheads; one is across from the Barton Warnock Education Center.

SEE PAGE 123 FOR INFORMATION ON OTHER HIKING TRAILS AT BIG BEND RANCH STATE PARK.

Big Thicket National Preserve

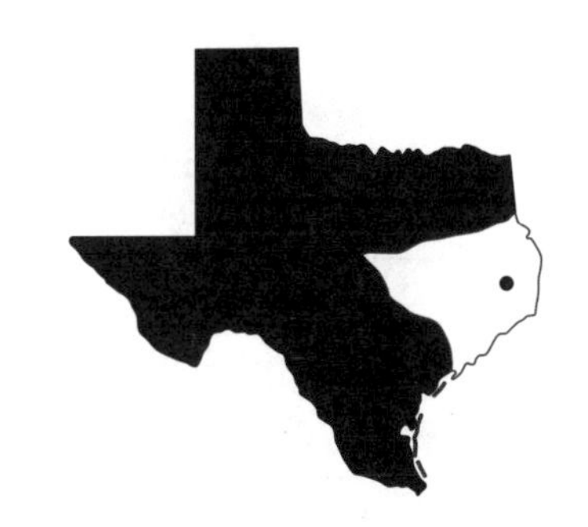

For Information

Big Thicket National Preserve
3785 Milam
Beaumont, TX 77701
Headquarters 409/839-2689
Visitor Center 409/246-2337

Backcountry Camping Information

For those individuals or small family groups who wish to experience backcountry camping, several camping zones have been established in isolated portions of some of the preserve units. Backcountry camping zones are designated in portions of 9 of the preserve units/corridors. Backcountry camping is suspended in all areas open to hunting from October 1 through January 15.

The purpose of these backcountry camping zones is to provide a minimum impact "wilderness" type experience. For this reason, backcountry use is limited to a maximum of 5 days, and group size is limited to eight persons. A visual and noise separation must be maintained between camped groups.

A free backcountry permit is required, and must be obtained in person at the beginning of the trip. You may obtain permits at three locations:

1. The Visitor Center on FM 420 in the Turkey Creek Unit. It is open daily from 9 a.m. to 5 p.m.
2. At Preserve Headquarters in Beaumont at 3785 Milam, weekdays between 8:00 a.m. and 4:30 p.m.
3. The Woodville Office on US 287, ½ mile northwest of the US 69/287 junction. It is open weekdays 8:00 a.m. to 4:30 p.m. Maps showing the specific zone locations are provided with the permit.

For those who are coming earlier or later than these hours, special arrangements can be made to register you at some convenient point and time at the start of the trip. Please phone ahead of time to make these arrangements: Visitor Center (409/246-2337); Headquarters (409/839-2689); Woodville Office, (409/283-5824).

There are no hiking trails linking one unit to another. Water and toilet facilities are not available in the backcountry zones. Fires using camp stoves are allowed in wooded areas; open fires are allowed only on sandbars along the Neches River. Pets and motorized vehicles are not allowed on preserve trails. Horses and mountain bikes are prohibited on all trails except on the Big Sandy Horse Trail. The possession of food or beverage in glass containers is prohibited. No camping is allowed within 25 feet of a lakeshore, stream, or other waterway, except on unrestricted sandbars within the Neches River watercourse. Pack out all trash and garbage; do not bury anything. And, one last reminder, a backcountry use permit (free) is required before overnight use on any unit of the Big Thicket National Preserve.

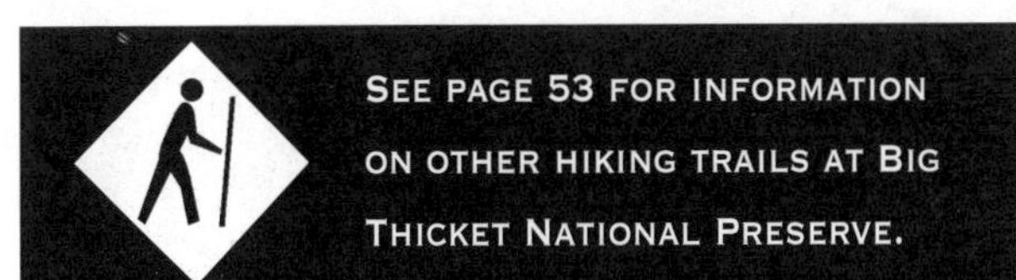

See page 53 for information on other hiking trails at Big Thicket National Preserve.

Before beginning an overnight canoe trip along the Neches River Corridor, check with a ranger for current and projected water conditions, weather forecasts, and road conditions at launch sites. Overnight camping on sandbars is permitted.

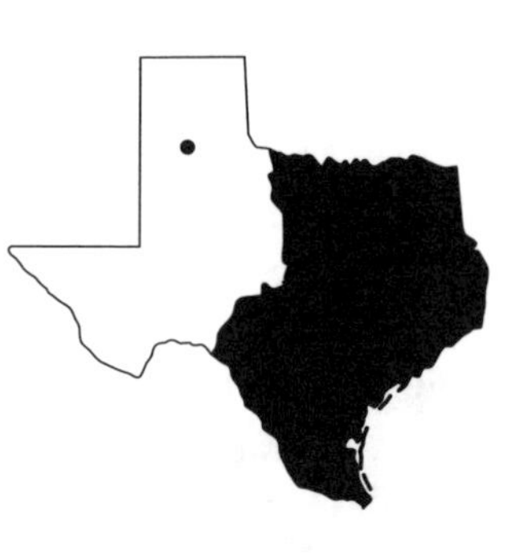

Caprock Canyons State Park and Trailway

FOR INFORMATION

CAPROCK CANYONS STATE PARK AND TRAILWAY
P.O. BOX 204
QUITAQUE, TX 79255
806/455-1492

LOCATION

Caprock Canyons State Park and Trailway is located 3 miles north of Quitaque. Although bordered on the north by TX 256, the park entrance is on the south and most easily accessible by traveling north through Quitaque on RR 1065. Quitaque is on TX 86, which runs east from I-27/US 87 at Tulia and west from US 287 at Estelline. The 15,160-acre park is named for the scenic and rugged escarpment that separates the tablelands of the Southern High Plains from the breaks and rolling plains to the east. Most of the area contains exposed red sandstones and siltstones.

TRAIL NOTES

Five hiking/backpacking trails, totaling 17 miles, are located in the park. They are:

Canyon Loop Trail (1½ miles)
Haynes Ridge Overlook Trail (2 miles)
Upper Canyon Trail (5½ miles)
Lower Canyon Trail (5 miles)
Canyon Rim Trail (3 miles)

Nearly 14 miles of trails are designated as equestrian trails. Two primitive camping areas for backpackers and one equestrian primitive camping area are provided in the backcountry. A hike or ride of about one mile is required to reach each of these areas. Open fires are not allowed in the primitive areas.

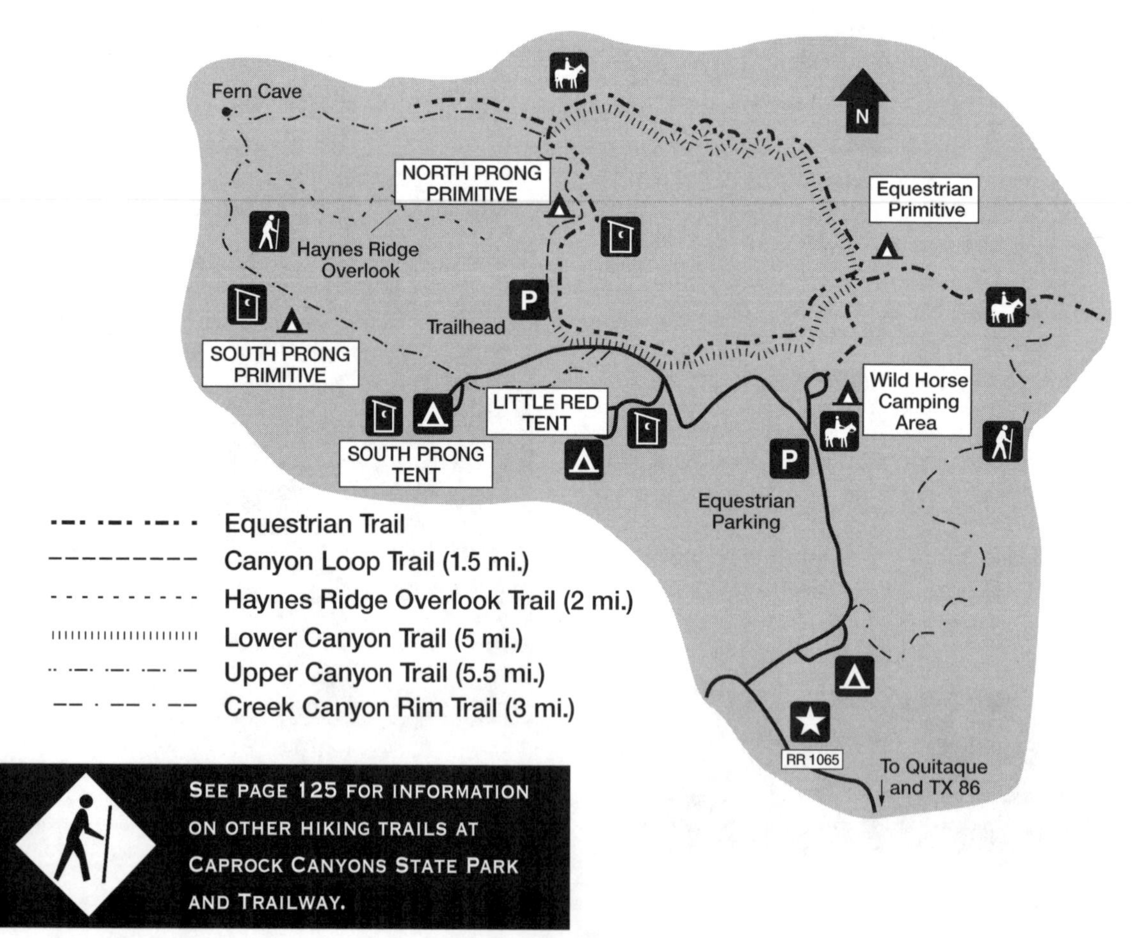

SEE PAGE 125 FOR INFORMATION ON OTHER HIKING TRAILS AT CAPROCK CANYONS STATE PARK AND TRAILWAY.

Caprock Canyons Trailway

LOCATION

The Caprock Canyons Trailway is the longest rail-to-trail conversion in the state of Texas. The 64-mile trail begins in South Plains, moves through Quitaque and Turkey as it passes within 3 miles of the state park, and ends in Estelline. In terms of its natural features, from west to east, the trail moves through the cultivated fields of the Texas high plains, drops into the rugged canyons of the Caprock Escarpment, and winds down into the famous Red River Valley.

TRAIL NOTES

The 64-mile-long multi-purpose trailway offers a unique and exciting recreational experience for hikers, bikers, and equestrian trail riders. The entire length of the trail is open for use, but as this guide went to press it was still under construction. Facilities shown on this map may not be complete and/or operational.

All trail users must obtain an entrance permit to use the parking area and trailway. Overnight campers must obtain permits at Caprock Canyons State Park headquarters. Day-use fees may be paid at the state park or at one of the volunteer pay stations located at each trailhead. Pick up a copy of the trail map at the state park; it contains valuable information on each of the 6 sections of the trail, such as the location of the backcountry campsites, the estimated completion time for each user group, and the phone number of a local shuttle service concessionaire for the trailway.

Sections of the trailway are quite remote; traveling the trailway alone is not recommended. All water, equipment, and supplies needed for the trip should be carried because services are limited. Drinking water stations and equestrian water tubs are available at many trailheads and developed primitive camping sites, but the availability of water is not dependable. During freezing weather and through the winter, water is usually not available. Portable phones may be useful for reporting problems and emergencies. Rattlesnakes are common; always watch where you put your hands and feet. Ground fires are not allowed.

The 742-foot Clarity Tunnel is located about 13 miles east of the South Plains parking lot and 4½ miles southwest of the Monk's Crossing parking lot. Round-trip is about 9 miles. Day-hikers wishing to see the Clarity Tunnel should access the trailway at Monk's Crossing and hike southwest. A population of Brazilian free-tailed bats inhabits the tunnel and main migrations and populations occur from April through October. Do not touch bats—alive or dead!

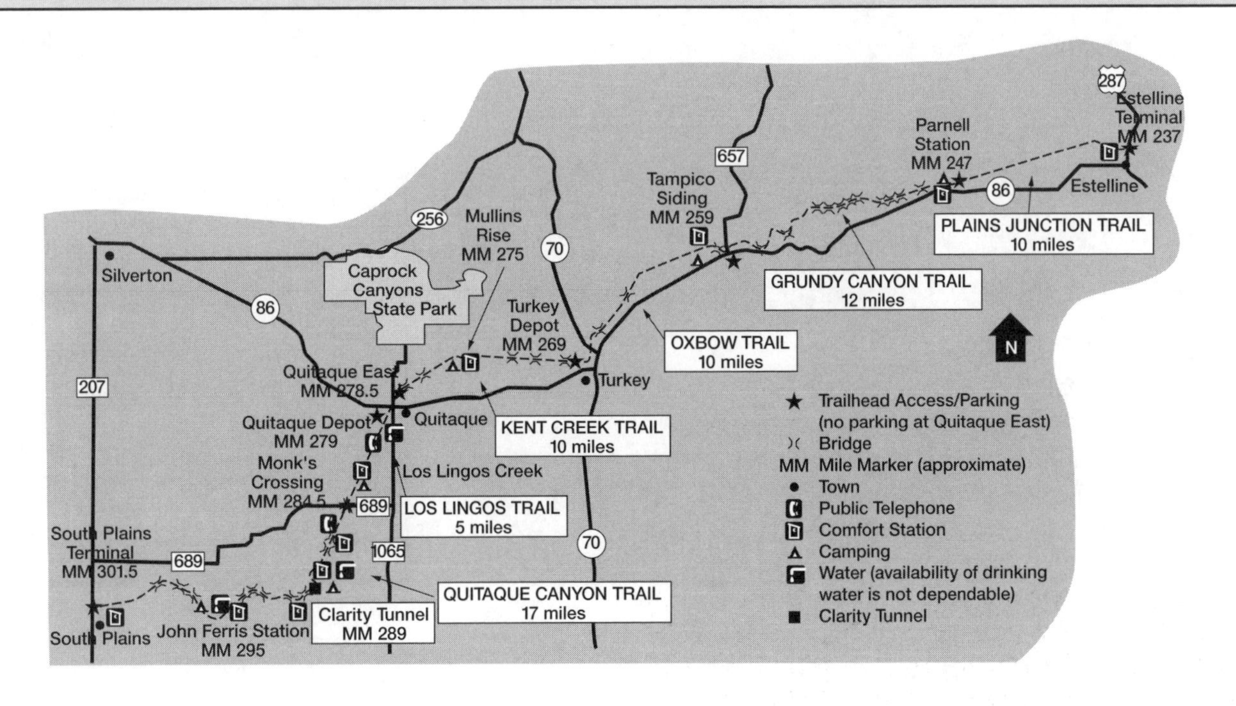

Choke Canyon State Park
North Shore Equestrian and Camping Area

FOR INFORMATION

Choke Canyon State Park
South Shore Unit
P.O. Box 1548
Three Rivers, TX 78071
512/786-3538

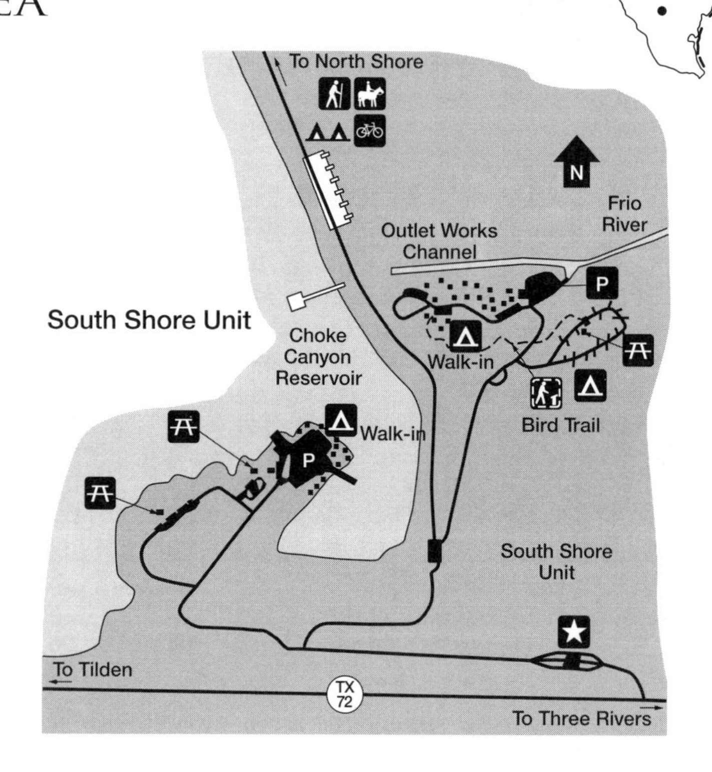

LOCATION

Access to the North Shore Equestrian and Camping Area is through the South Shore Unit of Choke Canyon State Park. The South Shore Unit is located 3½ miles west of Three Rivers off of TX 72 on Choke Canyon Reservoir. The 385-acre park provides access to the 26,000-acre reservoir, the Frio River below the dam, and 1,700 acres of uncrowded South Texas Brush Country scenery that has been named the North Shore Equestrian and Camping Area.

North Shore Equestrian Camping Area

Fence Boundary
Fence Boundary
Power Line
Paved Road to Dam
Boat ramp
N

TRAIL NOTES

A paved road across the dam leads to the facilities, which include 18 miles of designated trails for hiking, biking and horseback riding, and 4 primitive group camping areas. The terrain ranges from grassy shrubland to rugged and rocky and semi-rocky soil. Trail users need to bring adequate water for human consumption; lake water may be used for horses. Sanitary facilities are not available, and all litter and garbage must be packed out. There is a 45-horse limit; neither corrals nor horse rentals are available. Because of the remoteness of the group camping area, there is an 8-person minimum requirement. Fees include a per person entrance fee, a per horse daily fee, and a fee for primitive overnight camping. The area is closed one month each fall during hunting season; check schedule. Contact park for reservations and additional information.

Colorado Bend State Park

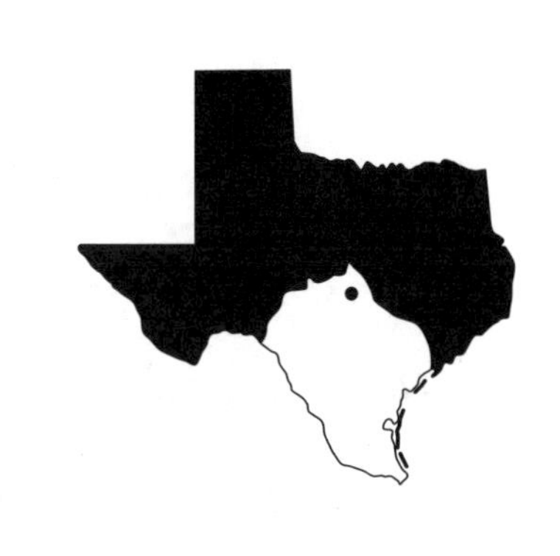

FOR INFORMATION

Colorado Bend State Park
P.O. Box 118
Bend, TX 76824
325/628-3240

LOCATION

This state park is on the Colorado River about 10 miles above Lake Buchanan, west of Lampasas and southeast of San Saba. From the intersection of US 281 and US 183 in Lampasas, take FM 580 west for 24 miles to Bend. From San Saba, take US 190 about 4 miles to FM 580 and travel southeast for 13 miles to Bend. From Bend, follow the signs 4 miles to the park entrance. The headquarters and main camping area are 6 miles past the entrance on the gravel road.

The access road into this 5,328-acre park is subject to flooding; after rain, several locations on the unpaved road may be difficult for standard two-wheel-drive vehicles to negotiate. It is advisable to leave the park if heavy rain is expected. Gorman Falls and several wild caves are accessible only through guided tours. The park is closed for wildlife management hunts—usually December through January.

You're never too young to fish . . . and what better place to learn than at Colorado Bend.

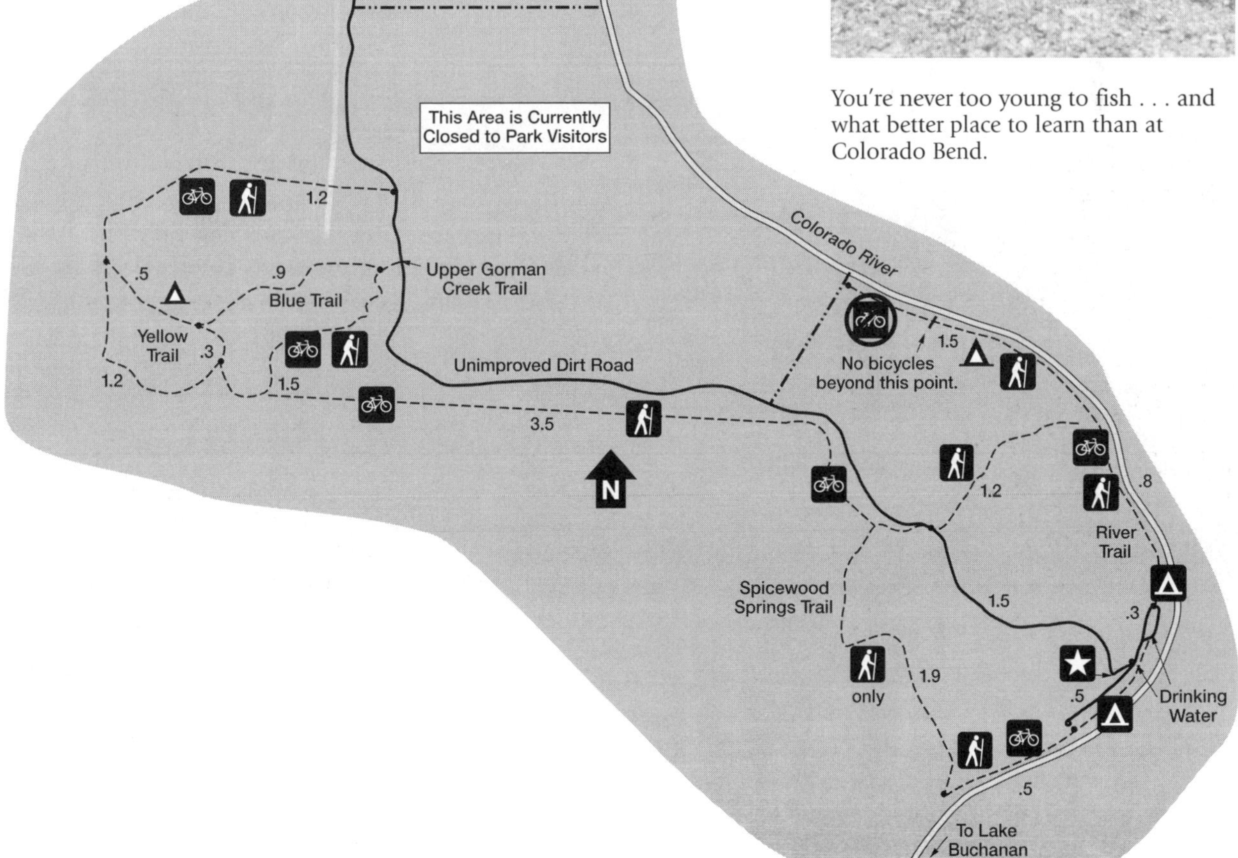

BACKPACKING TRAILS

TRAIL NOTES

There are 16 miles of hiking and 14 miles of bike trails at Colorado Bend State Park; one trail is designated for hiking only, but the other trails are for hiking and mountain biking. The Spicewood Springs Trail passes through fragile stream environments and is closed to bicycles. The 5.7-mile Upper Gorman Creek Trail and the River Trail are old dirt roads where hiking and all-terrain bicycling is permitted. Bicyclists should stay on designated trails and should always yield to hikers at all times. The dirt park road can also be used for mountain biking.

The Upper Gorman Creek Trail has a double-loop trail with a designated primitive camping area for backpackers. One loop is marked as the yellow trail and the other as the blue trail. A 1.2-mile trail that returns to the road is not marked. The River Trail has one designated primitive camping area for backpackers. Campfires are prohibited; cooking shall be done only on containerized fuel stoves. All garbage shall be packed out. Drinking water is provided at 2 locations in the park but must be carried by backpackers; composting toilets are provided at 4 locations at the park, but are not available at the 2 backcountry campsites.

Camping at Colorado Bend State Park is primitive only, but these folks don't seem to mind; the surroundings are quite scenic.

The Spicewood Springs Trail passes by this beautiful pool of clear water—a sharp contrast to the usual color of the Colorado River that is a short distance downstream.

GORMAN FALLS

Some areas of the park are currently closed to park visitors; they are being allowed to revert to their natural condition. Although the Gorman Falls area is closed, guided tours are now available on weekends. The Gorman Falls Tour is a 1½-mile round-trip hike over hill country terrain to below the falls; the Wild Cave Walking Tour takes you to Gorman Cave; and the Wild Cave Crawling Tour takes you through several relatively small and progressively more difficult caves. Reservations are recommended for some of the tours; a small tour fee is charged. Phone the park headquarters for tour schedule and other information.

Davis Mountains State Park

FOR INFORMATION

DAVIS MOUNTAINS STATE PARK
P.O. BOX 1707
FORT DAVIS, TX 79734
432/426-3337

LOCATION

Davis Mountains State Park is located 4 miles northwest of Fort Davis; from just north of Fort Davis on TX 17, go west on TX 118 to Park Road 3. This 2,709-acre park is located in the rolling foothills of the scenic mile-high Davis Mountains, the most extensive mountain range in Texas.

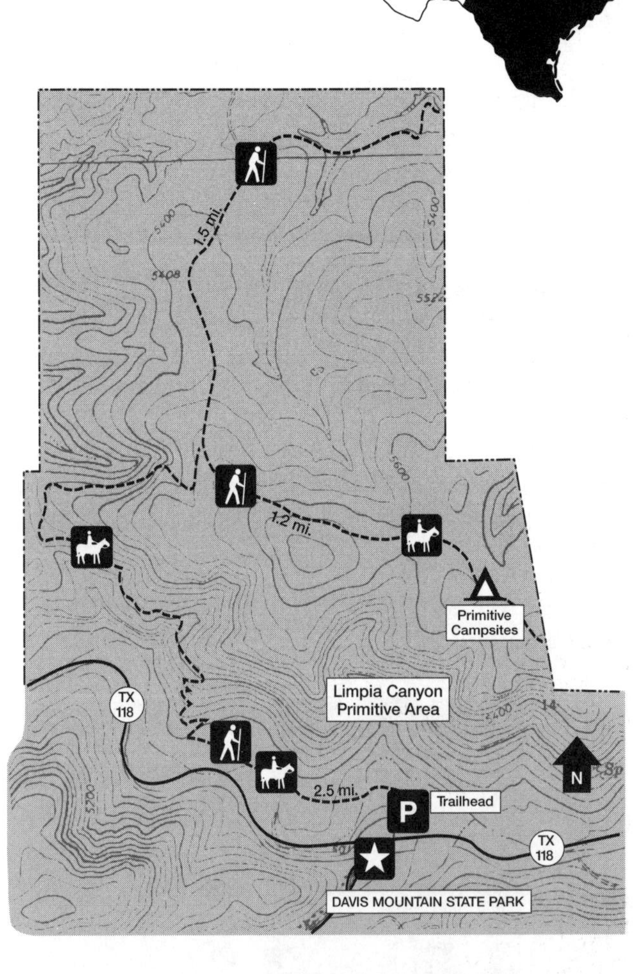

TRAIL NOTES

The northern half of the park, north of TX 118, has been designated the Limpia Canyon Primitive Area. This 1,400-acre area includes 6.5 miles of backcountry hiking trails with 6 primitive campsites, and a secured parking area. Users of this area, for day or overnight, must pay an activity fee or possess a valid Texas Conservation Passport. All users are required to read and sign a trail-use agreement and sign out on the daily log. Only then will the combination to the highway gate be given and access permitted. All vehicles will park in the designated area located north of TX 118 and just east of the park headquarters.

A maximum of 4 persons can occupy each of the primitive sites, which are reached by hiking 3 miles with an 800-foot elevation gain. To avoid impacting the primitive area, campers need not camp right at the numbered post when choosing a campsite—just anywhere around the general area. There is no water located in this area; it is recommended you carry at least one gallon of water per person per day. Hike with a partner whenever possible. Wear appropriate backcountry gear, including footwear. Be prepared for sudden weather changes. Use containerized fuel stoves only; open wood or charcoal fires are not allowed. Pack out all of your food garbage and trash, and bury your human waste according to proper backcountry ethics. All hikers **MUST** sign in on the daily log upon their return; *anyone who doesn't sign in is assumed lost and will pay for the cost of the search effort.*

Equestrian use of these trails is allowed and primitive equestrian camping is allowed in designated area. No facilities provided. All riders must stay on the trail; shoes for horses are recommended.

Davy Crockett National Forest/Four C National Hiking Trail

For Information

Davy Crockett National Forest
Rt. 1, Box 55 FS
Kennard, TX 75847
936/655-2299

Backpacking is permitted anywhere in Texas' national forests and primitive camping is allowed anywhere unless posted otherwise. A recent restriction is that camping within the boundaries of red-cockaded woodpecker colonies in the national forests in Texas is prohibited. Boundaries are identified by trees with green markings and/or signs. Permits are not needed for primitive camping although it is best to contact the office for detailed information. A detailed map of the Davy Crockett National Forest may be purchased from the Davy Crockett National Forest office.

College students enjoy hiking the 4-C Trail at spring break.

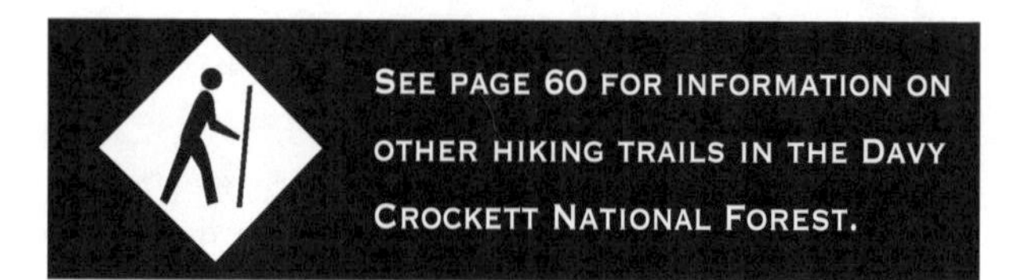

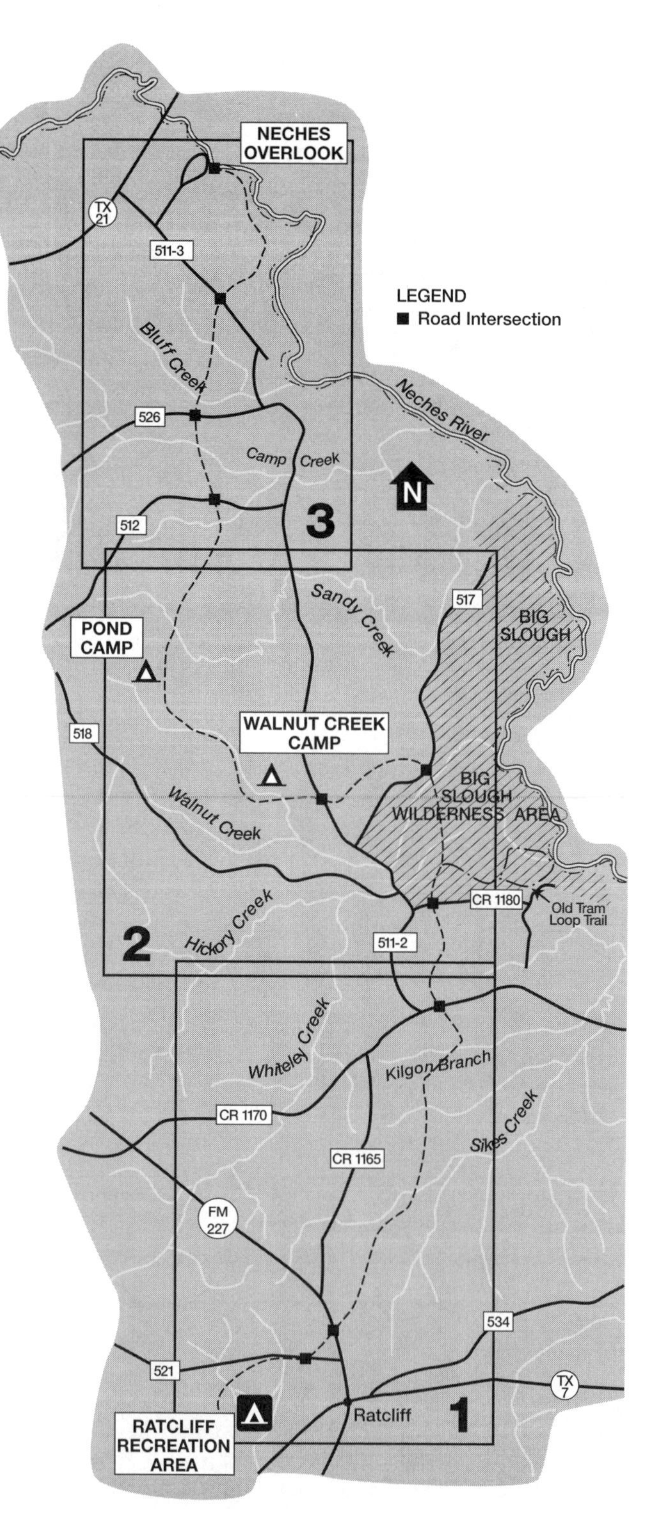

TRAIL NOTES

The name 4-C is derived from the Central Coal and Coke Company, which logged the virgin timber from land which now constitutes a bulk of the Davy Crockett National Forest. The sawmill was located at Ratcliff Lake and most tramways where the trail is located were built by the company. The forest, which the hikers now enjoy, is a second growth forest that came back after the company completed their logging operation in the early 1920s. The trail passes through the Big Slough Wilderness Area.

The 4-C trail is 20 miles long, begins at Ratcliff Lake in the parking lot near the concession stand, and ends at the Neches Overlook. This trail stays in the national forest; one exception being about one mile which goes over Champion Paper lands. The trail is marked with white rectangular paint spots and is easy to follow. It goes through many forest ecosystems which vary from bottomland hardwoods to dry upland pine sites. Unique features of the trail include a 300-foot footbridge that circles an old millpond and a 480-foot-long raised walkway across one of the boggy sloughs.

The 4-C trail can be hiked year-round and receives maximum use during spring, fall and winter months. Extra care should be taken during deer season, due to hunters in the area. There are many streams in the area, but using the water for drinking purposes is not recommended.

The Walnut Creek Campsite is located on a small ridgetop near Walnut Creek about midway on the trail. There are five tent pads for backpacker-type tents, a trail shelter, and a pit toilet. The Pond Campsite is located near Mile 13 of the trail on the edge of a small man-made pond.

The trail is designed as a hiker trail and, therefore, horses and off-road vehicles are prohibited. Take care with fire and remove all rubbish and garbage. Do not cut on or remove shrubs or plants.

These backpackers are getting their campsite organized for the overnight stay at a primitive campsite.

Many hikers choose to day-hike portions of the 4-C Trail.

Four C Hiking Trail (Ratcliff Topographic Map)

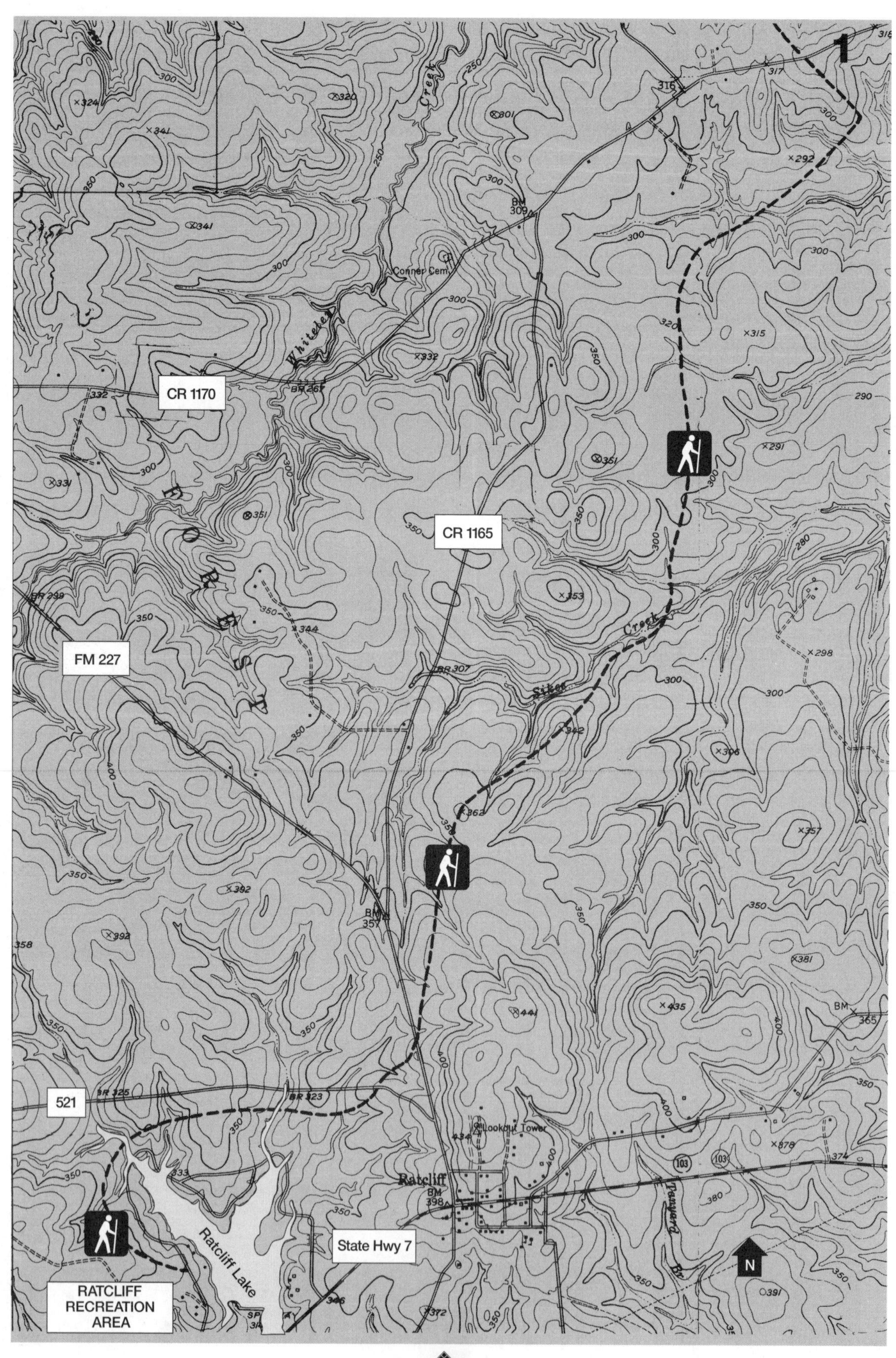

Four C Hiking Trail (Kennard Topographic Map)

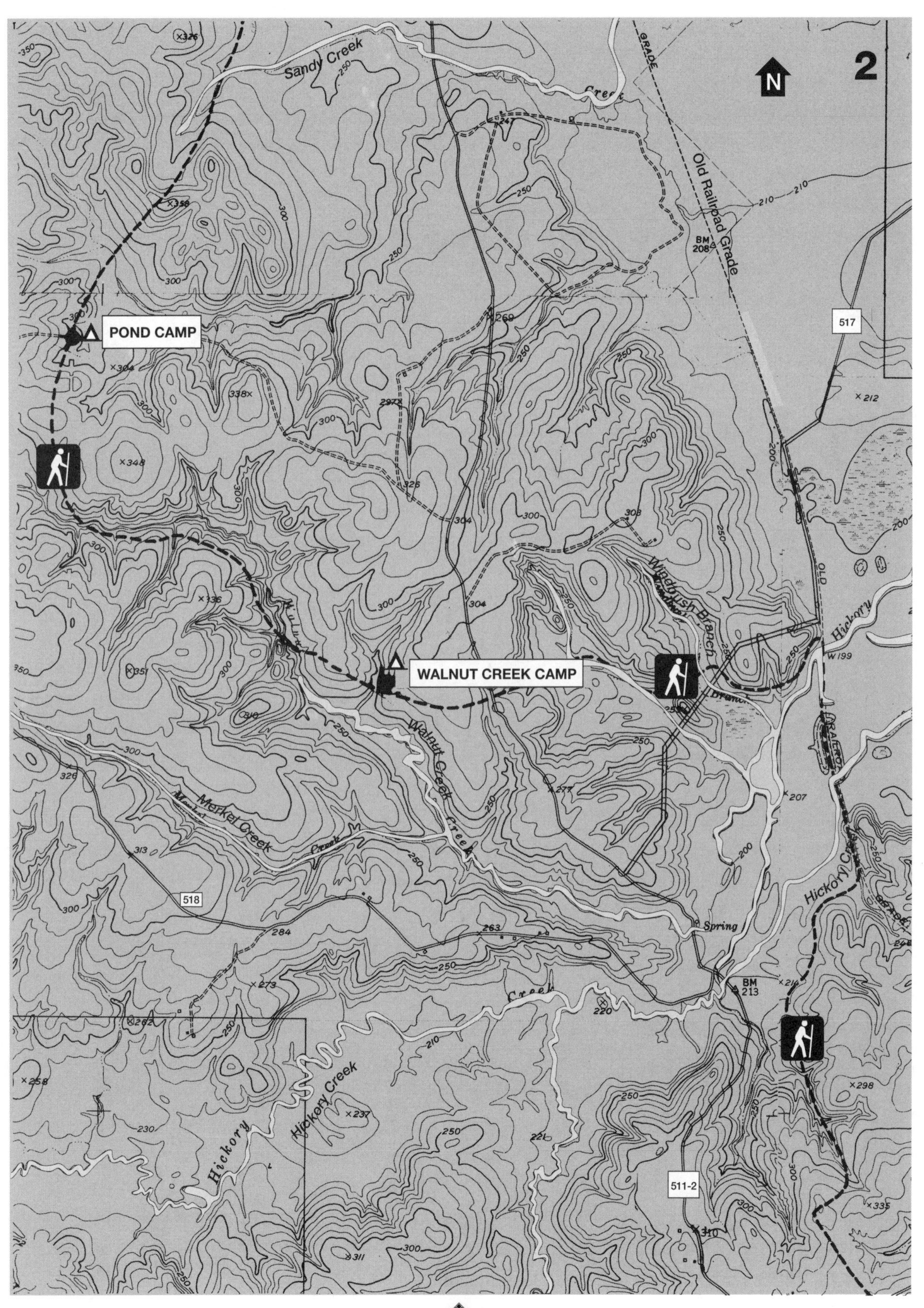

Four C Hiking Trail (Neches Topographic Map)

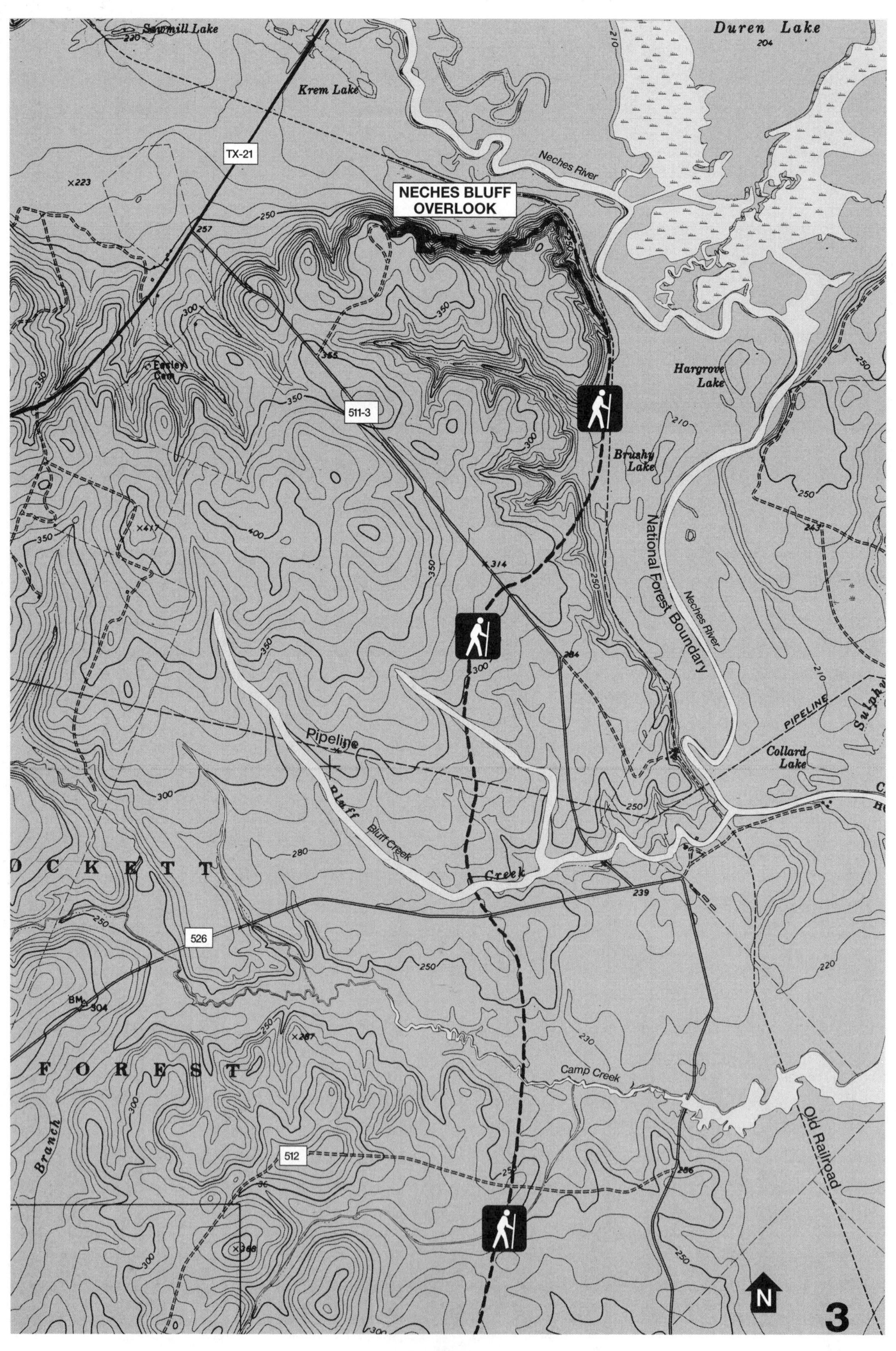

DEVILS RIVER STATE NATURAL AREA

FOR INFORMATION

DEVILS RIVER STATE NATURAL AREA
HCR 01, BOX 513
DEL RIO, TX 78840
830/395-2133

LOCATION

Devils River State Natural Area is located west of US 277 between Sonora and Del Rio. If you are coming from Del Rio, the turn off is 43 miles north, from Sonora it is 47 miles south. To reach the park headquarters, turn off on a county maintained dirt road named Dolan Creek Road and drive west for 22 miles. This natural area encompasses 19,988 acres. Access to Dolan Falls is only through the Nature Conservancy of Texas; there is no access through the park.

Reservations Are Required—The park is open 7 days a week and is currently accessible by reservation only; make camping and lodging facility reservations through the Central Reservation Center. Park tours include visitation of archaeological pictograph sites and a canyon tour of Devils River area and springs. Contact the park for times and prices. Tours are scheduled at 9:00 a.m. and 1:00 p.m. when staff is available to guide them; thus, all tours are on a pre-approved basis only. All persons entering the natural area for the day or overnight must have a permit. Visitors can buy permits at the headquarters office between 8 a.m. and 5 p.m. , or self-register at the same location after 5 p.m.

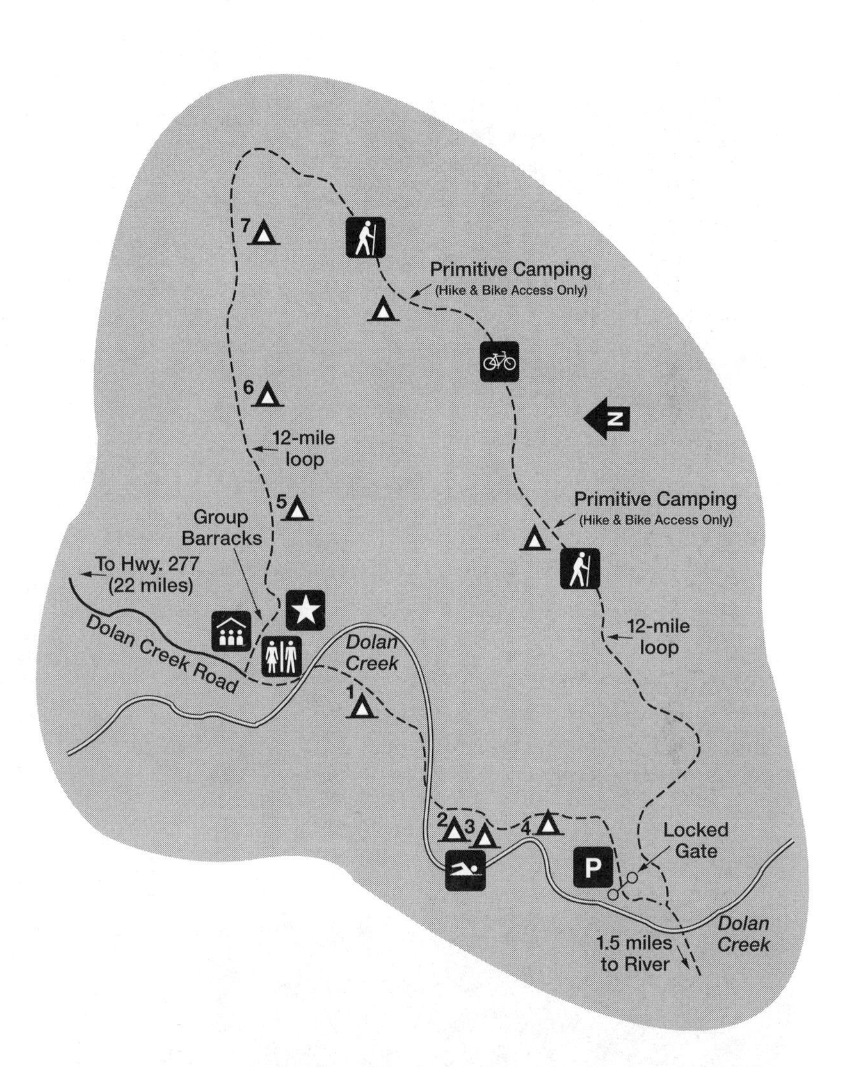

TRAIL NOTES

There are 7 primitive campsites available; all are vehicle accessible. Potable water is not available; bring your own drinking water; restroom facilities are very limited. A hike-and-bike loop trail is 12 miles in length; 2 primitive campsites for hike and bike are available along this trail. Hiking and biking are allowed *only* along the East Canyon road and along the main river road from designated camping areas. Hikers and bikers *must* remain on designated trails; cross-country travel is not allowed. Parking for river access is at the locked river gate on the main road; access to the river from this point is 1½ miles and can be reached by foot, bicycle, or park tour. There is a primitive camping area along the river for canoeists arriving from Baker's Crossing for a one-night stop. The park is a put-in point only for canoes. All canoeists must call ahead to schedule put-in. Put-in time 9:00 a.m. only.

Dinosaur Valley State Park

For Information

Dinosaur Valley State Park
P.O. Box 396
Glen Rose, TX 76043
254/897-4588

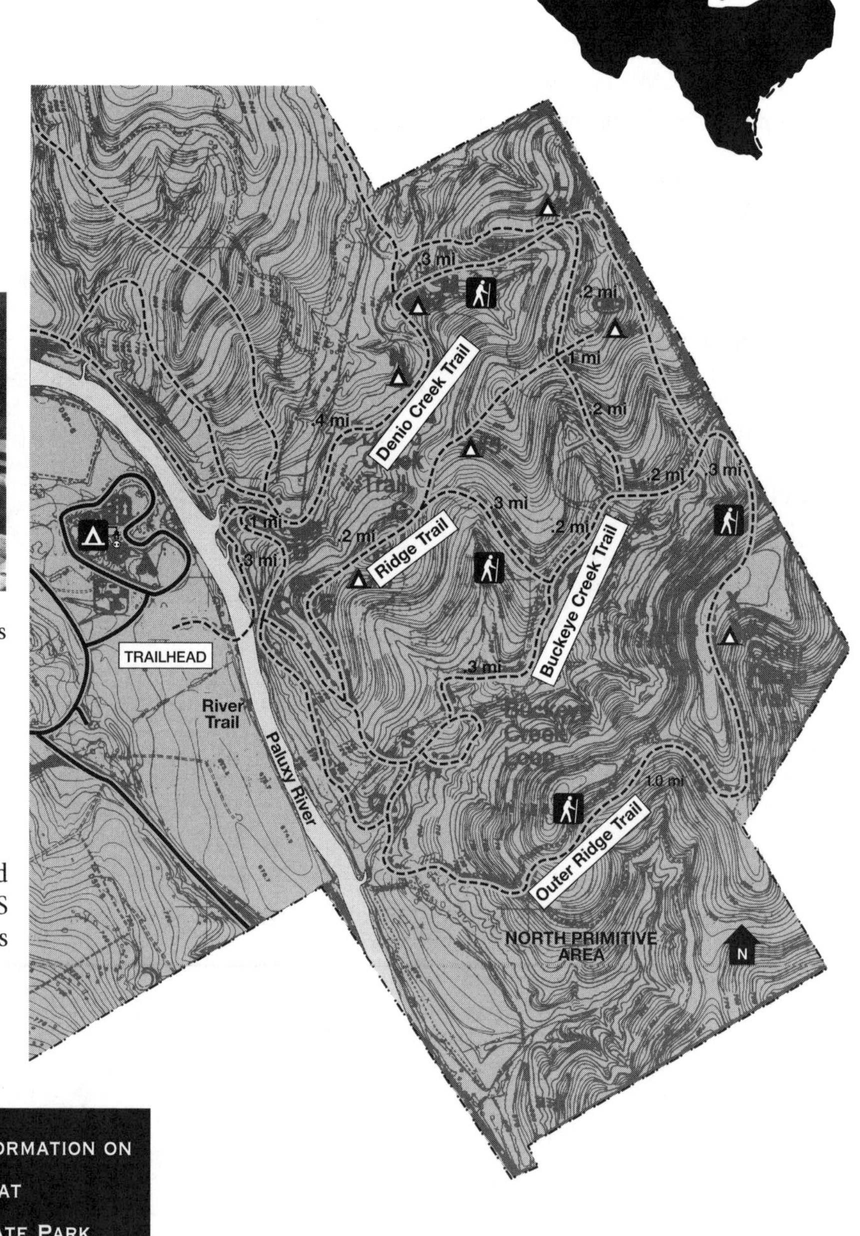

These dinosaur tracks, as well as 2 fiberglass models of dinosaurs that stand 45 and 70 feet tall, are definitely impressive exhibits.

Location

Dinosaur Valley State Park is located about 5 miles west of Glen Rose via US 67 and FM 205. The 1,525-acre park is along the Paluxy River.

See page 21 for information on other hiking trails at Dinosaur Valley State Park.

Trail Notes

A 10-mile trail system is located in the North Primitive area. Hikers are aided by a color-coded trail system: some trails are marked in white, some in blue, and some in yellow. For backpackers there are 7 primitive camp areas without any facilities; water is available at the trailhead. Overnight camping is permitted only in designated primitive camping areas. Campfires are not permitted in the primitive area due to the lack of natural firewood and because of the possibility of wildfires. Cooking shall be done only on containerized fuel stoves. All garbage and litter shall be packed out of the area for disposal in trash receptacles located at the trailhead. Burying garbage is not permitted. Hikers are asked to stay on the trail. Flash floods are a natural phenomenon in this area. During periods of heavy rain, stay on or move to high ground. Do not attempt to ford swollen creeks. Be prepared to wait it out, as the creeks will subside in a few hours after the rain stops.

Enchanted Rock State Natural Area

FOR INFORMATION

ENCHANTED ROCK STATE NATURAL AREA
16710 RANCH ROAD 965
FREDERICKSBURG, TX 78624
325/247-3903

TRAIL NOTES

Approximately 7 miles of trails exist; the main hiking trail that circumvents the several granite domes is 4 miles long but other access trails lead to the primitive camping areas as well as create a series of loop trails suitable for exploration and shorter hikes. Hiking in a clockwise direction, the distance from the trailhead to the Walnut Springs primitive camping area is 1.2 miles; the distance from the trailhead to the Moss Lake primitive camping area is 1.9 miles; the distance from the trailhead to the Buzzard's Roost primitive camping area is 3.4 miles; and the complete main trail loop is 4 miles.

The 3 primitive camping areas are accessible via the loop trail. These backcountry camping areas provide opportunities for a more rugged outdoor experience for backpackers: water is not provided; composting toilets are located adjacent to the trail at the designated camping areas; all garbage and litter shall be packed out; and cooking shall be done only on containerized fuel stoves, because campfires are not permitted in the primitive areas. *Bicycles are not allowed on the trails.*

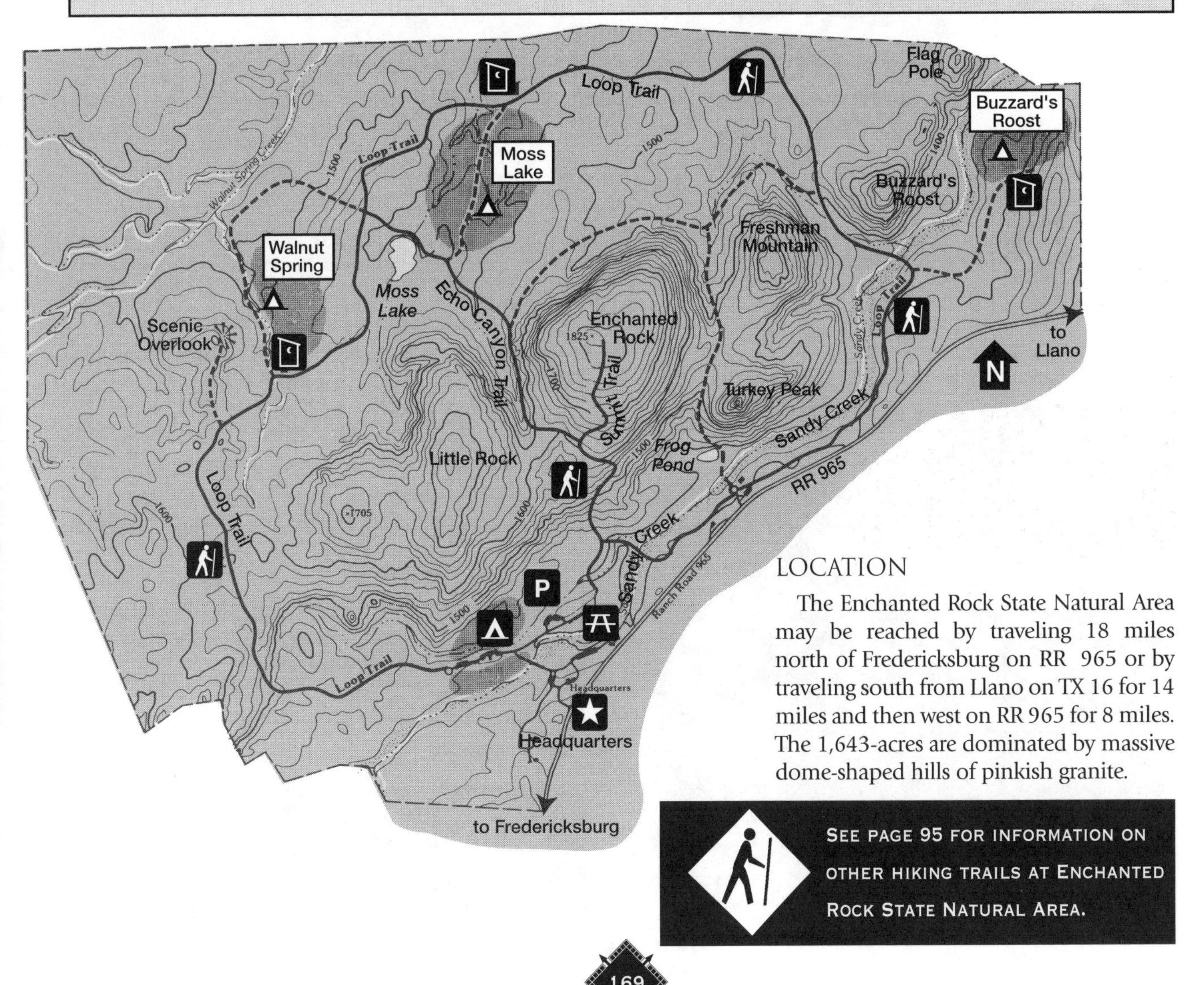

LOCATION

The Enchanted Rock State Natural Area may be reached by traveling 18 miles north of Fredericksburg on RR 965 or by traveling south from Llano on TX 16 for 14 miles and then west on RR 965 for 8 miles. The 1,643-acres are dominated by massive dome-shaped hills of pinkish granite.

SEE PAGE 95 FOR INFORMATION ON OTHER HIKING TRAILS AT ENCHANTED ROCK STATE NATURAL AREA.

FAIRFIELD LAKE STATE PARK

FOR INFORMATION

FAIRFIELD LAKE STATE PARK
123 STATE PARK RD. 64
FAIRFIELD, TX 75840
903/389-4514

LOCATION

Fairfield Lake State Park is located off I-45, 6 miles northeast of Fairfield on FM 488 to FM 2570, then northeast to FM 3285 to Park Road 64. The 1,460-acre park is situated on the southern end of the 2,400-acre Fairfield Lake.

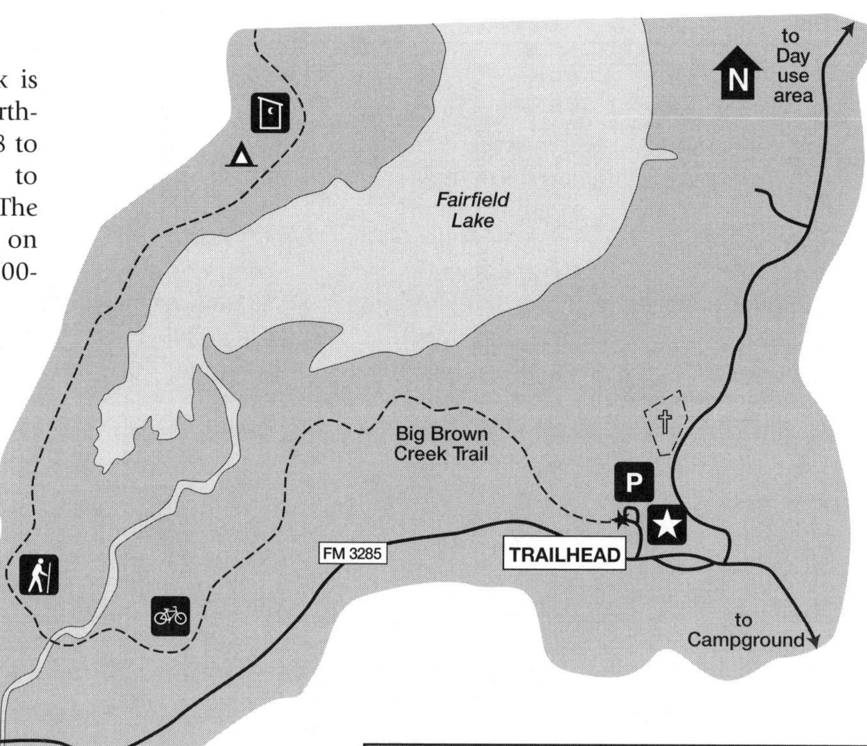

TRAIL NOTES

The 3-mile Big Brown Creek Trail (one way) is a hiking trail that leads to a backcountry camping area. This backpacker's camping area has water, flush toilets, and charcoal grills, so it can hardly be classified as primitive. The first 1½ miles of this trail have interpretive signs to identify many of the trees and other plants; several trailside benches are provided for rest stops. The trail leads through heavily wooded areas, dominated by various oaks and hickory, and then traverses a low, swampy area, where it crosses one of the primary creeks feeding the lake. Several ponds and streams can be seen along the way, providing a haven for many types of waterfowl and wildlife.

The first 1½ miles of the Big Brown Creek Trail is a nature trail with interpretive signs to identify many of the trees and plants.

SEE PAGE 23 FOR INFORMATION ON OTHER HIKING TRAILS AT FAIRFIELD LAKE STATE PARK.

GUADALUPE MOUNTAINS NATIONAL PARK

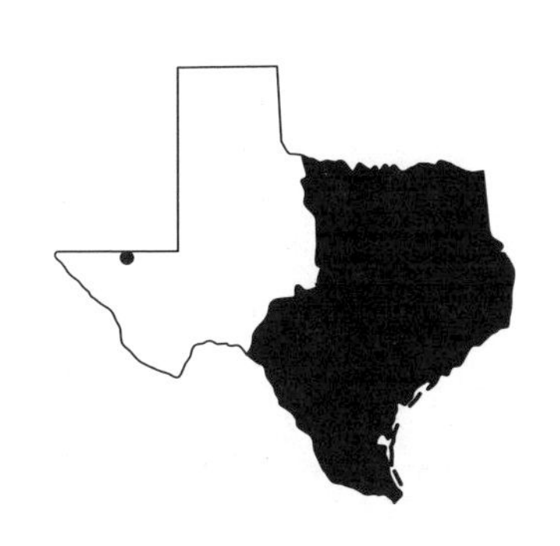

FOR INFORMATION

GUADALUPE MOUNTAINS NATIONAL PARK
HC60, BOX 400
SALT FLAT, TX 79847-9400
915/828-3251

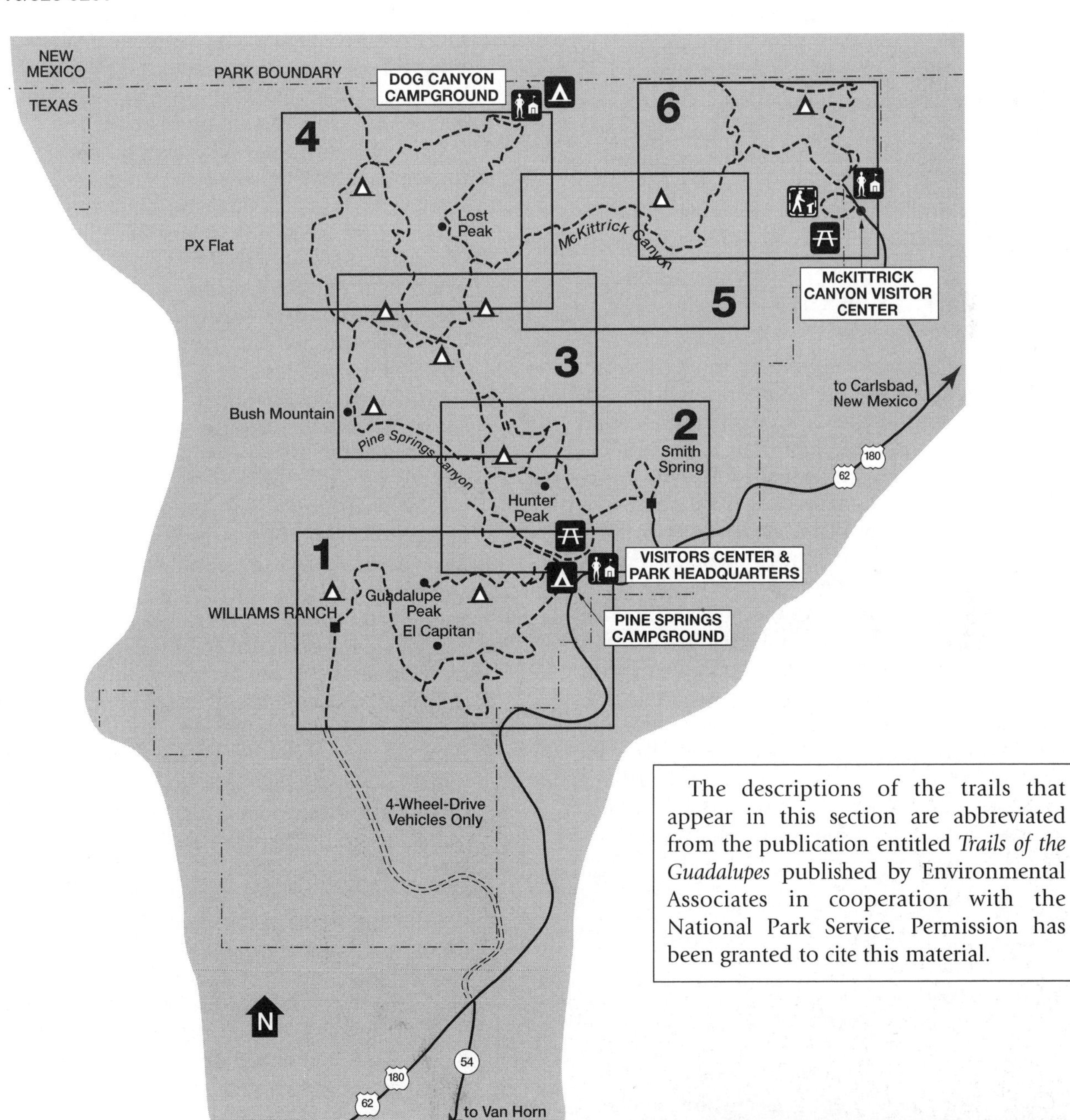

The descriptions of the trails that appear in this section are abbreviated from the publication entitled *Trails of the Guadalupes* published by Environmental Associates in cooperation with the National Park Service. Permission has been granted to cite this material.

SEE PAGES 131–133 FOR INFORMATION ON OTHER HIKING TRAILS AT GUADALUPE MOUNTAINS NATIONAL PARK.

LOCATIONS

▲ **Headquarters Visitor Center**—On US 62/180, 55 miles southwest of Carlsbad, New Mexico, and 110 miles east of El Paso, Texas. Open daily 8:00 a.m.–4:30 p.m. (MST) in winter, 8:00 a.m. to 6:00 p.m. in summer.

▲ **Pine Springs Campground**—¼ mile west of the Visitor Center. Picnic tables, flush toilets, and drinking water available.

▲ **Dog Canyon Campground**—In the Dog Canyon area of the park, 59 miles from Carlsbad, NM. Water, picnic tables, and flush toilets available.

▲ **McKittrick Canyon Visitor Center**—7 miles northeast of Headquarters Visitor Center on US 62/180 to McKittrick Canyon turnoff. Another 5 miles northwest to end of road.

BACKCOUNTRY POLICIES AND SAFETY SUGGESTIONS

The park contains more than 80 miles of rugged mountain trails. Many are in poor condition and some routes are ill-defined. In most cases, wildlife trails or old wagon trails have been followed. Rock cairns have been placed to facilitate following routes, and please do not disturb them. Signs are located at trail junctions. In many places, trails are steep.

Before venturing into the park's interior, backpackers must make thorough preparations and check in at the Headquarters Visitor Center or at the Dog Canyon Ranger Station to obtain a free backcountry permit. They should also check in upon their return. The park has established policies for use of the backcountry trails that are designed to protect the varied fragile resources of the park while allowing for the enjoyment of the user. The following list of backcountry policies and safety suggestions has been compiled from several sources of information distributed by the park:

1. Do not shortcut trails as this practice tramples vegetation, encourages erosion, and starts additional trails.
2. Pack out all garbage and trash associated with your trip. Do not bury garbage as animals will dig it up.
3. For disposal of human waste, dig a shallow "cat hole" 6–8 inches deep to stay within the "biological decomposer" soil layer. Cover the area when finished.
4. No open fires are permitted in the backcountry. Containerized fuel stoves may be used at the designated campsites.
5. Use only the designated campsites to avoid spreading the impact of camping. The sites are within ½ day of each other.
6. Backpackers should obtain permits from either the Headquarters Visitor Center or the Dog Canyon Ranger Station.
7. When obtaining the backcountry permit, hikers must specify which of the designated campsites they will occupy on each night of their trip.
8. Do not trench around tents because this kills vegetation and starts erosion problems.
9. If you plan only a day-hike, sign in and out on the register at the trailhead.
10. Three persons in a group is the safest number for backcountry hikes. That way if one person should be injured, another can stay with him while the third goes for help.
11. Carry plenty of water. Carry a minimum of 1 gallon per person per day. There is no water in the high country, so planning is imperative.
12. High winds are common, especially in the spring. The rainy season is about July through mid-September. Be especially prepared for wind and rain at those times. An exhausted hiker, unprotected from cool mountain rains, can become a victim of hypothermia.
13. Always carry a topographic map and compass and know how to use them. Trails are ill-defined and difficult to follow in places. A map and compass can help you regain your bearings if you get off the trails.
14. Do not attempt to descend the escarpment front, mountain sides, or into canyons unless you are on a trail. You can easily become trapped by cliffs both above and below you.
15. Guard against extreme fatigue. An overtired hiker is accident-prone. Make frequent short rest stops, even if you are in a hurry.
16. Carry a first-aid kit whenever you hike.
17. Watch for rattlesnakes whenever you hike. Chances are you won't see any, but it is possible.
18. Please respect and care for the land you walk over and camp upon. Do not disturb plants and animals. It should provide as much enjoyment for those who follow as it did for you.
19. If you become lost and can't determine your position from map and compass, move to an open area and stay there. You will be easier to find and will conserve your energy.
20. Wear a hat and sunglasses as protection against the hot desert sun. A day's exposure without protection can cause extreme eye pain. Wear a long-sleeve shirt and use sunscreen lotion.

21. The danger from sun exposure can't be overemphasized. Take frequent rest stops and drink plenty of water.
22. Trails are steep and rocky and the footing is poor, so good hiking boots are important. Never attempt a long hike in boots that have not been broken in properly.
23. Your hike will be safer and more enjoyable if you are in good condition. Follow a conditioning program before making long or strenuous hikes and backpacking trips, especially if you are not accustomed to the heat and 5,000–8,700-foot altitudes.
24. The park is an excellent winter hiking and camping spot, as long as one is equipped for winter hiking and camping. The temperatures can be severe, the snow can be deep, and the wind can be extremely strong.
25. Long pants should be worn as protection against the spines and stickers.

MAP 1 (SEE PAGE 174)

▲ **Guadalupe Peak Trail**—The view from the 8,749-foot summit is outstanding. The hike is 8.4 miles round-trip and is a strenuous hike over a steep trail. After leaving the floor of the canyon at Pine Springs Campground, the ascent is steady and involves a climb of about 3,000 feet. The Guadalupe Peak designated campsite is 1 mile from the summit.

▲ **El Capitan Trail**—Beginning at Pine Springs Campground, this horse/hike trail explores desert scenery and passes below the historic landmark of El Capitan. This trail swings off in a northwest direction along a ridge, and descends to the base of the escarpment near Shumard Canyon. A trip to Williams Ranch provides excellent views of the western side of the Guadalupe Mountains and the salt basin to the west. Round-trip is 18.8 miles.

MAP 2 (SEE PAGE 175)

▲ **Tejas Trail**—This trail starts at Pine Springs Campground and is one of the main access trails to the high country. The trail goes up Pine Springs Canyon before climbing steeply through a series of switchbacks. The ascent is difficult, involving a climb of more than 2,500 feet in 3.8 miles from the campground to the top of the ridge. The Pine Top campsite is 0.1 mile northwest along Bush Mountain Trail.

▲ **Bear Canyon Trail**—This trail is the other main access route from the Pine Springs Campground into the high country. It leads from the campground east to Upper Pine Springs, and then up Bear Canyon to the top of the ridge. The ascent to the top of the ridge is extremely steep. This 2.8-mile trail is more often used to leave the high country than to enter it.

▲ **Juniper Trail**—This trail passes through thick fir and pine forests. The distance from the top of the Tejas Trail to the Bowl is 1.5 miles. The loop trail from the campground up the Tejas Trail through the Bowl and down Bear Canyon Trail is approximately 9.4 miles.

▲ **Devil's Hall Trail**—This trail leads from Pine Springs Campground to Devil's Hall, a section of narrow canyon walls in the dry streambed of Pine Springs Canyon. This is a 5.0-mile round-trip, relatively level hike on the rocky surface of the canyon bottom. Access to this trail is via the horse trail to Guadalupe Peak.

▲ **Smith Springs Trail**—This trail begins at Frijole Historic Site. Smith Springs is a lovely oasis on a dry lower slope of the Guadalupe escarpment. This 2.2-mile round-trip loop hike also passes Manzanita Spring, which produces a pool of water often visited by wildlife. Interpretive signs introduce the geology, ecology, and history of the area.

▲ **Bowl Trail**—This trail begins 0.6 mile east of the Tejas Trail. It takes hikers to the top of Hunter Peak and then to the top of Bear Canyon Trail in 0.9 mile. The view from the top of Hunter Peak is spectacular.

▲ **Frijole Trail**—This 2.9-mile trail crosses the lower slopes of the Guadalupe Escarpment to connect Pine Springs Campground and the Frijole Ranch House. The trail ascends to join with the Bear Canyon Trail at 1.5 miles, then descends steadily to reach the ranch house.

There are numerous high vistas for hikers to enjoy when in the Guadalupe Mountains. Portions of the Tejas Trail from Pine Springs Campground to Pine Top are visible in the background.

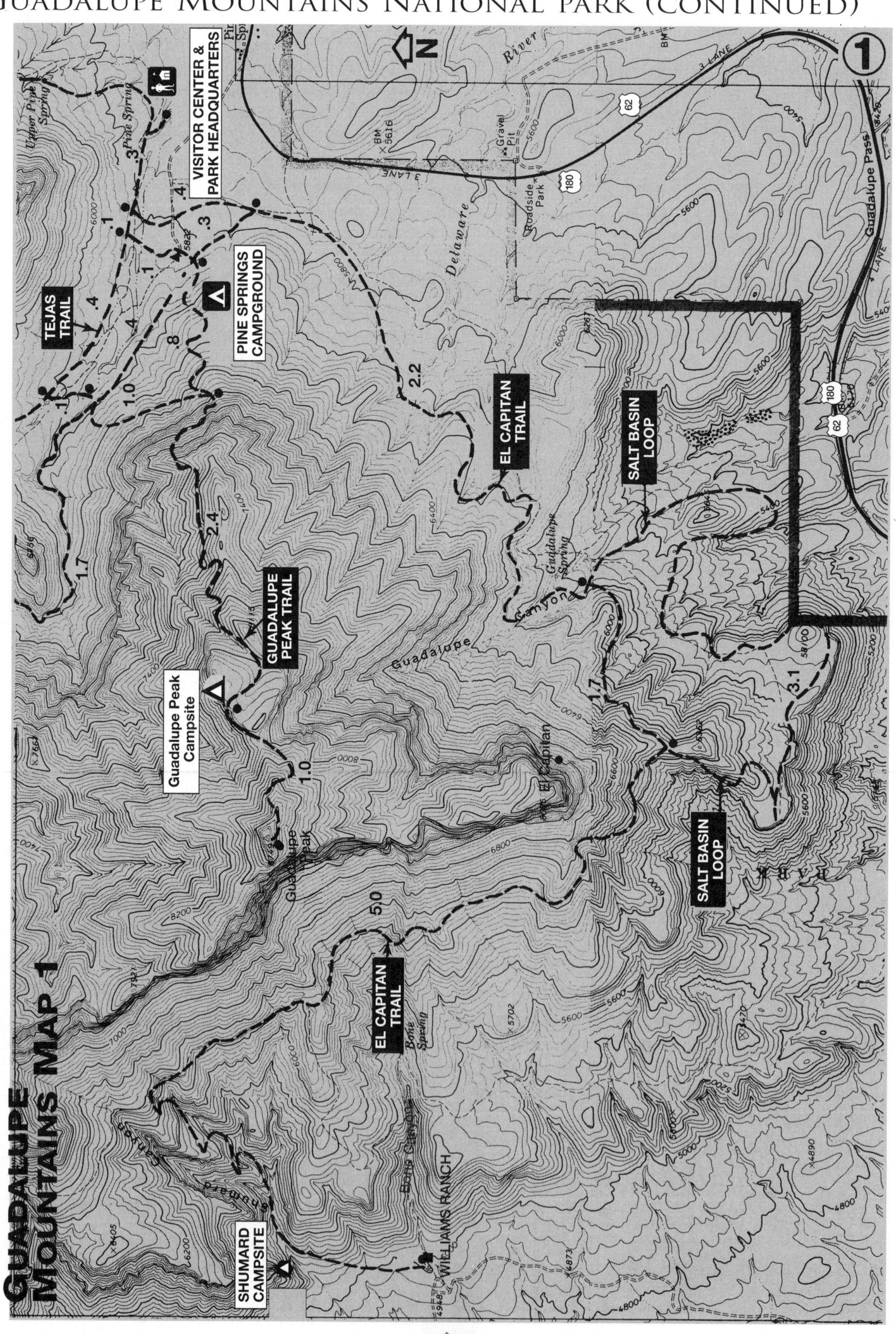
GUADALUPE MOUNTAINS MAP 1
VISITOR CENTER & PARK HEADQUARTERS
TEJAS TRAIL
PINE SPRINGS CAMPGROUND
EL CAPITAN TRAIL
SALT BASIN LOOP
GUADALUPE PEAK TRAIL
Guadalupe Peak Campsite
SALT BASIN LOOP
EL CAPITAN TRAIL
SHUMARD CAMPSITE
WILLIAMS RANCH
Guadalupe Peak
El Capitan
Guadalupe Canyon
Guadalupe Spring
Delaware River
Guadalupe Pass
Pine Spring
Upper Pine Spring
Bone Spring
Roadside Park
Gravel Pit
1

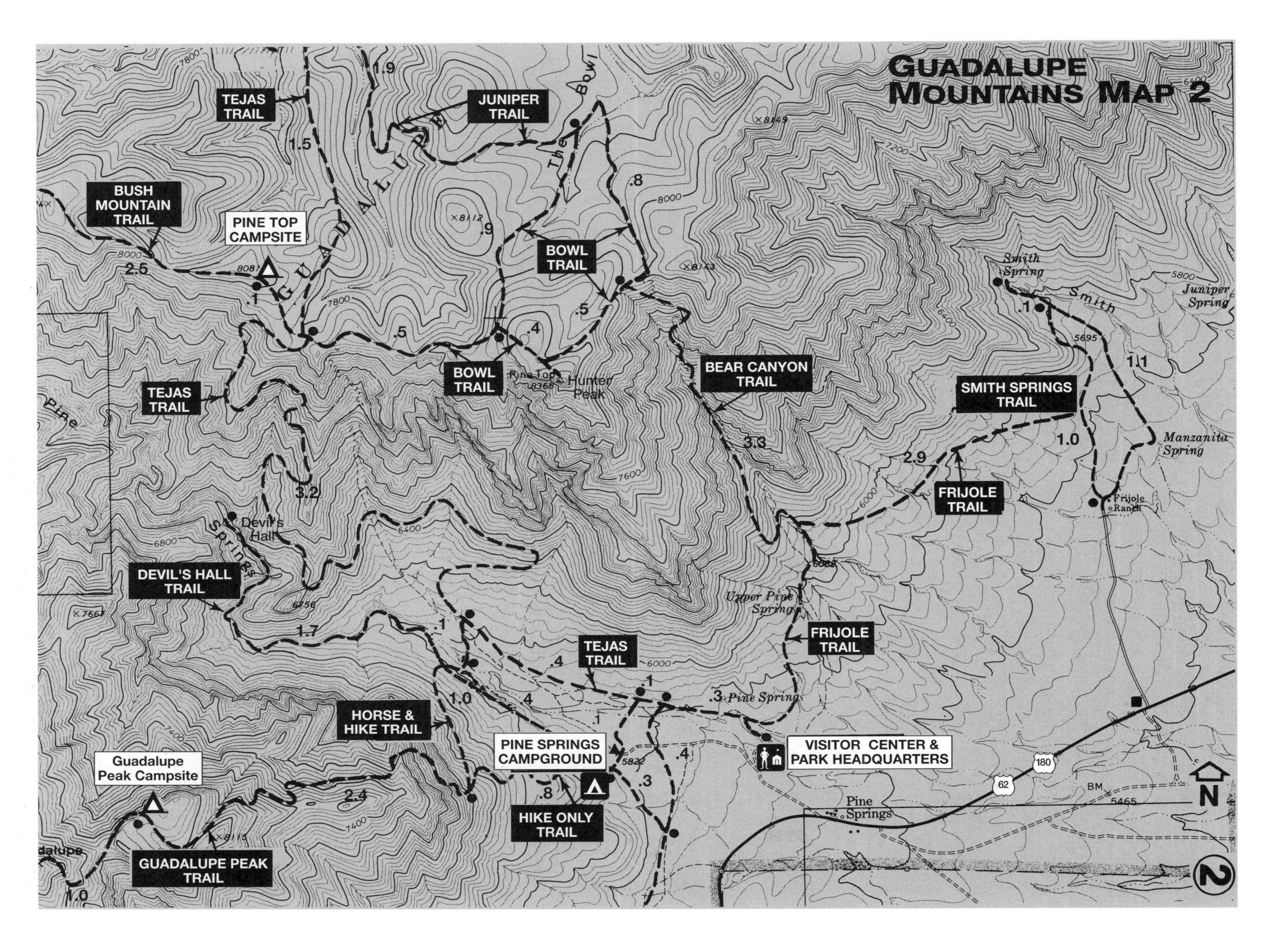
GUADALUPE MOUNTAINS MAP 2
TEJAS TRAIL
JUNIPER TRAIL
BUSH MOUNTAIN TRAIL
PINE TOP CAMPSITE
BOWL TRAIL
BOWL TRAIL
BEAR CANYON TRAIL
SMITH SPRINGS TRAIL
TEJAS TRAIL
FRIJOLE TRAIL
DEVIL'S HALL TRAIL
FRIJOLE TRAIL
TEJAS TRAIL
HORSE & HIKE TRAIL
PINE SPRINGS CAMPGROUND
VISITOR CENTER & PARK HEADQUARTERS
Guadalupe Peak Campsite
HIKE ONLY TRAIL
GUADALUPE PEAK TRAIL
Smith Spring
Juniper Spring
Manzanita Spring
Frijole Ranch
Upper Pine Spring
Pine Spring
Pine Springs
Devil's Hall
Hunter Peak
N
2

MAP 3 (SEE PAGE 177)

▲ **Bush Mountain Trail**—This trail leads to the summit of 8,631-foot high Bush Mountain. The Bush Mountain Campsite is approximately 0.2 mile south of the summit. The trail continues along Blue Ridge, descending to meet the Tejas Trail near the center of the park. Bush Mountain is the second highest mountain in Texas. This trail is unique in the variety of viewpoints it provides the backpacker. The Blue Ridge Campsite is located approximately 0.3 mile east of the Blue Ridge Trail junction.

▲ **Tejas Trail**—This trail descends through heavy forest growth to meet the Blue Ridge Trail and continues north to the Dog Canyon Campground.

MAP 4 (SEE PAGE 178)

▲ **Bush Mountain Trail**—Descending from Blue Ridge at its junction with Bush Mountain Trail, this trail goes 3.8 miles to the junction of the Marcus Trail at the north end of the park. Marcus Campsite is located at the junction of the Marcus Trail with the Bush Mountain Trail. Care should be taken to camp on high ground due to the danger of flooding from sudden rains. The trail drops about 2,000 feet in elevation from Blue Ridge as it descends into West Dog Canyon. The trail is not heavily used and is sometimes difficult to follow. Rock cairns help to identify the trail route.

A 2.9-mile trail leads from Marcus Campsite to Dog Canyon Campground. The Dog Canyon Campground is a major trailhead with a public access road from the north. This trail involves an ascent and a descent when hiked from either direction but is not extremely difficult. However, look for rock cairns. The trail passes near an old Mescalero campsite, recognizable by fire-blackened rocks.

▲ **Tejas Trail**—This trail leads from Dog Canyon Campground up through Dog Canyon, toward the summit of Lost Peak. From Lost Peak the trail descends gradually to a junction with the McKittrick Canyon Trail at 3.7 miles and continues south to the Mescalero Campsite. The trail involves considerable climbing when hiked from the north, and considerable descending when hiked from the south. The view from Lost Peak provides an unparalleled vantage point for viewing many of the canyons and ridges of the park. The Mescalero Campsite, located 4.3 miles from Dog Canyon Campground, is a sheltered campsite. The site is known as an old Mescalero Apache camp area.

▲ **Marcus Trail**—This portion of the Marcus Trail is 3.8 miles and goes from the Bush Mountain Trail junction to the Blue Ridge Trail. The trail ascends steadily along one side of West Dog Canyon. This ascent provides a good view into the canyon below and east to Lost Peak.

MAP 5 (SEE PAGE 179)

▲ **McKittrick Canyon Trail**—This trail follows the ridge that separates Devil's Den Canyon from South McKittrick Canyon. The McKittrick Ridge Campsite is located 2.6 miles east of the junction of Lost Peak Trail. The campsite is located about 100 yards north of the main trail. The trail continues approximately 3.1 miles before reaching the canyon floor, dropping some 2,380 feet in 2 miles of switchbacks. The trail passes near Turtle Rock, named for its silhouette as seen from the upper reaches of South McKittrick.

Backpackers headed into the backcountry area should always check the information board at the trailhead; the information posted there can be invaluable.

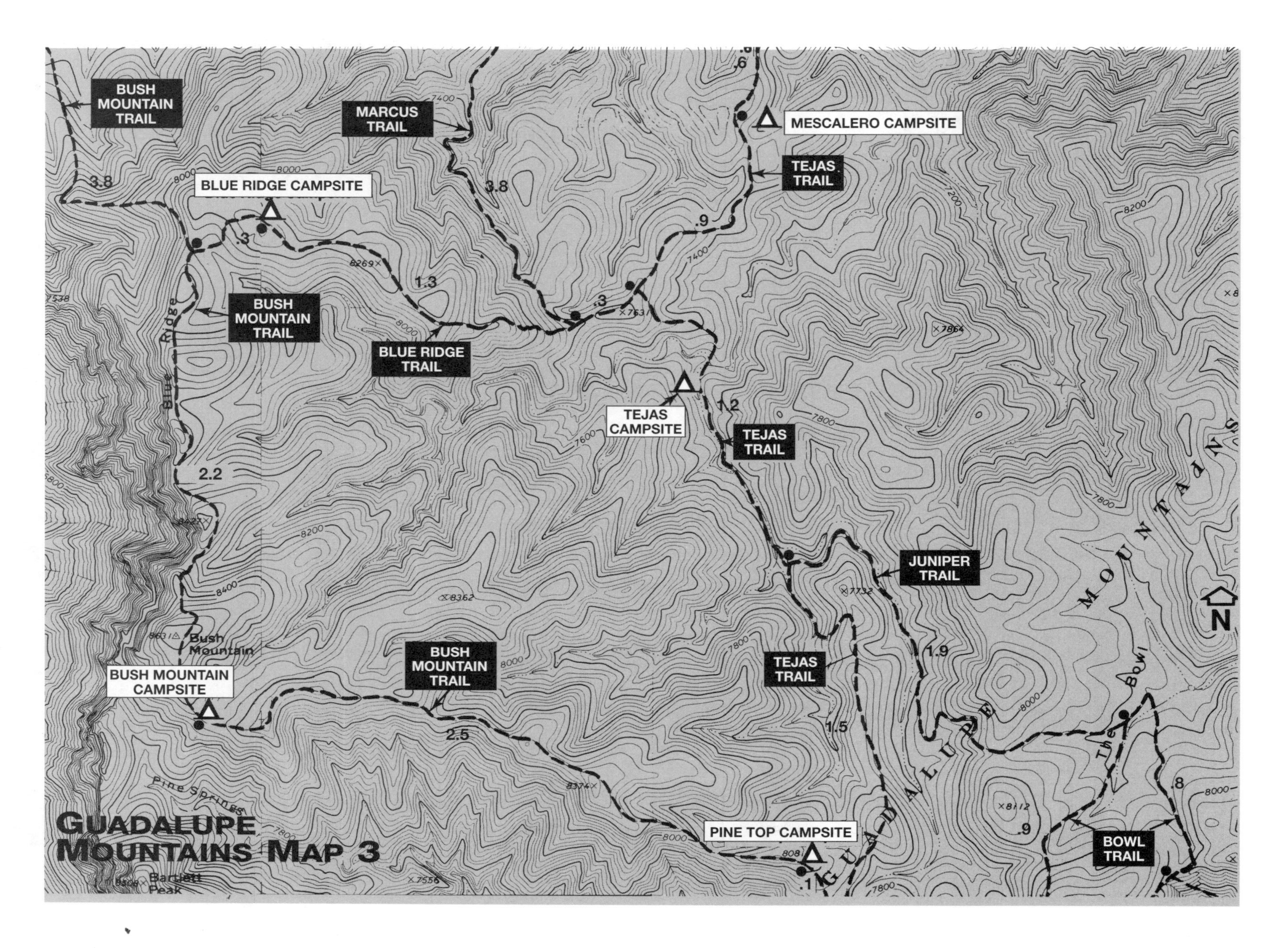

GUADALUPE MOUNTAINS MAP 3
BUSH MOUNTAIN TRAIL
MARCUS TRAIL
MESCALERO CAMPSITE
TEJAS TRAIL
BLUE RIDGE CAMPSITE
BUSH MOUNTAIN TRAIL
BLUE RIDGE TRAIL
TEJAS CAMPSITE
TEJAS TRAIL
JUNIPER TRAIL
TEJAS TRAIL
BUSH MOUNTAIN CAMPSITE
BUSH MOUNTAIN TRAIL
PINE TOP CAMPSITE
BOWL TRAIL
Blue Ridge
Bush Mountain
Pine Springs
Bartlett Peak
The Bowl
GUADALUPE MOUNTAINS
N
3.8
3.8
.3
1.3
.3
.9
.6
1.2
2.2
1.9
2.5
1.5
.1
.9
.8

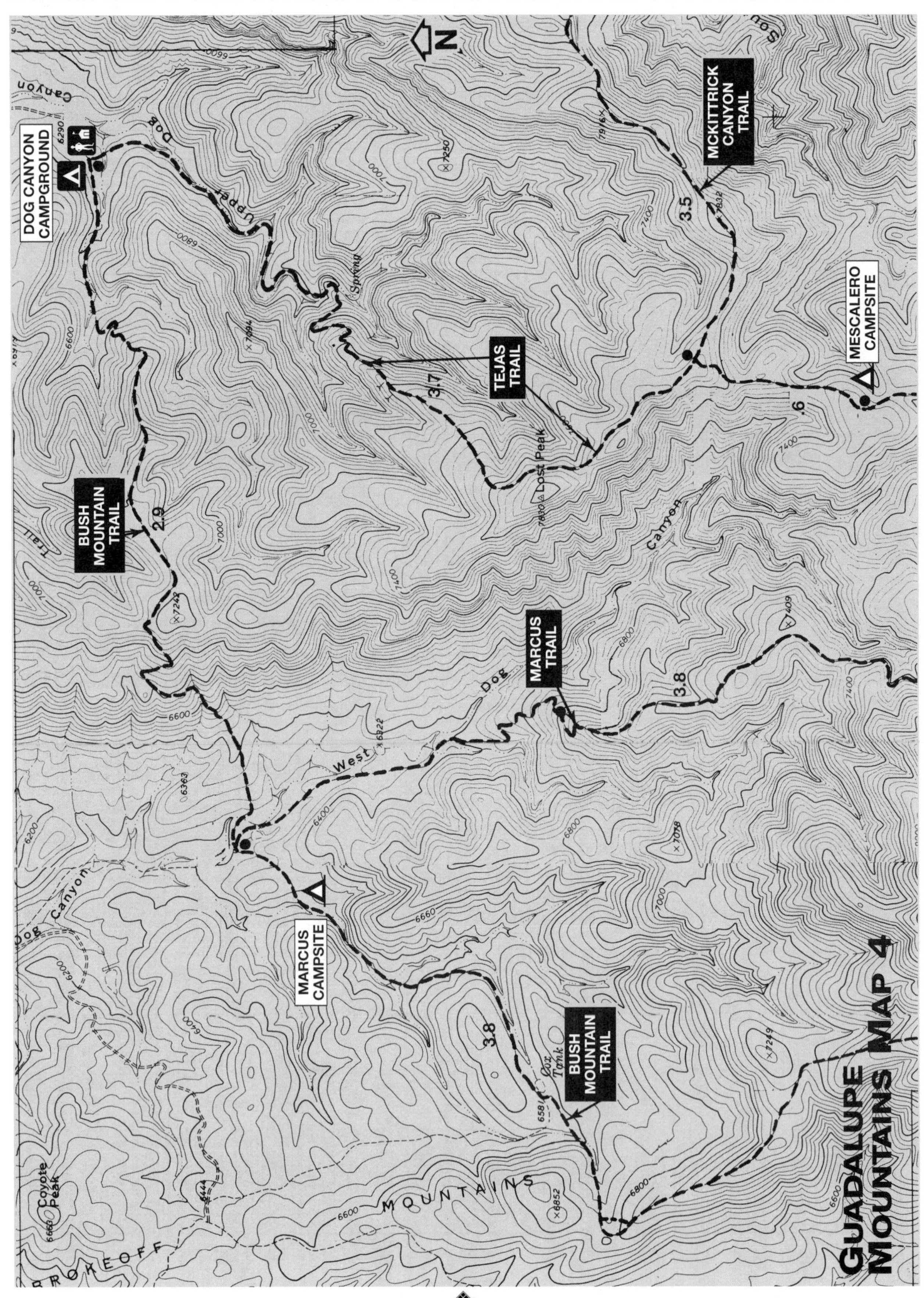

GUADALUPE MOUNTAINS MAP 4
DOG CANYON CAMPGROUND
MCKITTRICK CANYON TRAIL
TEJAS TRAIL
BUSH MOUNTAIN TRAIL
MARCUS TRAIL
MARCUS CAMPSITE
MESCALERO CAMPSITE
BUSH MOUNTAIN TRAIL
N
3.5
3.7
2.9
3.8
3.8
.6
Upper Dog Canyon
West Dog Canyon
Dog Canyon
Lost Peak
Spring
Cox Tank
Coyote Peak
MOUNTAINS
BROKEOFF

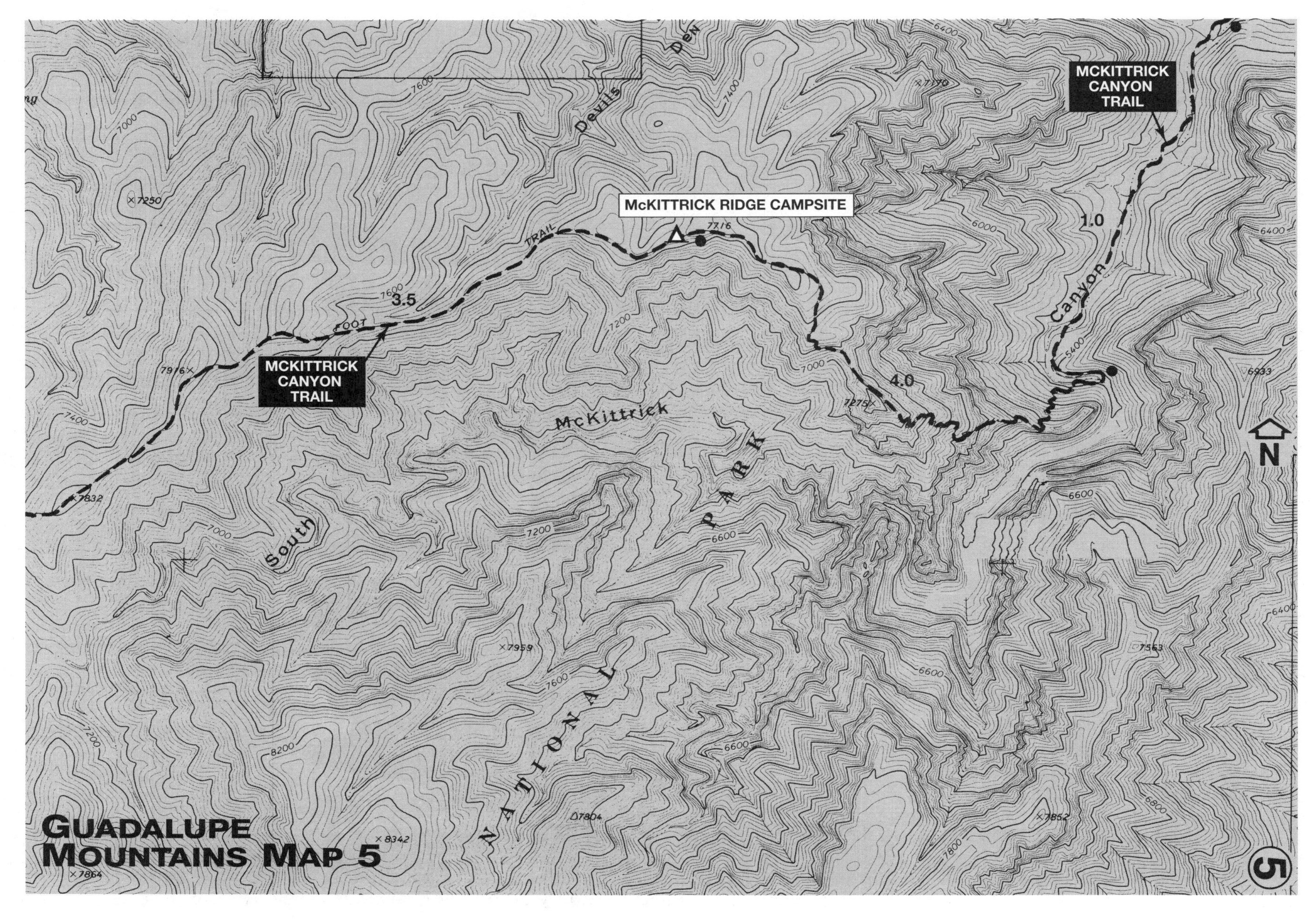
GUADALUPE MOUNTAINS MAP 5
5
N
MCKITTRICK CANYON TRAIL
McKITTRICK RIDGE CAMPSITE
MCKITTRICK CANYON TRAIL
1.0
3.5
4.0
Canyon
McKittrick
South
Devils Den
NATIONAL PARK
FOOT TRAIL

MCKITTRICK CANYON MAP 6
(SEE PAGE 181)

The entrance to McKittrick Canyon is located on U.S. 62/180, 7 miles northeast of Pine Springs Campground and 11 miles south of the New Mexico/Texas state line. The road from the highway to the parking area at the mouth of the canyon is approximately 5.0 miles long. The McKittrick Visitor Center is located at the end of the road, and offers restrooms, water, and picnicking.

McKittrick Canyon is unique among canyon communities in the park in the variety of vegetation occurring along its watercourse. The perennial spring-fed stream alternates from surface to underground as it travels through the canyon. The canyon is notable geologically, particularly in the large sections of the reef structure that are exposed. The canyon displays great diversity and beauty as grey oak, velvet ash, bigtooth maple, and little leaf walnut grow only a few miles from the creosote and mesquite of the west Texas desert. McKittrick Canyon is limited to day-use only. Hikers should remain on the trails and avoid wading in streams or trampling streambeds.

No restrooms or water are available at Pratt Lodge 2.3 miles into the canyon.

▲ **McKittrick Canyon Trail**—This trail follows the floor of McKittrick Canyon from the parking area past the Pratt Lodge (at 2.3 miles) to the Hunter Lodge. The Grotto Picnic Area is 1.1 miles from Pratt Lodge.

▲ **Permian Reef Geology Trail**—This 4.6-mile trail starts from the McKittrick Visitor Center and climbs 2,000 feet to the top of Camp Wilderness Ridge and ends at the state line. It passes through formations of the ancient Permian reef, and offers excellent views to the east and west. The Wilderness Ridge Campsite is 4.1 miles.

▲ An 0.8-mile nature trail is located adjacent to the McKittrick Canyon Visitor Center.

McKittrick Canyon has a certain mystique about it that few places have. Its beauty changes with the seasons. If you haven't experienced it . . . what are you waiting for? Just do it!

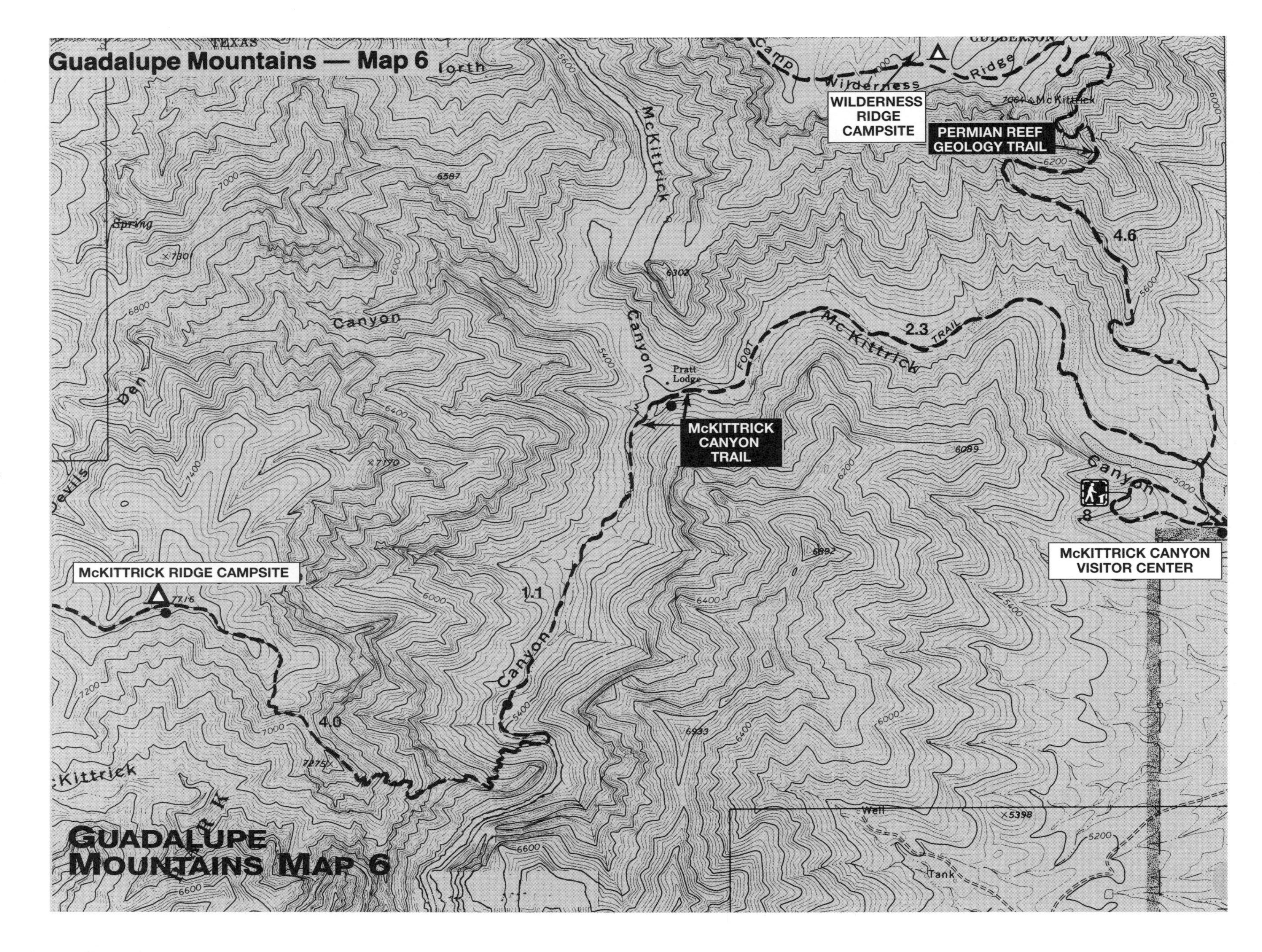
Guadalupe Mountains — Map 6
WILDERNESS RIDGE CAMPSITE
PERMIAN REEF GEOLOGY TRAIL
McKITTRICK CANYON TRAIL
McKITTRICK CANYON VISITOR CENTER
McKITTRICK RIDGE CAMPSITE
McKittrick Canyon
Pratt Lodge
Mc Kittrick FOOT TRAIL
Canyon
Wilderness Ridge
Spring
Den
4.6
2.3
1.1
4.0
8
Well
Tank
GUADALUPE MOUNTAINS MAP 6

HILL COUNTRY STATE NATURAL AREA

FOR INFORMATION

HILL COUNTRY STATE NATURAL AREA
10600 BANDERA CREEK RD.
BANDERA, TX 78003
830/796-4413

The 40 miles of multi-use trails at Hill Country SNA are designated for hikers, mountain bikers, and horseback riding. Bikers must yield to hikers and horses; hikers also yield to horses.

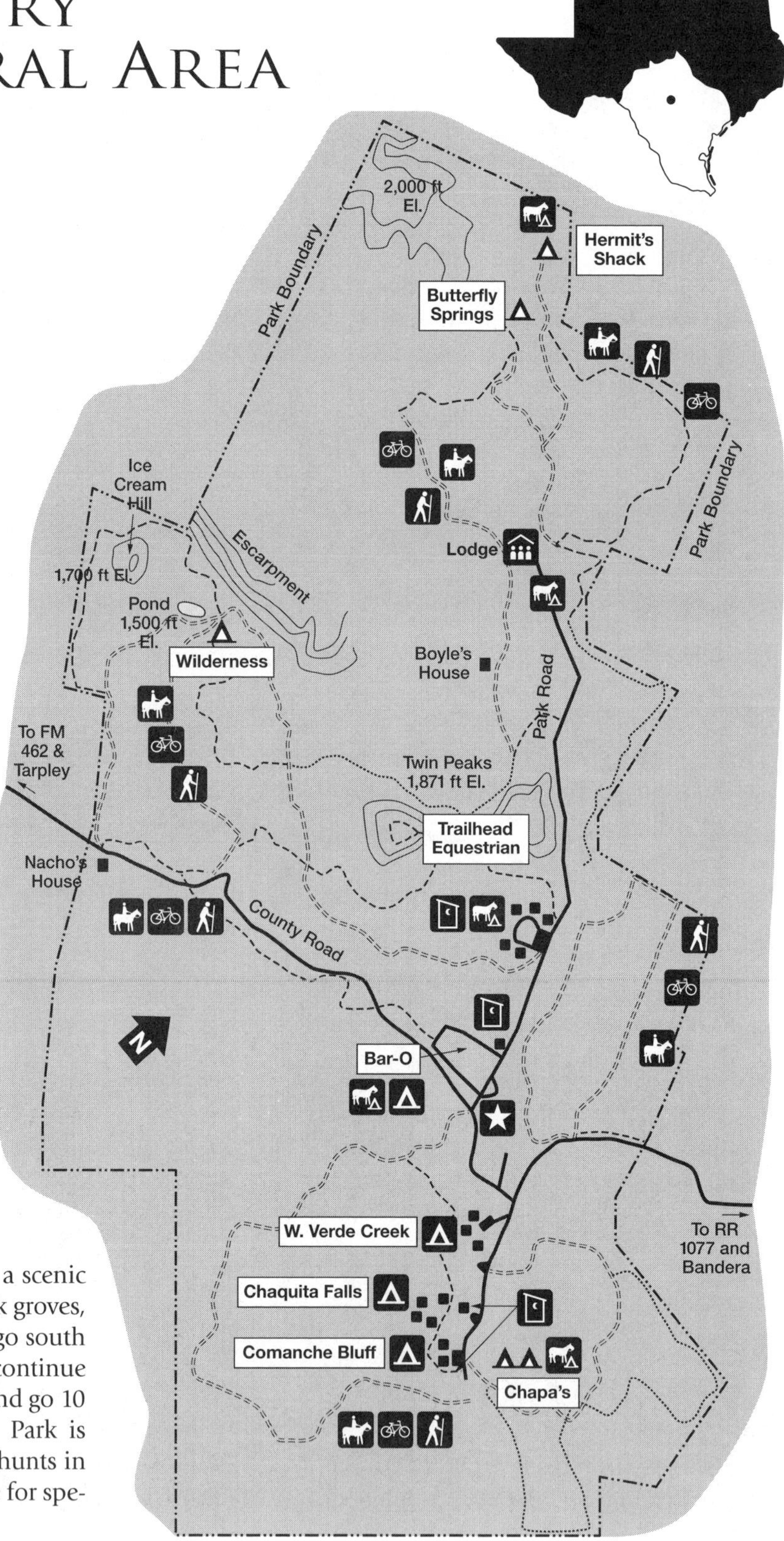

LOCATION

The Hill Country State Natural Area is a scenic mosaic of rocky hills, flowing springs, oak groves, grasslands, and canyons. From Bandera, go south on TX 173 across the Medina River and continue for about ¼-mile to FM 1077, turn right and go 10 miles to the end of the blacktop road. Park is open year round. Closed only for public hunts in December and January. Phone park office for specific dates.

TRAIL NOTES

This 5,370-acre area is operated to provide a "back-country" experience for a broad spectrum of outdoor enthusiasts; it offers primitive camping, off-road bicycling, hiking, and horseback riding. There are 40 miles and 23 designated multi-use trails, 3 designated camping areas for backpackers located 2½ to 3½ miles from trailhead parking, and 6 other camping areas with nearby parking. Overnight camping is permitted only in designated camping areas. Bring drinking water because potable water is not available; all water must be treated. Campfires are permitted only in fire rings. Only collection of deadwood on the ground is permitted. Dogs must be on a leash or tied at all times and they cannot be left unattended.

There are 3 designated swimming areas on West Verde Creek and moderate fishing opportunities for catfish, perch, and largemouth bass. Horse rentals are available from nearby ranches. Phone Bandera County Convention and Visitors Bureau for information (830/796-3045).

A more detailed trail map is available from park headquarters that shows contour lines, trail names, trail mileage, etc. The map on previous page merely displays the location of camping areas and the trail system in general; however, it should be helpful when planning a trip.

PRIMITIVE CAMPSITES

Hike-in primitive campsites for backpackers:

- ▲ *Butterfly Springs*—3½ miles from trailhead (no horses).
- ▲ *Hermit's Shack*—3½ miles from trailhead. Equestrian camping allowed.
- ▲ *Wilderness Camp*—About 2½ miles from trailhead. No horses allowed.

Walk-in developed campsites (with parking 50–100 yards from camping areas; no horses allowed): *West Verde Creek, Chaquita Falls,* and *Comanche Bluff.*

Camp areas open to equestrian use: *Bar-O, Hermit's Shack, Chapa's Group, Trailhead* and *Group Lodge.*

The Hill Country State Natural Area is often described as a scenic mosaic of rocky hills, flowing springs, oak groves, grasslands, and canyons. Obviously, a photograph can't do it justice.

LAKE GEORGETOWN/ GOOD WATER TRAIL

FOR INFORMATION

LAKE GEORGETOWN
500 CEDAR BREAKS RD.
GEORGETOWN, TX 78628-4901
512/930-5253

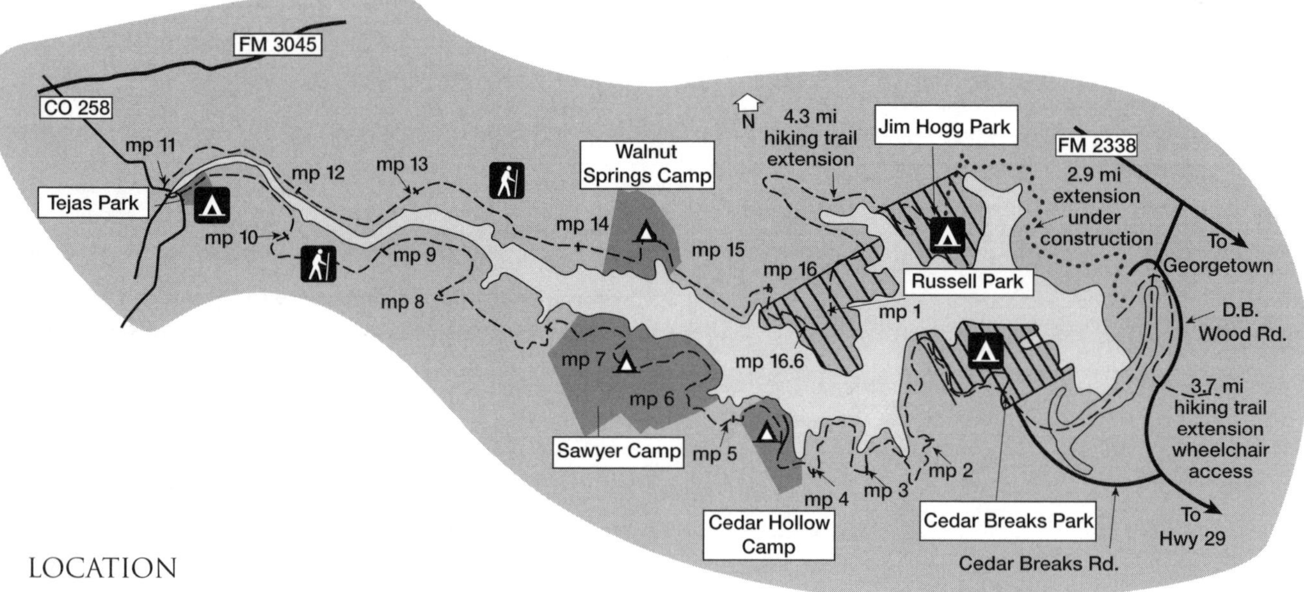

LOCATION

The Good Water Trail is located at Lake Georgetown, 4 miles west of Georgetown on FM 2338. The 16.6 mile Good Water Trail is named in honor of the Tonkawa Indians who made the land near the North Fork of the San Gabriel River their home.

TRAIL NOTES

The trail winds through more than 24 miles of countryside teeming with wildlife and traversed by numerous small streams. Backpackers may camp at Cedar Breaks Park or at one of 4 primitive campgrounds along the trail: Cedar Hollow Camp, Sawyer Camp, Tejas Park, or Walnut Springs Camp. The primitive campgrounds are non-fee areas; only Tejas Park has potable water.

Anyone using the trail is advised to check in and check out with the gate attendant at either Cedar Breaks Park, Russell Park, Jim Hogg Park, or Tejas Park. When checking in, you can also pick up a trail brochure from the gate attendant. The Lake Georgetown Visitor Center located at the Headquarters Building also has trail brochures. The trail is rough in spots; heavy footwear with strong ankle support is recommended. Fires are prohibited along the trail, but may be built in the fire rings located in the primitive campgrounds. Use only wood that is dead and fallen as well as the driftwood found along the lakeshore.

Mileposts (mp) occur at one-mile intervals along the Good Water Trail. Hikers may begin from one of seven access points. Russell Park is closed from October 1 to March 31 each year, but hiking trail parking is available, just inside the main entrance. Bikes are allowed on the new 4.3-mile trail extension from Russell Park to Jim Hogg Park as well as the new 3.7-mile trail extension from Cedar Breaks Park across the dam via the road that has been closed to vehicle traffic. The 2.9-mile trail that will connect these 2 trails is under construction; when completed the Good Water Trail will make a complete circle around the lake.

Lake Mineral Wells State Park and Trailway

For Information

Lake Mineral Wells State Park and Trailway
100 Park Rd. 71
Mineral Wells, TX 76067
940/328-1171

Location

Lake Mineral Wells State Park and Trailway is situated only 4 miles from the center of town. The park contains 3,282 acres, which include the 646-acre lake, and may be reached by traveling 4 miles east from the city of Mineral Wells on US 180, or 15 miles west of Weatherford on the same highway.

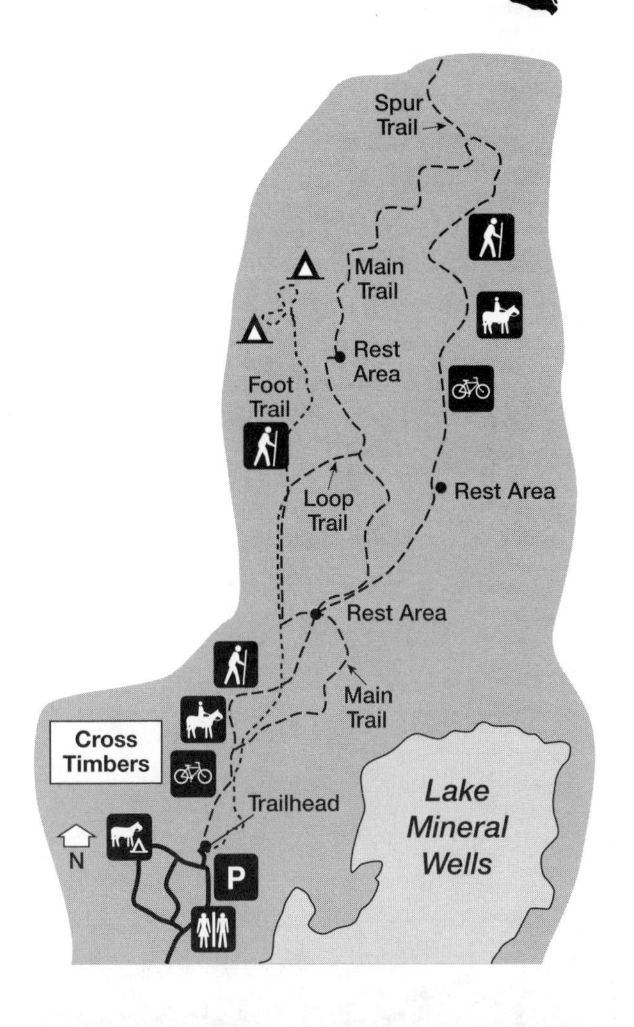

Trail Notes

A 2½-mile hiking trail (5 miles round-trip) begins at the trailhead, traverses the canyons along the creek, and leads to 2 primitive camping areas for backpackers. Erosion has created rolling to hilly terrain dissected by deep canyons. Thick brush rims the deeper canyons, and upland woods contain ash, juniper, sugarberry, and Texas oak, in addition to the other oaks. A 16-mile round-trip trail is available for horseback riding, hiking, and all-terrain bicycling. The trailhead to both of these trails is north of the Cross Timbers equestrian camping area.

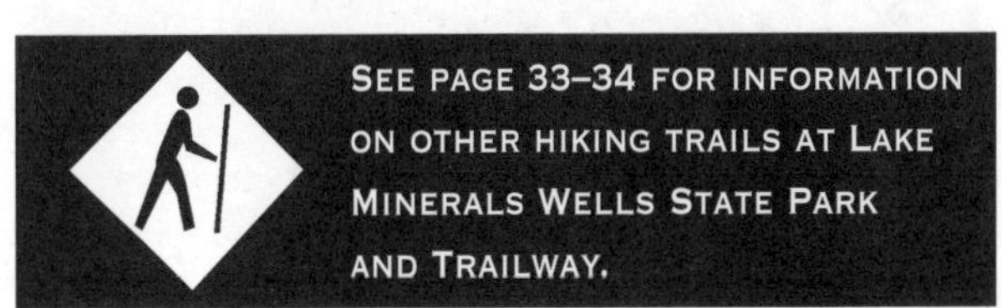
See page 33–34 for information on other hiking trails at Lake Minerals Wells State Park and Trailway.

Perhaps the 646-acre lake at this park might be considered the focal point of recreational activities, but the availability of many miles of multi-use trails certainly puts hiking, mountain biking, and horseback riding as close seconds.

Lake Somerville State Trailway

For Information

Lake Somerville Wildlife
Management Area and Trailway
6280 FM 180
Ledbetter, TX 78946-7036
979/289-2392

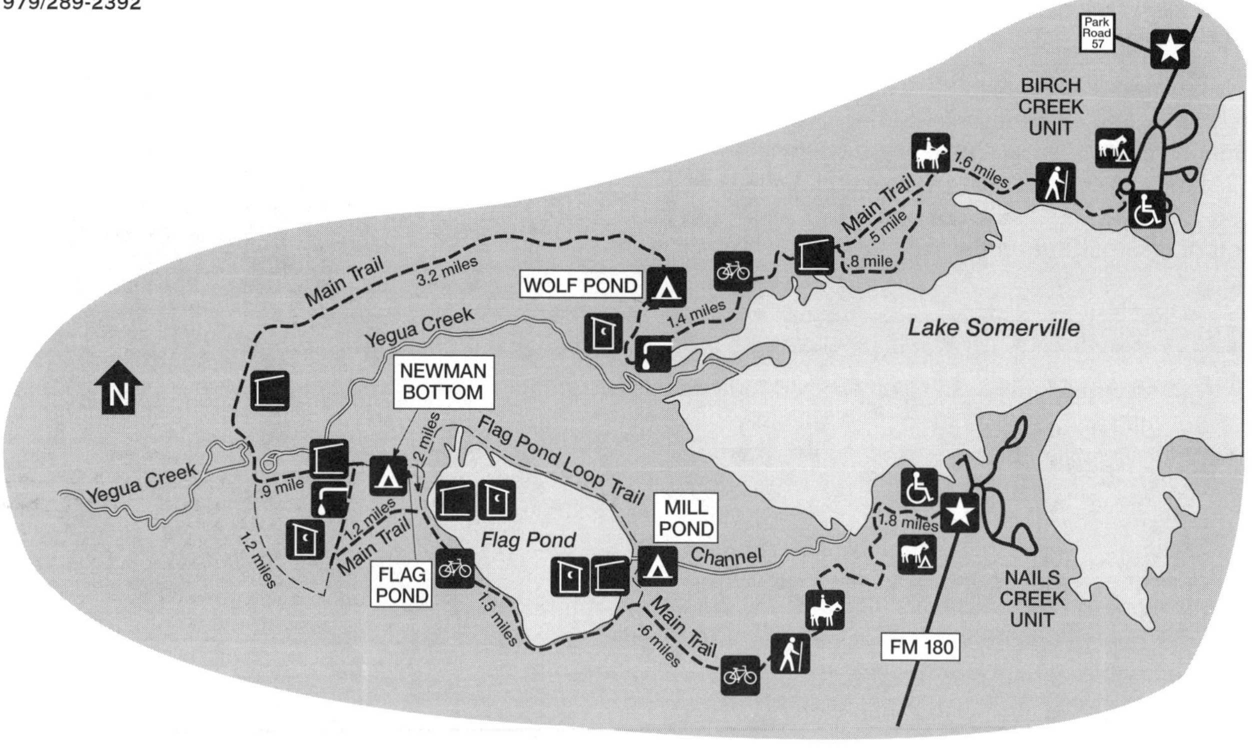

See page 70 for information on other hiking trails at Lake Somerville State Park and Trailway.

Location

The Birch Creek Unit is reached via TX 36, west of Somerville on FM 60 to Park Road 57. The Nails Creek Unit is reached via US 290 from FM 180 between Giddings and Ledbetter or from Burton via FM 1697 and FM 180.

Trail Notes

The Lake Somerville Trailway System, located around the west end of the reservoir, connects Birch Creek State Park with Nails Creek State Park via 13 miles of trails for hiking, mountain biking, horseback riding, backpacking, birding, and nature study. Flag Pond Campground, located approximately 4 miles from Nails Creek and 9 miles from Birch Creek along the trailway, provides wildlife viewing opportunities. Campgrounds for equestrian and backpackers are located along the trailway. Well water for horses only is available at Newman Bottom and Wolf Pond; chemical toilets are in the area. The trailway passes through dense stands of yaupon, post oak, hickory, blackjack oak, and water oak forests, past scenic overlooks and water crossings.

Lake Texoma/ Big Mineral Equestrian and Hiking Trail

For Information

LAKE TEXOMA
351 CORPS ROAD
DENISON, TX 75020-6425
903/465-4990

Location

The Big Mineral Equestrian and Hiking Trail is located on the west side of the southernmost arm of Lake Texoma. Trailheads are at the Brushy Creek Section and the Walnut Creek Section of Big Mineral Resort east of US 377; access is from Gordonville on FM 901 (see vicinity map).

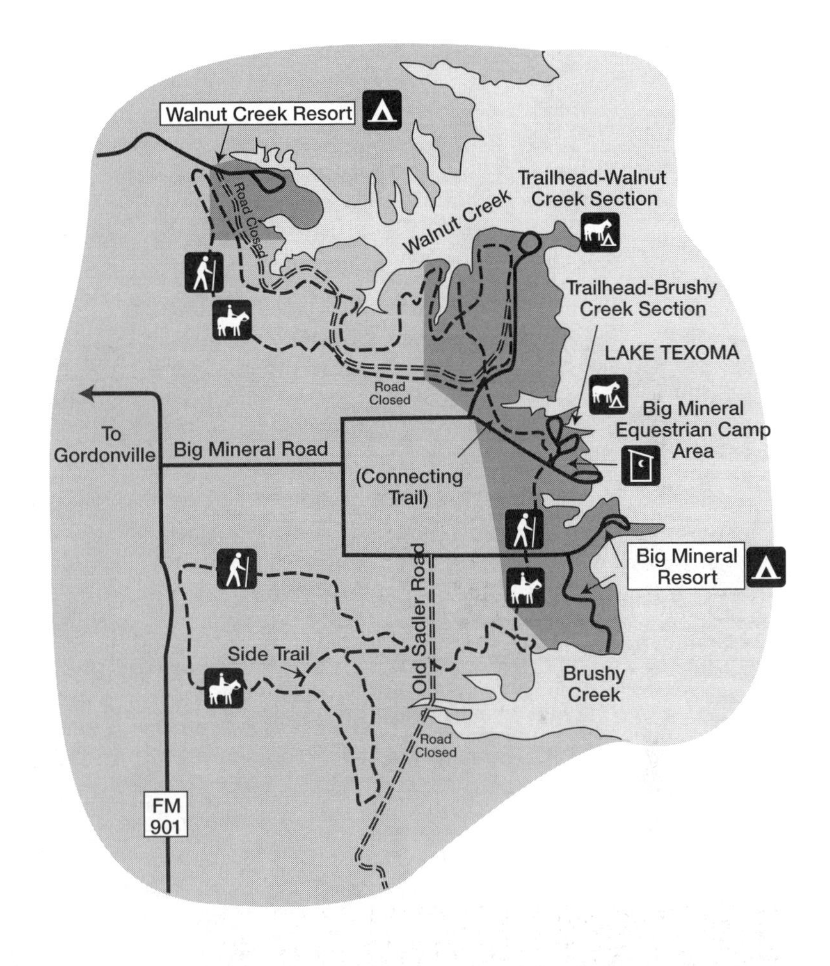

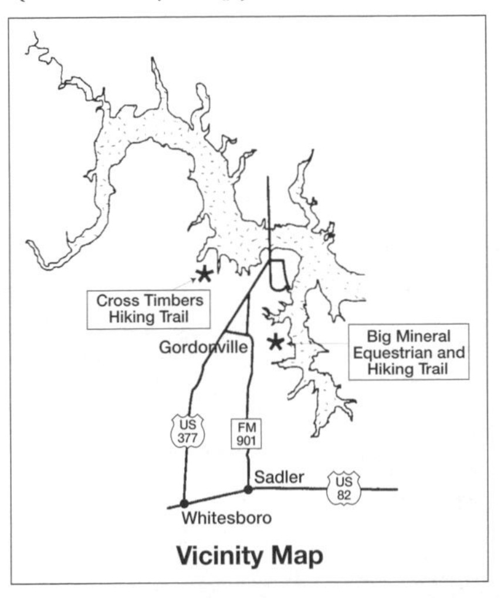

Trail Notes

The Big Mineral Equestrian Trail system is made up of two main trails, the Walnut Creek Loop and the Brushy Creek Loop. They are, however, joined together with a short connecting trail. The Walnut Creek Loop is about 10 miles long; it meanders through both bottomland woods and upland meadows. The Brushy Creek Loop is some 13 miles long and also traverses both upland and bottomland areas.

Each trail has several spurs leading to the lakeshore that are currently marked with blue and white ribbons. The main trails are marked with orange and white. Both trails together offer nearly 25 miles; because both riders and backpackers will be using the trail, both groups should watch out for each other while on the trail. There is ample parking and primitive camping at the trailheads. A unisex vault toilet, complete with hitching post, is also located along the trail. Gates that occur along the trail are designed to be opened without dismounting. The trail was constructed and is maintained by the Big Mineral Equestrian Trail Riders Association.

In the summer, camping is by permit only; free permits may be obtained at the project office. Horses and backpackers should remain off the trail during deer hunting season. Motorized vehicles and mountain bicycles are not allowed on the trail. Horses are not allowed in the developed public campgrounds and should be ridden at a walk in primitive camps.

Lake Texoma/Cross Timbers Hiking Trail

For Information

Lake Texoma
351 Corps Road
Denison, TX 75020-6425
903/465-4990

Location

The Cross Timbers Hiking Trail, designed for the enjoyment of backpackers and hikers, is located along the southern shoreline of Lake Texoma. The 14-mile trail begins in Juniper Point Recreation Area (north of Whitesboro off of US 377 near the Willis bridge to Madill, OK) and ends at the Rock Creek Camp Recreation Area. (See vicinity map, page 187.)

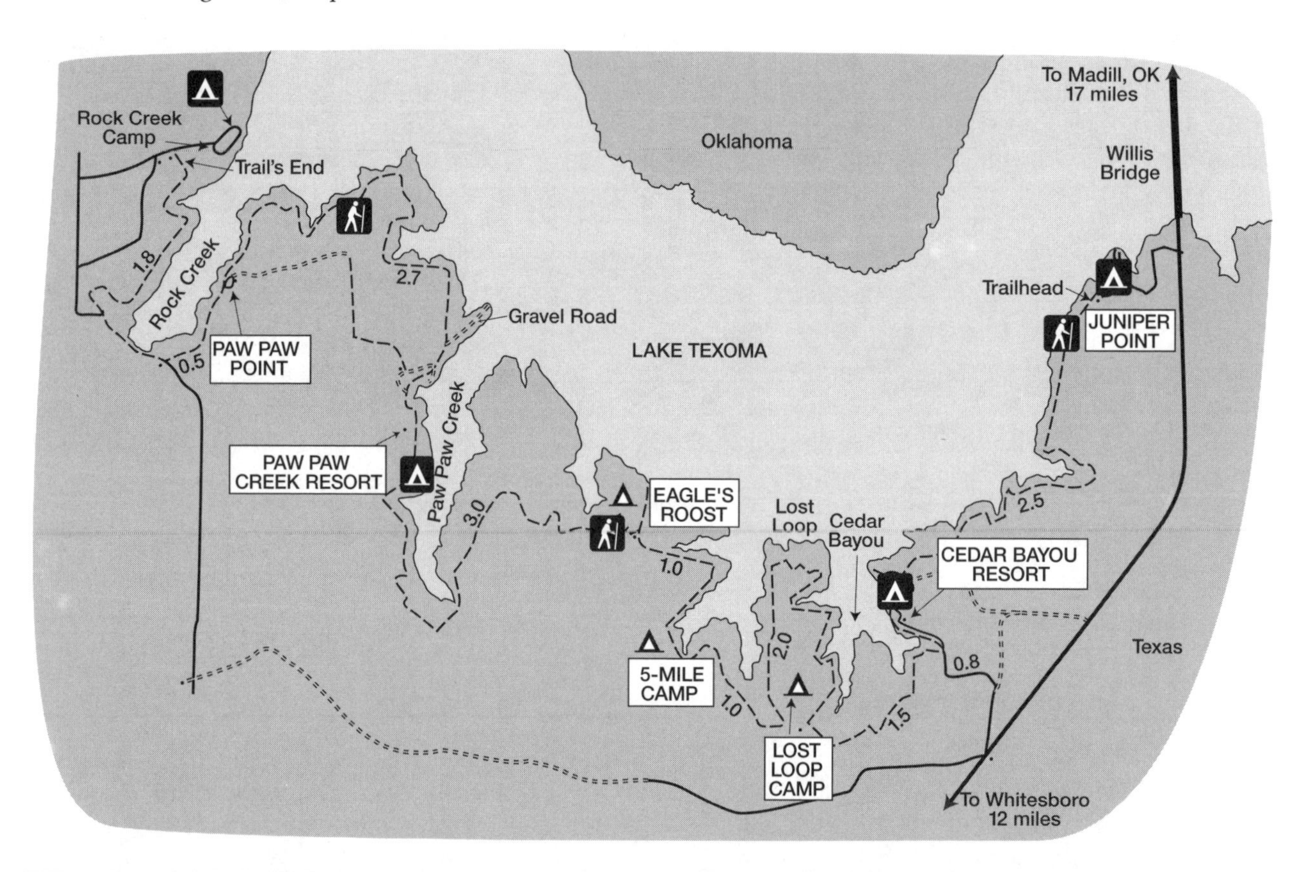

Trail Notes

Between Juniper Point and Cedar Bayou Resort, the hiker/backpacker travels high above the lake on the rocky ledges that make up the shoreline. From Cedar Bayou to Paw Paw Creek Resort the trail meanders through a blackjack oak woodland and takes the hiker through many changes of elevation. Between Paw Paw Creek Resort and Rock Creek Camp the trail is much flatter and the tree cover more sparse. The trail is well marked and mileposts have been erected along the way as reference points.

You may wish to camp along the trail in one of the 3 wilderness camps. Five-Mile Camp, Lost Loop Camp, and the Eagle's Roost Camp are available between Cedar Bayou and Paw Paw Creek resorts. These camps are primitive and have no water or conveniences; a permit is required. The permit may be applied for in person at the Lake Texoma Office, or obtained in advance by mail.

Lost Maples State Natural Area

FOR INFORMATION

Lost Maples State Natural Area
37221 FM 187
Vanderpool, TX 78885
830/966-3413

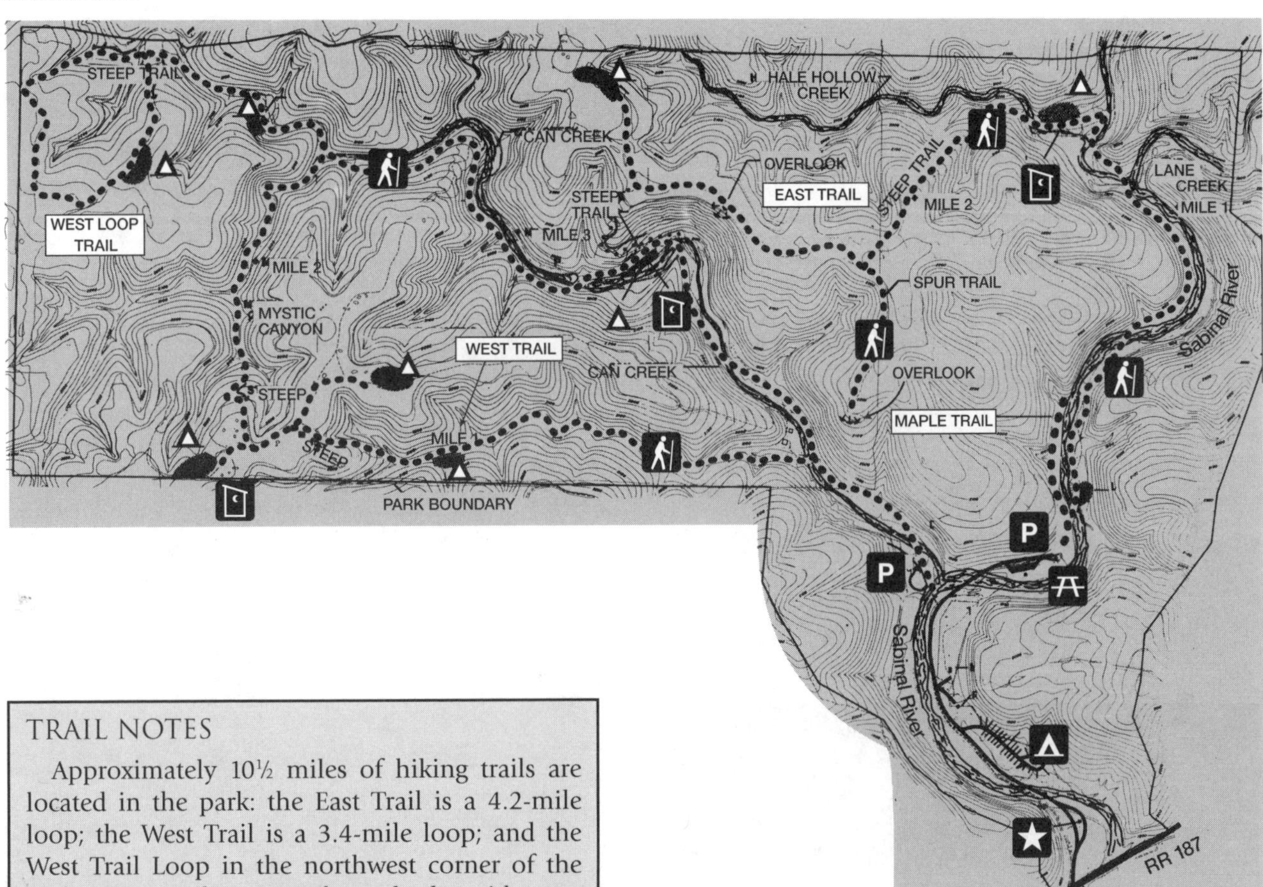

TRAIL NOTES

Approximately 10½ miles of hiking trails are located in the park: the East Trail is a 4.2-mile loop; the West Trail is a 3.4-mile loop; and the West Trail Loop in the northwest corner of the park is 1.8 miles. Several overlooks with spur trails are located at high vantage points along the primitive trails. There are portions of the trail that are quite strenuous; grade changes of several hundred feet are encountered on several trails. Proper shoes, wearing apparel, and physical condition should be considered when planning the route; water should be carried.

The Maple Trail, popular with day-hikers, is a developed nature trail approximately 1,400 feet long. Eight designated primitive camping areas with 3 composting toilets are accessible to hikers. Ground fires are not allowed; only containerized fuel stoves are acceptable.

LOCATION

Lost Maples State Natural Area is located 4 miles north of Vanderpool on RR 187. If traveling from Kerrville, take TX 39 west, then south on RR 187. If traveling from Bandera, take TX 16 west, then RR 470 southwest and RR 187 north.

See page 105 for information on the nature trail at Lost Maples State Natural Area.

PADRE ISLAND NATIONAL SEASHORE

FOR INFORMATION

PADRE ISLAND NATIONAL SEASHORE
(20420 PARK RD. 22)
P.O. BOX 181300
CORPUS CHRISTI, TX 78480-1300
361/949-8068 VISITOR STATION
361/949-8171 HEADQUARTERS
361/949-8175 (FOR RECORDED MESSAGE ON TIDES, WEATHER, BEACH CONDITIONS, ETC.)

Backpacking at Padre Island was quite an experience! Did I enjoy it? Yes! Do I plan to do it again? No.

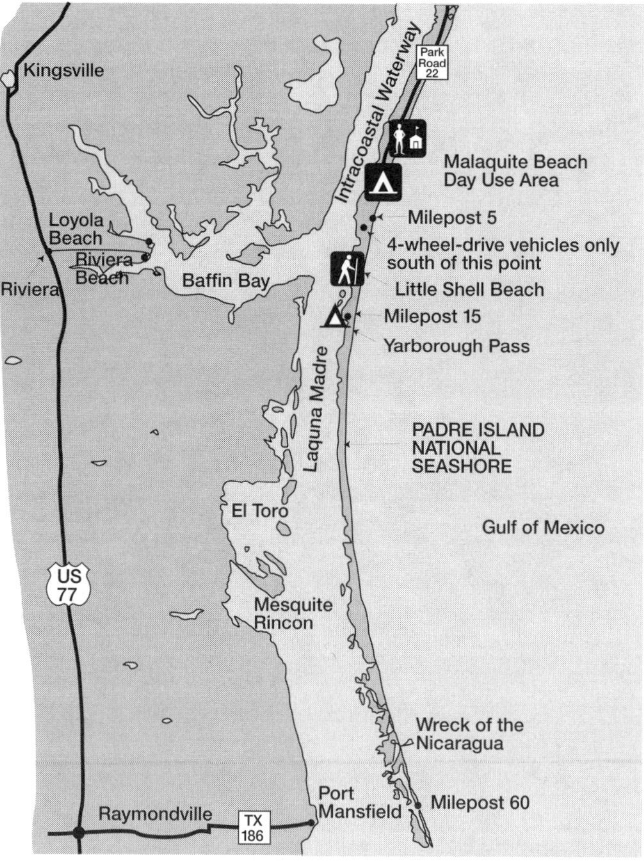

SEE PAGE 107 FOR INFORMATION ON OTHER HIKING TRAILS AT PADRE ISLAND NATIONAL SEASHORE.

TRAIL NOTES

Hiking and backpacking in Padre Island National Seashore are, to say the least, arduous experiences. An information sheet is available for those who plan to "rough it" down the island so that they may be properly prepared for the trip and adequately warned of the hazards to be encountered.

You should check at the Visitor Center before starting your trip. There are no trails on the island, but you may hike or drive a 4-wheel-drive vehicle almost the entire length of the beach. The sand on much of the beach is very loose and walking is slow and arduous. The heat, humidity, insects and rattlesnakes make it inadvisable to hike through the grasslands.

You may camp and build fires on the beach on the seaward side of the sand dunes; there is usually plenty of driftwood that can be used as firewood. You may not camp, build fires, or drive ATVs in the dunes or grasslands or mudflats.

It is about 60 miles from Malaquite Beach south to the Mansfield Channel and about 35 miles from the Channel to the southern end of the island. There is no potable water between Malquite Beach and Mansfield Channel. You will have to carry your water with you on any extended trip.

Topographical maps of the National Seashore may be obtained by writing to the U.S. Geological Survey, Denver, Colorado 80225. Eight maps cover the area from Malaquite Beach to the Mansfield Channel.

Pedernales Falls State Park

For Information

Pedernales Falls State Park
2585 Park Rd. 6026
Johnson City, TX 78636
830/868-7304

See page 109 for information on other hiking trails at Pedernales Falls State Park.

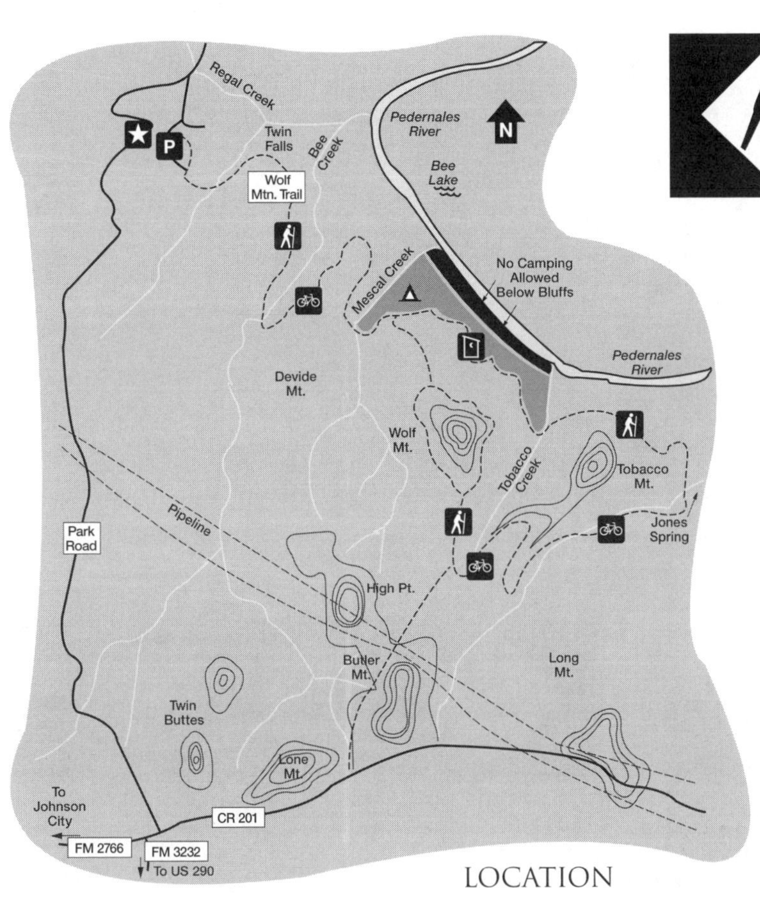

The Wolf Mountain Trail has become a popular biking trail.

Location

Pedernales Falls State Park may be reached by traveling 9 miles east of Johnson City on FM 2766, or by traveling west of Austin for 32 miles on US 290, then north on FM 3232 for 6 miles.

Trail Notes

The 7½-mile loop known as Wolf Mountain Trail is popular among hikers, backpackers, and mountain bikers. Overnight camping is permitted in the designated primitive camping area only, which is located approximately 2½ miles from the trailhead. The primitive camping area has 4 natural boundaries—Mescal Creek, Tobacco Creek, the trail, and the rock bluffs. No camping is allowed below the bluffs; no pets allowed overnight.

Campfires are not permitted in the primitive area due to the lack of natural firewood in the area and because of the possibility of wildfires. Cooking shall be done only on containerized fuel stoves. Chemical toilet facilities are located adjacent to the trail at the designated camping area. Drinking water should be carried in; it is available at the parking lot. There are springs in the area but the water is not recommended for human consumption.

The river area is subject to flash flooding and rising water. An automatic early flood warning system is installed at the park. There are towers with sirens located along the river from the falls area downstream to the primitive camping area. When a siren is heard, leave the river area immediately.

SABINE NATIONAL FOREST/ TRAIL BETWEEN THE LAKES

FOR INFORMATION

SABINE NATIONAL FOREST
(201 SOUTH PALM)
P.O. BOX 227
HEMPHILL, TX 75948
409/787-3870 OR 2791
TOLL FREE 1-866-235-1750

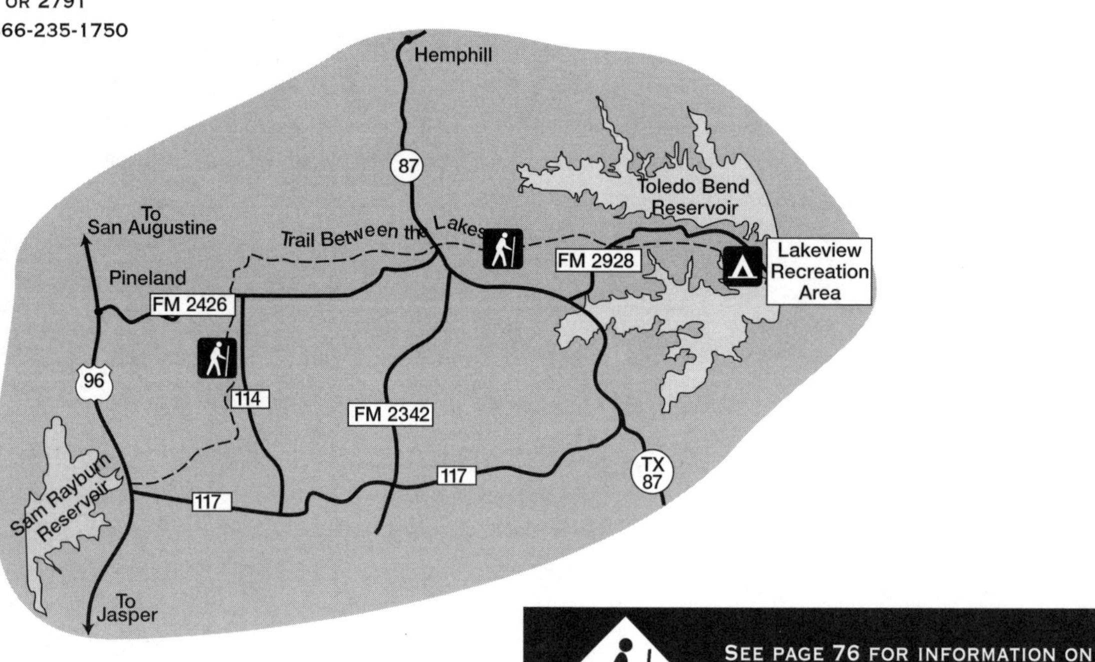

SEE PAGE 76 FOR INFORMATION ON OTHER HIKING TRAILS IN THE SABINE NATIONAL FOREST.

TRAIL NOTES

Hiking and backpacking are permitted anywhere in the national forests in Texas and primitive camping is allowed anywhere unless otherwise posted. Permits are not needed for primitive camping, although it is best to contact the office for detailed information. A detailed map of the Sabine National Forest may be purchased from the Sabine National Forest office.

The Trail Between the Lakes is a 28-mile hiking trail that extends from Lakeview Recreation Area on the Toledo Bend Reservoir to US 96 within sight of the easternmost point of Sam Rayburn Reservoir. The trail was built through the joint effort of the Golden Triangle Group of the Sierra Club and the U.S.D.A. Forest Service; members have adopted sections to maintain. A portion of the trail is adjacent to Toledo Bend Reservoir, and many portions lie along streams or special wildlife areas. The trail crosses roads at many locations, so it's easy to plan shorter hikes of varying lengths. Pick up a trail map from the forest office; it displays the numerous road crossings in great detail.

The trail is designated for hiking only; horses, off-road vehicles, and mountain bikes are not allowed.

There are many opportunities to camp in primitive or natural settings along the route, except in the Moore Plantation Wildlife Management Area during the deer season and in colonies of red-cockaded woodpeckers. The woodpecker colony boundaries are marked with aqua-green paint and boundary signs. Be careful with campfires, and if you "pack it in, pack it out."

Sam Houston National Forest/Lone Star Hiking Trail

FOR INFORMATION

Sam Houston National Forest
394 FM 1375 West
New Waverly, TX 77358
936/344-6205
Toll Free 1-888-361-6908

Backpacking is permitted anywhere in Texas' national forests and primitive camping is allowed anywhere unless posted otherwise. One restriction is that camping within the boundaries of red-cockaded woodpecker colonies in the national forests in Texas is prohibited. Boundaries are identified by trees with green or white markings and/or signs. Also, during the deer season, camping is limited to specially designated "Hunter Camps." Permits are not needed for primitive camping although it is best to contact the office for detailed information. A detailed map of the Sam Houston National Forest may be purchased from the Sam Houston National Forest Office.

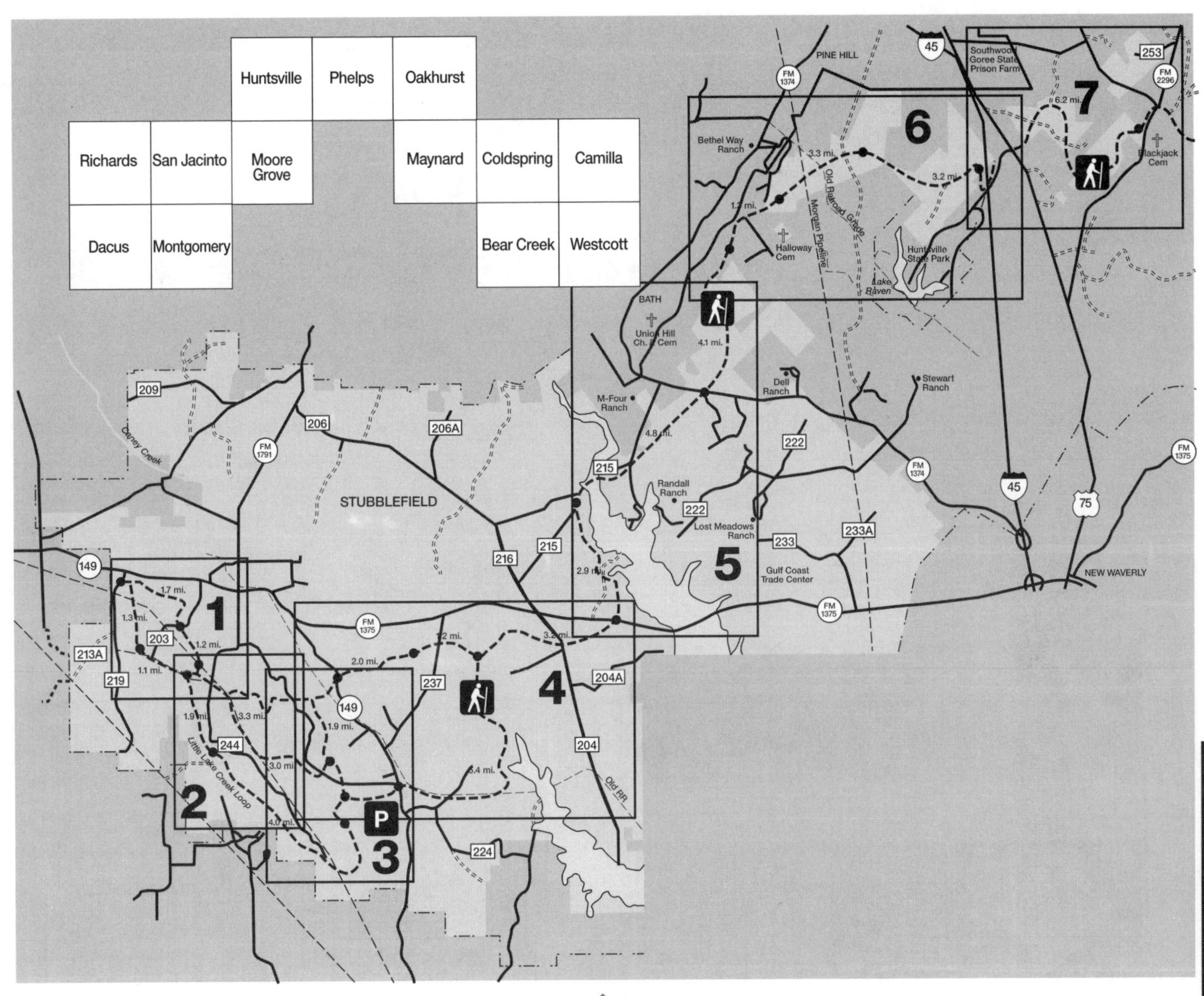

TRAIL NOTES

The Lone Star Hiking Trail has evolved through the efforts of a few thousand individuals belonging to a number of groups such as the U.S. Forest Service, the Boy Scouts, the Girl Scouts, the Youth Conservation Corp, the Sierra Club, and the Lone Star Hiking Trail Club.

The trail originated in 1968, when a small group of Sierra Club (Houston) members decided to help develop and support a long-distance overland hiking trail. They contacted the U.S. Forest Service and obtained permission to lay out the original portion of the trail, a 30-mile section in the Stubblefield area of the Sam Houston National Forest. Gradually, additional sections were added until the trail reached its present length of about 129 miles.

The Forest Service relies on volunteers to keep the trail open, clear, and well marked so that it will be enjoyable and attractive to hikers.

West of FM 149 above Montgomery, the western portion of the Lone Star Trail passes through the 3,855-acre Little Lake Creek Wilderness Area. On the eastern portion of the Lone Star Trail, west of the trailhead on FM 1725, the trail passes through Winters Bayou Scenic Area. This area is similar to the Big Thicket area. There are trail maps and brochures available at the New Waverly office providing detailed information about the Lone Star Trail. Obtain this information before planning hikes. Section maps in pdf format may be found at the Lone Star Hiking Trail Club website, www.lshtclub.com.

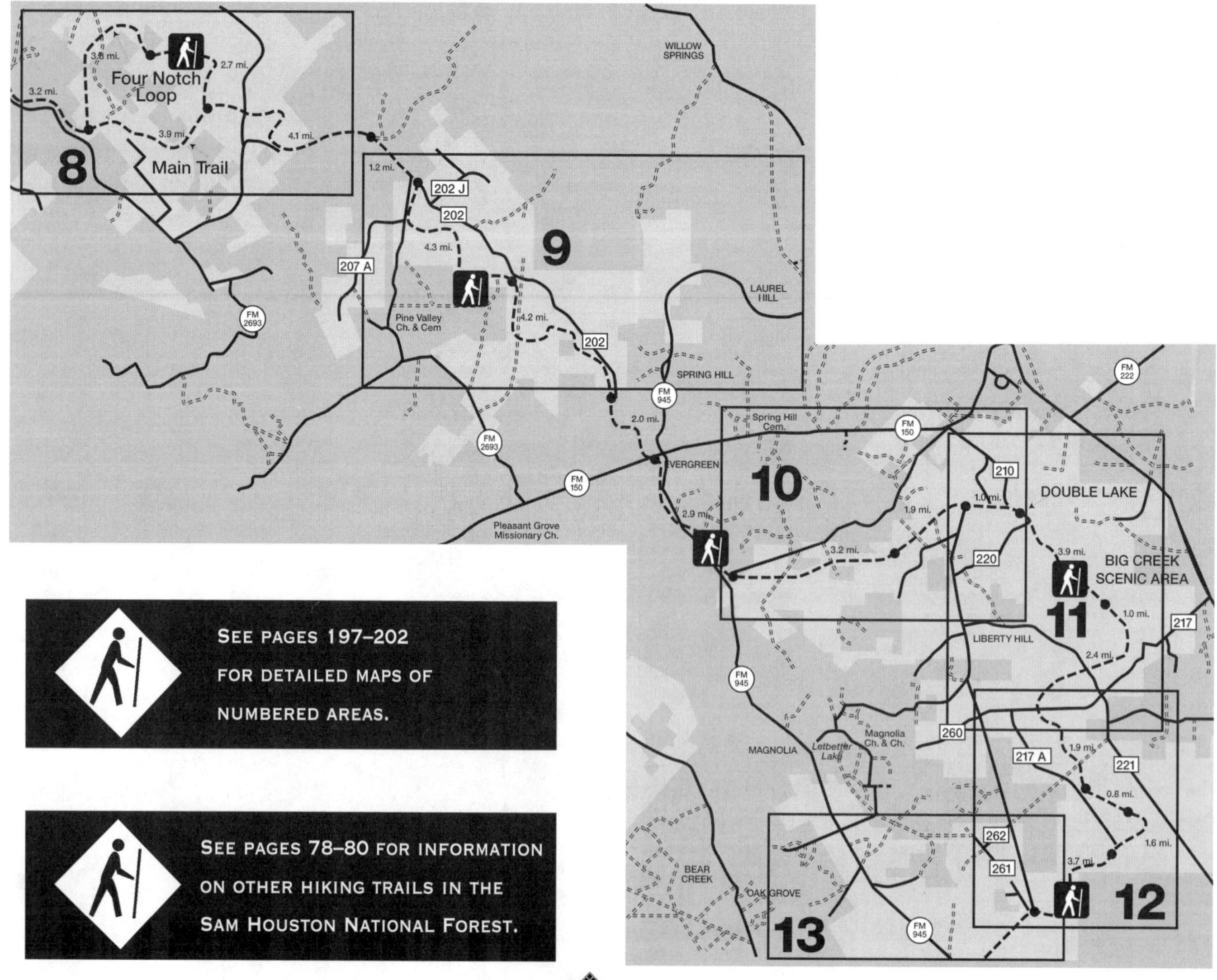

See pages 197–202 for detailed maps of numbered areas.

See pages 78–80 for information on other hiking trails in the Sam Houston National Forest.

BACKPACKING/HIKING INFORMATION

- ▲ Primitive Camping—"Backpacking" type camping is allowed along the Lone Star Hiking Trail. Hikers must "carry in and carry out all supplies and litter." Hikers must carry their own water. Certain areas are marked with three markers and are suitable for primitive type camping, but the hiker is not confined to these areas. The hiker is encouraged not to overuse any particular location and leave a minimum impact of his overnight stay along the trail.
- ▲ Water—Bring your own water. It is recommended that you do *not* drink out of the creeks and ponds along the trail.
- ▲ Hiking Time—A hiker can estimate covering one mile in about 30 minutes.
- ▲ Campfires—Campfires are allowed, but are restricted at certain times of year (example: during dry spell). If in doubt, check at the ranger station. If a hiker does have a campfire, clear the brush and pine needles around the campfire, and make sure it is extinguished thoroughly. It is preferable to carry and use a small cooking stove. (Carry out the empty fuel canisters.)
- ▲ Hiking Season—The choice times to hike on the Lone Star Hiking Trail are winter, spring, and fall. Long distance hiking is not as enjoyable during June, July, or August because it is generally very hot, humid, and a prime time for insects. Avoid hiking on the trail during hunting season.
- ▲ Hunting Season—The hunting season is normally from mid-November through the beginning of January. Check with the county or your local sporting goods shop for the exact dates, which vary each year. *Do not hike during hunting season!*
- ▲ Litter—Please have at least one person in your group tie a plastic bag to their belt to collect litter along the trail. Please pick up any litter, *even if it is not yours!*
- ▲ Insects—During the hot months (particularly June, July, and August) it is advisable to carry and use insect repellent that is suitable for repelling ticks, chiggers, and mosquitoes.
- ▲ Wet Road—Be careful not to get stuck when driving on secondary dirt roads after a bad rain.
- ▲ Creeks/Rivers—At certain times of the year (mainly January, February), the water level of the larger creeks and the San Jacinto River will rise. Until permanent, all-weather type hiking bridges are implemented, the hiker may have to make a detour around these flooded areas.
- ▲ Trail Length—Approximately 129 miles long.
- ▲ Trail Purpose—For hikers only; off-road vehicles, bicycles and horses are not allowed on the Lone Star Hiking Trail.
- ▲ Trail Status—During 1978, the eastern section of the trail in the vicinity of Double Lake was declared a National Recreational Trail.
- ▲ The forest is typically prescribed burned in October through March, depending upon weather and fuel conditions. Hikers and backpackers should check at the ranger station to see what prescribed burning is planned, if any.

You shouldn't be in too big of a hurry when you hike the trails in the Big Creek Scenic Area; there's just too much to see.

Trail Marking System

Aluminum markers 2 x 4 inches, attached to trees 10 to 50 yards apart, 5′–6′ high.

Trail goes straight ahead.

Trail turns left.

Trail turns right.

Special attention.

Primitive overnight stopover site.

Orange tape strip on marker: major loop or alternate to main trail.

White tape strip on marker: crossover (link) between main trail and a major loop.

Triangle marker: old style marker still seen on some parts of trail. Some have mile markings on them.

The 129-mile Lone Star Hiking Trail is maintained through the efforts of numerous volunteers.

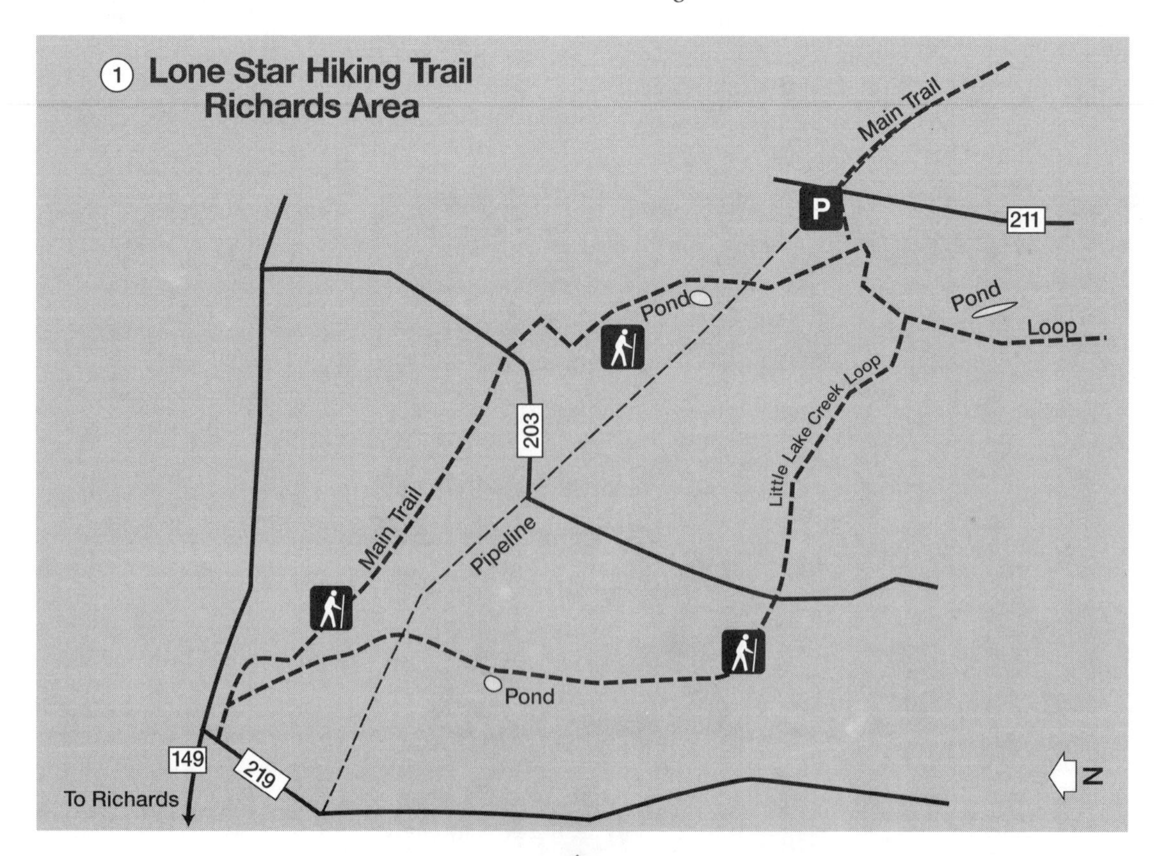

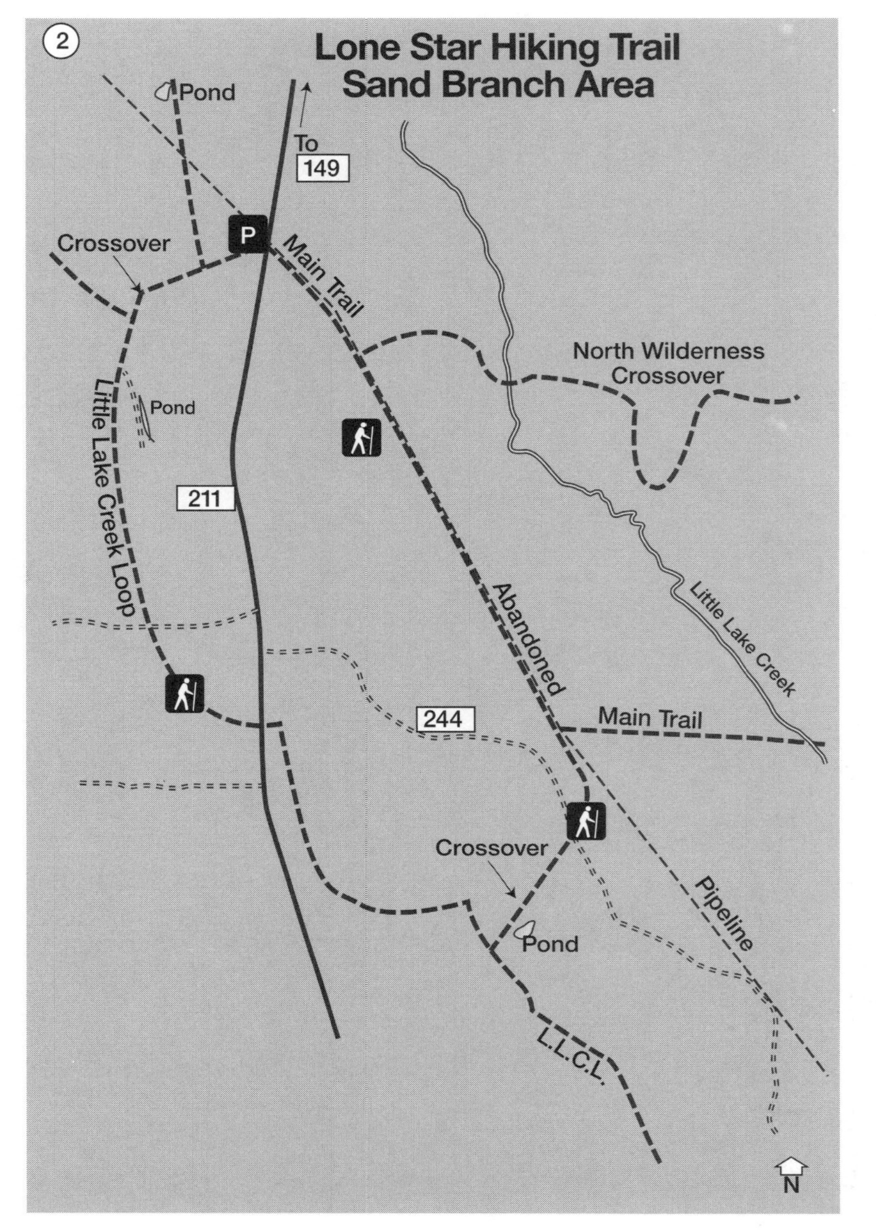
2
Lone Star Hiking Trail
Sand Branch Area
Pond
To
149
P
Crossover
Main Trail
North Wilderness
Crossover
Pond
Little Lake Creek Loop
211
Abandoned
Little Lake Creek
244
Main Trail
Crossover
Pond
Pipeline
L.L.C.L.
N

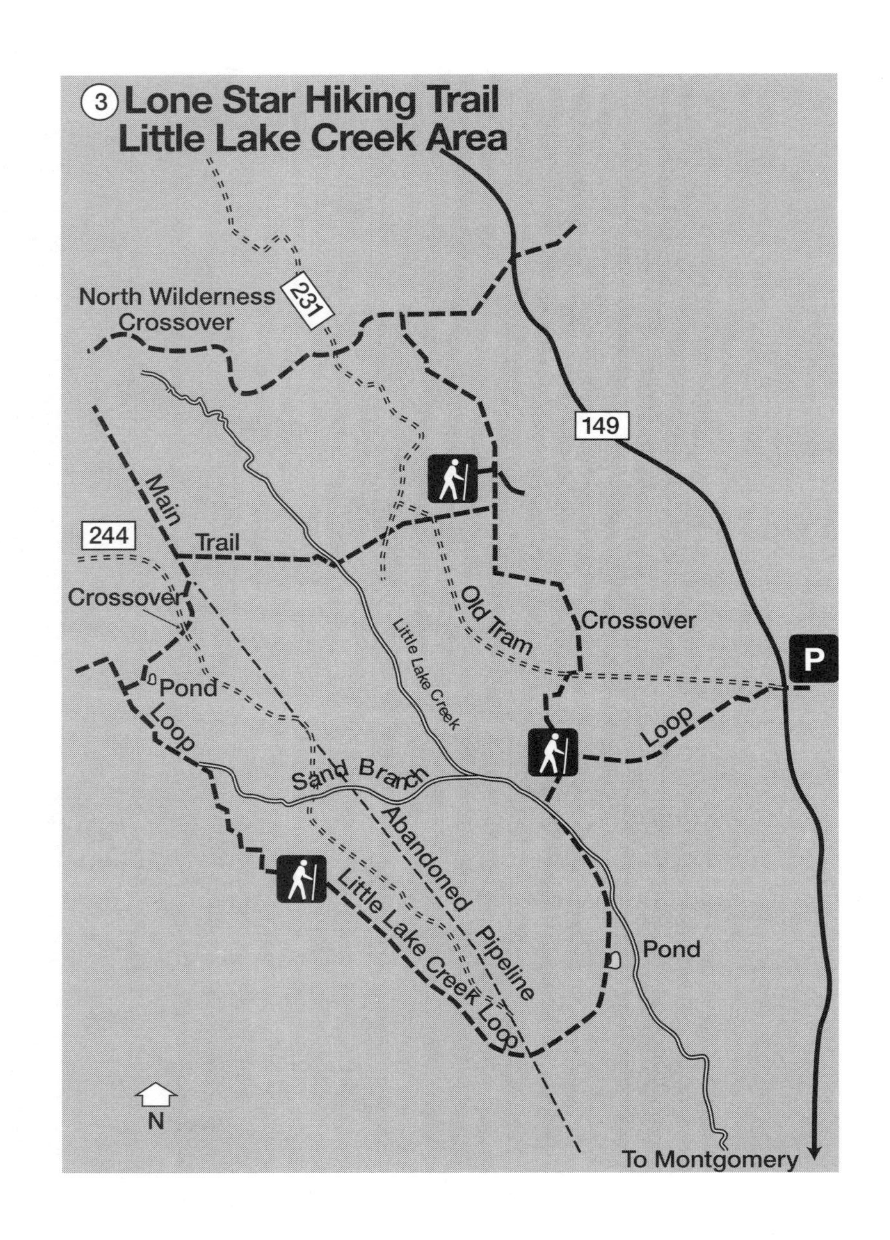
3
Lone Star Hiking Trail
Little Lake Creek Area
North Wilderness
Crossover
231
149
Main
Trail
244
Crossover
Old Tram
Little Lake Creek
Crossover
P
Pond
Loop
Loop
Sand Branch
Abandoned
Pipeline
Little Lake Creek Loop
Pond
N
To Montgomery

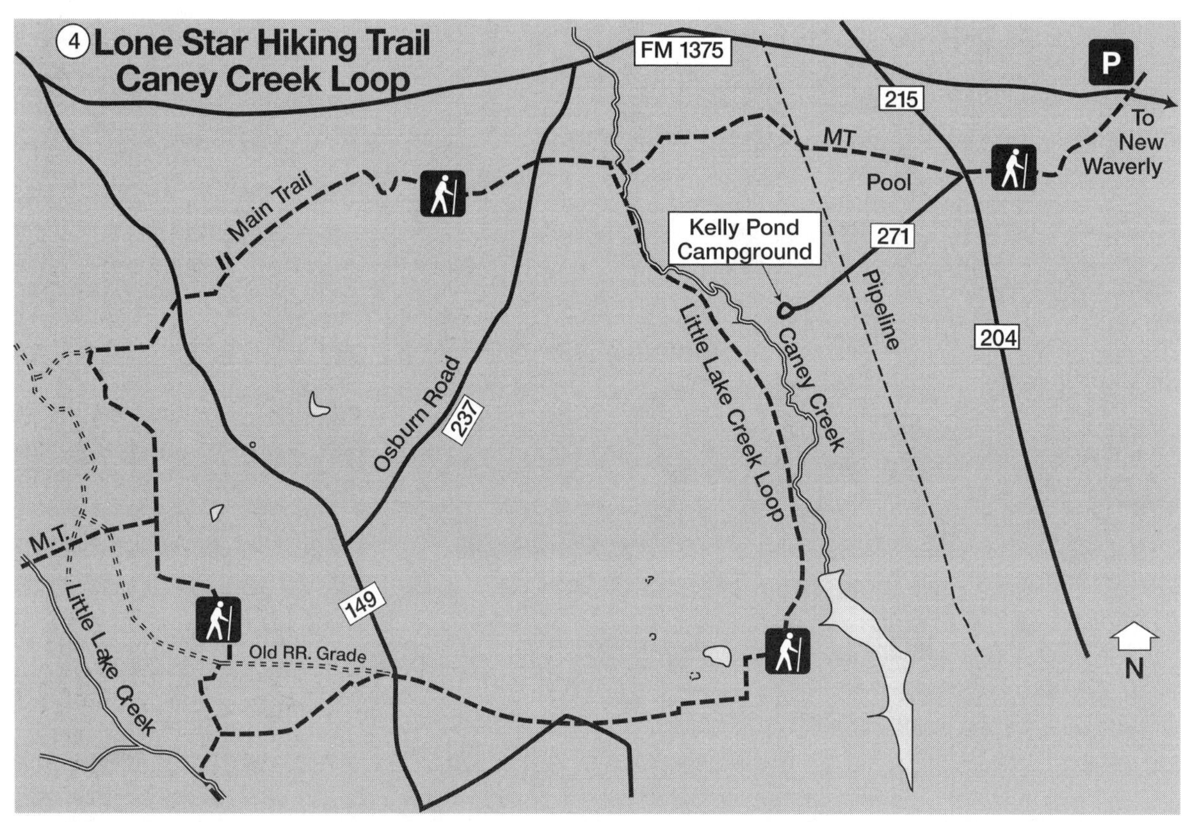
4 Lone Star Hiking Trail
Caney Creek Loop
FM 1375
P
215
To
New
Waverly
MT
Pool
Main Trail
Kelly Pond
Campground
271
Pipeline
204
Caney Creek
Little Lake Creek Loop
Osburn Road
237
M.T.
Little Lake Creek
149
Old RR. Grade
N

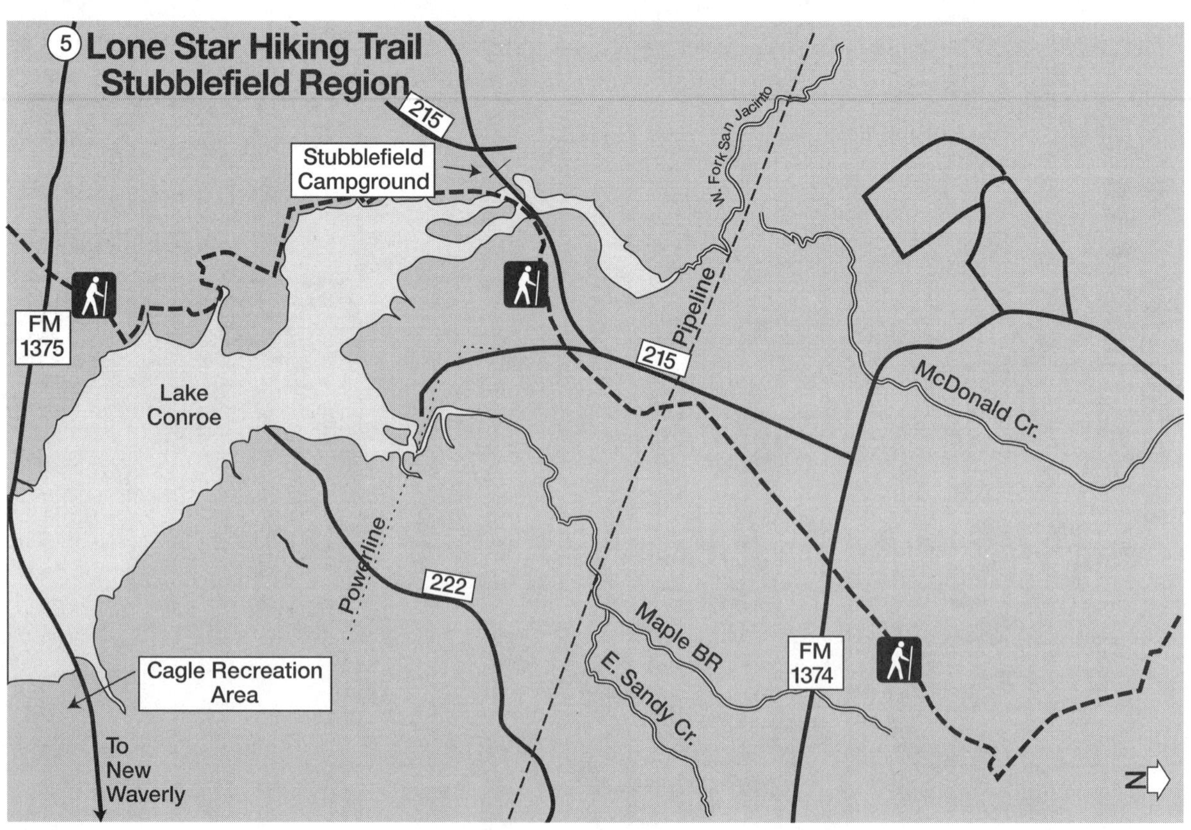
5 Lone Star Hiking Trail
Stubblefield Region
215
Stubblefield
Campground
W. Fork San Jacinto
FM
1375
Pipeline
215
Lake
Conroe
McDonald Cr.
Powerline
222
Maple BR
E. Sandy Cr.
FM
1374
Cagle Recreation
Area
To
New
Waverly
N

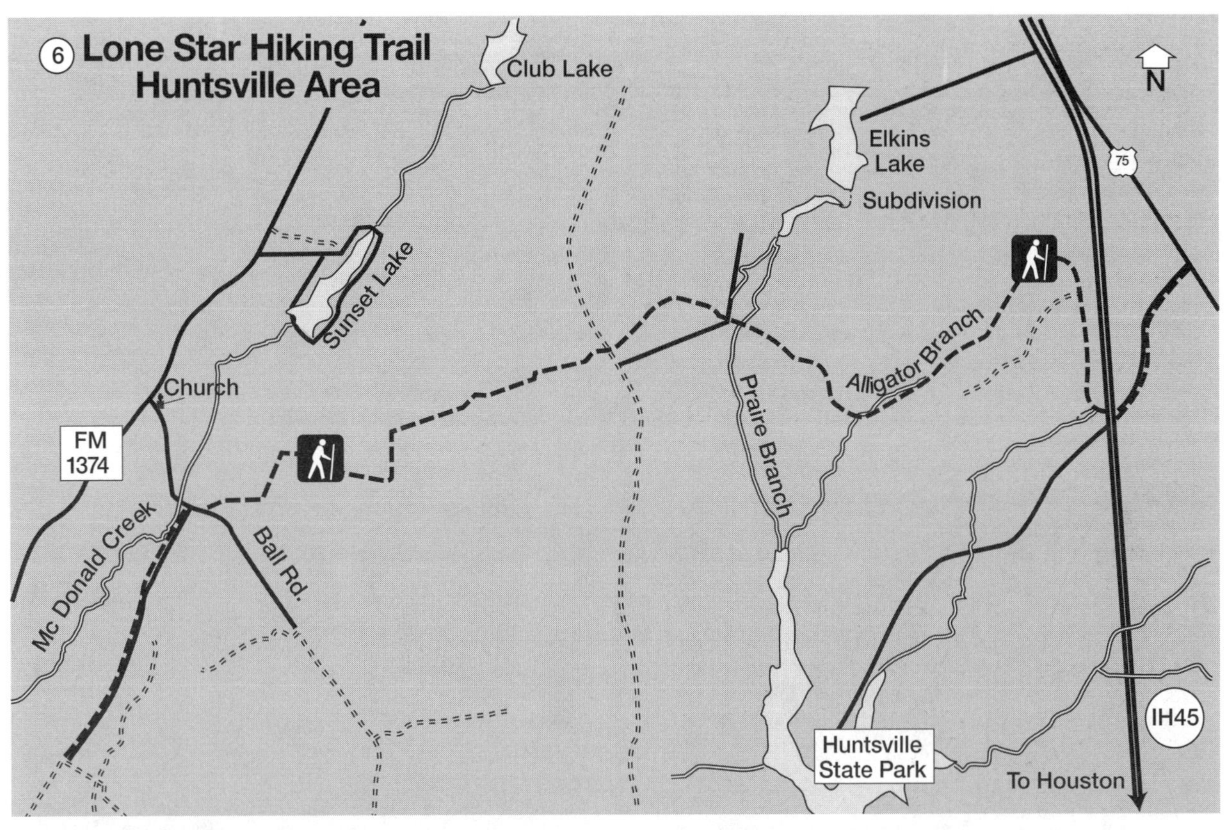

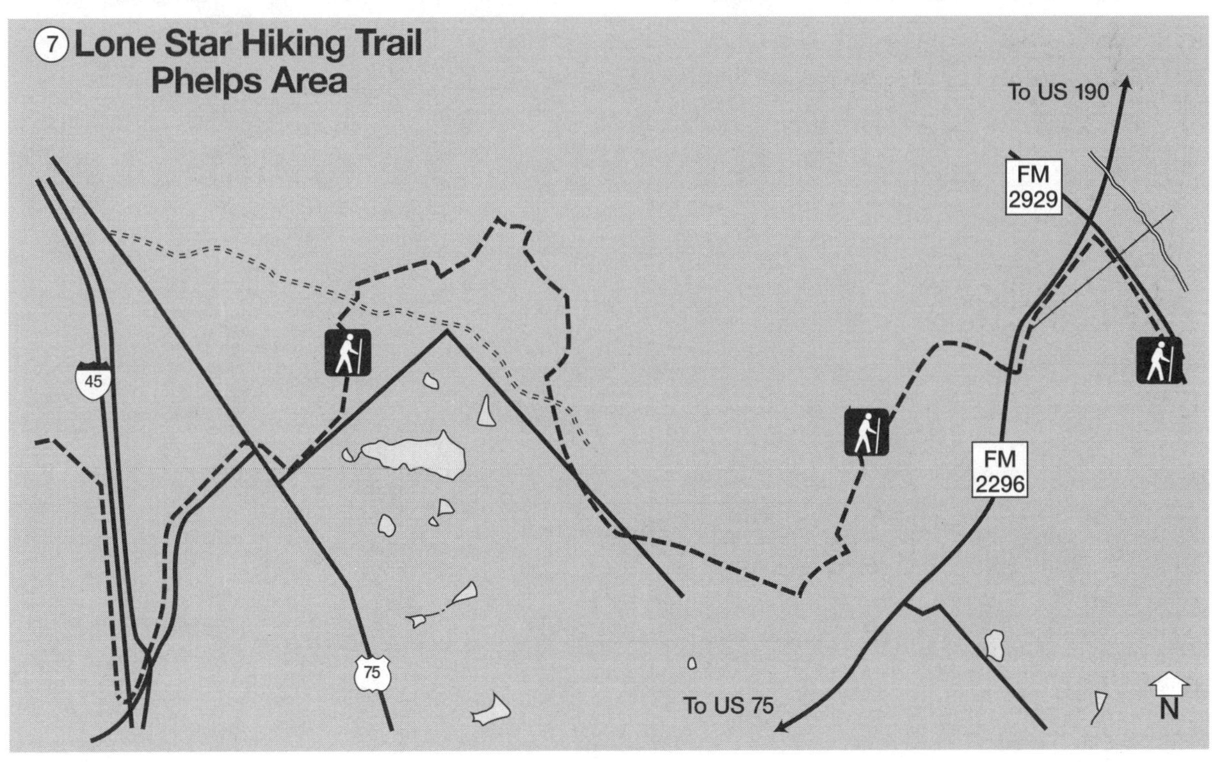

BACKPACKING TRAILS

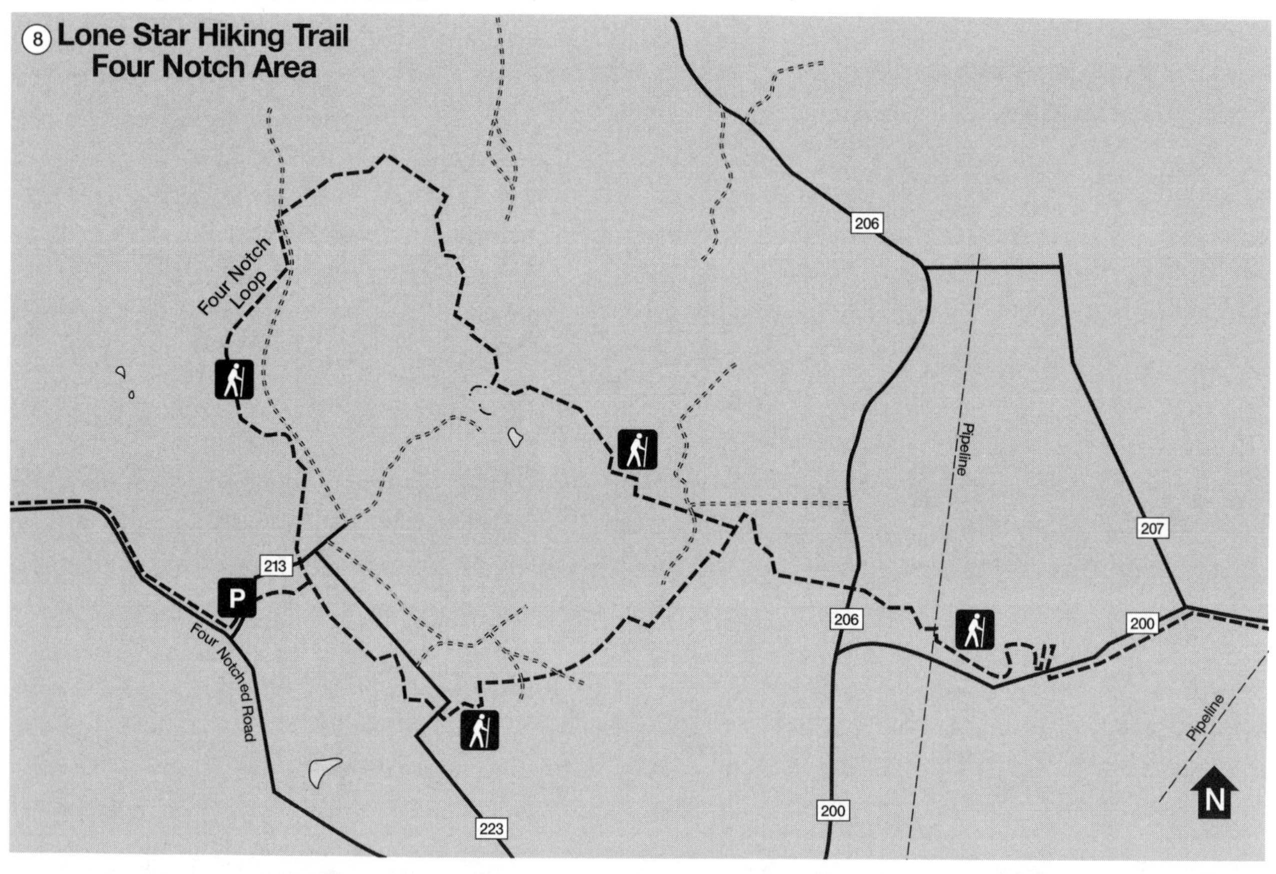
8 Lone Star Hiking Trail
Four Notch Area
Four Notch Loop
206
Pipeline
207
213
P
206
200
Four Notched Road
Pipeline
N
200
223

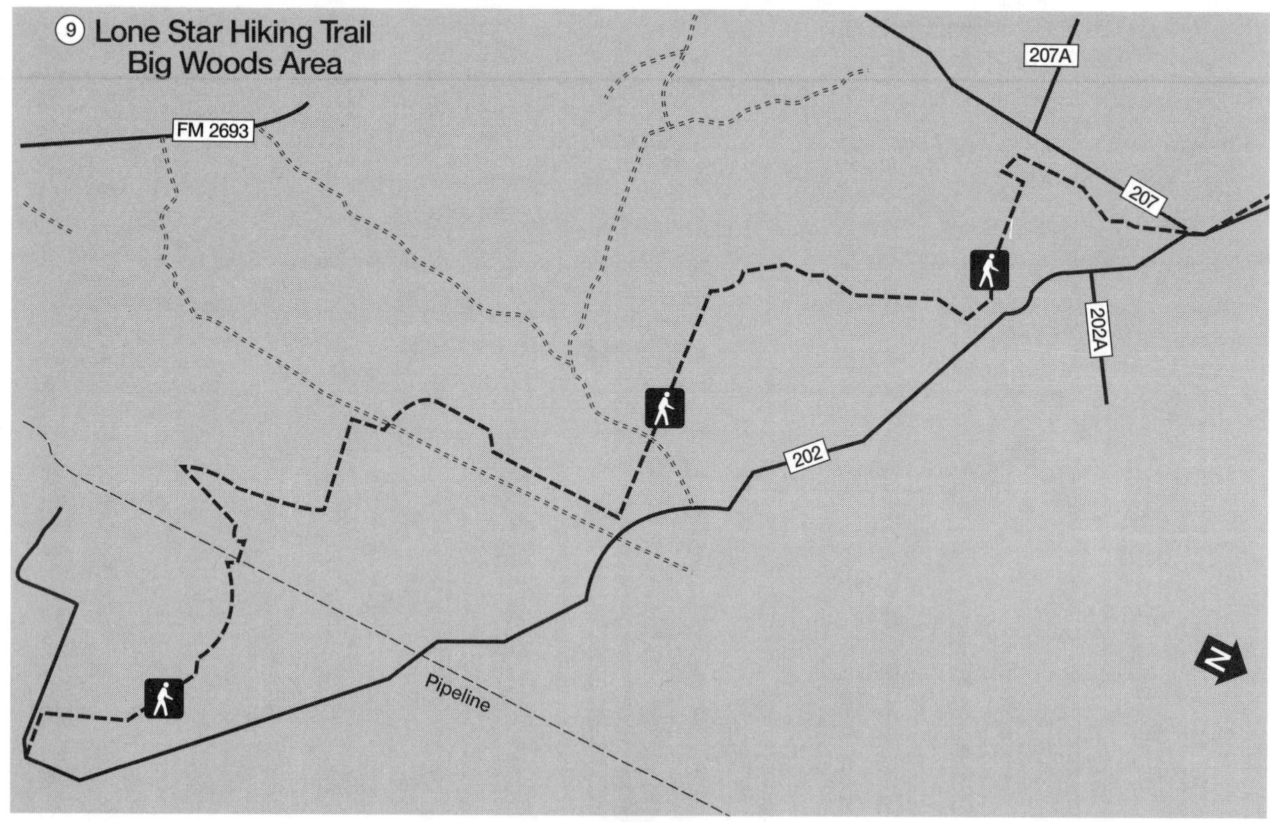
9 Lone Star Hiking Trail
Big Woods Area
207A
FM 2693
207
202A
202
Pipeline
N

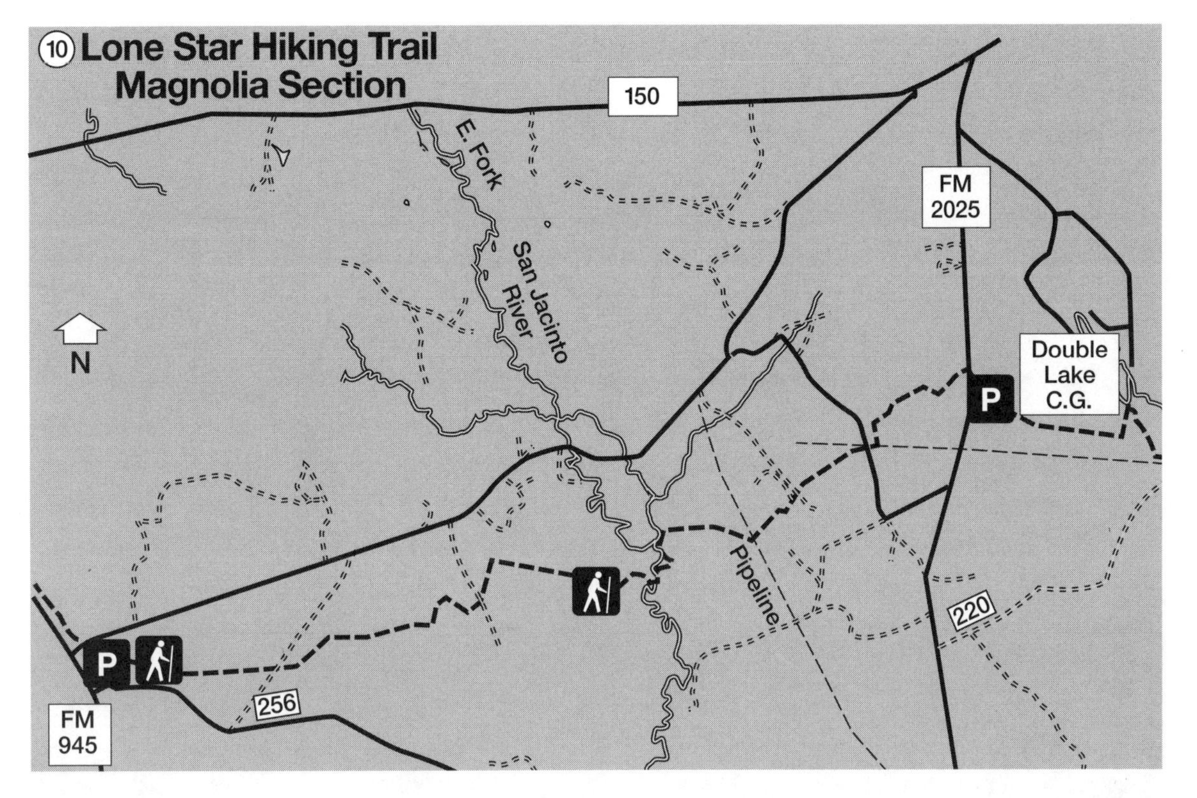

10 Lone Star Hiking Trail
Magnolia Section
150
E. Fork
San Jacinto
River
FM
2025
Double
Lake
C.G.
N
P
Pipeline
220
P
256
FM
945

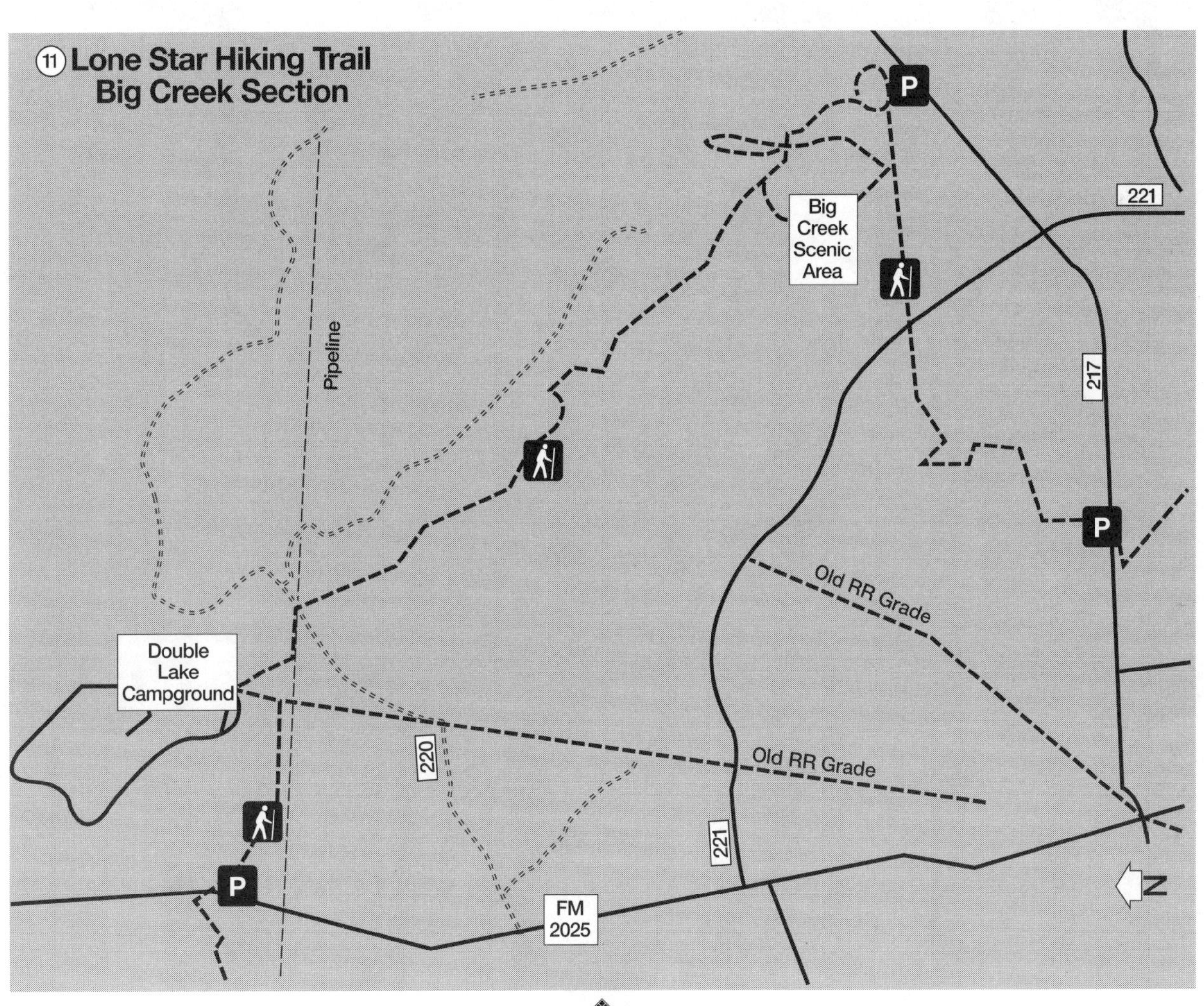

11 Lone Star Hiking Trail
Big Creek Section
P
Big
Creek
Scenic
Area
221
Pipeline
217
P
Old RR Grade
Double
Lake
Campground
220
Old RR Grade
221
P
FM
2025
N

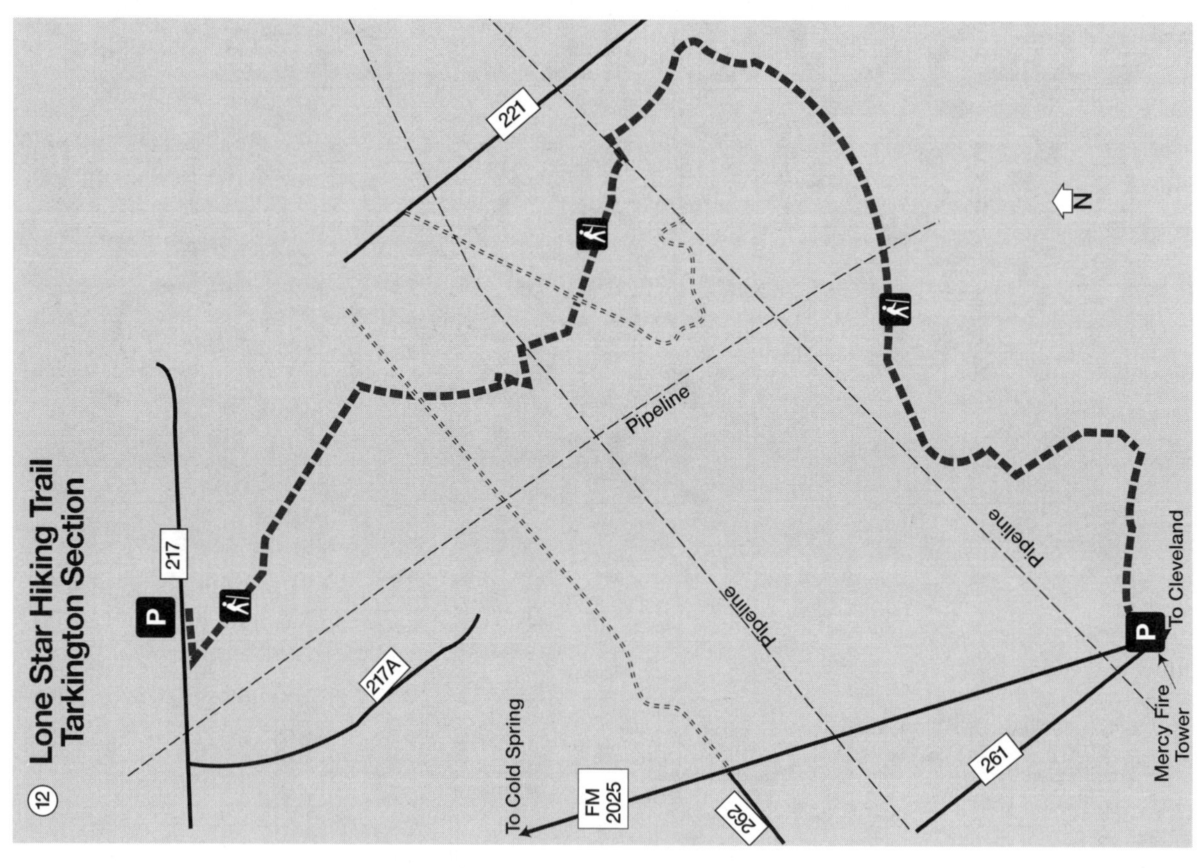
12
Lone Star Hiking Trail
Tarkington Section
P
217
217A
221
Pipeline
Pipeline
Pipeline
To Cold Spring
FM 2025
262
261
P
To Cleveland
Mercy Fire Tower
N

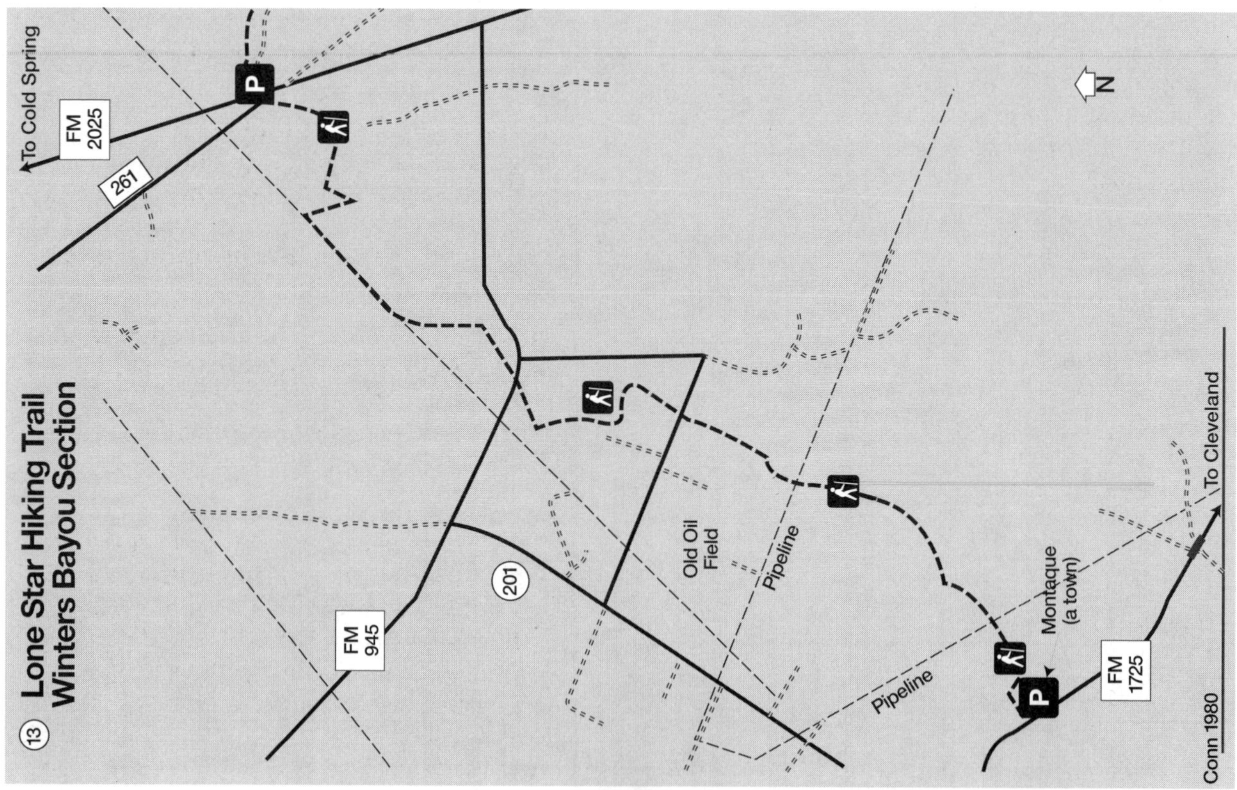
13
Lone Star Hiking Trail
Winters Bayou Section
To Cold Spring
FM 2025
261
P
FM 945
201
Old Oil Field
Pipeline
Pipeline
Montaque (a town)
P
FM 1725
To Cleveland
Conn 1980
N

Appendix

Resources for Further Information

National Forests & Grasslands in Texas
415 S. First St., Ste.110
Lufkin, TX 75910-3088
936/639-8501
www.southernregion.fs.fed.us/texas

National Park Service
Southwest Region
P.O. Box 728
Santa Fe, NM 87504
www.nps.gov

National Wildlife Refuges, Southwest Region
P.O. Box 1306
Albuquerque, NM 87103
www.fws.gov/southwest/refuges

Texas Parks and Wildlife Department
4200 Smith School Road
Austin, TX 78744-3291
512/389-8950
1-800-792-1112 (For Information Only)
www.tpwd.state.tx.us

U.S. Army Corps of Engineers
Federal Building
819 Taylor Street
P.O. Box 17300
Fort Worth, TX 76102-0300
817/334-2705
www.swf-wc.usace.army.mil

Guadalupe-Blanco River Authority
www.gbra.org

Lavaca-Navidad River Authority
www.lnra.org

Lone Star Trail Hiking Club Trail
www.lshtclub.com

Lower Colorado River Authority
www.lcra.org/index.html

Recreational Opportunities on Federal Lands
www.recreation.gov

Sabine River Authority
www.sra.dst.tx.us

Texas Department of Transportation
1-800-452-9292 (Travel Information)
www.dot.state.tx.us
www.traveltex.com

Trinity River Authority
www.trinityra.org

Reservation Systems

For Texas State Parks
Central Reservation System (**CRS**)
Texas Parks and Wildlife Department
Reservations may be made by e-mail, Internet, fax or phone
Reservations and cancellations: 512/389-8900
www.tpwd.state.tx.us/park

For several LCRA parks: Lake Bastrop, Lake, Fayette, and Black Rock Park at Lake Buchanan
Reservations available through the **CRS** or the TPWD (see above)

For select parks at the Army Corps of Engineers' lakes, National Park Service, and the USDA Forest Service recreation areas (Double Lake and Cagle RA in the Sam Houston National Forest)
Reservations available through the National Recreation Reservation Service (**NRRS**) by toll free telephone (1/877-444-6777) or by Internet.
www.reserveusa.com

INDEX

F

G

H

I

J

K

L

M

N

O

P

Q

R

S

T

U

V

W

Z

About the Author

Mickey Little, Ed.D., is professor emeritus of health and physical education at Texas A&M University, where she was founder and director of the Outdoor Education Institute. An avid camper, backpacker, and outdoor photographer, Dr. Little is the author of more than a dozen camping and hiking guides. She lives in the Hill Country near Johnson City, Texas, and continues to explore the outdoors.